Athleticism in the Victorian and Edwardian public school

ATHLETICISM IN THE VICTORIAN AND EDWARDIAN PUBLIC SCHOOL

THE EMERGENCE AND CONSOLIDATION OF AN EDUCATIONAL IDEOLOGY

J. A. MANGAN

 The Falmer Press

(A member of the Taylor & Francis Group)

London • New York • Philadelphia

UK   The Falmer Press, Falmer House, Barcombe, Lewes, East Sussex, BN8 5DL

USA   The Falmer Press, Taylor & Francis Inc., 242 Cherry Street, Philadelphia, PA 19106-1906

© Cambridge University Press 1981

First published by the Press Syndicate of the University of Cambridge, The Pitt Building, Trumpington Street, Cambridge CB2 1RP in 1981

Published 1986

Library of Congress Cataloging in Publication Data

Library of Congress Cataloging in Publication Data is available

Main entry under title:

Athleticism in the Victorian and Edwardian public school
Mangan, James A.
LC 86-13386
ISBN 1 85000 134 0 (pbk.)

Printed in Great Britain by Taylor & Francis (Printers) Ltd, Basingstoke

For Doris

Contents

APPENDICES

Illustrations

Tables

Acknowledgements

The debts accumulated in the writing of this book are many. In the first place, without the generous permission of the headmasters of the survey schools to make use of their archives and meet staff, it would not have been possible. I greatly appreciate, therefore, the interest and co-operation of Mr B. M. S. Hoban (Harrow), Mr I. D. S. Beer (Lancing), Mr R. B. Bruce-Lockhart (Loretto), Mr Roger Ellis (Marlborough), Rev. M. Bossy, SJ (Stonyhurst) and Mr J. C. Royds (Uppingham). In addition, Mr Ellis was instrumental in opening doors to other sources of material, notably the Headmasters' Conference and Mr Bruce-Lockhart's reflections on his years in the public school system were a most helpful contribution to my efforts to achieve a balanced perspective.

Thanks are due in large measure to the late Gerald Murray, formerly librarian and archivist of Marlborough College, whose considerable enthusiasm for this project, remarkable energy and great kindness produced a stream of letters, papers, suggestions and contacts without abatement over five years – all of which proved invaluable. I owe a special debt to him.

The issues of this inquiry were discussed with a large number of assistant masters and housemasters who all gave freely of their time to assess the past and the present. In particular I would like to thank Mr Raymond Venables, Mr James Morwood and Mr A. L. Warr of Harrow; Mr B. W. T. Handford, Mr R. M. Reeve and Mr A. H. P. Beater of Lancing; Mr Peter Wood and Mr E. C. Barclay-Smith of Loretto; Mr E. G. H. Kempson, Mr Michael Preston and Mr Michael Birley of Marlborough; Father F. J. Turner, Mr B. Fitzgerald and Colonel A. P. F. Shaw of Stonyhurst; Mr T. B. Belk, Mr B. Matthews and Dr M. Tozer of Uppingham. Others, rather too numerous to mention here, are thanked most sincerely. From all I gained insights.

I am obliged also to the retired headmasters, staff and old boys who wrote to me, often at great length, of their school experiences. My use of their material in text and note is, I hope, a satisfactory tribute to its value. Sadly it is not possible to thank in person the late G. A. N. Lowndes, author of that model of educational scholarship, the *The Silent Social Revolution.* I will remember with great pleasure his skill in recalling his Marlborough schooldays and in setting them in the wider context of a changing society, one June morning in his delightful house overlooking the Green in Marlborough.

Several distinguished scholars of various aspects of the English public schools – Professor Geoffrey Best, Professor J. de S. Honey, Professor P. C. McIntosh, Dr T. W. Bamford and Mr Patrick Scott – offered general advice and encouragement. Their kindness is gratefully recorded as is the support and encouragement given by two colleagues, Dr H. Hutchinson of Glasgow University and Mr W. Marker of Jordanhill College.

I must also express my gratitude to those librarians in schools, colleges, universities and public libraries who so efficiently located and procured even the most obscure sermon. I am more than grateful to Mrs Jean Robertson of Glasgow University Library for her skilful assistance, to Mr Stanley Gillam of the London Library for his permission to read the manuscript autobiography of John Addington Symonds and to Dr C. J. Wright of the British Museum Department of Manuscripts for a stimulating discussion on the literature of athleticism as well as for more orthodox assistance in locating material. I should like to thank also the staffs of the library of the Department of Education and Science, the National Library of Scotland, the Mitchell Library, Glasgow, Hamilton Public Library and the Lanarkshire Reference Library for help at various times.

The archivists of the Record Offices of many of the English counties obligingly investigated their archives for material on the public schools and several notified me of interesting and useful items in their possession. The school papers and correspondence provided by Miss A. Green of Berkshire, Mr Brian Smith of Gloucestershire and Mr B. C. Jones of Cumbria have been especially useful. In addition, the archives of the Headmasters' Conference and the Society of Jesus were opened to me by Mr R. St J. Pitts-Tucker and Rev. F. Edwards, SJ respectively. Mr Stephen Green, the curator of the MCC supplied valuable statistics on public school cricket. I am indebted to them all for their courteous attention.

In addition, to those already mentioned, I should like to thank the following for permission to use material: Professor Margaret Sutherland, editor of the *British Journal of Educational Studies* for allowing the inclusion of an early article of mine in the chapter on the literature of athleticism; Mr T. D. G. Sotheron-Estcourt for the Harrow papers of T. H. S. Sotheron; the Editor of *Punch* for various cartoons and verses; the National Portrait Gallery for the photograph of Frederick William Farrar; Sherborne School for the photograph of G. M. Carey and the Parker Gallery for the print of Stonyhurst College.

Two acknowledgements remain. When teaching commitments clashed exhaustingly with the demands of research Dr T. R. Bone, the principal, and the governors of Jordanhill granted me a period of study leave. It was an act of considerable generosity and I owe them much. Finally, the most profound thanks of all are to my wife. Her interest and support have been so wholehearted that her effort on my behalf can only be described as a labour of love.

Prologue

Five years after the Great War an aggressive pamphlet entitled *The Public Schools and Athleticism* appeared. It was a condemnation of the excessive interest in games in the schools by an obscure schoolmaster, J. H. Simpson.[1] It struck an unpleasantly discordant note amid applause which had begun some sixty years earlier and which, in an atmosphere of post-war nostalgia, had risen to a crescendo.

Simpson was more than a critic. He sought understanding as well as reformation. He asserted that games were an ostentatious and pervasive feature of the public school system, and argued that the study of this 'athleticism' was crucial to a comprehension of the system as a whole. Despite this observation there has been no close scrutiny of athleticism in the public schools.[2] This is a regrettable omission. The ideology strongly influenced the schools between 1860 and 1940; its widespread adoption had extensive educational and social repercussions. No history of the British public school and no record of British educational ideologies can be complete without a consideration of this controversial movement.

This book, therefore, is an attempt to rectify a longstanding omission. The intention is to trace the growth and consolidation of this once powerful ideology and to investigate the means by which it was created and sustained. But first, four problems must be resolved: what precisely is a public school, which schools are to be studied, what is the relevance of the term 'ideology' and finally, what exactly was athleticism?

There has never emerged an exact and universally acceptable definition of a public school.[3] This is not for want of trying. A wide variety of writers have struggled with the problem.[4] The definition adopted in this book is Vivian Ogilvie's since it combines clarity, comprehensiveness and qualification, and would meet with widespread understanding and acceptance. Ogilvie assures us that the

1

principal characteristics of a public school are: it is for the well-to-do, expensive, predominantly boarding, independent of the state, but neither privately owned nor profit making. He points out, however, that there are illustrious public schools which fall out of line in one or other particular: these constitute exceptions within the general rule. The rule (in its full-blown form) 'is an independent, non-local, predominantly boarding school for the upper and middle classes'.[5]

The public schools so defined are diverse in origin, history and type. At least six important nineteenth-century groupings may be discerned. The most famous group was the 'Great Public Schools', the subject of a royal commission set up in 1861, the Public Schools Commission or Clarendon Commission (after the chairman, Lord Clarendon).[6] The schools investigated were Eton, Harrow, Rugby, Winchester, Shrewsbury, Charterhouse, Westminster, St Paul's and Merchant Taylors.[7]

Throughout the nineteenth century, the period of the great expansion of public school education, other groupings emerged or were consolidated. The most amorphous was the large group of Denominational Schools: Roman Catholic, such as Stonyhurst (1793), Ampleforth (1802), Ratcliffe (1847) and Beaumont (1861); Quaker, such as Sidcot (1808) and Bootham (1823); Methodist, such as Kingswood (1848), Leys (1875) and Ashville (1877); and other Protestant Nonconformist, such as Mill Hill (1808), Caterham (1811) and Bishop's Stortford (1868). All were formed to provide an alternative education to that provided by the schools of the Established Church following the reform of the Penal Laws in the late eighteenth century.

A further grouping was the Proprietary Schools. These were financed initially by shareholders who purchased the right, in consequence, to nominate pupils. Cheltenham was the first: 'There were 650 shares, each share entitling the holder to nominate one pupil (usually, of course, held by the parent). If the proprietors should fail to nominate pupils, then the governors could do so.'[8] Other schools of this type include Marlborough (1843), Rossall (1844), Malvern (1865) and Dover College (1871).

Edward Thring became headmaster of Uppingham Grammar School in 1853. He transformed this small, unprepossessing local grammar school into an expensive national boarding school for the upper classes. A similar process of transformation occurred at several other institutions, including Sherborne, Tonbridge, Repton, Giggleswick, St Bees and Sedbergh. These schools became known on this account as 'Elevated Grammar Schools'.

A little before Thring in Rutland raised Uppingham to the ranks of a school for the wealthy, Nathaniel Woodard in Sussex had embarked on a more ambitious project: a network of Anglican middle-class schools throughout England. Originally only one, Lancing College (1848), was intended as a school for the better-off, but ultimately this was to be the fate of them all. By the time of his death in 1891 there were six Woodard boys' public schools: Lancing (1848), Hurstpierpoint (1849), Ardingly (1858), Denstone (1868), King's College, Taunton (1880) and Ellesmere (1884).

Finally, there were a number of schools financed and owned by a single individual, usually the headmaster: the Private Venture Schools. One such school was Loretto, a small boarding school outside Edinburgh, founded in 1827 by the Rev. Dr Langhorne, an English curate of the Scottish Episcopal Church. In 1862 Loretto was purchased by Hely Hutchinson Almond who modelled it on the lines of an English public school. By the end of the century it had become a small but famous public school in his hands. Other schools of this type include Merchiston (1833), Radley (1847), Bradfield (1850), Bloxham (1860), Monkton Coombe (1868), Wrekin (1879), Wycliffe (1882), and Abbotsholme (1889).

The distinguished social scientist Robert Merton has written of two species of academic investigator: the 'European and the American'.[9] The 'European' is preoccupied with interaction that should logically occur; the 'American' is concerned with relations that empirically exist. 'Europeans' interpret grandly from a short supply of material; 'Americans' interpret scantily from a mass of evidence. It is the possible weakness of the 'European' approach which concerns us here. A paucity of material, claims Merton, is no obstacle to the 'European' in his confident use of documents as indicators of extensively held views. Furthermore, the more often and the more emphatically a generalisation is aired, the greater the likelihood of its adopting the guise of a fact.

All this is relevant to historical studies of the English public school. Some recent works have been general in scope.[10] In J. de S. Honey's study of the public school as a community, for example, the 'sampling universe' is the whole system. And the evidence accumulated is unavoidably fragmentary. All historical studies, of course, face the problem of incomplete records: the result of material lost through accident, indifference or calculation. Optimistically, all that can be done is to echo the words of one scrupulous social historian and state bluntly that we are dealing with intangible evidence which is difficult to assess; but that sifting this evidence is valuable and the general impressions obtained are worthwhile.[11] Yet the question still remains as to how representative such evidence is. Can it be effectively claimed, for example, that it was the adoption of the pastoral role of the assistant master which changed the master–pupil relationship in the public schools and to produce as evidence an original model for Mr Chips, an extract from the death speech of Potts of Fettes, an old boy's autobiography, *Stalky and Co.*, and details of the emergence of a small and esoteric society of pious assistant masters?[12] There is a strong temptation to ask: what of happenings in the many unmentioned schools?

These comments should not be taken as an attack on a distinguished historian of the public schools. The debt owed to him by subsequent inquirers is considerable. But there are real methodological problems to be confronted here. In a study of athleticism in the public schools what is the 'universe' to be? If it is to be the 'total universe' and all the public schools are to be investigated the problems are formidable. The quality of the sources for each school varies greatly. At the same time a detailed study of scores of schools would take many years. One possible remedy from the social sciences – a random sample – might leave out schools which played a leading role in the development of the ideology and this could result in vital historical omissions. It is clearly unsuitable.

However, an investigation of one school from each of the groupings discussed earlier – Great Public Schools, Denominational Schools, Proprietary Schools, Elevated Grammar Schools, Woodard Schools and Private Venture Schools – would provide a systematic analysis of the growth and consolidation of athleticism in a cross section of the public schools that would help avoid the excesses of Merton's 'European' academic. Such an approach, of course, precludes confident generalisations about the entire public school system. However, it assists the building up of systematic knowledge of a cumulative character;[13] the detailed information gathered would provide material for future generalisations which would rely on substantial evidence rather than arbitrary selection; new or amended hypotheses could be offered on the basis of fresh material and weaknesses in earlier general studies could be revealed.

But perhaps most important of all, this approach permits the study in depth of individual schools, allowing detailed investigation of *variation in interpretation* of ideological fashion which general commentators are careful to suggest occurred but, understandably, to which they can devote little space themselves;[14] a variation attractively described by Bernard Darwin: 'What are truisms at Rugby, are paradoxes at Harrow, and an Eton custom would prove a revelation at Marlborough.'[15]

This type of analysis has been called appropriately 'intensive–comparative'.[16] No methodological approach possesses all the advantages or escapes all the shortcomings. Any analytical scheme is partial. Some things are analysed, others unexplained. However, as we have already seen above, the intensive–comparative approach has the virtue of being complementary to the general survey. It serves it in a monitoring role; and provides it with source material. To fulfil this dual purpose this study of athleticism will break new ground. It will be intensive and comparative; the 'total universe' will be the public school system and British upper-class society between approximately 1850 and 1950 – the relevant years; the 'sampling frame' will consist of all the schools in existence in this period and the case-studies will be made up of a sample of schools from the several sets described above.

In 1905, about the time that athleticism was at its height and school athletic success was a noted asset in the scramble for status and pupils, the *Harmsworth Encyclopedia* published a list of the names of 'the most famous' public schools of the period. They were:

Bedford, King Edward's School (Birmingham), Brighton, Charterhouse, Cheltenham, Christ's Hospital, City of London, Clifton, Dulwich, Eton, Haileybury, Harrow, Lancing, the Leys, Malvern, Manchester Grammar School, Marlborough, Merchant Taylors, Mill Hill, Repton, Rossall, Rugby, St Paul's, Sherborne, Shrewsbury, Stonyhurst, Tonbridge, Uppingham, Wellington, Westminster and Winchester, together with the Scottish schools Fettes, Glenalmond, and Loretto.[17]

This catalogue of the distinguished contains examples from the six groupings mentioned above, and will provide the sample for this book. The following schools will comprise the case-studies: Harrow (Great Public School), Stonyhurst (Denominational School), Marlborough (Proprietary School), Uppingham (Elevated Grammar School), Lancing (Woodard School) and Loretto (Private Venture School).[18] These particular schools have been selected because of the richness of archive and secondary source material associated with them and because of the importance of certain of them (for example, Marlborough and Loretto) in the evolution of athleticism. In addition, they have been chosen because they are widely scattered throughout the United Kingdom and so offer the possibility of interesting evidence of variation in regional response to ideological diffusion, and quite independent ideological patterns in response to local factors.

Ideologies,[19] it has been argued, are essentially the outcome of man's need for imposing intellectual order on the world.[20] Whatever their purpose a plethora of definitions exists. At the crudest level an ideology may be defined as a set of principles held by individuals or groups. At a more subtle level it may be regarded as a set of principles which determines action by providing a means of distinguishing between acceptable and unacceptable ideas. Even more expansively it is the whole complex of ideas and feelings linking the members of a group together with the means whereby these are established;[21] it embraces not only what is believed but the means of ensuring belief. There are further definitions to be considered. Some have regarded ideologies as forms of deceit, as pseudo-principles, obscuring the real reasons for action.[22] Others have considered that ideologies are simply value-judgements disguised as statements of fact to give them credibility.[23]

These several definitions are all useful conceptual tools with which to explore athleticism as an ideology in the public schools.[24] One purpose of this study is to demonstrate that it embraced a complex of ideas and feelings deliberately and carefully created through ritual and symbol; that it was, on occasion, a form of 'pseudo-reasoning', a deliberate rationalisation for ambitions such as status and power; and that it constituted value-judgements masquerading as facts to reinforce commitment. There is no one simple meaning of ideology in the context of public school athleticism. The term is a conceptual alembic. To reinforce this critical point by employing a different metaphor: the meanings resemble the layers of an onion, one hides within another. A fact that must be consistently borne in mind in the ensuing chapters.

The concept of athleticism, of course, may also be variously interpreted.[25] The *Shorter Oxford Dictionary* defines it in neutral and unsubtle terms as 'the practice of, and devotion to, athletic exercises'. In contrast two scholars, in the similarity of their interpretation, form a small, but sharp comminatory chorus with a large modern audience. In their view athleticism was a malign fashion. The most distinguished historian of the English public school saw athleticism in crude pathological terms: 'the late Victorian schools nurtured vices of their own. Probably the most important was the worship of the athlete with its attendant deification of success, and the mere physical virtue of courage';[26] and the most recent historian of British physical education has been no less harsh in his judgement: 'By athleticism is meant the exaltation and disproportionate regard for games which often resulted in the denigration of academic work and in anti-intellectualism'.[27]

Edward Lyttelton, an observer of the ideology in action in the nineteenth century, took a more balanced view.[28] Athleticism had dangers: particularly distraction from intellectual pursuits. It also possessed advantages: the stimulation of health and happiness and good moral training. Lyttelton readily admitted athleticism was 'a training shackled by many an antiquated abuse and sadly marred by countless stupidities',[29] but he felt it played a valuable part in the education of the higher classes.

Cyril Norwood, early in the twentieth century, attempted to distinguish between 'over-athleticism' – the attachment of wrong values to games, and athleticism – 'part of the ideal of the English [educational] tradition'.[30] He saw the latter as the attempt to implant certain ideals of character and conduct through the games field: 'a game is to be played for the game's sake . . . no unfair advantage of any sort can ever be taken, [yet] . . . within the rules no mercy is to be expected, or accepted or shown by either side; the lesson to be learnt by each individual is the subordination of self in order that he may render his best service as the member of a team in which he relies upon all the rest; and all the rest rely upon him: . . . finally, never on any occasion must he show the white feather.' Norwood concluded: 'If games can be played in this spirit, they are a magnificent preparation for life.'[31]

Today it is fashionable and to a degree wise, to look askance at such a naive and frequently abused faith in the educational virtues of the playing fields as demonstrated by Norwood and his ilk; but at the same time it is as well to remember that we are reacting, possibly predictably, with extremism to extremism. It is perhaps salutary to recall that English education has embraced the belief in the efficacy of sport *inter alia* for character building since Tudor times.[32]

Lyttelton and Norwood remind us of a period truth. Athleticism was all its critics claim of it; yet it was more. The clichés of modern conventional judgement must be resisted; the validity of contemporary generalisations must be challenged. They owe much to fashion, less to impartiality. If athleticism often degenerated into the self-absorption of Caliban, it frequently aimed to effect the selflessness of Ariel. Apparently it was *sometimes* successful. According to Philip Mason, for example, the games-trained officers from the public schools won an engaging fidelity from the Indian soldier, for their selfless leadership. Mason borrowed a description from the philosopher George Santayana to depict this imperial elite at its best: 'Never since the heroic days of Greece has the world had such a sweet, just, boyish master.' The reason, it appears, lay in a simple fact. 'Hardy as Spartans and disciplined as Romans' these masters carried the qualities they had learned on the games field into their military careers and led with boyishness, decision and courage.[33]

Reality is occasionally attractive. By virtue of its obscenity, the 'athleticism' described by T. C. Worsley in *Flannelled Fool* does not have to be the entire truth for all public schools and public school boys. Mason may have access to an equally valid reality. And Ray, the decent games player in *Tell England*, might have had just as much substance in the flesh as Cayley, the brutal athlete in *The Harrovians*.[34] In a passage totally contradictory of his later outspoken attack on public school games cited above, even E. C. Mack discovered virtue in their imperial consequences. He argued that the training largely acquired on the games field was the basis of courage and group loyalty that created 'responsible, honourable boys, willing to give their lives unquestionably to the preservation and expansion of Empire',[35] and considered that if world conditions had remained as they were in 1870, there was much of substance in the argument that public schools were worthy institutions, admirably serving the interests of the upper classes. The empire and the public school boy's contribution to it lasted beyond 1870. Mason's valedictory embraced the Indian army of the twentieth century.

The purpose of this brief defence of athleticism is not to gloss over deficiencies but to strike unaccustomed balance; it is an attempt to break a lance in the interests of accuracy. The public schools' considerable concern with games was not wholly vicious. It had nobility; it did reflect 'love of the open air, of sport and pluck and fair play'.[36] To borrow (and slightly adapt) Robert Nisbet's striking phrase, athleticism was 'a neologism born of moral passion'[37] as well as a Simpsonian term of justifiable disparagement. Physical exercise was taken, considerably and compulsorily, in the sincere belief of many, however romantic, misplaced or myopic, that it was a highly effective means of inculcating valuable instrumental and impressive educational goals: physical and moral courage, loyalty and co-operation, the capacity to act fairly and take defeat well, the ability to both command and obey. These were the famous ingredients of character training which the public schools considered their pride and their prerogative.[38]

The extract below supplies a period flavour of the once wide-spread educational certainty surrounding games in the public school system:

Many a lad who leaves an English public school disgracefully ignorant of the rudiments of useful knowledge, who can speak no language but his own, and writes that imperfectly, to whom the noble literature of his country and the stirring history of his forefathers are almost a sealed book, and who has devoted a great part of his time and nearly all his thoughts to athletic sports, yet brings away with him something beyond all price, a manly straightforward character, a scorn of lying and meanness, habits of obedience and command, and fearless courage. Thus equipped, he goes out into the world, and bears a man's part in subduing the earth, ruling its wild folk, and building up the Empire; doing many things so well that it seems a thousand pities that he was not trained to do them better, and to face the problems of race, creed and government in distant corners of the Empire with a more instructed mind. This type of citizen, however, with all his defects, has done yeoman's service to the Empire; and for much that is best in him our public schools may fairly take credit.[39]

The situation is clear from this and similar pronouncements. For many in the Victorian and Edwardian public schools, games became 'the wheel round which the moral values turned'.[40] It was a genuinely and extensively held belief that they inspired virtue; they developed manliness; they formed character. At the same time there were certainly casuists who used moral argument as a cover for simple pleasure. There were also opportunists, especially housemasters, who saw the value of games in terms of control and publicity.

The truth of the matter is that the ideology involved virtuousness, indulgence and expedience; it embraced idealism, casuistry and opportunism. It was, in fact, a complex manifestation. And as we shall now see, its origins were equally complex.

Part I

The growth of the ideology

I

Reformation, indifference and liberty

Tranquillity, reform, renewal: these are appropriate terms describing the condition of mid-nineteenth-century Britain. After the repeal of the Corn Law Act in 1846 'the storm of controversy dies rapidly down into a pleasantly exciting breeze before which the country drives "sails filled and streamers waving" past the dangerous reefs of India and the Crimea into the halcyon weather of Palmerston's old age'.[1] Legislation had brought peace; the Chartists were subdued; fears of revolution were allayed. At the same time there was to be no return to aristocratic paternalism, to wealth based predominantly on land, to nicely ordered relationships of feudal landed society. It was a time of change.

Despite the fears of the defeated Protectionists, the economy moved firmly towards a free trade policy. There was a steady growth in prosperity.[2] The nation experienced a shift in moral emphasis from a belief that the common good was best served by the self-interested action of the entrepreneur to a realisation of the need for collective responsibility. State provision for the poor, Factory Acts for the new proletariat and the consumer, symbolised the stirring of a collective conscience.[3] But the end of a simple-minded adherence to the Entrepreneurial Ideal was further indicated by the various Companies Acts between 1856 and 1862. The subsequent creation of joint-stock companies gave rise to a wealthy industrial plutocracy of directors and managers. The business aristocracy was born.

It was an era, too, when the middle classes themselves, growing in size and prosperity,[4] were losing patience with restricted educational and occupational opportunities and the demonstrable incompetence of an unskilled administration.[5] The Roebuck *Report on Army Maladministration during the Crimean War* (1856) resulted in army reforms that lasted for the next twenty years. By the

Universities Acts of 1854 and 1856 restriction of entry to Oxford and Cambridge on religious grounds was abolished. The formation of the Administrative Reform Association in 1855 reflected the intense agitation at the time for an end to patronage and the adoption of competition for positions in the administrative machinery of the state. Pressure for reform in 1853 had already achieved adoption of the principle of competitive entry to the Indian Civil Service; the following year came the Northcote-Trevelyan *Report on the Organisation of the Permanent Civil Service*; and 1855 saw the setting up of a commission to examine civil service candidates: 'Great Britain by imperceptible degrees acquired a Bureaucracy'.[6]

It was also the key period for the growth of the leading professions.[7] While the Institute of Civil Engineers had been founded in 1818, the Law Society in 1831 and the Royal Society of Architects in 1834, it was not until the Medical Act of 1858 that the 'registered medical practitioners' appeared. By the mid-1850s accountants were organising societies and institutes; others, for example mechanical engineers and naval architects, quickly followed suit.

Then, too, the interest of the British people was increasingly directed overseas; from now on 'the soldier, the emigrant and the explorer . . . take and fill the imagination'.[8]

These developments, a new prosperity, the rise of the industrial aristocracy, the growth of the professional middle class and the growing preoccupation with 'Britain overseas' against a backcloth of industrial, commercial and imperial expansion, led directly to the rebirth of that unique phenomenon of British society: the public school. They supplied the clientele, the finance and a training rationale.

There remains a fourth and major contribution to the successful regeneration of the public school: moral reformation. The savage conditions of the eighteenth- and early nineteenth-century aristocratic schools are recorded soberly in various histories of English education. Generations of scholars have attributed their transformation into places of order, some learning and improved piety in large measure to Thomas Arnold.[9] Yet the extent of Arnold's influence on public school education is the subject of contemporary reappraisal. One scholar has been so heretical as to state that Arnold is said to have reformed the public schools yet there is precious little evidence of it.[10] Whatever the limitations of his educational reforms, it was his success in projecting a personal moral image that was of considerable importance to the successful growth of the public school system. He had the facility to capture the headlines on religious, social and political matters.[11] And he was well served by an early adulatory press.[12] In consequence, he became for many mid-Victorians a symbol of the desire for moral reform that sprang out of an earlier era and owed much to Edmund Burke, Hannah More, John Wesley and the Clapham Sect.[13] He was in accord with the mood of his time: a reformation of manners which characterised mid-Victorian middle-class society. To a middle class starved of idealism and frightened of reality, he represented a noble educational ideal: 'to advance the Kingdom of God and His righteousness' through his pupils. His ambition, as he proclaimed it, was the creation of Christian gentlemen, and he pursued it with obsessional intensity. To this end the older boys at Rugby were encouraged to see themselves as 'the champions of righteousness especially selected to combat the ever watchful forces of evil'.[14]

Arnold's adult life was a passionate crusade against this abstraction.[15] He made it almost tangible in its reality. T. W. Bamford states, 'Evil was something positive that Arnold could almost see and feel. When faced with it he would rise in anger, and would, indeed, on occasion completely lose his self-control.'[16] In this crusade he was ruthless and sometimes frenetic. He flogged, expelled and harangued in its interest. To the middle-class public he seemed to 'cleanse the temple'. He appeared to be everything the god-fearing parent wanted in a schoolmaster: moral, strong, caring and clever. He restored the soiled and tattered reputation of the public school by means of powerful and effective impression management.[17] He reassured the new middle-class clientele that their sons would be safe in his bosom. Conviction, idealism and reassurance were his great interlinked contributions to the revitalisation of the English public school.

In time Vaughan at Harrow, Cotton at Marlborough and Thring at Uppingham among others, played their part in organisational, disciplinary and curricular reform. As a result the Hogarthian conditions of vice, squalor and brutality of earlier decades were at least mitigated, morality was powerfully preached if less widely practised and a new system of control was devised that curbed the worst excesses. The growing middle class were mollified and eventually became enthusiastic. If they disliked the former licence and savagery of the 'Great' public schools, they appreciated the exclusiveness and contacts they provided. With the worst elements of these schools now repressed, those who could afford to, joined, and those who could not, imitated. The results are as familiar as the earnestness of Arnold: the expansion of existing schools and the creation by a variety of means of literally scores of others.[18]

II

By the end of the sixth decade of the century the terms tranquillity, reform, renewal, used earlier to describe mid-nineteenth-century Britain, would serve adequately to describe the public school system. Stability has been established out of recurring disorder; popularity had swollen numbers; a more adequate organisational framework was being developed; the formal curriculum was undergoing reform. Curricular reform was not so much associated with the classroom, however, as with something else: the newly enlarged or created playing fields.

From 1850 onwards, games were purposefully and deliberately assimilated into the formal curriculum of the public schools: suitable facilities were constructed, headmasters insisted on pupil involvement, staff participation was increasingly expected and the creation of a legitimating rhetoric began. The individual response of each school to the general trend, as has been noted already in the prologue, has been remarked upon by historians but not investigated in any detail. To trace the origins of this movement in the six schools of this study and to locate significant differences in early interpretation is the main purpose of the next two chapters; but first it is necessary to expose a commonplace historical inaccuracy.

Pierre de Coubertin once asserted that from a moral point of view, no system could stand higher than the English athletic sports system as understood and explained by Thomas Arnold.[19] It must be made quite clear that the conviction that Arnold was responsible for the 'athletic sports system' of the public schools, although widely held,[20] is, in the unmerciful expression of a recent commentator, 'a specific erroneous belief'.[21] It does not accord with the evidence and should be firmly rejected. It was in no way the outcome of his idealism, organisational perspicacity, concern with the dangers of idleness or simple enthusiasm. Arnold appears to have been insensitive to the possibilities of an athletic ethos with team games as the instrument of moral conditioning, as a mechanism of control, as a desirable antidote to vandalism and even as a means of personal enjoyment. In plain fact, at no time in his life did Arnold appear to be much interested in such activities. As a Winchester schoolboy, games had no strong attraction for him. An afternoon on the downs overlooking the school devoted to the attack or defence of an imaginary fort provided 'the summit of schoolboy happiness'.

At his own small school at Laleham on the Thames, which he established in 1819 at the age of twenty-four, he organised, encouraged and participated in a number of physical activities, but games were not among them.[22] He went from Laleham to Rugby as headmaster in 1828 and in Stanley's full description of his work at Rugby there is no mention of concern for the value of these activities.[23] His most positive action was to watch benignly the boys on Big Side.

The reader searches his sermons in vain for the exhortations and apologias that are to be found in the sermons of later headmasters. For all his obsession with sin, Arnold was blind to the moral possibilities of cricket and football that later public school masters saw with such clarity and preached with such certainty. And a search of his journals and letters for an awareness of such possibilities would be equally fruitless.[24]

More significant still, in Arnold's own contributions to educational theory there is not a single reference to physical activities. In his article on Rugby School for example, in the *Quarterly Journal of Education* in 1834,[25] he described the content and organisation of the curriculum of the school in some detail without a mention of games. Yet within a decade of his death they were part of the pedagogical equipment of staff and the formal curriculum of several public schools. And in an article entitled 'On the Discipline of Public Schools' in the same journal a year later, he offered a narrow interpretation of the term discipline and was concerned to mount a defence of corporal punishment rather than to consider the possibilities for both corporate and self discipline that the games field might offer – a commonplace association of ideas in later decades.

There are other pointers to Arnold's negative attitude to games. Charles Lake became one of the earliest Arnoldian neophytes; on his own admission a devotee of games while at Rugby, he was converted to a love of Arnold by Arthur Penrhyn Stanley, whereupon he abandoned games 'almost as a matter of course' and spent his time in the more mature business of walking and discoursing in an attempt to be an Arnoldian man, not 'a fine muscular specimen who could outfight and outplay all his foreign foes and rivals' but 'an adult in mind and ideals'.[26] And finally, in striking contrast to the athletic assistant master of the 1890s, Arnold's ideal assistant master was characterised only by the behaviour and standards of a Christian gentleman, a clerical garb, first-class mental ability and a desire to travel to broaden the mind. The truth of the matter has been succinctly stated by David Newsome: Arnold's ideal of Christian man did not attach any great importance to the physical.[27]

The responsibility for the early stimulus that led in time to a fully-matured ideology of athleticism with a well-developed moral component lies with others. C. J. Vaughan became headmaster of Harrow in 1845, G. E. L. Cotton, of Marlborough in 1852, Edward Thring, of Uppingham in 1853, Henry Walford, of Lancing in 1859 and Hely Hutchinson Almond, of Loretto in 1862. It was such headmasters as these rather than Thomas Arnold who took the then novel step of encouraging pupils and staff to consider games as part of the formal curriculum, and so began a trend which was to become a notable feature of the public school system as a whole by the last quarter of the century.

Until the advent of Vaughan, Cotton, Thring, Walford and Almond, boys' leisure activities at Harrow, Marlborough, Uppingham, Lancing and Loretto were broadly similar. In the first instance staff were not responsible for the boys outside the classroom. The situation at Marlborough, described by one pupil in his diary, applied also at the other schools: 'For the strictness with which they conducted their actual teaching, masters atoned by an almost total indifference to the way in which a boy employed his leisure.'[28] The staff were scholars. They had no official part in the control or organisation of the boys' free time and most certainly none in their games. Nor were games the main part of the boys' extra-curricular activities. The location of the schools in rural surroundings and the absence of bounds meant that a large part of the boys' free time was spent exploring the countryside, fishing, hunting small animals and nesting.

At Marlborough, although established mainly for the sons of clergymen, the pupils were saintly neither in person nor practice.[29] On the opening day of the college, 20 August 1843, they indulged in a brutal frog hunt in the school grounds, beat the creatures to death and 'piled the bodies high'. This activity typified their recreational habits for a decade. From rural parishes of the western counties, they were much given to poaching, trespassing and nesting.[30] The 'squaler', a piece of cane about eighteen inches in length topped with a piece of lead and thrown with great efficiency at rabbits and squirrels, rather than the cricket bat was in everyday use.[31] The analysis of the diary of a Marlborough schoolboy on p. 20 provides a clear picture of the everyday amusements of the time.[32] And the more intellectual enjoyed the liberty to pursue their esoteric pleasures. William Morris, at Marlborough from 1848 to 1851, 'never played cricket or football' but explored the pre-Celtic long barrows above Pewsey Vale, the stone circles of Avebury and the Roman villas at Vennel.[33]

At Lancing, the official historian records: 'There were, in fact, no organised games for some considerable time and small boys amused themselves with marbles or "chiving" or climbing trees; the older boys passed the hours of leisure in haphazard ways, sometimes with a book, sometimes with a pretence at cricket, sometimes with a saunter over the Downs',[34] and an old boy wrote joyfully of his Lancing schooldays in the middle of the century: 'what could we do with our freedom then, except range over the glorious unspoilt countryside'.[35]

Pre-Almond Loretto in the 1850s in the hands of the Langhorne brothers 'had no adequate separate playground . . . within the school precincts and none at all without'.[36] The boys fled to the local golf course and shared it fully with the players.

At Uppingham under Holden, the headmaster before Thring, some played hockey, cricket, fives and swam, but 'a larger proportion of the boys rambled'. T. G. Bonney, the famous naturalist, remembered Holden's liberality with affection and gratitude, and attributed his interest in natural history to it.[37] He collected birds' eggs, dug for fossils and sketched the stone coffins of Liddington churchyard.

At Harrow, amusements before the era of athleticism included bird-shooting, nesting, duck-hunting and even for a while, beagling, in addition to cricket, football, racquets and hares and hounds, but the most popular entertainment was 'toozling' or chasing and killing birds in the hedgerows. A pupil recorded in his diary in the late 1830s:

Went out shooting, over Hedstone fields and having no sport, put down the gun and found a Joe Bent in Hedge adjoining private road, which was killed after a splendid run by M. Tufnell. Found a robin in same hedge, which, after an

The diary of Boscawen Somerset: content analysis of daytime leisure entries

a) 25 February – 24 June 1851

Countryside excursions	Visits to Marlborough	Bathing	Games	Illness	Confined to school grounds	Miscellaneous*	No details or entry not clear	Total leisure entries
42	14	5	4 (Including two occasions when he was confined to school grounds and played cricket, and a third occasion – a whole holiday – when he played cricket, was out first ball and went off nesting)	10	6	12	16	109

* Miscellaneous includes study (1), chess (2), music practice and egg blowing (1), watching bathing (1), high jumping (2), kickabout (2), 'laid up in field' (1), packing eggs (1) and general packing (1).

b) 19 September – 18 December 1851

In the autumn and winter months Somerset apparently felt free to devote more time to games. During the period 19 September to 18 December 1851 he shared his time more equally between football and rural forays. In late November the weather was particularly cold and there were several skating afternoons on local ponds.

Countryside excursions	Games (football)	Visits to Marlborough	Skating	Miscellaneous*	No details or entry not clear	Total leisure entries
28	23	13	7	5	12	88

* Miscellaneous includes bathing in September (2), walking in school fields (1) 'made out proportions for boat' (1) and backgammon (1).

exceedingly brilliant run, was killed by Mr. Torre. Had an animated run with Joe Bent. Home by Church Fields. N.B. Game plentiful but blackbirds wild. First eggs taken, Missle Thrushes.[38]

Stonyhurst proves an exception to the rule of freedom existing in the other five schools – an idiosyncracy that will become commonplace in this study. The liberty of the pupil to do as he pleased in his own free time was not an acceptable principle or practice. The Jesuits were continental in their educational philosophy and practice. They faithfully transplanted continental habits in English soil. They brought with them to Stonyhurst their traditional 'surveillant' or 'Hofmeister' whose function was to exercise unflagging supervision of the pupils 'to establish and maintain order, to prevent evil and repress abuse'.[39] The rules of surveillance were meticulous and laid down century after century in Jesuit publications such as *Ordre de Jour pour le Collège des Pensionnaires de la Flèche*, *Observations Relatives à la bonne Tenue d'un pensionnat* and *Practical Manual of the Prefect*. The supervision was unrelenting.[40]

In contrast to the other schools, exploration of the countryside was tightly circumscribed and consisted of formal walks in escorted crocodiles. For their games the boys were restricted to a large playground on the south side of the school, which three prefects (members of the Jesuit staff) patrolled constantly. In the early days the playground was not fenced but breaking bounds was not easy. The famous naturalist, Charles Waterton, an early Stonyhurst pupil, recorded:

At Stonyhurst there are boundaries marked out to the students, which they are not allowed to pass, and there are prefects always pacing to and fro within the lines, to prevent any unlucky boys from straying on either side of them. Not withstanding the vigilance of these lynx-eyed guardians, I would now and then manage to escape and would bolt into a very extensive labyrinth of yew and holly trees, close at hand.[41]

The unremitting surveillance of Waterton's 'lynx-eyed guardians' which, in the words of the Schools Inquiry Commission was 'the most peculiar feature of the discipline'[42] at Stonyhurst, as we shall discover in due course, was to block the thrust of athleticism there.

Before 1845 the picture is clear. With the single exception of Stonyhurst the schools of this study were characterised by the pupils' substantial liberty to roam over the local countryside and the restriction of staff concern to the classroom. In all the schools sponsored, systematised and compulsory games were as yet unknown.

2

Licence, antidote and emulation

By the end of the nineteenth century athleticism was to marshal a coherent set of educational arguments for its existence and become the hallmark of an acceptable public school. By a process of observation, borrowing and assimilation it was to become a remarkably uniform manifestation. Then, a further process of reappraisal, ideological and organisational reconstruction commenced. And its decline began. Its evolution is analogous with the formation of an ancient river: its sources are minor tributaries; its main force is a broad and powerful stream; its mouth is a silted and sluggish delta. However integrated its main confluence, its origins, at least in the schools of this study, were markedly diverse. This diversity can be seen clearly from the separate investigation of each of the six schools which follows in this and the next chapter.

As the young master in *Tom Brown's Schooldays*[1] G. E. L. Cotton may have preached the virtues of games for developing co-operation, unselfishness and sound character, but his principal motive in introducing games at Marlborough is to be found in the disciplinary problems that faced him on his arrival there as headmaster in 1852: poaching, trespassing and general lawlessness. These problems had been compounded by a dramatic rise in school numbers. In 1843 there were 200 pupils; by 1848 the number had risen to over 500. Consequently 'the bully had become more ferocious, the poacher more audacious and the breaker of bounds more regardless of the law'.[2] The situation had become so serious that Cotton's predecessor, M. Wilkinson, had been faced with an insurrection which led to his resignation and which the college's historians have described as a 'great rebellion'.[3] Cotton joined 'a large disorganised . . . turbulent community'.[4]

His first priority, therefore, was to gain control over a considerable body of fractious pupils who had antagonised the neighbourhood and bullied the staff. He set out his plan of campaign in his 'Circular to Parents' of June 1853[5] in which he argued for organised games, improved cultural amenities and a reformed syllabus. His main objective was to keep the pupils 'as much as possible together in one body in the college itself and in the playground'. He saw organised games as the means to this end. How he proposed to 'encourage' games was carefully described in the 'Circular'. He claimed that games at the school were imperfectly organised and the facilities hopelessly inadequate, and proposed that the boys' money, frequently spent on questionable amusement, should be spent instead on 'constant and wholesome' recreation. He, therefore, recommended direct subscription to games clubs so as to develop the athletic amenities of the school and seduce the pupils away from the local farms and estates.

Games were not the exclusive subject of the 'Circular' nor the only recreational 'amusements' he wished to promote. House libraries, carpentry and scientific occupations were further ambitions. He also ventured to suggest a 'modern side' which eventually became a reality in 1858, but the 'Circular' is of special importance for the evolution of athleticism because it constitutes a statement of intent to include games as part of the formal curriculum of the school. It marks a turning-point in the development of public school education. Cotton's 'Circular to Parents' was the epitaph to unsupervised leisure.

In seeking to restrict the boys to the college, Cotton was faced with a dilemma. If vandalism was to be curbed, if good relations with the community were to be fostered, if a respectable image was to be successfully cultivated, there had to be some form of control over the boys. At the time the common distinction between a private and public school was the freedom from supervision the boys enjoyed in the latter.[6] And Cotton was quite clear in his own mind about this distinction. In his 'Circular' he referred to 'the liberty which is necessary if Marlborough is also to confer the advantages, and be conducted on the principles of English public schools, under which any system of entire and compulsory restriction to College premises is quite impossible'.[7]

His original and Machiavellian solution was to introduce a policy of staff involvement in school games. He appointed young games players as masters who, through their enthusiasm, drew the boys onto the playing fields and kept them there. The most successful of these custodians were E. A. Scott, C. M. Bull and Charles Bere.[8]

Scott was a key figure in the development of rugby football, racquets and fives, and also had a large part to play in the introduction of colours and house matches. Bull proved a more than adequate inspirational leader and drove his boys relentlessly on the games field.[9] Bere was responsible for introducing rugby to Marlborough. The boys' appreciation of his contribution to their recreation is suggested in the diary of Henry Palmer, one of his pupils. The entry for 10 March 1854 reads '. . . had a splendid game of football . . . Bere was heartily cheered as this was his last game with us, he probably leaves tomorrow.'[10] Other notable sporting masters under Cotton were George Branson, something of a sporting eccentric who hurled himself into the rugby 'squashes' of the time in a tall hat (games at that time were played in ordinary clothes), Henry Richard Tomkinson, educated at Rugby in Cotton's house and a fine all-rounder who became Cotton's brother-in-law, and John Sowerby who, as assistant master under Wilkinson, collected the reluctant, the enthusiastic and common-room volunteers for cricket games on half-holidays. Such men earned this accolade some years later: 'Marlborough's great reformation was accomplished in her games. These brave masters came amongst us and reformed our cricket in a slight degree; they altogether reformed our football turning it from a private farce into a great school institution.'[11] It must be added that they were also the successful instruments of Cotton's sensible and cunning expedience. Through their efforts, wrote his wife after his death, 'a civilised out-of-door life in the form of cricket, football and wholesome sports took the place of poaching, rat hunting and poultry stealing'.[12]

While his young masters played, Cotton preached. A feature of public school literature in the nineteenth century is the published sermons of headmasters. They were the repository not only of moral cliché and high-minded exhortation, but also of personal idealism and educational philosophy. They were a form of public testimony intended to demonstrate the pastoral concern and intellectual power of the preacher. Through school sermons the public judged the tone of the school and the church estimated the headmaster's suitability for preferment. Publication was an exercise in publicity no headmaster, ambitious for himself and for his school, could ignore. All the great headmasters and many obscure ones published their sermons.

In his published sermons Cotton carefully rationalised his efforts

1 Stonyhurst idiosyncracy: religious, social and geographical isolation resulted in versions of both football and cricket which were far more idiosyncratic than those of most public schools as this etching of Stonyhurst football illustrates.

2   G. E. L. Cotton, often considered to have begun the athleticism movement but whose role in this regard has been exaggerated. His innovations probably owed much to the Harrow headmaster, Charles Vaughan.

at keeping order – it was hardly desirable that team games should be
publicised as instruments of seduction and appeasement. He gave
the Graeco-Renaissance concept of 'the whole man' a Christian
emphasis. The argument was straightforward. God was the
Creator of our bodies as well as our minds. His workmanship
included physical as well as mental powers and faculties. In developing both we served Him who made us, no less surely than
when we knelt in prayer.[13] Cotton was careful to emphasise the
correct moral imperative implicit in physical effort. Only when
such striving reflected religious goodness was it blessed.

It has been suggested that if Hughes was the first in literature to
glorify athletics as a moral discipline, Cotton was the first to do so
in practice.[14] The claim is far too dogmatic. Cotton cannot be said to
have glorified athletics. He knew the inevitable outcome of such an
attitude at Marlborough. He had few illusions about his pupils. The
schoolboy world, he once remarked, was one of 'low morality, of
neglect of holy things, of discouragement of earnest goodness'.[15]
Unsurprisingly, therefore, he spoke out firmly against an 'immoderate interest' in athletic pastimes:

Perhaps its least evil is, that it retards the course of that education which is to fit you
for doing your duty to God and man. It must also engender a certain amount of
self-will, a feeling of self-importance, a desire for self-indulgence. The applause
here bestowed upon success in games is apt to blind a person to his own ignorance,
to make him indifferent to the faults of his character, to prevent him from realizing
the fact that he will be judged very differently when he passes from boyhood to
manhood. Above all this immoderate interest in mere amusement is inconsistent
with the sober spirit of watching unto prayer. It intrudes not only into time of
study, but into times intended for holier occupations. Thus by a strange perversity
we employ God's gifts for our own injury.[16]

Interestingly, Henry Palmer wrote in his diary, 'Cotton told me I
was going the way of all cricketers because I failed in my
repetition.'[17]

Despite the cumbrous pieties of Cotton's sermons, due to his
influence, from the middle of the nineteenth century the Marlborough boys' variations on traditional English field sports gradually became a thing of the past and games began to dominate their
thoughts. Evidence of the impact of the new ideas is available in
Palmer's diary. It provides an interesting contrast with the diary of
Boscawen Somerset. Between February and June 1854 Palmer's
diary contains ninety-seven leisure entries. He played games on sixty-
three afternoons and explored the countryside on only thirteen

occasions. And these outings were restricted to sedate Sunday walks among the beeches of Savernake. Whereas Somerset roamed the Downs, Palmer journeyed between stumps and goalposts, a practice very familiar to later generations of Marlborough boys.

Cotton left Marlborough in 1858 to become Bishop of Calcutta. He ensured the perpetuation of his reform by influencing the governors to appoint G. G. Bradley (1858–70) as his successor.[18] The latter's enthusiasm and support for games guaranteed their place in school life.[19] Cotton achieved his ends at Marlborough: institutional survival and pupil compliance. But he also ushered in a movement for which the public school system would pay a high price in bitter criticism, savage contempt and ridiculed stereotypes. Cotton may be likened to the godfather who was happy to take part in the baptismal ceremonies but who would have been dismayed, if he had lived, to find himself responsible for a not particularly congenial set of godchildren.[20]

Be that as it may, the important point is that one of the origins of athleticism lay in the utilisation of games as a form of *social control*. Cotton's educational rationale disguised the nature of the enterprise and legitimated the action. An ideology was born, not because of the nobility that supposedly arose from the action, but because an argument made an action acceptable. As Cyril Norwood, a later headmaster of Marlborough wrote: 'Cotton went to Marlborough . . . to create a school out of mutineers, and he consciously developed organised games as one of the methods by which the school should be brought into order.'[21]

II

On Tuesday, 22 February 1853, certain members of the fifth and sixth forms of Harrow School held a meeting at which, 'It was decided that a Club should be established at Harrow, to be called the Harrow Philathletic Club, with the view of promoting among the members of the school an increased interest in games and other manly exercises.'[22] A prospectus was subsequently printed and circulated.

It is an enthusiastic and constructive document which in some respects bears a close resemblance to Cotton's 'Circular to Parents', a similarity which could be more than fortuitous as will be seen in due course. It laid stress, for example, on the fact that, 'the encouragement of innocent amusements and recreation must tend greatly to the maintenance of order and discipline throughout the School'. Furthermore, members were pledged to the promotion and encouragement of a variety of games 'by pecuniary contributions'. It advocated the collection of subscriptions for games prizes, the encouragement of house matches and the foundation of a gymnasium. It asserted somewhat optimistically that 'those who play well, will be generally found to work well'; a premise that was to be subsequently disproved. Finally, it expressed concern about a general apathy and want of spirit and the considerable lack of interest in games. It argued that the main benefit of a sports club would be to disseminate throughout the school 'a stronger feeling of interest in manly exercises and amusements than now exists'.

This was an accurate prediction. In later decades the Philathletic Club was to be a body of enormous influence, prestige and power. The other schools eventually developed powerful games committees either exclusively of boys or a mixture of boys and staff, but Harrow Philathletic Club is unique in its early conception, and its influence. Its membership comprised thirty pupils elected from the sixth and fifth forms and was a 'corps d'élite' which ultimately organised, coerced and flattered the bulk of the school into a complicated system of regimented games playing. It was a significant instrument of both innovation and maintenance in the history of athleticism.

It is curious that the role of the club in the evolution of games has been neglected. Much has been made of the contributions of Cotton and Thring to this development. It has been stated that Marlborough and Uppingham were the matrix from which organised games sprang. McIntosh has written in this connection: 'The lead was taken not by the older schools but by such newly established schools as Marlborough and Uppingham'; [23] and again: 'It was in two Philistine schools, Marlborough and Uppingham, that athleticism made its most significant advances in the eighteen-fifties.'[24] Yet it is a fact that the Harrow Philathletic Club literature predates Cotton's 'Circular to Parents' and Thring's first-day inspirational efforts on the Uppingham school cricket field when he joined the boys in a game of cricket. The 'Prospectus', the 'Rules' and the 'Circular to Old Boys'[25] represent a carefully planned attempt to systematise and extend physical exercise throughout the school. The scheme is at once as ambitious, revolutionary and extensive as that of Cotton and it was committed to paper *two months earlier* than Cotton's letter after a considerably earlier conception.[26]

This closeness in time of the appearance of the two circulars from Harrow and Marlborough excites both interest and conjecture in the absence of conclusive evidence. Of particular interest is the part played by C. J. Vaughan in the emergence of both these documents, and in the creation of the Philathletic Club itself.

Vaughan took up the headship of Harrow in 1845 at the age of twenty-eight. Like Cotton he was no athlete, rather a distinguished scholar. According to J. E. C. Welldon, who questioned Vaughan's contemporaries, he hated games.[27] At Rugby he had been greatly influenced by Arnold's idea and with Arthur Penrhyn Stanley and William Charles Lake formed the famous group of Arnoldian disciples who spread Arnold's doctrines throughout the school. He preferred the more elevating and mature practice of discussing religious and philosophical matters during walks in the Midland countryside to playing games. At Cambridge his interests remained spiritual and intellectual. Subsequently at Harrow he expressed constant anxiety over his pupils 'sowing to the flesh' rather than 'sowing to the spirit'.[28]

There is no evidence to show that Vaughan desired to lead by example and usher boys onto the playing fields as in the case of Thring, or that he had evolved a considerable educational philosophy which embraced those fields as in the case of Almond. His sermons, in contrast to those of Cotton, are notably free of any rationale for the introduction of physical activities. On the contrary, with pure Arnoldian didacticism, when he piously reminded his boys that spirit, mind and body in that sequence was the concern of the school, he reflected mournfully that 'at a place like this you are constantly tempted to invert that natural order'.[29] He could deliver a sermon on the formation of character and ignore the games field completely. On the single occasion when he conceded virtue in what he considered the obsessional interest of Harrow boys in games, it was to find spiritual satisfaction in the manner in which they acted to merge the individual in the community thus developing an awareness of membership of the body of Christ!

Yet Vaughan is something of an enigma. While some commentators judged him indifferent to games and while he maintained a low profile in connection with them, it should not be overlooked that the strenuous Charles Kingsley was a friend who regularly preached and dined at Harrow,[30] that Vaughan himself was extremely enthusiastic about the success of his own house in school games[31] and that in the Philathletic Club circular it is noted that the plans for the club had met 'with the entire approbation of the Head Master'.[32]

There is a certain logic in the argument that the reign of the previous headmaster, C. Wordsworth, rather than that of Vaughan should have seen the inception of the Philathletic Club. In him we find that blend of intellectualism, piety and physical talent so common to nineteenth-century muscular Christians. As a boy at Winchester (1820–5) he was a brilliant academic and 'the best cricketer, footballer, fives (bat and hand) player and runner in the school, and on account of this was known as "The Great Christopher"'.[33] He played in the first match against Harrow in 1825 (his brother Charles was captain of the Harrow eleven)[34] and at Cambridge remained an enthusiast, playing tennis, cricket and billiards as well as rowing and shooting. Gradually, however, intellectual interests became uppermost and by the time he was appointed to Harrow he was in the traditional mould of the headmasters of the time: theologian and classicist. Not a whisper for or against games came from his chapel pulpit[35] and there is no record of him taking an interest in the boys' games. He represented the old orthodoxy, his physical skills subordinated to his professional image. His conventionality, which defied logic, emphasises the radicalism of Cotton, Thring and Almond, and more subtly that of Vaughan.

The irony is that Wordsworth might usefully have retained and used his great games ability at Harrow, for under him indiscipline flourished and in consequence numbers fell off. In 1845 Vaughan came to repair the damage and paradoxically, in view of his own unathletic inclinations, it was in his time that organised games became established. The time was ripe. The same practical circumstances that dictated Cotton's actions at Marlborough also shaped the behaviour of Vaughan whatever his personal inclinations or spiritual reservations. He was faced with difficulties remarkably similar to those which were to face Cotton eight years later at Marlborough: a failing school, indisciplined pupils, and the hostility of the local community.

The wildness, brutality and irresponsibility of Harrow boys of the time is extensively recorded.[36] Torre recalled that in the years before Vaughan many boys kept a dog and cats, the one to kill the others. He mentioned another popular activity – stone-throwing – and described fights between the Harrow boys and the navvies building the London and North-Western Railway.[37] Another Harrovian of the period referred to stone-throwing as 'the prevailing vice of Harrow' and described how boys used to exchange fire with the school's professional bowler and ground keeper who never moved about without a pocketful of stones.[38] And yet another provided particularly gruesome details of the years before Vaughan's headmastership: 'Stone-throwing was the principal leisure occupation of the boys and they performed with deadly accuracy. No dog could live on Harrow Hill. Ponies frequently lost their eyes if they had to pull their owners' carts near the school.'[39] Considerable ill-feeling among the locals resulted from such behaviour and from the carelessness of the boys on their runs through the countryside.[40] Such actions led to the advice offered privately to Vaughan on his appointment as headmaster, to sack the 69 boys remaining after Wordsworth had left and start afresh.[41] Vaughan ignored this advice. He won the confidence of parents and numbers rose to 283 by 1847.[42] His school was no longer in danger of extinction but he then faced a further problem equally familiar to Cotton: a large number of unruly boys with unregulated and unsupervised leisure, precisely the situation that had brought the school to its knees under Wordsworth.

Vaughan reacted to this problem by introducing Arnoldian practice.[43] In particular he greatly extended the power of the prefects (referred to as monitors at Harrow) in an attempt to curb indiscipline.[44] Details are available in his famous apologia on the Platt/Stewart affair of 1854, which he wrote to Lord Palmerston,[45] himself a distinguished Old Harrovian, who was incensed by the tyranny of boys over boys he considered implicit in the monitorial reforms. Vaughan's arguments closely resembled those of Cotton regarding the advantages of the prefectorial system. The task of the monitor was 'the enforcement of internal discipline, the object of which is good order, the honourable conduct, the gentlemanlike tone of the houses and of the school'. The alternative, he argued, was 'the unceasing espionage of an increased staff of subordinate masters'; a system which, as already discussed, was repugnant to a true public school.

Like Cotton, Vaughan saw the possibilities in games for expending boys' energy and keeping them within bounds; but while Cotton relied on masters to persuade boys onto the playing fields, he put his faith in his monitors. This link between his monitorial system and organised games is clear from a number of sources. In a circular sent by 'an Assistant Master' of the school to parents in April 1854, it was stated that the prefectorial reforms had been

devised expressly for the organisation of games: 'such is the intention, such is the tendency and such is the main effect of the Monitorial System at Harrow'.[46] It is no surprise therefore to find that the
monitors were ex-officio members of the Philathletic Club, an
arrangement that clearly suggests the influence of the school
authorities. Then again the Platt/Stewart controversy itself arose
out of the newly introduced monitorial supervision on the football
pitch which gave Platt the right to punish Stewart, a point which
The Times in the subsequent furore completely failed to
appreciate.[47] E. C. Mack noted the close relationship between the
monitorial and games systems and maintained that with the improved organisation of the prefect system under Vaughan, games
became a regular means to perfect the more manly moral ideals. He
also asserted that 'while Vaughan did not further athleticism as did
Cotton, his [monitorial] system readily served it'.[48] Vaughan *did*
further athleticism of course, precisely by means of his monitors
just as Cotton did by means of his masters. Both did so largely
unintentionally, but both did so for exactly the same reasons – as a
means of controlling and supervising unruly pupils.

In any consideration of the innovational similarities of Cotton
and Vaughan it is important to recall that they were close friends as
well as professional colleagues. They had been at Cambridge
together and Vaughan was responsible for Cotton going to Rugby.[49]
During their respective headships they maintained continual contact. Vaughan delivered sermons at Marlborough on several
occasions.[50] and it was he who gave the sermon at Cotton's consecration as Bishop of Calcutta in 1858. As headmasters it would be
most unlikely that they failed to discuss their mutual problems or
mull over possible solutions. It is entirely reasonable to suggest that
they attempted broadly the same solutions to the same problems,
some form of 'police force' and the introduction of organised
games, as a result of such discussion and reflection. It is further
possible that since Vaughan was the senior and more experienced
headmaster (he had been headmaster for seven years before Cotton
obtained his appointment), and since the idea of the Philathletic
Club had been mooted as early as 1852, a year earlier than Cotton's
'Circular' appeared and even before Cotton became headmaster of
Marlborough, the idea of organised games as an antidote to vandalism, trespassing and indiscipline at both Marlborough and Harrow
owed as much, if not more, to Vaughan as to Cotton.[51]

A somewhat sophisticated approach on the part of Vaughan to

the introduction of organised games, namely permitting the initiative to be seen to come from the boys through their apparent creation of the Philathletic Club, would be entirely in keeping with his technique for handling relationships with his pupils. A large part of his success at Harrow lay in his careful diplomacy in dealings with the boys.[52] His was the iron fist tucked well into the velvet glove. In all his major reforms he moved gently, first sensibly winning the boys over to his side. He had, apparently, an intuitive understanding of boys and was well aware of their conservatism. It would not be surprising, therefore, if he set up a monitorial system *inter alia* to supervise games, and waited several years before the introduction of further games reform by means of the Philathletic Club. He waited, in fact, until the improvement of facilities would make reforms viable, and in 1849 games facilities were extended by six acres.[53] Another reason for the specific timing of the creation of the club is suggested in the 'Prospectus' – as a remedy for a considerable decline in the school's interest in games. This was a state of affairs too dangerous to tolerate. To do so would be to risk a return to the bad practice of former days.

Whether Vaughan was the 'éminence grise' behind Cotton's reforms and the conception of the Philathletic Club or merely, in the case of the latter, a sensible opportunist gratefully endorsing a useful disciplinary tool or a realist bowing to popular demand, or all these things is not absolutely clear. But there are good grounds for postulating that he had a more active role in the promulgation of organised games at both Marlborough and Harrow than has been hitherto appreciated.

Despite Vaughan's deliberate utilisation of games as an instrument of social control, he appears to have been less concerned than Cotton to provide an underpinning educational rationale for public consumption. With the onus of responsibility on the boys rather than on the masters there was perhaps less need to justify the action. While at Marlborough ideological support and organisational implementation occurred simultaneously, at Harrow, from the evidence available, ideological argument for a games system followed implementation. It was not until the 1860s and 70s that pupils, staff and old boys began to put forward a respectable set of ideological arguments.

Lack of early rhetorical support and uncertainty over the precise extent of Vaughan's contribution, however, should not distract attention from the fact that Harrow possessed and implemented a set of plans for the organisation of games *before* both Marlborough and Uppingham. Despite what has been asserted in some quarters, as we have seen above, at least one of the older schools played as important a part as the newer schools in the evolution of athleticism. Nor should the fact be overlooked that systematised games at Harrow as at Marlborough arose primarily out of organisational expediency.

III

In 1857 Lancing College was established on a spur of the Sussex Downs overlooking the Adur estuary,[54] a year before Cotton left Marlborough for Calcutta and two years before Vaughan mysteriously withdrew from Harrow into obscurity.

It was the conception of Nathaniel Woodard. Woodard was the son of an Essex country gentleman and one of a large family so that his father was unable to give him a public school and university education. He was a religious boy and wished early to become a clergyman, but his lack of degree made this impossible. In 1834, however, due to the kind support of relatives, he took up residence as a rather elderly undergraduate at Magdalen Hall (now Hertford College), Oxford. His academic ability was only moderate; he took six years to graduate, but in 1841 he achieved his childhood ambition. He was ordained by the Bishop of London and appointed curate in the parish of St Bartholomew, Bethnal Green. There, he became greatly interested in the education of his parishioners. He won a considerable reputation for energy, initiative and concern, and managed to provide them with a school. 'Romish' views on confession, however, resulted in a controversy with his bishop which led to his dismissal.

As a consequence of the Bethnal Green dispute, Woodard was offered and accepted the curacy of New Shoreham in Sussex by the incumbent William Wheeler, himself of High Church leanings. The population of Shoreham, a small south-coast port, were mostly lower-middle-class tradesmen and sea captains. Woodard found them irreligious, illiterate and dangerously impractical. The captains were so ignorant of the science of navigation as to be unable to use a quadrant. As a result, on 11 January 1847 he opened a day school for the middle classes in the drawing room of the New Shoreham vicarage. One intention was to offer them useful training in navigation and general educational skills, but a more profound purpose was to draw them off 'from the bad influence of their present principles';[55] in short, to wean them away from their godless, ignorant way of life. This was clear from the curriculum of the new school: it was to be 'a Religious and good sound Commercial Education with the elements of Latin and French'.[56] The religious element was pronounced. The day began with attendance at matins; religious habits were noted in the mark book; 'good religious habits' won prizes: 'useful and Religious books'!

In 1848 Woodard extended his Shoreham scheme to include boarding facilities for 'young gentlemen, sons of clergy and others'. It was an action stimulated less by idealism than by pragmatism. He wished to cater for a moneyed middle-class clientele in order to create a reserve fund for times of crisis and a reproduction fund for new foundations. By the following year there were two schools at Shoreham: St Mary's Grammar School (a day school for the lower middle class) and St Nicolas' Grammar School (a boarding school for the professional class). They were soon to merge and within a few years to become SS Mary and Nicolas School, Lancing, eventually to be known as Lancing College. The main elements of Woodard's ambitious educational scheme, which in time he hoped would span the whole of England, were now evident: an education for the middle class with a strong religious emphasis within a boarding system.[57]

Woodard's ideal of a network of schools throughout the length and breadth of England was never realised. Funds, though substantial, were insufficient for adequate endowments, but one year before Woodard's death the scheme comprised 'eleven schools, representing an investment of hundreds of thousands of pounds . . . In the South were SS Mary and Nicolas, Lancing; St John's, Hurstpierpoint; St Saviour's, Ardingly; and St Michael's, Bognor; St Chad's, Denstone; St Oswald's, Ellesmere, and St Anne's and St Mary's, Abbots Bromley; St Winifred's, Bangor, and the day school at Dewsbury all functioned in the Midlands. King's College, Taunton, was established in the West.'[58] The boys' schools, in their urgent desire for public school status, as we shall see shortly, comprised a solid corpus of schools committed to athleticism.

Of the schools created by Woodard, Lancing College with its origins in his first boarding school, St Nicolas' Grammar School, was the socially superior. Its clientele were lesser gentry and the professions. From its inception Woodard claimed for it the status of a public school.[59] At Shoreham before its move, however, it was small and shabby and was hard pressed to claim the position to which it aspired. B. W. T. Handford has written, 'there was a certain pathos in the condition of the school at this time'.[60] Indeed, it was originally advertised realistically as a 'public school for the sons of gentlemen of restricted means'. In Handford's opinion, it was only on taking up residence on Lancing Hill that the college became recognisable as a genuine public school. Instrumental in this social elevation, he has asserted – significantly – were the provision of reasonable games facilities, the rapid development of organised games and a house system. With these essentials the school could be, and was, advertised confidently as 'a public school for the sons of gentlemen and persons in affluent circumstances[61] and the fees were considerably increased. The importance of adequate playing fields in the quest for an unassailable image was again demonstrated some years later by the drive to improve these facilities in the 1880s, when numbers remained disappointingly static. The relatively makeshift character of the games facilities and accessories in comparison with better schools was held to be responsible. Men of wealth, it was argued, would scarcely consider Lancing a leading public school.[62]

An admirer has suggested that respect for the public school system taught Woodard that true education was an indivisible whole, affecting body, mind and soul 'operative no less on the playing field than in the classroom', and that this was the reason he provided his schools with playing space.[63] If this is so, it must be said there is no direct evidence of his appreciation of a holistic argument for games. Unlike Thring and Almond he never articulated a philosophy of physical education. In his surviving sermons and educational pamphlets there is no record of any reflection on physical education provision in his schools or an awareness of the possibilities of moral learning inherent in team games.[64] Equally he does not appear to have joined in the games of his boys. Although he had certain affinities with Kingsley in his social conscience, he was no muscular Christian.

In fact, Woodard does not appear to have been greatly interested in games. When he set up his first school, St Mary's Grammar School in 1848, he showed greater concern for its organisation than for that of the subsequent schools he founded. It is interesting to note, therefore, that like Arnold he appeared to find little educational value in team games. While he provided gym poles in the garden, and a design for a larger school in Shoreham included a gymnasium and a fives court,[65] he revealed no apparent concern for games as an element of the curriculum.

And in general he made no radical contributions to the public school curriculum. His aim was to extend the provision of a past age rather than pioneer change in the manner of Sanderson of Oundle, Reddie of Abbotsholme or Almond of Loretto. The Schools Inquiry Commission highlighted this conservatism by revealing the complete absence of science teaching at Lancing, and the existence of a solidly classical curriculum.[66] On the evidence available, the provision of playing fields, such as they were, certainly in the case of Lancing, can be more reasonably attributed to Woodard's great concern to provide it with the image of a public school,[67] rather than to a personal philosophy of education or physical education.

Woodard had a free hand in the appointment of masters and headmasters.[68] And it would appear that to further a public school image at Lancing he speedily appointed games enthusiasts to the staff. In 1855, on the eve of Lancing's move to its new home, William Sterne Raymond joined the school. It was a revealing appointment. He was a good scholar *and* an all-round athlete: swimmer, jumper, footballer, runner, cricketer. To these sporting talents he added a passionate nature, a simple character, a vivacious manner and a sincere Christianity; yet another mid–century Kingsleian muscular Christian.

His appointment was a logical outcome of Woodard's ambition for it was to Raymond that the status–conscious Lancing owed its organised games and early games facilities. Shortly after his arrival Lancing Cricket Club was systematised and house matches started. He constructed the first cricket ground on the Dyke Field, and in conjunction with two local professionals coached and played in the school eleven. He also founded Lancing football. As a direct consequence of all this, Raymond was, in Handford's telling phrase, 'perhaps the first to begin the work of changing St Nicolas' School, Shoreham, into a public school'.[69] This was certainly the most important historical outcome of his actions, but whether it had a personal motive is unclear. One important reason for his enthusiasm for games that is clear, however, was the release they offered 'from sins of the grosser kind', the 'inward conflict with the demon lust' and the 'enormous evil of unchastity'.[70]

Raymond was not a public school boy but the product of Bury St

Edmund's Grammar School, Suffolk. It was mid-century Cambridge that provided him with the opportunity to develop his games-playing ability, and the changing climate of opinion concerning the role of assistant masters about this time allowed him the opportunity to teach boys outdoors as well as indoors. He died prematurely in 1863, but by then he had laid the foundations of organised games at Lancing and given the school the first layer of a public school patina.

While Raymond's influence was restricted to Lancing, the general change in the climate of opinion regarding the role of games, and the role of staff in relation to them within the Woodard school system as a whole, was considerably facilitated and accelerated by E. C. Lowe who joined Woodard in 1849. Lowe was assistant master at St Nicolas' School, Shoreham, for a term before taking up the headship of St John's, Hurstpierpoint, which opened in the year he entered the system. He remained there as headmaster until 1872. From 1873 to 1891 he was provost[71] of Denstone College. He then returned to Lancing in 1891 as provost and was reappointed in 1896 for two further years.[72] Throughout his career, therefore, he was a distinguished and influential member of the Woodard system.

His significance for this study lies in the fact that he preached unceasingly both the virtues of 'bodily education' and the desirability of a public school life style for all the Woodard institutions with passionate conviction. In 1856, for example, in a sermon entitled 'The Image of God' he argued that physical education was important to ensure a manly presence, in turn important because external appearance was a 'sure index of the man within'.[73] Thirteen years later he took up cudgels with Sir John Coleridge and in an open letter on the virtues of the liberal system of education offered by the society at St Nicolas' College, he wrote of games and playground exercises that he found them highly important and connected with many beneficial moral results;[74] a point made with similar conviction in his evidence to the Schools Inquiry Commission in 1865. The members of the commission could scarcely have doubted his sincerity; the inspector who visited Hurstpierpoint reported that muscle was as much admired there as at any other public school.[75] Finally, in 1878 in a pamphlet in which he looked back over thirty years in Woodard schools, he made a statement of commitment which was quite unexceptional in public school annals for its stereotypic catch-phrases:

An important element of public school training must always be looked for not in the mere excellence of games and athletic sports but in the organisation by boys of a system which calls out their individual powers, gives reasonable self-reliance, teaches forbearance and fair play, and prepares boys for that knowledge of man and manners which in practical utility may dispute the palm with book knowledge itself.[76]

Lowe is an important figure in the history of the Woodard schools. His influential position in the society ensured the development of the right social image not only for Lancing but for the other schools of the system.

In 1859 Henry Walford became headmaster of Lancing. This was a startling appointment. Walford was out of sympathy with 'the austerity and mysticism implied in the Oxford Movement'[77] while Woodard, for his part, was a confirmed disciple of Pusey, Newman and Keble, and believed it was his mission to apply Tractarian Theology to the education of the middle classes.[78] This very divergence of theological views had caused Walford's resignation from the post of assistant master at Lancing which he had held from 1852 to 1855. Yet he was appointed to the headship of the school four years later. The truth of the matter was that Woodard badly needed a headmaster of demonstrably rugged Christianity.

The Woodard system had suffered during the early 1850s from accusations of 'Popish practices', especially sacramental confession. This had given the schools an undesirable image as places of womanish piety and effeminate Puseyism. Largely because of this the then headmaster of Lancing, John Braithwaite, had committed the cardinal sin of public school headmasters: by 1858, after seven years in his charge, the school's numbers had not increased. Braithwaite was a mild and nervous man. Walford's forceful masculinity was in strong contrast. So despite his reservations about Tractarianism he was chosen to replace his opposite in appearance and conviction, and retrieve the fortunes of the school. It was a decision on the part of Woodard that underlines both his practicality and his strong desire to see Lancing a successful public school.

In terms of image Woodard chose well. Walford was a tall, heavily built extrovert, who had been at Rugby under Arnold and encouraged the Lancing boys to think he was the original 'slogger' Williams in the celebrated fight in *Tom Brown's Schooldays*.[79] He radiated a 'manly ethical Christianity' that was to prove a valuable asset to Lancing. He had, in fact, certain similarities in appearance and function with the symbolic Rev. Bernard Colquhoun in

Keddy: a story of Oxford by the obscure Edwardian novelist
H. N. Dickinson. Colquhoun.

stood six foot two in his thick woolly socks . . . he reminded one of the Village
Blacksmith, and the muscles of his brawny arm were considered very taking by
admirers. His appearance made plain black cloth look like the roughest tweed; his
surplice was a suit of mail. In modern days it is surely hard to exaggerate the value
of a man like this. For if anyone were found to say or hint or fear that Christianity is
the religion of weaklings and cowards, Mr. Colquhoun would give a contrary
argument that would not be soon forgotten. It would not be the first time that
orthodoxy has resulted from muscular force.[80]

Walford not only looked the part, he performed the role of muscular Christian quite adequately. He played cricket with the boys,
introduced compulsory games and supported this step with standard ideological arguments from the pulpit.[81]

He was one of a new generation of public school headmasters
who were not simply scholars, but also games players. Temple,
Butler, Thring and Almond, to name but a few, typified the new
men. In appointing Walford, Woodard was calling attention to the
normality of Lancing as a public school; and, in addition, selecting a
man with the type of virile image attractive to parents and pupils.
His stratagem worked. Puseyism was slowly forgotten, masculinity was emphasised and numbers steadily increased.[82]

As significant as Walford's appointment were his senior staff,
W. S. Raymond, the games-playing cleric already discussed, and
A. C. Wilson.[83] Wilson was also a committed supporter of games.
He specialised in producing unbeaten teams. His house cricket team
was unbeaten in ten years and several times beat the rest of the
school. Included in his personal notebook and press cuttings for his
own and others' edification and stimulation, was the following
homily: 'The great value of a school is that it is, or ought to be, a
place of moral discipline, and this discipline is taught as much in the
playground or cricket field as in the classroom.'[84] Walford,
Raymond and Wilson were the first housemasters of the new
Lancing on the Hill. On this site, therefore, it had three masters[85] in
the most powerful positions in the school who welcomed and
promoted the new games system so indispensable to a genuine
public school. With these enthusiasts in authority, games facilities
and a games ethos quickly developed, a state of affairs that reflected
events in the more firmly established public schools up and down
the country such as Marlborough and Harrow.

It was neither disciplinary necessity nor ideological conviction

that provided the major impetus for the development of games at
Lancing. There is no record of serious indiscipline. Numbers, an
important factor as we have seen, were small. Lowe, Walford,
Wilson and Raymond were ideologically committed to a greater or
lesser degree, but Woodard, the central figure who recruited them
all, was not. He sought first and foremost the security of an upper-
class identity for Lancing mainly for reasons of insurance. It was a
case of emulation for acceptance and survival.

IV

Cotton's encouragement of games is considered by Honey as significant for the development of the Victorian public school; but he
finds it difficult to understand how the message spread; Cotton's
masters gained few headships and he himself left little in the way of
propaganda.[86] This chapter throws some light on the problem. It is
not a matter of seeking evidence of cultural diffusion from a single
influential source. Even within the narrow context of the three
schools considered above, there is evidence of parallel innovation as
a product of similar organisational problems; equally the extant
records suggest that imitation of the greater by the lesser played its
part in the diffusion process.

Indeed the contribution of Cotton himself, it is suggested, needs
to be looked at closely. There are grounds for believing that
Vaughan played a more positive part in the introduction of organised games and in the stimulation of athleticism at both Harrow and
Marlborough than has been recognised hitherto. He faced the same
school problems as Cotton, earlier than Cotton, and his school
produced a blueprint of solutions earlier than Marlborough. It is a
distinct possibility that Cotton's reforms owed something to him.

If Vaughan's role in the development of the games cult is not
wholly clear but may well have been underestimated, that of the
Harrow Philathletic Club certainly has been overlooked. Its system
of organised games pre-dates developments at both Marlborough
and Uppingham. This being the case it is difficult to see how the
newer nineteenth-century public schools can continue to be regarded as the exclusive seed beds of the athleticism movement.

3

Idealism, idealists and rejection

Edward Thring (1821–87) inherited a love of the open air.[1] His father, John Gale Thring, was an energetic squarson, rector of the parish of Alford in Somerset and squire of the estate of Alford Manor. It was written of him: 'He had the fondness of the English country gentleman for outdoor life, and was known as the best and boldest rider in the county of Somerset.'[2] Boldness and pleasure in physical action were qualities Thring himself displayed in time. Denied the extensive acres of Alford (he was a younger son) and the leisure of the wealthy rural churchman and possessed of a teaching vocation, Thring transformed indulgence into virtue and riding to hounds into the educational pursuit of leather balls on games fields.

Between 1853 and 1887 Thring transformed Uppingham from a backward grammar school into a national public school. But the school's transformation was as much the consequence of the formative years of his life as of the years of his headship. Thring himself stressed that the schoolboy was father to the schoolmaster. And the schoolboy participated successfully and enthusiastically in a variety of physical activities. At Eton he played cricket, football and fives, raced allcomers and played 'at the Wall'. A contemporary recorded that 'his pluck and muscle were peerless'.[3] Pleasures, habits and enthusiasms that lasted his lifetime, were established and consolidated in the shadow of Windsor.

There were less attractive experiences which were to lead to fortunate consequences for others. Thring was at Eton towards the end of the pre-Clarendon era. He later described the cruelty, the squalor, the official indifference and lack of privacy in a graphic sketch of life in the rat-infested Long Chamber which housed fifty-two boys:

Rough and ready was the life they led: cruel, at times, the suffering and the wrong; wild the profligacy. For after eight o'clock at night no prying eye came near till the following morning; no one lived in the same building; cries of joy and pain were equally unheard; and excepting a code of laws of their own, there was no help or redress for anyone.[4]

When he became a schoolmaster he was moved, in his own words, 'to try to see if I could not make the life of small boys at school happier and brighter'.[5]

In the manner of the nineteenth-century clerical headmaster Cotton eventually left Marlborough for a bishopric.[6] Vaughan was ambitious for similar promotion from Harrow, but was foolishly indiscreet.[7] In contrast, Thring was a professional schoolteacher. His eyes were not fastened upon prestigious bishoprics, restful canonries or wealthy colleges. His ambition was to teach children, and it arose from his experience in the national schools in Gloucester where he took up a curacy in 1847 after leaving Cambridge. It was there that his concern for the less capable child was aroused, a feature that was to characterise his career at Uppingham. He was obsessed by a desire to stimulate comprehension in the unorganised heads of his working-class boys, so distant from the 'brain world of the Cambridge Honours man'[8] In 1886 in his address to the Education Society on his election as president, he reflected on the influence the Gloucester period had had on his subsequent career, declaring that everything he most valued in educational thought, practice and experience stemmed from it.

The strain of his Gloucester work resulted in a crisis of health in 1848, but while he recuperated he did not lose sight of his destiny and acquired further educational experience as a classical examiner at Eton, Rugby and King's College, Cambridge, from teaching private pupils at Great Marlow and from work in the parish school of Stubbings outside Maidenhead. In 1853 he applied for, and obtained, the headship of Uppingham Grammar School in Rutland. He was thirty-two.

Thring was a sensualist. He had a Wordsworthian passion for nature, a Kingsleian delight in bodily exercise and a seldom revealed, but honest pleasure in sex.[9] J. H. Skrine, his Arthur Penrhyn Stanley, considered that he was concerned with the 'antithesis of life to intellect', worshipped life and identified life with feeling rather than mental effort, and 'spent too much time doing to talk much about books'. His temperament, Skrine concluded, was rude and practical.[10] It was an impression he made on the less admiring. When he preached at Harrow the boys nicknamed him

'Old Sheep Folds' on account of his thumping, antiphonic, collo-
quial delivery.[11]

Those commentators who were close to him during his life, J. H.
Skrine and W. F. Rawnsley, leave an impression of an energetic,
intense, opinionated, deeply religious man, a man of the senses
rather than intellect, distrustful of intellectual subtlety, delighting
in robust directness. It is not surprising, therefore, that his favourite
contemporary writers were novelists and poets such as Scott,
Tennyson and Kingsley rather than scientists and philosophers such
as Darwin, Mill and Bentham, nor that he was contemptuous of
agnostics and aesthetes however accomplished. To Thring,
Herbert Spencer was 'a most consummate donkey' and Charles
Swinburne 'the greatest blackguard in Europe'.[12]

These characteristics and predilections make him a candidate for
inclusion in the school of muscular Christians and indeed his close
affinity with Charles Kingsley has been remarked upon. It has been
observed that his ideal of manliness, while chivalric in the manner
of his favourite authors, Scott and Tennyson, moral in the manner
of Farrar and Arnold, Christian in the manner of the children's
writers, Mrs Gatty and Mrs Ewing, 'owed most to Kingsley's ideal
of healthy manliness'.[13] And while Thring held the view that education included the imparting of knowledge as well as the implant-
ing of Kingsleian Christian manliness, in his view the latter was the
supreme aim. Character is a common synonym for manliness in the
language of the period and Thring conventionally valued character
far more highly than mere brains.[14] The experiences of his own
schooldays and early manhood at Gloucester, his wholesome sensuality, his religious fervour and Kingsleian values determined the
shape of Uppingham. It was to be unique.[15]

In the first place it was to provide an education relevant to the
needs of each boy. To this end he expanded the traditional curriculum to include music, drawing, languages *and* games. Since assessment of individual need required sound assessment of the individual he aimed firstly *inter alia* at a pupil–teacher ratio of thirty to
one and a permanent staff who knew the boys well. Secondly,
pupils at his school were to have privacy and dignity; to this end he
established private studies and dormitory cubicles for each boy,[16]
and while giving great power to his prefects he ensured by a system
of careful checks that their power was sensibly restricted. Thirdly,
it was Thring who was to define the educational needs of his pupils.
His concern to provide a training of 'true men' was paramount.

Learning was not to be dictated by eventual occupation or educational tradition but by the educational ideals of Edward Thring.

His concept of education was in essence the Graeco-Renaissance ideal of the whole man: character, intellect and body in harmony. He preached: 'Life is one piece . . . health of body, health of intellect, health of heart all uniting to form the true man.'[17] There could be no separation of parts in sound educational practice wherever the whole training of the heart, mind and body was undertaken. A clear idea of the official ideology of Uppingham under Thring is provided by a group of his pupil-neophytes, who, for reasons of conviction or diplomacy, echoed his philosophy in *School Delusions: essays by the sixth form*, a pamphlet published in 1860. A delusion to be carefully avoided, which recurs throughout this set of essays, was the belief that education comprised the single-minded pursuit of academic success when in reality 'the hard worker and hard player is almost certainly the best man'.[18] In practical terms, at Thring's Uppingham the choice was not between games and learning. Education embraced both.

For Thring was a period rarity. He possessed a philosophy of physical education – with physiological, aesthetic and psychological components: 'The life builds the body. A bad life builds an ugly, unhealthy body; a good life builds a good and healthy body.' Cotton made a passing reference in his sermons to the philosophy of the whole man; Thring devoted his educational life to its theory and practice.

It was not all dogmatism translated into action. Expedience played some part. Thring fully understood the value of the games field for breaking down antagonism between masters and boys and sought to reverse 'a principle of opposition'. He maintained that relationships would prosper if masters showed themselves 'capable of understanding and advancing all manly pleasures', and so he sought a 'unity of purpose' between master and boy in all good things including those refreshing activities of the playing field. And while there was no pressing need at Uppingham on Thring's arrival to develop games as an instrument of social control, in time, as the school grew in size,[19] good relations with the local farmers did become a necessary concern. Thring's diary contains a record of the complaints and fears of the local yeomanry.[20]

Harrow and Marlborough, as has been seen, produced early blueprints for organised games playing: the Philathletic Club 'Prospectus' of April 1853, and Cotton's 'Circular to Parents' of June

1853. At Uppingham, Thring's earliest influence was one of example: 'On the tenth of September, 1853, I entered on my Headmastership with the very appropriate initiation of a whole holiday and a cricket match in which I recall I got 15 by some good swinging hits to the great delight of my pupils.'[21] This participation was to become a habit, proudly maintained. He reported to the Schools Inquiry Commission that he played cricket and football with the boys 'very much indeed'.[22] He played fives until his forty-ninth year; a longevity that was the admiration of his pupils.

Despite a common belief to the contrary, Thring had no blueprint for a school when he arrived at Uppingham.[23] As the school developed so his ideas developed. But he organised as well as reflected, and played. During the first fifteen years he searched tirelessly for games fields;[24] he built fives courts, a bathing pool, a pavilion and the first gymnasium in an English public school – offering tempting if esoteric prizes for the exercises: a goose, a pork pie and a pot of jam;[25] he introduced athletic sports and systematised cricket and football; he probably inaugurated a Committee of Games and certainly offered a Champion's Cup for the best athletic all-rounder. To achieve all this he spent his own money gladly, and pressed masters for theirs.[26] By 1867 he had created physical education facilities for some 300 boys.

Thring's 'triumphalist admirers'[27] portrayed a simple man of exuberant physicality, a then fashionable muscular Christian. The image has persisted.[28] However, the last decade has seen an attempt to present a more rounded, dignified portrait of the man in an age less addicted to traditional public school mores.[29] A simple-minded enthusiasm for athletes and athletics is not, of course, the entirety of Thring's personality. As his recent apologists argue, he struggled against narrow muscularity; he was far more than a games zealot. Yet at the same time he lent his considerable support to games. His appearance at cricket, football and fives, his energetic pursuit of playing fields for his school, his songs of devotion, his speeches of exhortation and his works of educational philosophy, counted for more in the long run than anxious comment in his private diary, infrequent admonishments in the school chapel, resistance to the appointment of a cricket professional and reluctance to champion rugby union football.[30]

His ideal of the educated man was noble, its lineage ancient, his promulgation sincere. But there remains standing at the shoulder of the thoughtful educational figure, a charismatic reformed squarson exuding the odour of exuberant clean-living, a sheaf of sermons for boys in one hand and a cricket bat in the other. An inspiration to action. And the public school world was only too willing to be inspired to play; but was far less moved by his idealism. Ultimately his educational ideas 'fell flat' in the system and even his own school abandoned many he cherished.[31]

The concern here, of course, is less with the man than with his role in the rise of athleticism. In this context he must be considered as a willing and influential contributor to the popularisation of physical activities in school, but an unintentional contributor to their glorification. Like Cotton he was a piper whose tunes provoked a frenzy he failed to contain. He created a force that took control of his school after his death and distorted his educational ideals.[32] He strove for the *aurea mediocritas*: in fact he began a movement eventually characterised by enthusiastic excess. But for the purposes of this study he demonstrates one thing in particular (together with Almond as we shall now see), namely that athleticism did not arise simply out of sensible expedience or calculating imitation, but also out of considered and applied educational theory.

II

Nine years after Edward Thring arrived at Uppingham, Hely Hutchinson Almond (1832–1903) bought a small private school called Loretto at Musselburgh outside Edinburgh. Almond was twenty-nine. He had drifted into teaching.[33] His first choice of a career had been the Indian Civil Service but he was an unsuccessful applicant and in 1857 he was offered a teaching post at Loretto through the good offices of a distant relative and Oxford contemporary, Charles Langhorne. Charles and his two brothers, Thomas and Alexander, ran the school between them. Almond remained a year, moving in 1858 to the post of second master at Merchiston Castle School before purchasing Loretto in 1862, and returning as headmaster.

One of Almond's first actions as a new headmaster was to rent a games field, Pinkie Mains. It was the first in the history of the school. He quickly added a gymnasium. These radical innovations were in part the result of contrasting experiences of his own education, first in Glasgow and then at Oxford. The Scottish education of his own youth was severely scholastic; he had little to do with his afternoons 'but roam aimlessly about the streets and road'. The antidote to this boredom he subsequently discovered at Oxford.

In 1850 he went to Balliol, the recipient of a Snell exhibition. He was a successful scholar but it was the Isis that 'opened his mind to the existence of a new set of values. His love of the open air, his passion for health, his appreciation of manly endurance, his reverence for loyalty and public spirit were . . . the gifts of the river'.[34] In old age Almond clung to the belief that the Balliol eight did him more good than all the academic prizes he had won. It was, in fact, the whole ambience of the English university that excited him: the unexceptional co-existence of physical exercise and academic learning.

Almond always maintained that his early educational experiences reflected the unsound values associated with health of Scottish society. This conviction was so important to the development of Loretto that his official biographer, R. J. Mackenzie, devoted a chapter to Almond's condemnation of Scottish opinion and practice regarding matters of physical well-being. It demonstrates the full extent of Almond's alienation from the Scottish educational and social systems; he castigated the 'bookish' Scot and applauded the manly English. With romantic indulgence he portrayed the English squire and country parson jointly as the harmonious embodiment of a tradition 'of bodily vigour and manly life'. In his flattering opinion their beneficial influence impregnated the English public schools and universities – those 'champions of the physical virtues'. The result, he maintained, was a virile and influential upper class and a sane educational system. Scottish lairds, Almond conceded, stood for manliness, but reneging on nationalism, and with younger sons who were not to be found in the religion of the people as in England, they had little influence. Scottish universities for their part, were peopled with professors whose opinions on matters of physical health stood in marked contrast with the attitude of the Oxford or Cambridge don. The Oxbridge tutor saw the river and the cricket field as educational agencies; the Scottish professor too often regarded them as mischievous distractions or, at best, childish amusements. To add to the distressing burden of an uninfluential gentry and an anti-athletic intelligentsia there was the Scottish bourgeoisie, swept along on a wave of unrelenting commercialism and mawkish religion. They were Almond's real foes. They shuddered at the thought of open bedroom windows; they prophesied rheumatism for the youth in his cold morning tub and bronchitis for the cross-country runner; they were scandalised by the coatless and shocked by the capless, and in the main they thought games an immature occupation for adults and a frivolous one for boys.

It was their conventions that Almond challenged, ridiculed and rejected. The harness of irrational convention cut deeply into his reasoned individualism. He pledged himself to the overthrow of 'Mrs Grundy' and to the elevation of the Goddess of Reason. To this end 'he spent much of his time and energy demonstrating the absurdity and even wickedness of the regulations which Society ordains . . . nor did he confine himself to demonstrations and denials. He conceived the idea . . . of an organised attack upon the presiding genius of conventional society.'[35] In his aggressive individualism he gained much strength from the ideas of John Stuart Mill propounded in his famous *Essay on Liberty*. In particular, as a deliberate and ostentatious eccentric in the interests of good health, Almond was reassured by this appropriate passage:

Precisely because the tyranny of opinion is such as to make eccentricity a reproach, it is desirable, in order to break through that tyranny, that people should be eccentric. Eccentricity has always abounded when and where strength of character has abounded; and the amount of eccentricity in a society has generally been proportional to the amount of genius, mental vigour, and moral courage, which it contained.[36]

In truth, on matters of health Almond had experienced something akin to a Pauline conversion on an English river. A suitable stream was not a feature of Musselburgh but meadows were plentiful. He populated them with his own pupils engaging in healthy English educational practices. But he went further. It was his ambition to apply all the rules of health to school life, so he set about establishing a regimen of sound living that embraced diet, dress and exercise. In this way he hoped to nurture 'a group of evangelical schoolboys' who would spread his gospel throughout society.

In creating his system of physical education he drew inspiration not only from his personal experiences, but also from the writings of Herbert Spencer, John Ruskin and Archibald MacLaren. In 1861 Spencer published his *Education: intellectual, moral and physical*. In it he asserted that the first requisite for success in life was to be a good animal, and a nation of good animals was the first condition of national prosperity. Consequently, he argued, children must be trained to bear the physical wear and tear of life's struggle. Attention should be paid to their diet, clothing and exercise. Some of his caveats and imperatives are wholly Almondian, in particular: 'The

3 H. H. Almond, headmaster of Loretto 1862–1903, visionary, rebel and reformer

4 Loretto dress in 1901: Almond felt strongly about the need for comfortable healthy clothing. Here in old age he is typically coatless and tieless, while Sandy O'Neill, his headboy, wears the famous Loretto uniform: short trousers, sensible boots and open-necked shirt.

physical education of children . . . errs in deficient feeding, in deficient clothing, in deficient exercise . . . and in excessive mental application', and 'Growth is the dominant requirement to which all others must be subordinated.'[37]

Spencer furnished Almond with both a powerful rationale for his own physiological Darwinism, as well as a personal challenge. As Almond conceded in a letter to Spencer written in 1900:

I owe so much to you that I feel myself bound to make an acknowledgement . . . Some twenty-five years ago I, for the first time, read your Essays on Education. The sentence in which you say that while so many try to rear the finest bullocks or horses, no one ever tries to rear the finest men, took hold of me as no other sentence I have ever read has done. My eyes were opened by it to what seemed to me a mass of prejudice and folly on which our decendants will look back as we look on the customs of savages; and I made a solemn vow that there should be at least one exception to your well deserved taunt.[38]

It is inevitable that Almond be labelled a muscular Christian.[39] He matched the archetype Kingsley in personality and practice. Like Kingsley he preached the period virtues of developing the broad chest, the tireless stride and the strong body for Christ. Like Kingsley, he abhorred ascetics. He urged his boys to consecrate their healthy bodies as a 'living sacrifice to God'. He appealed to them for a vigorous and manly religion. Was 'an ailing emaciated body . . . more pleasing to God than the powerful frame, and the ruddy glow and the buoyant energies of health' he rhetorically demanded of them?[40] Pious, compassionate, volatile, nervously intense, physically exuberant, he had all the hallmarks of that odd breed of religious, introverted extroverts epitomised by Kingsley. He shared their pantheistic inclinations. Kingsley wept over the death of a tree.[41] Thring sought consolation in 'the rush of life in the tree and the grass'.[42] Almond for his part would abandon his school for long periods in later life and seek the pleasures and consolations of nature in his highland cottage at Loch Inver.[43]

With his passion for nature, it is not surprising that he was strongly influenced by Ruskin's writings on education. Ruskin's opinion that 'a chalk stream does more for education than a hundred national schools with all their doctrines at Baptismal Regeneration into the bargain'[44] struck in him a responsive chord. He attempted to combine physical and aesthetic education by introducing 'Long Grinds' for the whole school in the Border countryside in spring and autumn, a 'break' during the summer term, provided the pupils kept out of towns and stayed in the country air, and, from 1870, periods in the Highlands for selected groups of boys of weak constitution, under examination pressure or whom he merely wanted to know better.

Almond shared Thring's conviction concerning the value of gymnastics in school. Uppingham's proud boast is that it was the first English public school to have a gymnasium. Thring's admiration for German education[45] resulted in his appointing a German, George Beisiegal,[46] as the first gymnastics instructor. He took up his post in January 1860. A gymnasium was built at Loretto in the 1860s and a visiting instructor appointed, a Mr Roland, who had a gymnasium in Edinburgh.[47]

Thring looked to Germany for a system of exercises; Almond found his in the works of Archibald MacLaren[48] whose ideas were published in three volumes: *A Military System of Gymnastic Exercises for the use of Instructors* (1862), *Training in Theory and Practice* (1866), and *A System of Physical Education Theoretical and Practical* (1869). From MacLaren, however, he took much more than exercises for biceps and pectorals. MacLaren's second book was devoted largely to diet, sleep, hygiene and dress, which were to become 'the main feature of life at Loretto'. The third book included details of the influence of systematic exercise on the physical growth and development of boys including tables of physical measurements. Almond measured his pupils at least three times a year[49] and acknowledged his debt to MacLaren in the *Lorettonian* in January 1886. MacLaren had also published six articles on physical education in *Macmillan's Magazine* between 1860 and 1864, and it is likely that, because of their earlier timing which corresponded with Almond's purchase of Loretto, they had an even greater seminal influence on him.[50]

Almond drew freely on the ideas of his inspirationalists. The nature of his own originality lay in synthesis, application and persistence. He blended the ideas of Ruskin, MacLaren and Spencer into a conceptual and practical whole which went under the name of 'Lorettonianism', as Almond called his gospel of good health. For forty years he never compromised in its application. The physical care of his boys was the main work of his life and 'Lorettonianism' was 'the informing principle of the community'. It constituted an elaborate and systematic programme of health education covering food, clothes, physical exercise, sleep, fresh air and cold baths. As Thring was wedded to the concept of creating a new kind of school, so Almond was wedded to the idea of establishing a great new educational ideal.

Yet to a degree Loretto resembled a remedial health centre with its wholesome and plentiful food, daily cold baths, open windows in dormitory and classroom, regular physical activity throughout the day (morning and afternoon) and clothes and footwear designed for sensible living. This emphasis on 'the scientific training of the young human animal' did result, in fact, in Loretto becoming a place for the special care of boys of poor physique and weak constitution, an eventuality well described in one of Almond's own letters: 'A narrow-chested poorly-nourished boy came here in 1844. He improved greatly in the next two years, chest from $29\frac{1}{2}$ inches to 35, weight from 6 stone 11, to 8 stone 4, and I was quite happy about him. He was also tall for his age growing from 5 ft. $1\frac{1}{2}$ to 5 ft. 7 in the time. He never appeared in our medical books except for a weak knee till November 3rd. 1887, and there was no other ostensible cause for his doing so . . .'[51] Paradoxically Almond regretted his success in attracting feeble boys to his school, considering it a distortion of his educational ideals.

Almond has been described as the Wesley of the public school system.[52] It is an apt simile. He desired reformation rather than revolution and wished his school to exist within a traditional framework.[53] Despite reservations about the English public school system, he consistently claimed public school status for Loretto.[54] He stated explicitly that it was only in that form that he cared for the school's perpetuation, but wrote regretfully of Loretto as 'the only public school which at present, is fighting the battle of rationality'.[55]

While he had reservations about the wider system, he cherished those educational ideals associated with the games field which came to distinguish the more normal public schools. He endorsed, preached and publicised the simple creed: I believe in games for the training of a boy's character. Tristram wrote of him that he regarded the development of character as far more important than the inculcation of knowledge, and reported his anger at the publication of Kipling's 'The Islanders'; for 'Almond himself had always looked on athletic games so entirely as a means of training character'.[56]

It must not be overlooked that Almond balanced a 'science of health' with a 'scheme of ethics'. His adoption of the latter element meant that the educational emphasis at Loretto was in some respects quite orthodox: 'First – Character. Second – Physique. Third –

Intelligence. Fourth – Manners. Fifth – Information'.[57] And within this scheme of ethics the standard order of moral worth was delineated: 'Games in which success depends on the united efforts of many, and which also foster courage and endurance, are the very life blood of the public school system. And all the more self-indulgent games or pursuits contain within themselves an element of danger to school patriotism and might, if they permanently injured the patriotic games, cause public schools to fail in their main object, which we take to be the production of a grand breed of men for the service of the British nation.'[58] In short, Almond, along with many public school colleagues, believed that while some games promoted selfishness and were therefore inferior, cricket and football promoted unselfishness and were consequently superior.

In the possession of a fundamental anti-intellectualism Almond also reflected certain primary public school values. His 'intense practicality of temper' caused him to disparage 'impractical erudition', while a 'racy . . . vigour' produced in him a positive dislike of fine scholarship. He loathed the examination system. He was opposed to school scholarships for fear of harm done to children 'pale with learning'. He believed 'an exaggerated value' was assigned to the 'seedy professor' and dwelt with pleasure upon the rude superiorities of a more muscular generation.[59] He sought a suitable religious hero in support of his own views, and was in no doubt as to the choice St Paul might have made between 'vigorous manhood, full of courage' and 'the languid, lisping babbler about art and culture'.[60] The outcome at Loretto was the subordination of scholarship to fitness.[61] R. J. Mackenzie, for the most part appreciative of his former headmaster, was gently critical of Almond's intellectual stance. He considered that while Almond was often stimulating, the systematic working through of a syllabus did not suit his butterfly approach. Furthermore, he found Almond's defence of a classical curriculum for boys mystifying, commenting that Almond completely failed to perceive that 'a scientific system of intellectual education was a necessary counterpart of his physical and social propaganda'. His approach to learning, Mackenzie concluded, was not a fortunate one for the encouragement of school study.[62] Significantly, when Tristram became headmaster on Almond's death he felt obliged to improve academic standards.[63]

Loretto's combination of the conventional and the unconventional is nicely brought together in a little-known fictional tale of Loretto life, *Steady and Strong* written by R. M. Freeman, and the book is a work of unrelenting propaganda in which idosyncratic 'Lorettonianism' and mainstream public school morality-training are smoothly blended and find their fullest expression in breezy pronouncements from the Head:

I wish to make [Chudleigh] the most *manly* school, and I only value skill in athletics so far as it is a token of genuine manliness. Be careful to understand well what I mean by this term 'manly'. . . . I want each of my boys to be foremost in braving pain and facing danger, to take a licking without flinching, to stop the most violent rush at football, to stand up to the swiftest ball at cricket, to play an uphill game pluckily, to run races gamely, in short, to 'funk' nothing . . . the force of the brain hangs upon the health of the body, – and, what is of greater importance, . . . a robust, healthy frame, strengthened by constant air and exercise, and tempered by the wholesome toils of an athletic life, is the best safeguard against that most deadly form of moral degradation, which has wrecked so many thousands of our English boys and young men . . . For these reasons I set the greatest store by the laws of health and exercise.[64]

The conventional schoolboy hero is Reginald Owen, a delicate boy, who under the Head's scientific regime grows into a powerful, if exhibitionist, youth:

He had acquired more accomplishments, especially of a physical kind, in his one term at Chudleigh than in his whole time with worthy Doctor Hyde . . . He scarcely ever passed a five-barred gate without vaulting it, or saw a convenient rail or branch without performing upon it 'circles', and 'back-shoots', and 'upstarts', and 'rises', and various other exercises; he 'swarmed' all the flag-staffs and tele-graph posts in the neighbourhood . . . Even indoors, his athletic exhibitions were not laid aside; he was constantly practising lying with his head on one chair and his heels on another – raising himself from the ground by a poker laid over the top of a door – doing the 'balance' on the arms of the armchairs.[65]

The spirit of Almond pervades the book as that of Arnold in *Tom Brown's Schooldays*. Freeman's novel however, is an act of homage that *faithfully* reproduces the Almondian regime.

Almond is still regarded as a unique zealot.[66] Yet his ideas on exercise now diluted into truisms would find much sympathy among modern cardiologists.[67] And there is more to Almond than the period unconventionality of his rigorous concern with the physiological, and his efforts to tumble the card castles of the Scottish bourgeoisie. He was a stereotypic muscular Christian, quite conventional in his robust religious beliefs. Many of his educational objectives were indistinguishable from those of the more staid English public schools. Almond supplies images of contrast and similarity; he embodied normal as well as deviant elements of athleticism. His importance to the history of the ideology lies in his influence in propagating its standard values, by both precept and example. His writings were widely published and his pupils achieved stunning success on the fields of Oxford and Cambridge. He devoted his later years to publicising his 'gospel' in many journals and newspapers including *Field, Health, Journal of Education, New Review, Nineteenth Century, Scotsman, Spectator, Tatler* and *The Times*. In 1880 Loretto had five rugby blues and one cricket blue at Oxford; in 1881 eight out of nine Lorettonian under-graduates played rugby for Oxford and of the eight, one was captain of the cricket eleven and another president of the University Boat Club. In 1884 Loretto had eleven full blues at Oxford and seven played in the University Match. Between 1884 and 1891 four Lorettonians held the captaincy of the university fifteen and in 1900 the captains of both university rugby teams were from Loretto. Consistent, if less spectacular, representation was a feature of the last three decades of the nineteenth century. Almond's publications and the boys' representative honours brought Loretto extensive publicity, and served to advance the cause of athleticism and to establish its educational soundness.

At the same time, it remains true that Almond's special contri-bution was his preoccupation with physical health rather than social control, or even morality. He supplied a component to the move-ment that leaned heavily on physiological argument and a belief in educational and social reform. His was a new sacerdocy,[68] the systematic theology of which was constructed out of a profound study of the principles of sensible living. He represents a distinctive strand in the spreading web of athleticism in the nineteenth-century public school.

III

There is more than a superficial resemblance in the educational roles of the Society of Jesus founded by Ignatius Loyola and the Society of SS Mary and Nicolas founded by Nathaniel Woodard.[69] In nineteenth-century England these societies had a broadly similar objective: the re-establishment of a truly Christian way of life through the provision of an educational system for the ignorant and the ignored of the middle classes. It is true that the Jesuits were, in theory and practice, socially, if not intellectually, more egalitarian. The Ignatian ideal was to serve an aristocracy of talent, not of birth. And so the Jesuits catered for a wider spread of population than the

Woodard Corporation, and in time possessed public, grammar and elementary schools.[70] But the middle class were not to be neglected; their wealth and influence would be valuable assets for the survival of the faith. Day schools were set up in cities with large Roman Catholic populations to cater specifically for middle-class Catholic boys. This account of the Jesuits in Glasgow in 1859 is a description of a general aspiration:

At the moment there was not in all Glasgow a single Catholic school of higher class than the ordinary poor schools and yet there was a Catholic population of more than 100,000, being one fourth of the whole population . . . If we can inspire the parents with a little higher ambition and lead these to secure for their children the goods of education as well as those of fortune, they will be well able to take rank as Gentlemen in Glasgow and the Church will no longer be in the extraordinary condition in which it now finds itself, when almost the entire Catholic population belongs to the lower and uneducated ranks of life.[71]

In this cultivation of the more socially influential, the practice of the Society of Jesus was considerably in advance of the Society of St Nicolas. Some three hundred years before Woodard, Ignatius had felt the need to woo the richer sections of the community in order to subsidise the whole system, and to win the support of the powerful. Aristocratic schools thus became a feature of the Jesuit educational system. This tradition accounted for the establishment of boarding schools for wealthy Catholics when the Jesuits returned to England on the easing of the Penal Laws: Stonyhurst in 1793, Mount St Mary's in 1842 and Beaumont in 1861.

Stonyhurst differed in one important respect from its sister colleges. Its ancestry went back to Elizabethan England. It had its origins in the seminary for English Catholic boys at St Omer founded in 1592 by the Society of Jesus, following its expulsion from England after a series of anti-Catholic Acts culminating in the 1585 Act against the Jesuits.[72] By this Act Catholics were not only forbidden to celebrate or be present at mass; they were 'forbidden to found new schools or to teach their children at home under penalty of £10 for each month, if a schoolmaster was kept who did not conform'.[73]

The outcome was the establishment of several schools on the mainland of Catholic Europe, among them St Omer. The seminary was forced to move twice in the two hundred years before the Jesuits returned to English soil, on each occasion following further troubles for the Order. In 1762, the parliament of France having set its face against the Society of Jesus, the masters and pupils moved secretly to Bruges in Belgium. There the school was given sanctuary for some eleven years until the suppression of the Jesuits by Pope Clement XIV at the instigation of the Bourbon sovereigns forced a removal to Liège into the beneficial care of a powerful and tolerant prince–bishop, Charles, Count Welbruck. In 1793 the school's existence was threatened by the revolutionary armies of France and the whole school fled again, this time to England via the Meuse and Rotterdam.

Among the scholars at the English seminary of the Bruges period was Thomas Weld, who owned several estates, including the mansion and lands of Stonyhurst in the Ribble Valley in North Lancashire. He offered Stonyhurst to the homeless seminarians from Belgium as a refuge. They took up residence on 29 August 1794. The Order was still proscribed by the Catholic church, and the new occupants were known as 'the Gentlemen from Liège'.[74] There were about two dozen in all.

An English sanctuary was made possible by the relaxation of the anti-Catholic laws following the first of the Catholic Relief Acts in 1778. As a result of this Act, Catholics could once more legally purchase and inherit land, and the persecution of the clergy by common informers was abolished. Both these improvements were of obvious importance to the survival of an English Catholic school run by clerics. Thirteen years later the second Catholic Relief Act gave further freedom and security to church members: churches, chapels and mass were legalised and in the words of David Mathew, the historian of English Catholicism 'with the passing of the Relief Act of 1791 the acute difficulties within the Catholic body diminished'.[75] And it may be added, Catholic institutions such as Stonyhurst could now exist once more.

From the first moments and for the best part of eighty years Stonyhurst was characterised by a considerable cultural, geographical, religious and educational distance from mainstream public school life. This fact requires emphasis because it was the major reason for the idiosyncratic nature of the school and for its rejection of both the animus and emblems of athleticism.

During the famous nineteenth-century trial of the Tichborne Claimant, it was disclosed that the group of Stonyhurst students known as 'The Philosophers' was an institution, which confused and puzzled English judges and barristers.[76] There was much else to bewilder those of an orthodox English education, for Stonyhurst pupils were excluded from contact with Protestant culture and

Protestant public schools by virtue of a long exile, legal discrimination and virulent anti-Catholicism. It was an exclusion bred out of centuries of suspicion and slow to dissipate. When, in 1874, Stonyhurst played its first cricket match against a non-Catholic school, Rossall, a Protestant newspaper expostulated:

How the Rossall pupils could have desired, or the Rossall masters could have sanctioned any match of the kind we are entirely at a loss to conceive. However it is some comfort to know that the Protestant youths were thoroughly well beaten, as they richly deserved to be. But have the Rossall masters never read the Bible? or have they forgotten the consequence – as recorded in its pages – of allowing Israelites to mingle in the Moabite games and dances? All these comminglings with Papists act as so many enticements to idolatry, and the masters who do not see this are unfit to manage a Protestant school. We would advise parents who have sons at Rossall to keep a sharp look-out.[77]

At the same time insularity was deliberately sought by Catholics. Discussion by Catholic educationalists in the second half of the nineteenth century on the nature of the higher education of educated Catholic youth, for example, was full of fears of contamination by the Protestant world.[78] In particular, the idea of the creation of an Oxford or Cambridge hall or college as distinct from a Catholic university, caused much anxiety and had to be vigorously defended by the Jesuit, E. I. Purbrick. It is interesting to note that one cause for concern was the fear of over-indulgence in games. In a statement that sheds light on attitudes and standards at Stonyhurst, Purbrick, with an orthodox Jesuit regard for intellectual rigour, suggested this might be avoided quite simply by a searching terminal examination, power 'to weed the College', a fairly stiff entrance examination, scholarships and other means to be devised as experience might suggest.[79] Purbrick taught and administered at Stonyhurst for over fifteen years, and his comments would seem to reflect the traditional Jesuit attitude to learning and corresponding Stonyhurst values.[80]

The Jesuits, as distinct from the Catholic community, were further isolated because of the peculiar antipathy they generated. It was an antagonism felt as much by English Catholics as by English Protestants. The followers of Loyola with their unsavoury reputation, whether justified or unjustified, caused the Catholic community to fear an arousal of Protestant hostility against all Catholics. Furthermore Jesuit independence of mind occasionally annoyed the Catholic establishment. Their nineteenth-century support of a moderate definition of papal infallibility, for example, aroused the anger of Cardinal Manning[81] who considered them disloyal to the Pope. Manning typifies the jealousy, resentment and irritation the Jesuits engendered among English Catholics. He 'criticised them historically as an English Archbishop and his hand lay heavy on them as an administrator'.[82]

At Stonyhurst cultural segregation was reinforced by geographical location. John Gerard, writing at the turn of the last century, opened his chapter on Stonyhurst life with the remark that North Lancashire in 1894 was considered by many as remote and inaccessible, yet a hundred years earlier it had been vastly more isolated. He pointed out that in consequence the college had of necessity to work out its own history in its own way relying solely on its imported traditions. During the early years, in the face of widespread hostility it was clearly an advantage to be a hermitical community in the depths of rural Lancashire. But later when the Jesuits' position in English society eased, and recognition as a public school was desired, its long established traditions made assimilation more difficult than for Beaumont, its sister school in the south opened in 1861, and deliberately run on more normal public school lines.[83]

There was yet another even more potent reason for separateness however: the long-established Jesuit pattern of educational training. It has been wisely written that in order to understand the Jesuit system of education 'in any country at any period, there is need of studying its great educational document, the *Ratio Studiorum . . .* the kernel, the core, the soul of Jesuit pedagogy'.[84] This statement may be less valid in the second part of the twentieth century but was wholly applicable for the entire period of the nineteenth. Furthermore, regarding athleticism, the substance of ideological dismissal lay in this sourcebook of the Jesuit educational process. For this reason it requires scrutiny.

On deciding that education was to be a concern of the Society, Loyola wrote what has been called an educational tract, the fourth part of the *Constitutions* of the Society. A great deal of effort, consultation and refinement was to take place before a complete educational system was devised however. The *Monumenta Paedagogica* of the Society contains records of various schemes devised by members of the Order which were investigated for their value and which supplied 'the pedagogic atmosphere that preceded the definitive *Ratio*'. In 1586 the first *Ratio* appeared. Extensive analysis by the best scholars and ablest teachers of the Provinces followed.

The result was an amended edition in 1591. More criticism followed, and in 1599 a shorter, less prolix *Ratio* was issued. This had 'the force of law for all Jesuit Colleges until the suppression of the Society in 1773'. Its influence did not end there. 'It has served', stated the Jesuit historian McGucken in 1932, 'to perpetuate the Jesuit tradition . . . to hand on to the modern Jesuit school the same spirit that animated the Jesuit College of the seventeenth century.'[85]

After the restoration of the Society a revised edition of the *Ratio* was issued in 1832. The changes were comparatively small but the Provinces were allowed to adapt the curriculum to the needs of the countries in which they were located. Stonyhurst adapted its curriculum to suit the requirements of London University Matriculation (more science and mathematics); but when in 1895 access was permitted to Oxford and Cambridge the Jesuits returned with relief to a traditional predominantly classical curriculum, with the result that J. M. Jeffries, a Stonyhurst pupil who experienced the post-1900 curriculum, wrote tersely in his autobiography: 'My education was extremely classical!'[86]

The definitive *Ratio Studiorum* of 1599 was not only the product of consultation among Jesuits. It drew on the writers of the classical world notably Quintilian, the Roman rhetorician, on educators of the Renaissance universities of the period, the Spanish pedagogue Vives, the German Protestant Johann Sturm and the Brethren of the Common Life, a religious order. In short, 'the traditional conservatism of Spain, the cosmopolitan experimentation of France . . . and the literary and artistic flowering of the Italian Renaissance all have their traces in the *Ratio* which was admittedly a synthesis of contemporary education'.[87] The outcome of synthesis, discussion and careful selection was a uniform and distinctive type of education: the Jesuit type. The *Ratio* symbolised the uniformity of the Order, a unity animated by identical principles, objectives and methodology. It constituted 'a standard instruction in standard thoughts'.[88]

What the *Ratio* serves to illustrate in the context of athleticism is Jesuit autonomy and conservatism. Pride in a well thought-out and strongly established educational system of their own resulted in a reaction to the educational fashions of the English upper-class school which was diffident, cautious and even patronising. Fealty also produced a serious-minded, scrupulous approach to academic learning that would not permit idleness nor allow staff to look indulgently on the intellectually lazy no matter how well they played games.

Despite all the careful attention to detail in drawing up a system of classical education for its colleges, the teaching of the academic syllabus was not the primary work of the Order. Education in the faith was the main object of the Jesuit school 'at every time, in every country, under every condition'. To this end Jesuit teachers were urged: 'Speak of God in class, every chance you get; there will be no lack of opportunities if only you seize hold of them.'[89] In addition, to educate in leadership was the special aim of the upper-class Jesuit school. This stress on leadership was strikingly similar to that of the Protestant public school. The aim of the English Jesuit boarding school was not simply the making of good Catholics. Such a process could be achieved by missionary work; it did not require schools. The schools were to produce educated Catholic gentlemen, able to take their proper place in the world and to act as forceful leaders of Catholic thought and action.

However close in ambition to the Protestant public schools the objectives might be, the *means* of realisation remained distinct. Educated gentlemen and forceful leaders were formed by an endless process of direct and indirect moral indoctrination, but the games field was never in theory or in practice a major site for this. In a sober paper entitled 'Moral Training and Instruction in the Catholic schools connected by the Jesuit Order in Great Britain and Ireland' written for an international inquiry into moral education in 1907, the Rev. Michael Maher, Jesuit director of studies of the seminary at Stonyhurst, dismissed the moral role of games fields in a single sentence, mentioning only that subordination and co-operation were qualities associated with those places. 'The essential character of the moral teaching and training in our system lies in . . . the direct and indirect religious and moral instruction, the Sunday work and the weekday work, the lessons and the religious exercises, together with the general tone of the school arising out of community of belief and aspirations, a view of life and principles of action among masters and boys.[90] The exclusive nature of the sturdy, moralistic tone struck by Jesuit mentors in their English public schools is beautifully exemplified in the following more colourful statement: 'Be men of grit, men of enthusiasm, without which life is but a poor limp affair. Be men of loyalty – men of Catholic loyalty – for your religion will but serve to stiffen your loyalty, and I have seen more loyalty . . . in the Catholic than in the

Protestant schools. It could scarcely be otherwise, for patriotism is the rare rich bloom of religion and the finer the soil, the more vigorous the bloom.'[91]

It must not be thought, of course, that the Jesuits undervalued or ignored physical exercise. In his *Stonyhurst Memories* Percy Fitzgerald, describing the school in the 1850s before the advent of orthodox football and cricket, recalled that 'games were a great and notable feature of our . . . life'; only 'a few recluses' opted out.[92] The high point of the games season was the Stonyhurst football[93] 'Grand Matches' at Shrovetide, which lasted three days, but there was also handball and second bounce (both types of fives), bandy (a kind of hockey), Stonyhurst cricket[94] and twenty-mile walks to Pendle, a local mountain. Nor did these exhaust the list. Once again a schoolboy diary, that of B. E. James, furnishes clear evidence of a wide range of activities: James played football and a great deal of cricket but he also played rounders, went skating, shot-putting and running on the fells.[95]

It is unquestionably true that throughout the nineteenth century and after, physical activities were as important to Stonyhurst pupils as to most schoolboys, and were actively encouraged by the staff – but only in order to develop healthy bodies. While the Benedictine writer, Bede Jarret, in *Living Temples* might find moral virtue in games,[96] the Jesuit author, William Lockington, in his *Bodily Health and Spiritual Vigour* was concerned only with the production of physical stamina to sustain the priest in the saving of souls[97] – a more than symbolic contrast.

An interesting fact of Stonyhurst life which has attracted little attention among students of athleticism is the common practice, *some sixty years* before Cotton recruited his young muscular masters, of staff participation in the boys' games. Fitzgerald wrote of the 'Grand Matches' that 'the masters – strong athletic men – caught the prevailing fury and fought on different sides'.[98] Another, who recalled with affection the masters' enthusiasm for games was a 'Catholic Barrister': 'In the playground they were the unconstrained sharers in our sport.'[99] And in 1903 His Majesty's Inspectors were favourably impressed by the staff involvement 'in the playground and the cricket field'[100] and suggested that it helped promote excellent relations despite the considerable supervision and restraint to which the boys were subjected. They failed to note, however, its unique longevity as a tradition.

Stonyhurst gradually adopted the games, developed the facilities and to a small extent the sporting rituals and symbols of the Protestant public schools.[101] But encouragement and involvement at no time represented ideological commitment of a moralistic nature or lapsed into smiling compliance with brown-cheeked hedonism. As at Lancing the motivation above all was for the sake of acceptance and integration into the public school system.[102] But for the first sixty years of the nineteenth century Stonyhurst remained indifferently aloof from its non-Catholic peers. Its masters played with the boys as they had always done; it played its own games, even its own cricket; later still it found no overt attraction in the ideological pronouncements that were beginning to characterise other schools from the 1850s onwards; and it permitted little freedom to the pupils to control and organise their leisure activities. Those who talk of athleticism as a phenomenon of the public schools must exclude the Jesuit institution of Stonyhurst from the generalisation. Both athletic idealism and indulgence were firmly repressed. There, religion was, and was to remain, the source of moral soundness and the adversary of moral corruption.

IV

An examination of the early stages of the evolution of athleticism in the six schools of this study is now complete.

Events at Harrow, Marlborough, Lancing, Uppingham and Loretto – Stonyhurst clearly stands apart – in the middle of the nineteenth century demonstrate unmistakably that the well-heads of athleticism were strikingly diverse in nature: the strategic and tactical responses to disciplinary problems of pragmatists, the different experiences, philosophies and paradigms of ideopraxists and the desire for acceptance of humble emulators. Cotton, Woodard and, in all probability, Vaughan, supplied the practical dynamic; Thring and Almond supplied the ideological. Public school historians have been rebuked for their preoccupation with the nineteenth-century headmaster,[103] but four of these men were headmasters and illustrate his importance as an agent of change. Butler's words concerning the nineteenth-century headmaster of Harrow, that his power was autocratic, masters his nominees and the tone his direct responsibility have relevance in a wider context.[104]

The growth of athleticism was characterised by diffusion *and* parallel innovation. There was interchange of ideas and individual conclusion. Vaughan and Cotton appear to have set up a dialogue;

Almond and Thring worked literally in splendid isolation.

Isolation elsewhere brought about a complication which must be acknowledged in any attempt to refine generalities concerning the widespread influence of the movement. Stonyhurst's aloofness from many developments associated with athleticism, particularly the school's continuing disdain for the rhetoric of ideological commitment, amounts to substantial rejection. This fact and the anticipation at Stonyhurst, by several decades, of one significant manifestation of the games movement, namely the involvement of the masters in the boys' games, without any of the institutional pressures that produced Cotton's machinations, together add fresh subtlety to the history of public school athleticism and the development of games in English education.

In conjunction with the emergence from the historical depths of the Harrow Philathletic Club, such facts muddy the placid waters of settled opinion.

4

Compulsion, conformity and allegiance

It was written of Eton in 1898:

> There are fifty fives courts where before there was one; twenty games or there-abouts of cricket as against three; compulsory football for every house four or five times a week; to say nothing of beagles and athletic sports in the Easter Term, and rowing and bathing daily through the summer. There are house colours for football and school colours for football, cricket, rowing, racquets; there are challenge cups, senior and junior . . .

and the writer continued,

> What is true of Eton is, I believe, true, *mutatis mutandis*, of the other great public schools; the comprehensive net of athletics has closed around them all, sweeping in our boys by shoals, and few are the puny minnows that swim through its meshes. And yet the whole system is entirely modern, most of it a development of the last forty years.[1]

This picturesque metaphor contains the essence of an educational revolution. Between approximately 1860 and 1900 from diverse origins and parallel with continued variation in interpretation, there developed a broad measure of conformity with regard to the major features of athleticism; supportive ideological statements appeared, considerable investment in the machinery of games playing was made, compulsory games were introduced and an intense enthusiasm on the part of many pupils became evident. These various features did not display a steady, uniform growth, at least, not in the six schools of this survey. Progress towards conformity was uneven, dependent *inter alia* on the philosophy, inclinations and power of individual headmasters and their staff, on the wealth and goodwill of parents, old boys, masters and well-wishers, on the rapidity with which facilities could be developed, and not least on the strong-minded independence of some boys and on the single-minded enthusiasm of others.

The impression is sometimes given of a change of ethos producing uncomplicated pupil acquiescence on an ever increasing scale. One commentator, for example, while scrupulously careful to emphasise our lack of precise knowledge of the timing of events, the variation in timing between schools and the order of 'seminal elements', implies an ordered progression to uniformity due to 'a subtle but organised drive by authority' and omits any reference to pupil resistance and rejection.[2] In fact, conformity was resisted, delayed, even in part thwarted by some pupils. Yet despite these obstacles, seldom considered by educational historians, it is certainly true that by 1900 all the schools of this study showed marked similarities in the provision of facilities and in the compulsion to use them, and five out of six schools – the exception, already noted, was Stonyhurst[3] – subscribed loudly and consistently to the moral ethic allegedly inherent in athleticism and had produced in most of their pupils an obsession with games.

The opening quotations of this chapter overlook one significant development: the ideological underpinning of considerable investment in games facilities. Investment in games 'plant' in the nineteenth-century public school on such a scale required a persuasive rationale. A wholesome set of educational arguments to justify the creation of such resources had to be marshalled and spread among the influential, the wealthy and the clientele. The pursuit of allegedly sound educational objectives through the medium of the games field had to be expounded and persistently re-emphasised to sustain the believer, placate the critical, win over the naive and effect a cover for the indulgent.

There was, however, another dimension to the process of indoctrination. Since all the boys were ultimately required to use the costly games facilities, it was desirable in the interests of morale and discipline to use every means possible to gain the goodwill of the uncommitted and to maintain the enthusiasm of the partial. One important means of doing this was the reiteration of the virtuous qualities of the games player in the school magazine. This constituted a simple and persistent attempt to 'sell' a desirable image to the school community; to link cause and effect; to produce mass identification with an 'ideal type'.

The *Pall Mall Gazette* of 16 July 1866, reporting the annual match at Lord's between Eton and Harrow, adopted a highly moralising tone to the detriment of the Eton team: 'Cricket is a game which reflects the character – a game of correct habits, of patient and well-considered practice – the very last game in the world in which any youth without the power of concentrativeness – nine tenths of education but voted a bore at Eton – is ever likely to excel. To any lover of education the play of Harrow was a treat, and that of Eton a disappointment. In Harrow we saw care and discipline, and patient labour; in Eton a wild erratic performance, no sign of training or mental effort . . .'[4] This was an interpretation of personal virtue that was to gain wide currency in the public school system and which in style and content was reproduced in the *Marlburian*, the *Lancing College Magazine*, the *Harrovian*, the *Uppingham School Magazine* and the *Lorettonian*.

The cumulative impact of the extensive literature of athleticism is dealt with fully in chapter 8 but attention is briefly focused here on the systematic support lent to the ideology and to that concrete manifestation of ideological commitment, the athlete hero, by the school magazine. Frequent opportunity was taken in this main vehicle of institutional propaganda to indoctrinate the reader. As playing fields were expanded and boys forced on to them, the magazines kept up a steady stream of messages, stressing the value of these new manifestations for the development of a noble type of boy. Intensity of proselytism ranged from the modest, rather impersonal assertion of an Uppingham correspondent, 'it is in our games as well as in our classrooms that character is moulded',[5] to the obsequious pronouncement of a Harrow editorial in defence of the power of the captains of the eleven, 'Look at the uniform judiciousness of their conduct, their high moral influence and above all their bodily strength. Is it not here that we must look for the very essence of what is a Harrow boy's idea of a gentleman?'[6]

On such carefully laid rhetorical foundations a solid superstructure of facilities was gradually erected. Over several decades all the schools accumulated a large acreage of land to provide playing fields, racquets, fives and squash courts, gymnasia and swimming pools. 'Machinery, machinery, machinery should be the motto of any good school . . . as little as possible ought to be left to personal merit in the teachers, as much as possible ought to rest on the system and the appliances', wrote Edward Thring.[7] A general appreciation of the soundness of this organisational principle as applied to games, for producing smooth discipline, acquiescent pupils and contented parents is demonstrated by table 1 on p. 71.

Large sums of money were obtained from governors, masters, old boys, parents and well-wishers for the purchase of land and the

Table 1 *Approximate games acreage owned or leased and used for major games in 1845 and 1900*

	1845	1900
Harrow	8	146
Marlborough	2	68
Uppingham	2	49
Lancing	0 (1848)	14½
Stonyhurst	2	30
Loretto	0	22

Note: The amount of land obtained, of course, was dependent on such factors as the wealth of benefactors and the number of pupils to be accommodated. For example at Lancing numbers rose to some 200 in the 1880s but fell to less than 120 by 1900. Being a small school like Loretto, therefore, the games fields were naturally fewer than elsewhere. What the table above clearly demonstrates is that between 1845 and 1900 games became an integral part of school life, and facilities were purchased and developed so as to ensure the compulsory participation of most pupils.

Sources: Harrow, E. D. Laborde, *Harrow School: yesterday and today*; Lancing: Mr B. W. T. Handford; Loretto: *School Register 1908*; Marlborough: Mr G. Murray and Mr. J. Warwick James; Stonyhurst: Rev. J. F. Turner; Uppingham: *School Prospectus (1974)*.

construction of amenities. The situation at Harrow was typical, not perhaps in the amount contributed – Harrow had especially wealthy benefactors – but in the facilities created and source and type of contribution. Between 1850 and 1900 well over £70,000 was collected for athletic facilities. Cricket and football fields were created and continually improved, a gymnasium was erected, a swimming pool was constructed and racquets and fives courts were built. Large contributions came from staff such as Vaughan and Bowen, memorial funds in honour of famous headmasters and loyal old boys, regular appeals, 'friends of the school', appreciative parents and affectionate former pupils. Details are to be found in appendix II.

By the end of the century the facilities created from these funds were maintained by a well-organised system of games subscriptions. A typical statement of accounts for the summer term of 1893[8] from the Marlborough Games Committee shows how the subscriptions raised by each house were used to pay for cricket professionals, ground staff, maintenance and the not ungenerous obligations of the host team (see table II, p. 72).

Hand in hand with these manifestations came the systematisation of games playing. The school registers, school histories and club

Table II *Marlborough Games Committee statement of accounts for summer term 1893*

Received

	£	s.	d.
By Cash in hand from Lent Term	2	16	2
,, Deposits at the Bank	120	0	0
,, Interest on Deposits	1	5	3
,, Donation to Cricket from the Common Room	8	0	0
,, Annual subscription from the Council, through the Bursar	26	0	0
,, Subscription from:-			

	£	s.	d.
A House	19	11	3
Mr. Champney's House	12	2	3
Cotton	11	17	9
Mr. Eve's	12	13	3
Mr. Galpin's	12	11	6
Mr. Gould's	15	4	0
Littlefield	12	4	6
Mr. Macdonald's	3	6	0
Mr. Madden's	10	4	3
Mr. Mansell's	3	6	0
Dr. Penny's	0	17	6
Mr. Pollock's	12	17	6
Preshute	13	9	3
Summerfield	3	7	3
Mr. Upcott's	3	13	6
	147	5	9

	£	s.	d.
	£305	**7**	**2**

Paid

	£	s.	d.
To Hide 2 quarters' salary to Michaelmas	48	0	0
,, ,, Hockey Team's Bill	2	14	0
,, ,, Cricket Team's Bill	41	17	7
,, Parmenter	41	5	0
,, Smith	41	0	0
,, Palser	21	13	4
,, Smart	16	5	0
,, Gregory	8	12	0
,, Smallbones	4	19	6
,, Boys for getting up plantains	1	1	9
,, Stabling and keep of the horse	3	2	10
,, Leather boots and repair to harness	3	14	2
,, Repairs to Club Property	10	19	11½
,, E. Foster (for luncheons)	7	6	6
,, R. Long (for 67 gallons of beer)	3	7	6
,, Stagg (for 99 dozen of ginger beer)	4	19	0
,, N. Drace (towards dinners at extra match)	1	6	0
,, ,, (captain's telegrams and postage)	1	2	2
,, The Treasurer (for postage)		2	3½
,, Policeman (on Cheltenham match days)		6	0
,, J. W. Brooke (for watering-carts)	1	7	0
,, Dale and Co. (for watering-cans)	0	13	0
,, Dock (for Brakes for Cheltenham XI)	3	10	6
,, Steel (for omnibus fares for Football team in February)		15	0
,, Gale (for printing)		13	3
,, Wells (for rolling ground)	2	15	0
,, Sutton and Sons (for grass seed)		7	2
,, Morrison (for tent, and Box to keep it in)	25	7	0
Total	£301	15	0
Balance to Michaelmas Term	£3	12	2
	£305	**7**	**2**

Signed,
R. ALFORD, Treasurer.
J. S. THOMAS, Bursar.

record books supply between them evidence of this, which is reproduced in table III below. The table illustrates a *trend*. It does not necessarily include the earliest 'foreign' matches, school teams or athletics meetings, but indicates when the recording of teams, fixtures and events became regularised. There were, for example, spasmodically arranged matches with local clubs, groups of old boys and sometimes university or college teams prior to the dates given in the table in several of the schools. The discrepancy in some cases between the date of the regular recording of school teams and 'foreign' matches means simply that for many years school teams played internal fixtures against various combinations of the remainder of the school.

The history of the forty years after 1860 is one of expansion and improvement. Internal games, usually in the form of house matches or their equivalent, gradually took up more and more time

Table III *Commencement of regular recording of matches, championships and teams*

	school cricket eleven	school football teams	athletic sports or championships	'Foreign' cricket matches	'Foreign' football matches
Harrow	1818	1850s	1850s	1818	1927
Marlborough	1849	1859	1867	1855	1887
Uppingham	1860	1864	1860	1865	1899
Lancing	1855	1863	1861	1869	1865
Loretto		(see below)		1863	1867
Stonyhurst	1861	1884	1866	1861	1884

Points associated with individual schools

Harrow: Harrow is unique in the above company. 'Foreign' cricket matches were regularised early in the nineteenth century with the establishment of the annual fixtures against Eton and Winchester. The retention until 1927 of Harrow football meant that until this time school football matches against external opposition were limited to the annual old boys' match.

Uppingham: Uppingham retained its own type of football until 1899 when it adopted rugby union and as at Harrow, external matches were therefore restricted to those with old boys until that date.

Lancing: The earliest Lancing games records have not survived. The above dates are taken from the extant records. But by 1860 it would seem there were regular football and cricket fixtures with Brighton College.

Loretto: As with Lancing, details of early school teams are lost. The extant records date from 1877. Due to Almond's strong principles Loretto did not have internal athletic sports meetings, only standards. Almond maintained that intra-school sports encouraged selfishness.

as they were discovered to be the most satisfactory way of stimulating enthusiasm for what eventually became almost daily visits to the playing fields. Hockey, swimming, gymnastics, racquets, fives, squash and fencing, some or all were added to the major games of football and cricket. The athletic championships, or in the case of Loretto athletic standards, became a regular institution.

A huge games-playing machine was ultimately constructed, efficiently serviced and periodically improved; oiled by the wealth of governors, staff, boys, parents and old boys; driven by an elitist group of masters and pupils who protected and promoted their principles and their pleasures with elaborate rituals and symbols of status and power; put to general use by constant reiteration of an educational ideal and, ultimately, by the crude technique of coercion.

II

It has been stated that the compulsion associated with games in the public schools came from the boys themselves.[9] The histories of the six schools of this study suggest the need for a more flexible interpretation of its origins.

The evidence from Marlborough suggests that the claim is an over-simplification. Certainly in a sermon preached at Marlborough in 1897, J. S. Thomas, the long-serving college bursar,[10] in his youth and early manhood a distinguished and enthusiastic games player, recalled that 'it is a historical fact that the compulsion was never imposed from above . . .'.[11] However this is a very puzzling comment in the light of Cotton's 'Circular to Parents' of 1853. And there is the early entry (1857) in the Marlborough College Cricket Club book for which he was also responsible: 'The Club will consist of all boys belonging to the College in the capacity of pupils . . . All will be forced to pay the regular subscription.'[12] Such a mandate, of course, does not get boys onto the playing fields and it appears that a distinction must be made between compulsory financial support and compulsory physical involvement. But since Cotton made subscription, if not participation, compulsory it is clear that at Marlborough compulsion in the area of the boys' games was not wholly the product of pupil pressure.

Then again, as we have already seen, Cotton's desire to have the mass of the boys play games is set out without ambiguity in his 'Circular'. In view of the enormous influence of the headmaster in school affairs, even those ostensibly the responsibility of the pupils (well exemplified by Thring in the specific case of compulsory games as will be seen shortly), it may be reasonably hypothesised that Cotton strongly 'encouraged' compulsory participation as well as compulsory subscription through the strategy, already discussed, of using games-playing masters. Thomas, in fact, indicated as much. His statement continued, '. . . it [compulsion] sprang up spontaneously in the various Houses; the leading boys in *co-operation with their masters* [emphasis added] resolving that it had become a necessity . . . Nothing could have been more mischievous than purposeless idleness which characterized many, for whom games had no special attraction.' The argument concerning the need for an antidote to purposeless idleness has a Cottonian ring. More to the point, the phrase 'leading boys in co-operation with their masters' scarcely places the onus of responsibility for compulsion exclusively on the pupils. It should also be noted in this context that the spirit which led to fierce games rivalry demanding total support from all members of the house only developed fully after Cotton's reconstruction of the house system in 1852;[13] a point surely not without significance. Clearly the truth of the matter is that Cotton and his staff had a large part to play in the introduction of compulsory games at Marlborough – a part that was all the more effective for being both direct and indirect. Cotton and his young masters were, to a considerable degree, responsible for the eventual state of affairs in the 1870s deprecated by correspondents to *The Times* and the *Marlburian*, namely that boys were subject 'to direct tyranny . . . and were all, with few exceptions, compelled to play all school games'.[14]

Henry Montagu Butler, who succeeded Vaughan as headmaster of Harrow, informed the Public Schools Commission that compulsory attendance at football was part of the internal government which, so far as was known, was originally established by the boys themselves.[15] Compulsory games fagging (fetching and carrying equipment by younger boys) had a long history at Harrow before 1864, and was certainly initiated by the boys. Compulsory games playing on the other hand appears to have been introduced in Vaughan's time, a by-product of the systematisation of games following the creation of the Philathletic Club. In *Harrow Recollections* Sydney Daryl, writing of the period shortly before Vaughan's retirement, made what appears to be the first reference to compulsory games at Harrow stating that every boy was now compelled 'to go down to footer' twice a week. He commented favourably on this apparently new and much resented compulsion: 'A great many people complain that football is made compulsory but far from coinciding in their views, I believe it to be one of the very best things that could possibly happen. Loiterers are kept out of mischief, health and appetite are promoted.'[16] Support for the claim that compulsory games began under Vaughan is also to be found elsewhere.[17]

Vaughan's role in the introduction of games at Harrow has already been discussed in chapter 2 and it was suggested that his contribution had been underestimated. It was argued that there are grounds for believing him responsible through his monitors for the systematisation of games, including compulsion. But it was also stated that the exact situation is far from clear. In which case any unqualified assertion is ill-advised.

The situation at Uppingham illustrates the need for care in interpreting even the apparently obvious. In his book of essays on education published in 1866 Thring wrote that he left control of school games in the boys' hands.[18] The first Uppingham Games Committee was formed in 1857. All five members were pupils. One of its early rules read: 'At least one game of football should be played each week and . . . non-attendance on field days should be punished by a fine.'[19] *Prima facie*, it would seem that the introduction of compulsory games at Uppingham was in fact the boys' doing. In all probability however, the committee was an extension of Thring's own authority; certainly it was formed on his initiative.[20] The truth of the matter was the boys did control games provided they complied with Thring's intentions. Thring kept and used a headmasterly veto.[21] That Thring subscribed to the principle of 'indirect rule' is clear from his own writing. On one occasion he wrote in his diary: 'Went this afternoon with . . . Althorpe and Clay [pupils] to choose the steeplechase ground. Could not help contrasting it to my own school life . . . surely this leading the school without destroying their freedom at all must have great effect.'[22] In short, a knowledge of Thring's method of implementing his policies brings to light the fact that he, not the boys, was the force behind the introduction of compulsory games.

If the validity of the theory that games compulsion was the innovation of the boys is somewhat weakened by the Marlborough, Harrow and Uppingham evidence, it is substantially weakened by that of Loretto, Stonyhurst and Lancing.

The introduction of compulsory participation in physical activities at Loretto was wholly Almond's decision.[23] It was part of a programme of good health habits which, as already mentioned, included such things as open dormitory windows, abstinence between meals, open-necked shirts, the abolition of waistcoats, sensibly designed boots and not least, cold baths.[24] Almond's pedagogical ambition was to develop a 'balance' between intellectual effort and physical activity. When he set his system before the Royal Commission on Physical Training (Scotland) he declared that his ideal daily timetable was: '6 hours study, 10 hours sleep, $1\frac{1}{2}$ hours at meals, 1 hour free after meals, 1 hour drawing or singing, $\frac{1}{2}$ hour prayers or assembly, $\frac{1}{2}$ hour in the gymnasium, $2\frac{1}{4}$ hours at games, 1 hour leisure.'[25] By 1870 this timetable was in operation. The physical education component was compulsory, an arrangement which was at loggerheads with Almond's self-proclaimed aim of education for individuality. Perhaps it was this obvious contradiction that caused one member of the Royal Commission to remark to him drily, concerning his much polished physical education programme: 'It does not appear you have spared compulsion!'[26]

At Stonyhurst, the boys' role in the introduction of compulsory games can be swiftly dealt with. Jesuit pupils had far less freedom to innovate than pupils in the Protestant schools. The modern games of cricket and football, for example, were introduced and run by members of staff. Father Clough and Father Welby introduced cricket, Father Baldwin introduced football, Father Robinson introduced hockey, and the famed prefects controlled and supervised daily play.[27] In 1890 the 'Football Notes' in the college magazine contained the brief information that a new rule had been introduced to the effect that instead of football being voluntary, all were obliged to play once a week.[28] While responsibility for the rule is not stated, the pattern of games control leaves little likelihood of it being the independent action of the boys.

As regards Lancing, the diary of a Lancing schoolboy, Samuel Roebuck Brooke,[29] for the years 1860–2, by great good fortune contains a record of the introduction of compulsory games at this Woodard school. It is a record that further exposes the power of the Victorian headmaster as an agent of change. Brooke was a clever, priggish boy, poorly co-ordinated and continually prone to colds and stomach ailments. Games were a source of misery and humiliation. This led to his meticulous chronicling of the introduction of compulsion at Lancing. His diary served as a catharsis; torment was released through the nib of his pen and the result is a unique first-hand account of the growth of compulsory games in one public school.

The first school entry was in February 1860. On Monday 12 March, Brooke played one of his infrequent games of football. The season was almost over and the extent of his relief is seen in the comment: 'I am glad and thankful to say that it will be the last of the kind for some time to come.'[30] The following day he avoided games 'and loitered about'. Within a few days the season closed and for the remainder of the school year little of moment occurred. On 9 October of the following school year Brooke wrote in his diary: 'The Football Season. Today the first game of football was played . . . I was not present, but I heard there was a considerable quantity of "compulsion", which augurs ill certainly, and I must say that things do look very badly.'[31] The threat of compulsion weighed lightly upon him, however, and for the rest of the week he spent his afternoons blackberrying in the valley below the school. His tranquillity was greatly disturbed when in the middle of the month the captain of football, R. W. Papineau, announced that the game was now compulsory both on Tuesdays and Saturdays on the authorisation of the new headmaster Henry Walford. Brooke's disgust was considerable, especially regarding the headmaster's involvement; a fact that suggests complete freedom from staff interference in earlier years. Despite 'the odious rule of 20th. inst.', Brooke 'skipped football' for the next five compulsory sessions, was subsequently interviewed by Papineau and, although a sixth former, was threatened with a beating. Compulsion was to be taken seriously.

The headmaster's desire to see the new ruling implemented was made clear the very next day when he used the chapel pulpit to set in place an ideological cornerstone for the subsequent edifice of compulsion, claiming that it was the duty of boys to join in 'the unity of sports' and urging them to submit with good grace to the reformation.[32] And within twenty-four hours of this exhortation Walford had taken the opportunity of exerting further pressure on Brooke by way of 'a few unusually kind words' on the subject. The combined forces of headmaster and captain of the eleven thrust Brooke onto the football field. For the rest of the term the struggle was abandoned; a mixture of coercion and persuasion had overcome brief resistance. Brooke continued his diatribe against compulsory games in his diary, rejoicing over 'injuries, visits and wet days', but submitted to the system. After Christmas at home[33] he returned resolved to resume the conflict. He immediately absented himself from football; his dereliction of duty was noticed and resulted in a 'jaw' from Papineau on the importance of setting an example. Papineau's assault on his freedom was again followed by official reinforcement: the headmaster declared to the school shortly afterwards that football on Tuesdays and Thursdays was 'utterly and thoroughly compulsory'. Brooke's reaction was predictable. 'Our playtime *is* our playtime!' he protested in his diary, and once more capitulated.[34] By the following year compulsory football was firmly established. A brief revolution among the boys over the twice-weekly compulsory game did occur in February 1862. Brooke thought this 'a very gratifying performance'; but as a consequence R. E. Sanderson,[35] the new headmaster, assembled the school, and declared football to be compulsory on Tuesday and Saturday afternoons *and* from 12 to 1.10 on Mondays, Wednesdays and Fridays. Brooke's only consolation was that one zealot's proposal for a fine of sixpence for non-attendance was not taken up. Brooke left at Easter 1862; his considerable torment was over.

There are gaps in Brooke's record of the introduction of compulsory games at Lancing. It is impossible, for example, to be precise about Walford's motivation, but we do have a detailed picture of determined innovation, spasmodic resistance and, ultimately, institutionalised compulsion which illustrates the formidable influence of the headmaster, a reliance on ideological underpinning and interestingly, since it is seldom considered, considerable reluctance on the part of many boys.

An accurate understanding of the development of games in the public school system requires us to recognise that at Uppingham, Loretto and Lancing the headmaster was a major influence in the introduction of compulsion; that at Stonyhurst the pattern of authority suggests that the Order rather than the boys was responsible: that at Marlborough the contribution of the headmaster and his staff was considerable. All this would suggest that uncritical acceptance of the exclusive role of the pupils in the introduction of compulsory games should be avoided, and the contribution of the headmaster reappraised. The nineteenth-century public school headmaster was more often than not an educational entrepreneur of energy and will: as H. D. Rawnsley wrote of Thring, 'he was the very pulse of the machine'.[36]

III

Neatness of conceptualisation in conjunction with brevity of exposition run the special risk of overlooking loose ends, squeezing out essential contradictions, distorting reality. The assertion that, 'between 1860 and 1880 games became compulsory, organised and eulogised in all the leading public schools'[37] is one example. It implies too rapid, smooth and complete a transition from haphazardness to regimentation, liberty to compulsion, coolness to euphoria. It fails to fit the facts at Harrow – indisputably a leading school; and the spread of compulsion, organisation and eulogy at the other schools of this study was erratic, more gradual and in some cases far from complete by 1880. While compulsion, organisation and eulogy did eventually characterise the public school games system, at least for the schools of this study, the time scale must be expanded from twenty to forty years, and the suggestion of a smooth metamorphosis accomplished between 1860 and 1880 must be regarded with some scepticism.[38]

Nothing more firmly gives the lie to the commonly drawn image of the relentless, all-consuming appetite of 'the tin God of Athleticism', which by 1880 had swallowed its victims, than the development of athletic sports. The Stonyhurst athletic championships faithfully reflect the situation at the other schools. Before they became permanently established they passed through a period of uncertainty and vicissitude. Inaugurated in 1866, they were held continuously until 1872; then held erratically until 1897; only then did they occur regularly.

Compulsion provides an equally striking mirror image. Bland assertions regarding the triumphant onward march of compulsion take little note of protest, incompetent implementation and partial rejection.[39] Harrow is a valuable case study in consequence: it serves notice to the complacent that intention is not always translated into reality, and official policy does not necessarily result in desired action.

At Harrow, although games had become compulsory during Vaughan's headship (1845–59), throughout the 1860s, 1870s and 1880s the compulsory system of school games, as distinct from house games,[40] was extremely unpopular with the mass of the boys, disorganised rather than organised and only compulsory for a minority. It was disclosed in *Harrow Notes* in 1885 that there had been several methods of avoiding compulsory games in past decades – by obtaining exemption from the head of school who had the right to 'let off' as many as he thought fit, by pleading 'extra school' or 'lines', by claiming the right to exemption after three winter attendances and by watching or playing in a house match. In addition, each monitor who 'went down' was able to release four others from attendance.[41]

Unpalatable home truths about the compulsory system of games first surfaced in the *Harrovian* late in 1869.[42] 'A Tyro' complained through the correspondence columns of the magazine that there was scarcely a boy who did not detest compulsory football and called for a removal of the incubus. The editors lamely admitted that he represented a large and increasing portion of the community, but advanced the argument that inadequate organisation was as much the cause of ill-feeling as compulsion, and laid the blame on the fact that school 'pick-up' games were lacking in the *esprit de corps* of house games. In reality, the situation was more chaotic than the careful half-truth of the editorial suggested, and only one head of Cerebus was silenced by this feeble retort. The issue was reopened in the magazine in October of the following year. This time an enthusiastic correspondent urged a tightening up of the compulsory system.[43] Attendance, he hinted, required more careful supervision. An article on compulsory football in the same number spelled out the facts behind his mild admonition. It demonstrated clearly that compulsory football was *not*, in truth, compulsory, since on any half-day only between 150 and 200 boys out of 500 could be found on the playing fields.[44]

The next year, 1871, attention in the magazine shifted to compulsory cricket. It now transpired that only about 90 boys were involved in cricket matches on half-days and that consequently over 400 boys were quite free to do as they pleased.[45] Autumn brought more unhappy statistics. 'Compulsion' collated the attendance figures at compulsory football on a typical half-day. Of 532 boys, 115 were exempted due to their position in the school, 17 were excused on a plea of three years involvement and 63 had obtained medical certificates of exemption.[46] Eight years later the situation remained much the same. Most boys, the editors of the *Harrovian* stated early in 1879, regarded compulsory football 'as an invention to prevent their life here becoming more pleasant'; and for the majority it was compulsory in name only.[47] Later in the year a writer on 'Loafers' noted a common but serious evil in the summer term: over 300 boys played no games.[48]

Complaints from the righteous about the attitude towards compulsion continued to appear in the correspondence columns.[49] In 1883 'A well-wisher to Harrow' wrote that the system of compulsory games was 'an absolute failure', badly organised, inadequately supervised and universally detested.[50] Two years later the school's compulsory games system was *abandoned*.[51] School games became voluntary; the logical outcome of events. Reality had long been a simulacrum of the ideal. Compulsion was still possible in house games at the discretion of the house captain. This had always been the most efficient method of compulsion; one Old Harrovian recalled a game of 'footer' under a particularly zealous house captain every day in the previous decade.[52] The houses retained compulsory games playing but the system of compulsory attendance at school games was now completely jettisoned, and the system in its more successful form settled down to a relatively frictionless existence.

C. C. Cotterill was an assistant master at Fettes from 1870 to 1890, and a keen admirer of Almond and his physical education system in nearby Musselburgh. In *Suggested Reforms in the Public Schools*, published in 1883, Cotterill pressed for the introduction of *daily* physical activity. It is impossible to estimate with any accuracy the effect of his book on the public schools of the time. In all probability he was in part inspiration, and in part symptom of an educational fashion;[53] but it is a fact that within fifteen years of his urging, a fully fledged system of daily compulsory games which came close to his ideal was in operation at Harrow, Marlborough, Lancing, Uppingham and Loretto.

In 1900 *The Times*, *à propos* of the call of the militaristic Eton headmaster Warre for an act of parliament to make boys of fifteen and upwards liable to compulsory military training at school, commented sardonically: 'There is no Act of Parliament to compel boys to play cricket yet there is no want of stability in the ordinance that they shall play cricket.'[54] It was an exact appraisal of the state of compulsory games at the time. Teething troubles which had gone on for an inordinately long time in some schools were over. A system had evolved that was stable, reasonably well organised, and tolerated where it was not enthusiastically embraced.

The various school systems were not all as meticulously structured as at Charterhouse which was seemingly an extreme example of brutal efficiency: 'All boys in the Lower School had to score eighteen points known as pricks (and play two run abouts during the football season) every week. A game of cricket or football counted four points, fives counted three, squash two, swimming one. Any boy who failed to play the requisite number of games was beaten with a toasting fork.'[55] But Gurner's description of Marlborough before the Great War was commonly applicable. At Marlborough, he observed, there were now ample playing fields, generous timetable provision and a games master who saw to it that the facilities were not wasted. As a consequence, 'Every boy who was not suffering from some specific defect took part in the various turn-outs, trials, pick-ups, house practices and nets which took place on every afternoon.'[56]

Generations of boys were now growing up for whom compulsory games were a commonplace institutional tradition rather than a revolutionary ill-organised innovation. Eventually no other reality could be conceived. To play games virtually every day became the norm. Protestors, instead of voicing demotic objections as formerly, became deviants in the eyes of the majority and 'obliged to votary under pain of severe physical torture', namely a beating.[57] In a stanza written at Marlborough, the poet, Charles Sorley, celebrated the new conformity with these caustic lines:

> O come and see, it's such a sight,
> So many boys all doing right:
> To see them underneath the yoke
> Blindfolded by the older folk.[58]

The adopted system, mocked by Sorley, was to continue in broadly the same form until the Second World War.

Conditions at Uppingham, Harrow, Lancing and Loretto as the nineteenth century drew to a close, show the schools to be loyal exemplars of the new tradition.

At Uppingham games became compulsory three times a week in 1889; subsequently the system was overhauled and reformed yet again to promote further development of 'wholesome rivalry'. To stimulate the keenest participation, a house league was created, substantially increasing the number of house matches. The result was that boys generally played five games of rugby football a week.[59] As for cricket, Roe, in his review of public school cricket of the time, wrote admiringly of the sight at Uppingham on a typical summer's day of 'eighteen simultaneous games on one ground'.[60]

Harrow, as we have seen, had now resolved its problem, and a complicated system of house and school matches operated like clockwork. 'When I was at Harrow,' wrote one former pupil, remembering his schooldays between 1891 and 1895 towards the end of Welldon's headship (1884–95) 'every boy had to play football every day of every week.'[61] Summer at Harrow witnessed an elaborate system of cricket games that promised little rest from the games field for the majority. Compulsory cricket eventually included sixth-form matches, fifth-form matches, colts matches, Philathletic games, house leagues, house games, house matches and Torpid (junior) house matches, leaving only 'a small body of unemployables . . . interested . . . in natural history and lawn tennis'.[62]

Lancing, too, went the way of public school flesh. In the late seventies all games were compulsory three times a week. By 1888 it appears that football was compulsory every day and cricket three times a week.[63] When, in 1901, some relief was provided from six-days-a-week winter games by making attendance compulsory only three times weekly, an editorial in the magazine expressed considerable concern lest this departure from established habits might produce 'degenerate boys imbued with the spirit of loafing'.[64] Resented innovation had become respected tradition.

At Loretto, of course, Almond had early perfected the organisation of the games; not as a paper exercise as occurred elsewhere, but in practice. In the autumn and early spring this meant 'big sides' two or three days weekly and 'small sides' three or four days and on the other days, soccer or shinty. Those boys not able to play football, played fives, or took walks or runs, and sometimes played golf, if fit for nothing more vigorous. In summer, according to a long-suffering pupil it was 'cricket et toujours cricket; sides twice a week and matches most Saturdays, with nets on the other days; the juniors . . . having sides every day except Saturdays'.[65] And on wet days there were runs: a 'Wallyford', a 'long Wallyford', a 'Falside', a 'Three Trees' or a 'Three Trees and Falside'.[66]

This glimpse of life at Loretto alerts us to the fact that an integral part of 'compulsory games' at all the schools, while technically not a game at all, was the compulsory run, 'grind' or 'sweat'. It is an interesting phenomenon because it was essentially an instrument of social control, rather than moral improvement. It was predominantly a device for occupying the poorer games player when no game was available, or a means of occupying all boys in impossible playing conditions. The following extract from the *Lorettonian* nicely illustrates its bad weather role:

Monday, Dec. 4	Pouring rain; Wallyford run
Tuesday, Dec. 5	Snow – Falside run
Wednesday, Dec. 6	Snowballing sides in Park and Orchard
Thursday, Dec. 7	Snowballing sides on field and Linkfield
Friday, Dec. 8	Partial thaw – long walks
Saturday, Dec. 9	Heavy showers of snow, then rapid thaw.

About thirty fellows did 'Three Trees and Falside' run (snow often knee deep); about as many went by train to Longniddry and waded home; while the small boys went by train to Prestonpans and walked home by Tranent.[67]

Loretto's runs were tough and idiosyncratic. H. B. Tristram recorded: 'Boys were taught to face the wildest day that our climate gives us . . . the north-easterly gales that made the waves break right over the road beneath Drummore, or the driving snowstorms that blocked the railways, never stopped them. On the day of the great snowstorm in January, 1881, they went a "Falside and Three Trees". The roads were filled hedge-high with snow, and a way could only be found through the fields by the side, while even there every now and then they would fall into a drift.'[68]

At most of the other schools runs were only a little less arduous, and no less consistent. Marlborough 'sweats' have been celebrated in verse by Charles Sorley in his 'Song of the Ungirt Runners'[69] who ran 'because they must, through the great wide air' of the Wiltshire Downs. Another Marlburian described a typical weekday sight any winter between 1890 and 1945: 'It is 3 o'clock, and all the favourite tracks are covered: red, white and blue, Preshute is going to Old Eagle; black and blue and blue and white, B1 and B2 to Rockley Warren or Rockley Copse; magenta and white, C3's objective in Trainer's; red and blue, A House is content with First Post.'[70]

Uppingham boys were accompanied on house runs by praepostors on bicycles with whips 'lashing out at any fellow with a stitch or a cramp' or were sent on timed runs to local villages with the penalty of a beating if overdue.[71] One Uppinghamian sang despairingly in the *Uppingham School Magazine* at the start of a new term: 'And soon, in regulated checks we'll go – a run to Manton.'[72] Pupils of Lancing were apparently treated more kindly and given the choice of a run, a fine or the gym. The victim of an unavoidable run, admitted one of the persecuted, proceeded 'to walk deliberately to his destination'.[73]

It should not be thought, even when the system was at its peak, that all avenues of escape for the unenthusiastic were blocked and that all but the sick trooped religiously out to the fields or ran to distant mileposts or villages. Sympathetic housemasters such as Oliver Hall at Uppingham and B. W. T. Handford at Lancing fought a rear-guard action in the interests of individuality and freedom of choice. And there were others. This fact permitted John Betjeman under the tutelage of C. W. Hughes, his Marlborough art master, to paint 'skies of cobalt and ultramarine' instead of chasing bruised, red cricket balls,[74] C. R. W. Nevinson to escape 'grim afternoons' on the games field and draw the 'lovely architecture of Rutland'[75] and the Meinertzhagen brothers at Harrow, due to the liberality with passes of their housemaster, R. Bosworth-Smith, to go wandering over the countryside to Ruislip reservoir, instead of fielding on the Sixth Form Ground.[76] Archaeology and natural history societies also offered a means of avoidance to the seriously profane. Professor D. Savory remembered a flourishing natural history society at Marlborough. By a fortunate rule members were permitted to miss one afternoon's compulsory cricket per week in order to study local flora and fauna.[77] In a pastich à la Goldsmith one iconoclast spoke for all:

> Oh, who can wonder if the Forest wields
> A spell more potent than the playing fields
> Where sullen fielders blinded by the sun,
> Hold the rare catch, and mourn the frequent run.[78]

Be that as it may, by 1900 a new era of games regimentation had arrived. Many pupils did spend much of their daytime 'leisure' in supervised activities on the games fields. The innovations of Cotton, Almond, Walford and Thring, extended and perfected, were now 'taken for granted' institutions.

IV

Early antipathy towards compulsory games, as demonstrated with particular vehemence at Lancing and Harrow, should never be interpreted as antipathy to games themselves. Once resentment over the curtailment of liberty was no longer an issue because those who had known the old ways had gone, and once radical reform had become conservative tradition and inadequate organisation more efficient, the enthusiasm of many pupils for the games field was expressed more strongly than ever.

Games had long been worshipped in the older public schools. Early cricket enthusiasts at Harrow were virtually professional in their involvement and commitment. A former captain of the eleven informed the Public Schools Commission that while fifteen hours was about the average time spent on cricket per week, those of extreme devotion, 'who certainly did next to no school work', played twenty hours of cricket weekly.[79] In the winter, he continued, the cricketers became footballers and 'it took up almost all the time they could give to it'.[80] His picture of Harrow zeal was corroborated by M. W. Ridley, a Harrow master.[81]

Early as it was at this time in the development of athleticism, the athlete 'ideal-type' was already delineated and hugely admired. George Russell has left an unflattering but not uncharitable description of the Harrovian hero of this period in his recollection of 'Biceps Max', captain of the cricket eleven and house autocrat. 'He beat us into mummies if we evaded cricket fagging', Russell recalled, and wondered even in maturity if Biceps Max would beat him with a tray if he met him in the club and 'contradicted him in conversation, confuted him in argument or capped his best story'.[82] His academic standing was low but little was thought of intellectual distinction in those days, remarked Russell; the concern was much more with his capability to make the highest score at Lord's.

Games then in the 1860s had a considerable hold on Harrow boys and were not without support from the masters. Most masters watched the boys' cricket with enthusiasm. Even Butler, headmaster at the time of the Public Schools Commission 'could talk cricket shop, ancient or modern, like Lilleywhite or R. H. Lyttleton'.[83] No doubt *Tyro* had both masters and pupils in mind when in 1866, following a year without defeat on football or cricket field, it began its editorial with this acidic remark: 'For the far too great number of our body who place athletic before intellectual results, the past year must have been one continual source of enjoyment and triumph.'[84] By the time of the Lord's match later in the year it had regained its proper sense of perspective and could proclaim: 'If there is one thing that *lives* more than another at Harrow it is cricket; at the noble game Harrow is indeed a king among schools.'[85] This would seem to be an immodest, but accurate reflection of the attitude and values of the majority of Harrovians of the period.

Only at Loretto, due to Almond's fanaticism, was there similar intensity of involvement in the early 1860s. Elsewhere enthusiasm grew steadily but for a while was less pronounced. Lancing was handicapped by poor facilities. For some years after Cotton's reform some Marlborough boys still hankered after access to the neighbouring countryside. At Uppingham it was always Thring's policy to permit his boys reasonable access.

By the mid-1870s, however, leisure horizons in all five schools were becoming restricted to the playing fields and a passion which grew into an obsession was being assiduously cultivated by the zealous. Rowland Prothero, when attempting in the 1930s to define the distinction between the youth of that time and his own, concluded:

Contemporary fiction represents the school-boys and undergraduates of today as more absorbed in the problems of adult life than in the puerile pursuit of athletics. But in the 'sixties and 'seventies their interests, if they were physically fit, raced in exactly the opposite direction. *No picture of them would be true if it did not emphasize their passion for games, and therefore my own enthusiasms are not so much personal as typical of the period.*[86] [Emphasis added]

The reasons for this situation will be examined at length in later chapters. The purpose here is to determine a sequence of events and to trace the evolution of an ethos, and any student of the school literature of the period must agree with Prothero's analysis and extend it into subsequent decades.

It is interesting to concentrate briefly on the Marlborough evidence because in all probability Marlborough was the most intellectual, and contained the most academically able boys, of the schools under consideration; yet here the new passion for the games field was very evident. The *Marlborough College Register* records 474 Oxford and Cambridge scholars and exhibitioners between 1880 and 1920.[87] Yet these boys 'who really brought credit to the school . . . were those . . . least thought of by their comrades. The heroes were the members of the cricket Eleven or the football Fifteen'.[88] Marlburian Cyril Alington, in his own words, 'went through a period of disgust with a world which appreciated athletic prowess more than intelligence' and wrote – anonymously – a bitter couplet for the school magazine, describing a place,

> Where Weight precedence gives, Worth seeks in vain,
> And heavy limbs can balance heavy brain.[89]

Anonymity was imperative: most of his friends were athletes. In terror of detection for some time, he eventually realised that they would hardly read 'the poetical parts of the paper'. A later Marlburian neatly summed up commonplace institutional values with a liberal use of assonance: 'The one kind of work that it's wicked to shirk, is the labour of willow and wicket.'[90] It was an accurate as well as euphonious comment. The new passion is reflected not only in the statements of Prothero and Alington but also in the contents of the school magazine presented in table IV on p. 92.[91]

Perhaps the central preoccupations of the boys are caught more graphically by listing merely a few of the themes of the many letters about games in the correspondence columns: the iniquity of running back at rugger, the unsuitability of tennis as a school game, the necessity of compulsory house gymnastics, the ungentlemanly habit of lying on the ball in rugby matches, the desirability of house grounds for football, Indian clubs versus dumbells, the attractions of lawn tennis house competitions, the over use of cricket nets, the need for a pole-vaulting event in the school sports, correct behaviour at school matches, the headgear of the Marlborough eleven at Lord's, the value of a housemaster's race for sports day and biased representation on the football committee.

Marlborough is a study in emphasis not exclusiveness. The evidence surviving leaves little doubt that, in the decades immediately before and after the turn of the century, games enthusiasm there was pronounced, heavily involved the majority, and was underpinned and legitimated by a powerful and explicitly formulated educational rationale. And Marlborough was a mirror in which all the other schools except Stonyhurst would have speedily recognised themselves.

This general state of affairs in the schools is indicated by such factors as the occasional and unsuccessful attempts of enterprising editors to direct the emphasis in the school magazines away from the interminable descriptions of, and arguments about, school games. One disillusioned set of editors of the *Harrovian* announced in 1872, 'The Philistine part of our population has indeed grumbled and abused in its own peculiarly forcible and persistent manner, when it has been pleased to think that sufficient space has not been allotted to the glorification of muscle.'[92] When, a year later, the editors of the *Uppingham School Magazine*, while careful to praise an earnestness in the school about 'outdoor work', raised the

Punch was a consistent critic of the late nineteenth-century games-cult which preoccupied public schools and universities and their products. In prose, verse and cartoon it ridiculed its various manifestations. It, therefore, provides an amusing yet mordant view of period values, attitudes and practices.

SEASONABLE ATHLETICS.

The stalwart Brothers Dick and Bob turn their Public School and College Education to good Account by taking their newly-married Wives (the gentle Sisters, Blanche and Violet) on a Walking Tour through the Midland Counties. Laden in the Manner we have tried to depict, these brawny Sons of Anak look upon Thirty Miles a Day as a mere Trifle.

5   This is the first cartoon the magazine published on the subject of the new 'public school and college education' and its devotees – a benign if amused depiction of strange new creatures. (*Punch*, 6 September 1873, p. 94)

FORM.

Public School Boy (to General Sir George, G.C.B., G.S.I., V.C., &c., &c., &c.) I say, Grandpapa,—a—would you mind just putting on your Hat *a little* straighter! Here comes Cudders—he's awfully particular—and he's the Captain of our Eleven, you know!"

THE NEW TYRANNY.

"Of course you needn't *Work*, Fitzmilksopp; but *Play* you must and *shall*!"

6   This cartoon, which appeared fourteen years after the one above, is far less charitable. It mocks the foolish pretentions of the athletic 'blood'. (*Punch*, 17 September 1887, p. 123)

7   The New Tyranny was, of course, compulsory games advocated with equal enthusiasm by robust masters and admiring parents. (*Punch*, 5 October 1889, p. 165)

ATHLETICS UNDER DIFFICULTIES.

Master (to Brown Secundus, who is doing a little private practice).
"How's this, Brown! Out of School! What for!"
Brown Secundus (innocently). "Sprained Wrist, Sir!"

8 (*Punch*, 31 March 1894, p. 155)

PREPARING FOR BLACK MONDAY.

Paterfamilias (reading School Report). "Ah, my Boy, this isn't
so good as it might be. 'Latin indifferent,' 'French poor,'
'Arithmetic nothing'!"
Tommy. "Ah, but look down there, Papa. 'Health excellent'!"

9 (*Punch*, 20 September 1890, p. 141)

Both these cartoons illustrate the firm resistance to academic learning of the
sturdy, well-adjusted, anti-intellectual public school boy of the time.

CONFIDENCES.

Miss Girton. "And do you like Browning?"
Muscular Undergraduate. "Well, to tell the truth, I'd as soon read a Time-table!"

10 *Punch*'s sardonic view of the ex-public school boy as Oxbridge 'hearty'
displaying a healthy distaste for poets and poetry. (*Punch*, 10 July 1897, p. 6)

Table IV An analysis of the pages and correspondence in the 'Marlburian' 1866–1966

Pages

	1866	1876	1886	1896	1906	1926	1936	1946	1956	1966
Sport	68 (37.4%)	72 (40.0%)	60½ (30.8%)	66 (32.8%)	69½ (35.9%)	54 (31.0%)	60½ (30.6%)	30 (31.6%)	32 (18.2%)	11 (11.7%)
All other	114 (62.6%)	108½ (60.0%)	135½ (69.2%)	135 (67.2%)	123½ (64.1%)	120 (69.0%)	136 (69.4%)	65 (68.4%)	144 (81.8%)	83 (88.3%)

Correspondence

	1866	1876	1886	1896	1906	1926	1936	1946	1956	1966
Sport	26 (53.1%)	19 (67.9%)	59 (46.5%)	33 (50.8%)	12 (32.4%)	3 (8.6%)	6 (40.0%)	1 (7.1%)	3 (8.6%)	2 (18.2%)
All other	23 (46.9%)	9 (32.1%)	68 (53.5%)	32 (49.2%)	25 (67.6%)	32 (91.4%)	9 (60.0%)	13 (92.9%)	32 (91.4%)	9 (81.8%)

N.B. 1916 is omitted. The Great War resulted in traditional team games being replaced in importance by military manoeuvres.

possibility of the danger of overestimating and over-emphasising such subordinate matters and proposed a mild reform – the reduction of space devoted to these topics – they admitted this would be distasteful to many.[93] It was. The next number brought complaints about the inclusion of a boring list of local flora by way of substitution.[94] The editors persisted with their new policy for some considerable time, insisting that all aspects of school life must find a place in the school journal. Due to the considerable criticism they encountered at one point a meek editorial stated that all they desired was that the games element should not become a tyrant.[95] Their idealism was unavailing. Eventually they weakly apologised for the re-emphasis on cricket and the exclusion of botany. They had learned that the magazine only sold when it gave substantial space to games.[96]

Biographies and autobiographies dealing with the schools of the period between approximately 1880 and 1900 provide a glimpse of a common reality. As it was at Harrow, so it was in large measure at Marlborough, Loretto, Uppingham and Lancing. In his biography of the Jesuit, C. C. Martindale, Peter Caraman remarks of Harrow in the 1890s, 'Days . . . were then spent in the minimum of necessary work and the maximum of congenial games.'[97] Richard Meinertzhagen thought, 'Too much was made of games . . . Boys became heroes because they were "games" prodigies.'[98] Of Harrow a few years later, Sir Stephen Tallents wrote that it was 'not only Spartan but Philistine. . . . All its emphasis was on athletics; brains and artistic gifts found few outlets and counted for next to nothing.'[99] Later still, looking back over twenty years as master and chaplain between 1917 and 1942, E. M. Venables reflected sadly: 'The evidence that the school took work at all seriously was far to seek . . . While nobody would wish to see pale-faced students displace the carefree, robust, vital "lads in coats of blue" with all their gaiety and laughter on the Hill . . . this is not incompatible with serious study and hard work.' But Harrovians did not consider that hard work was quite the thing. As Venables knew only too well: 'Games and everything connected with games came very much first.'[100] So much so that Francis Yeats Brown looked back to his Harrow schooldays with an acquired equanimity that still did not quite hide the sense of failure: '. . . it was discovered that I was short-sighted and that I was no good at cricket. Naturally enough, I became a person of no account.[101] By the turn of the century, without too much exaggeration, the *Public School Magazine* was prepared to define 'modern learning' thus:

> If you want an education
> Of the highest exaltation,
> You've only got to follow out this code.
> You must be quick in spurning,
> Every single form of learning,
> To get the education *à la mode*.
> You must give up Greek and Latin
> For of course there's more than that in
> This plan of education up to date:
> You must give up mathematics;
> All your conics and your statics
> Are needless for the athletician state.[102]

Care must be taken to avoid the gins and pitfalls of exaggeration but staff, pupils, observers and even humorists of the era present a stark, unsubtle image of the reality of life in the schools after 1880. Comment is too frequent, references too numerous, examples too widespread for the *Zeitgeist* to be rejected. There were, of course, rebels, protestors and reformers and they will be considered in due course. There were, as has been seen, narrow avenues of escape, guarded by sympathetic masters. Yet the evidence available leaves little doubt that in all the schools except Stonyhurst, many were now in the embrace of an ideology which had developed a standardised vocabulary of commitment, created an enthusiastic body of supporters through the liberal provision of facilities, and won a captive clientele through the introduction of compulsory games. By the evening of Victoria's reign there was considerable allegiance to the now widespread athleticism.

In 1875, *Punch*, with some prescience, anticipated a typical 'school report' twenty years on:[103]

SCHOOL REPORTS OF THE FUTURE

Dear Mr. Punch,

My experience of to-day justifies me, I think, in anticipating for my son's son, when he goes to a public school, some such School Report as the enclosed.

Your obedient Servant,

PETER PATERFAMILIAS.

Report for First Term of 1895

Name – 'PATERFAMILIAS SECUNDUS'.   SET II.

Subject	Place in Set	Remarks
1. Football	Back	Is not wanting in pluck – should allow more for the wind in his drop-kicks.
2. Boating	No. 7	Has overcome his 'screwing' propensity – hangs a little on the feather.
3. Racquets		Is getting to place his balls lower but has not yet broken himself of shutting his eyes on the stroke.
4. Boxing		Striking out better from the shoulder, but still will anticipate his parry.
5. Cricket	Point	A sure catch. Fair change bowler and is improving. Might bat squarer, and wants confidence.
6. Gymnasium		Parallel bars, good. Will do the 'back circle' next Term. Vaulting moderate.
7. Athletic Sports	First in Mile under 16.	Time in long races good, but trusts too much to his spurt. Does better at long jumping than high. Putting the weight, weak.
Conduct *Coach's Report* *House-Master's Report*		Painstaking – seems to have ambition. Obedient, except that he will practise fives in his bedroom.
Headmaster's Remarks on Form-Work		No observations; the weather having been so fine this Term that every day has been devoted to games.

ARNOLD BUSBY BROWN,

(Formerly Stroke of the Lady Margaret Eight, and Captain of the Cambridge Eleven)

HEAD MASTER.

If things didn't quite come to this, Cyril Heber-Percy's house-master at Harrow certainly showed willing, and an absolute clear-headedness about education priorities, when with deprecatory gentleness, he wrote to Heber-Percy's father in an end of term report: 'I don't think too much attention need be given to the very bad report he has received from Mr. Roebuck his classics master. He has played exceptional hard, and for the second year running we won the cock-house match.'[104]

The next four chapters will be concerned with the internal and external forces which produced and nurtured this blithe, absolute self-confidence.

Part II

The forces of ideological consolidation

5

Conspicuous resources, anti-intellectualism and sporting pedagogues

The English public school is invariably an island of mellowed buildings in a sea of well-kept playing fields. Nothing more strikingly illustrates the part that games have played in English upper-class education than the view down Music Hill, through Butler Gate and across the sweeping acres of Harrow 'footer' fields with its thirty-four pitches stretching to the Sheepcote Road. These spatial symbols of commitment, indulgence and privilege bear witness to the power of an ideology, the wealth of an institution and the devotion of its pupils, staff, old boys and parents. The latter were the financial source of the impressive facilities on which the public school boy ostensibly developed his character. It was the wealth of the upper classes which translated a value system into a set of actions by ensuring the purchase and maintenance of sufficient fields so that each member of a large school could find space to kick, chase and strike a ball.[1]

The Victorian economic substructure determined the reign of athleticism. All other causes were subordinate to it. Wealth released the potential of character. As Geoffrey Best has written: 'The economic substructure must always be there . . . the limiting terms of mid-Victorian British Society were prescribed by economic forces. Its "economic miracle", such as it was, alone made possible that unprecedented degree and diffusion of wealth that allowed its citizens, as consumers, to reveal their characters in the choices they actually made out of such an unparalleled variety of goods.'[2] Much of this wealth was accumulated between 1850 and 1873; a time of 'unchallenged British ascendancy over the family of nations in commerce and manufacture'.[3] Riches disproportionately held in the hands of the upper classes raised public school chapels, built the houses, purchased the playing fields and provided the security which permitted the occupation of these fields for several hours each day.

Security has been acknowledged as the key to an understanding of English education.[4] It undoubtedly opens the door to an understanding of events in the nineteenth-century public school. Economic security made possible a 'conspicuous consumption' of time in 'conspicuous leisure'. The terms are Veblen's. He saw these two phenomena as ostentatious symbols of upper-class status, denoting freedom from the preoccupation of earning a living. Leisure, however, as Veblen was quick to point out, did not connote passivity, but the 'non-productive consumption of time' in playing games.[5] He further suggested that both ostentatious consumption and leisure were invariably underpinned by a pseudo-rationale (in his pleasing expression 'a coloured make-belief of purpose') in an attempt to provide them with dignity. Veblen's theorising has substantial relevance for this study, yet he might have added a third element: conspicuous resources. Playing fields were themselves significant symbols of security and elitism. An analysis of the growth of games facilities in the schools is basic to an understanding of the means whereby athleticism grew powerful; it allows the study of a system of financial support without which ideological conviction and casuistic manipulation could not have prospered.

Of the schools investigated in this study Uppingham possesses the most complete records of the evolution of games facilities and is broadly representative of the other schools. It will serve, therefore, as a case study.

Thring, his staff, old boys and eventually the governors gave their money generously to build up the school's amenities. Thring, in particular, borrowed heavily from his father to pay for his school expenses and was often in considerable debt. When he went to Uppingham in 1853 he was anxious to develop adequate physical education facilities.[6] Among his early actions were the negotiation of a new bathing pool, the creation of a gymnasium, the extension of the Upper cricket ground, the renting of football fields and the search for a suitable meadow on which to hold athletic championships. All this was expensive and in the first twenty years of his headship there was no corpus of nostalgic old boys and proud parents ready to contribute their wealth to the school. The responsibility for the purchase of land and the development of amenities fell squarely on the headmaster and his staff. Fortunately many were men of private means.[7] Thring, therefore, instituted a 'Domus fund' to which the masters contributed, and which was in effect a system of corporate taxation for funding the expansion of the school.[8]

Details of the masters' financial contribution to the creation of games facilities are to be found in a document entitled 'A Statement of Capital Invested and Comparative Annual Expenditure of Trust and Masters 1853–1872'[9] presented to the governors of the school in 1872:

(i) Presented by Present Masters to the Trust since 1853:

	£
The Gymnasium	300
Two Fives Courts in Quad	100

(ii) Belonging to the Masters Conjointly:

	£
Two bathing places	250
Two Cricket Fields	300
Pavilion in Cricket Field	360

In addition, under an item entitled 'Comparative Annual Expenditure of the Trust and the Masters in carrying on the work of the School' it was revealed that masters were also responsible for the maintenance of the gymnasium, and those cricket fields and bathing places purchased or leased for the school. They also paid rent on several of these amenities.

The purpose of Thring's 'Statement' was to emphasise to the governors, with whom he had been involved in a long and bitter conflict over the development of the school, just how little they had done. It serves also to demonstrate the extent to which staff had supported not only facilities upon which athleticism was to flourish, but the whole physical structure of the school. In the nineteen years of Uppingham's existence under Thring, the total capital invested in 'plant' was £81,196. Of this the staff had contributed £74,103 (91¼%) and the trust £7,093 (8¾%).[10]

Masters continued to play a substantial part in the creation of games facilities after 1872, as the purchase of Fowler's Field illustrates. Soon after the famous Borth migration,[11] a field on the north-west side of the town belonging to a Mr Fowler was offered for sale. Unable to purchase it himself from lack of funds, Thring wrote to a wealthy assistant master, Howard Candler, urging him to buy it: 'It is in my opinion very important that Mr. Fowler's field should be in school hands; and much to the interest of the school that you should purchase it.'[12] The request is a good example both of Thring's ability to drum up financial support for his ventures and of the loyalty of his staff. Attached was an agreement to rent the field direct from Candler for twenty-one years, already arranged between Thring and other members of staff. Twenty-three masters had signed the document, pledging annual payments of several pounds each to the School Cricket Fund.[13] Candler obediently bought the field for £1220. His generosity did not end there. In safer times, the governors, who at the time of the flight to Borth were unwilling to risk funds on uncertain investments, bought the field from Candler for £1280.[14] Candler promptly handed the £60 profit to the Games Committee to be used for turfing the arable field. And then donated a screen of trees along the side overlooking the road.

By the end of the nineteenth century the burden of enlarging, developing and equipping Uppingham had passed from the shoulders of devoted staff to old boys, parents and the governors, who now had considerably more confidence in the school than in earlier times. The last great item of expenditure between 1853 and the Second World War was the governors' purchase, between 1919 and 1922, of the Middle Ground and an adjoining tract of land which together added up to some thirty-five acres. An old boy, C. C. Brook, immediately donated £5000 for levelling and preparation. Two years earlier Sir Harry McGowan, who had two sons at the school, had paid for a pavilion on the Leicester Road Ground (formerly Fowler's Field).

Day-to-day maintenance of the games equipment and facilities of the public schools, as has been seen briefly in chapter 3, was paid for in the main by regular annual subscriptions from boys and staff. School subscriptions were generally collected by house. In T. B. Rowe's house in 1869 the seniors paid 12s 6d and the juniors 10s 6d annually.[15] There were, in addition, house subscriptions also predominantly for the upkeep of games equipment and facilities. The *School Rules* circa 1880 state that new boys at that time paid an entrance feee of 5s, younger house members paid 14s and older boys 18s yearly.[16] Each year the 'School Games Account' was published in the school magazine: subscribers could thus see how their money was spent. The two contrasting examples on pp. 104–5 (table v) show clearly the increased complexity and sophistication of amenities of the post-Thring era. This progression led to the subscription system being abandoned; eventually a lump sum was added to school fees and the bursar took charge of the accounts.[17]

Uppingham provides an outline of a neatly interlocking system of facility provision and maintenance typical of the nineteenth-century public school. It depended to a considerable extent on the freely given wealth of individuals. In general, staff, old boys and governors provided the capital necessary for the construction of 'plant'; staff and boys contributed through the subscription system to meet 'running costs'; parents, old boys and staff donated additional luxuries.

'An English Public School,' remarked a *Guardian* editorial on public school expenses in 1892, 'like an English Ironclad, is an elaborate affair.' Funds had to be found to cover the cost not only of staff, board and lodging and sanatorium but also of adequate playing fields. These were indispensable. 'The value of physical training is felt – some say it is overfelt,' it added by way of explanation.[18] The observation was wholly accurate. Schools of the time stood or fell in public esteem by the quality of their wickets and the extensiveness of their games acres. Paul Ford admitted that the organisation of games at public schools was extremely expensive, but added realistically, 'Any school that would recommend itself to the British public must concern itself to see that its athletic appliances do not fall behind its neighbours.'[19]

Parents, old boys, staff, governors in the various guises of idealist, pleasure-lover and status-seeker found the cause of splendid wickets a desirable one. They were content to meet the cost. In educational matters few things demonstrate the wealth or the interests of the nineteenth-century upper classes as well as the expenditure lavished on the games fields of the public schools. Dingy classrooms contrasted strongly with superbly kept cricket squares and spacious football acres – symbols of the dominant values of the system and the wealth of Victorian society.

II

The theory that games 'got out of hand' in the public schools because schoolmasters failed to introduce alternative ways for pupils to spend their free time[20] is, unhappily, a considerable over-simplification. The causes of athleticism were several, intricately entangled, and involved factors both inside and outside the schools. Yet a mass retreat from dingy classroom to superb playing field, attractive enough in itself, was made all the more seductive by the limited number of extra-curricular activities available for many years. For much of the nineteenth century these were restricted to a debating society for senior boys, a natural history society or an archaeological society and a concert club.[21] The one notable exception was Stonyhurst where the Jesuit tradition of play-acting took

Table v

1882			

Expenditure

	£	s	d
H. H. Stephenson – salary	75	0	0
Cricket and football accounts	30	19	0
Barsby, wages	52	0	0
Sawdust, etc.	1	7	6
Boys' wages	13	10	4
Extra labour	4	5	6
Brown, bowler	16	10	0
Water works	5	0	0
Athletic prizes and expenses	35	7	6
Horse-hire	28	5	0
Ironmonger	10	1	0
Painting etc.	2	18	9
Carpenter	6	14	0
Printing	0	2	5
Rent of grounds	59	0	0
Taxes	2	17	3
Interest to bank	2	12	4
	£346	10	7

Receipts

	£	s	d
From the school – 1st term	108	14	8
” ” ” – 2nd term	119	16	4
” ” ” – 3rd term	84	6	4
Elevens' subscriptions	24	1	0
Captain of games (fines, entries etc.)	4	6	6
Rent for grazing	17	0	0
Surplus of Oakham Show subscription	1	16	0
From the masters	39	0	0
Right of way	0	1	0
	£399	1	10

	£	s	d
Expenditure, 1882	346	10	7
Debt, Christmas 1881	92	2	9
	£438	13	4
Receipts	£399	1	10
Total debt, Christmas 1882	£39	11	6

Uppingham School games accounts: growth of expenditure

			1908	

Expenditure

	£ s d	£ s d		£ s d
Salaries – Baldwin	55 0 0			
Bird	13 12 6			
Thorpe	57 4 0		Insurance –	
Cobb	19 3 5		Fire	0 2 0
Boys	27 1 0		Employers liability	2 17 11
		190 6 11	Hire of football stand	1 0 0
Extra labour		2 4 0	Pinney – sports prizes	10 2 0
Water rate (three quarters)		3 15 0	Scrubbing tent	0 2 0
Water for jump		0 7 6	C11 Thorpe – sports prizes	22 10 0
Rent: Leicester Road Ground		39 0 0	Rates	4 11 3
Garden		1 0 0	Green – for cricket lunches	23 12 0
Belgrave		4 0 0	Draper – for beer	1 2 2
New Ground		5 0 0	Wyon – for medals	2 10 0
Whitening		1 7 6	Washing	0 16 6
Umpires – Haileybury		10 0 0	Two cheque books	0 4 0
Scott		1 5 0	Dalby	1 13 0
Glenn		17 5 8	Bird – for carting etc.	7 0 0
Dolby		6 5 6	Hawthorn	8 12 6
Mrs W. Dean		24 5 9	White	0 6 6
Mrs L. Dean		0 5 6	Cliff	4 9 5
Rutland Agricultural Society		5 0 0	String	0 0 9
Fat Stock Show		5 0 0	Sellars	1 16 0
Baldwin's accounts –			Steward	1 7 0
Hockey		5 17 8	Nicholls	0 4 0
Cricket.................		21 1 9	Tickets to Rugby (Baldwin	
Football...............		5 13 5	and Thorpe)	0 7 6
Sports prizes		4 9 6	Balance in bank, 31 Dec	
Coltman..........................		37 11 6	1908	28 6 11
Curtis		1 13 6	Cash in hand, 31 Dec 1908 ..	15 2 1
Woodrock		5 2 0		
				£537 2 8

Receipts

	£ s d	£ s d		£ s d
Subscriptions			From house-masters'	
1st Term	121 15 8		cricket lunches	10 2 6
2nd Term	147 5 8		From Thorpe – part rent of	
3rd Term	135 13 4		garden	0 10 0
			M.R. dividend	3 1 3
		404 14 8	Interest	1 0 0
Masters' subscriptions	35 3 0		Sale of Committee of Games	
Fives' entrance fees	5 5 0		rules	1 14 2
Raven testimonial surplus	12 13 0		Balance in bank, 31 Dec	
Contribution to sports prizes	4 4 0		1907	39 0 11
Scott – for grazing Leicester			Cash in hand, 1 Jan. 1908	4 15 2
Road Ground	8 0 0			
Sale of nets	1 10 0			£537 2 8
From Cadet Corps for use of				
Leicester Road Ground	5 0 0			

up a considerable amount of time and effort.[22] No doubt, more clubs and societies would have reduced the strong interest in games. At the same time since a number of factors produced the reign of athleticism, the removal of any single one would not have been sufficient in itself to lessen the influence of the ideology substantially. Furthermore, despite the conscientious support of staff those activities which were available had a precarious existence at times.

It is worth noting also that the proliferation of clubs and societies, when it came, was the result of changes in pupil attitudes, parental expectations, intellectual standards and social values as much as the radicalism, liberality or perceptiveness of schoolmasters. In the interim there was much truth in the observation of Rufus, the captain of the eleven, in *Prelude*, Beverley Nichols's novel of Marlborough life: 'You know an awful lot of rot's talked about games at a public school. My pater seemed to think that it was the tradition of games that made me a dunce. He didn't see that it is because there are so many dunces like me that games sprang up at all.'[23]

Of course, upper-class dunces were not invariably born so; they were certainly made so by a process of intense conditioning by parents, peers and pedagogues. They were caught up, in fact, in the standards of their time. Discomfort in the presence of the intellectual of questionable masculinity and preference for a 'manly' image led to the general adoption of the ideal of the English male expounded to Harold Nicolson's uncle during his Rugby schooldays: 'It was taught on all sides that manliness and self-control were the highest aims of English boyhood: he was taught that all but the most material forms of intelligence were slightly effeminate: he learnt, as they all learnt, to rely on action rather than ideas.'[24]

As a result, lack of respect for learning, contempt for 'bookworms' and admiration for active muscle have been constant features of many public school boys throughout much of the schools' history. Precedent was firmly established by the 'Great Schools' as Nicolson reveals above. The Public Schools Commission reported in 1864 that their intellectual standards were distinctly unsatisfactory.[25] *The Times* offered a bald interpretation of the commission's more gently worded accusations. It commented that, on the evidence of the commission's findings, the public school system was a failure. And a failure even when represented by its better specimens – university entrants. Most had nothing to show for their schooling other than some Latin and Greek, a little English and a little arithmetic. Sadly, their knowledge of the former was most inaccurate and their knowledge of the latter contemptible. The newspaper attributed this academic ineptitude 'partly to the formidable competition of games and social life, and partly to overcrowded classrooms and poor equipment'.[26] The situation improved little, if at all, during the next forty years. Criticism of intellectual standards, while it could scarcely be more harsh, grew in volume. There were, of course, variations in academic performance. Stonyhurst achievements received praise from the Schools Inquiry Commission[27] and Marlborough's prowess in gaining university scholarships was shown by the same commission to be justly famous.[28] But the general position has been neatly summarised by Ogilvie. Character was cultivated; brains were disparaged. A handful won scholarships; the majority became solid men of their class.[29]

The disparagement of brains reflected nothing short of a general and virulent anti-intellectualism on the part of most boys and some masters. 'The "Highbrow",' wrote Ian Hay in a book inappropriately entitled in this context, *The Lighter Side of School Life*, 'is a fish out of water with a vengeance but he does exist at school – somehow.'[30] John Addington Symonds at Harrow, James Elroy Flecker at Uppingham, John Betjeman at Marlborough, Evelyn Waugh at Lancing, are some of the distinguished writers who bear witness from one generation to the next to the accuracy of Hay's testimony.[31] Such philistinism greatly offended Matthew Arnold and convinced him that the intellectual life and general culture of the upper classes had 'somewhat flagged since the last century'. He pointed an accusing finger at the 'Great Schools' and considered that intellectual vitality had passed from their classrooms to those of the second grade.[32] It was a naive view. Perhaps he was too easily impressed by Marlborough's knack of winning Oxford and Cambridge awards. In reality there was little to choose between the old and the new.[33]

The attitude to learning prevalent in the schools caused anxiety among the discerning in society. Periodically letters and articles of attack and defence would appear in national newspapers and journals. Protagonists and antagonists fought out a bitter conflict, for example, in the great athleticism controversy in the correspondence columns of *The Times* in 1889. There was a short but sharp exchange between A. W. Ready and H. H. Almond in the *New Review* in the mid-1890s. Sir Oliver Lodge resumed the struggle on behalf of the protestants in the *Nineteenth Century* in 1902.

Contributors to *The Times Educational Supplement* joined in battle in 1918 and the *English Review* in 1923 was the arena in which one of the last sustained attacks on public school anti-intellectualism was mounted.[34]

Some critics found insufficient space in newspapers and journals for condemnation and published whole books. One of the fiercest antagonists of the schools was S. P. B. Mais.[35] He had the advantage of first-hand experience of several schools as boy and master. With considerable authority therefore, he could write that public school products 'knew nothing, cared little, exhausted their keenness on games and considered anything but the most perfunctory interest in school work a gross breach of good form'.[36]

Accusations of limited cultural and intellectual horizons, ignorance of political, social and economic matters were frequently levelled at the schools – from within. Even at Marlborough, despised by true gentlemen for its talent for getting boys 'to acquire a power of interminable quotation',[37] discontent about the low quality of intellectual life was voiced from time to time. 'Adam House' in *David Blaize* was sufficient of a sore thumb to attract attention because 'even the juniors took an interest in all sorts of queer things like reading books . . . and knowing the difference between Liberals and Conservatives'.[38] At this bizarre establishment the daily paper was considered something more than the source of century makers in county matches.[39] Paul Trevelyan, the hero of *Prelude*, pushing aside momentarily memories of London dinners and theatres, crates of liqueurs, rose-tipped abdullahs and £20 notes from his mother, reflected bitterly on the fact that he and his fellow pupils – the future governing class – knew nothing about the conditions of the country; and argued that 'instead of writing Latin elegiacs . . . we ought to be learning what the socialists are saying. What Henderson and McDonald are thinking . . .'

Symptomatic of intellectual apathy were the constant editorials in the school magazines down the decades, bewailing the lack of material of sufficient literary quality.[40] On one occasion the editors of the *Lorettonian* were reduced to begging for a letter, having given up hope of any literary articles, and on another aired the general truth that 'when there is no football there is nothing with which to fill up the paper'.[41] The interrelated problems of a poor literary standard and a heavy sporting imbalance sufficiently concerned J. R. H. O'Regan, a Marlborough master, for him to make them the subject of a frank essay in a book published at the beginning of the twentieth century.[42] Poor quality material in the *Marlburian* was nothing new, however. As early as 1866, pleas from the editors for literary work fell upon deaf ears, while a request from a correspondent for the insertion of 'Charades, Conundrums and Compositions' – for the benefit of 'many members of the school . . . who felt, and not unnaturally, unequal to the task of perusing the undeniably clever but to them perhaps *too* clever literary articles' – met with immediate gratification.[43] Happily there were moments of relief. The *Marlburian* contained literary contributions of a high quality in the first quarter of the twentieth century when the contributors included Charles Sorley, John Betjeman and Louis MacNeice.

While the general picture in the schools is of low intellectual interest and effort, it is all too easy to commit the sin of omission. Care must be taken to avoid this. It is as well, therefore, to remember Arnold Lunn's words about Harrow to the effect that while academic standards were generally poor, the few motivated boys used never to lack for stimulation from able masters.[44] Motivated boys and clever staff existed in all the schools.

Headmasters were well aware of, and often deprecated the anti-intellectualism of their pupils. Even Welldon, for all his enthusiasm for games, did not entirely lack a sense of proportion. In *Gerald Eversley's Friendship* he wrote these almost frank words: 'Of the achievements of the intellect, if they stand alone, public school opinion is still as it has always been, slightly contemptuous, but strength, speed, athletic skill, quickness of eye and hand . . . command universal applause among schoolboys as among savages.'[45] Some headmasters were noted antagonists of the athletocrat. F. W. Farrar in particular, continually deprecated the poor intellectual efforts of the majority of Marlburians. 'Do not think that I disparage the physical vigour at which I daily look with interest,' he told them in a sermon, 'but it is impossible to repress a sigh when one thinks that the same vigour infused also into intellectual studies which are far higher and nobler, would carry all success and prosperity in life irresistibly before you.'[46]

Yet the attitude of others was ambivalent and must have been confusing to immature schoolboys. If headmasters frequently admired, and held up for admiration, the coolness of the talented athlete, too often they warned against the self-possession of the able scholar. Cotterill, in his *Suggested Reforms in the Public School*, exhibited the clearest symptoms of a general *mal de siècle*:

Cleverness – what an aim! Good God, what an aim! Cleverness neither makes nor keeps man or nation. Let it not be thought that it ever can. For a while it may succeed, but only for a while. But self-sacrifice, – this it is that makes and preserves men and nations, yes, and fills them with joy – only this. Big brains, and big biceps – yes, both are well enough. But courage and kindness, gentle manliness, and self-sacrifice – this is what we want.[47]

This deep-rooted Anglo-Saxon suspicion of brilliance was constantly revealed by headmasters. At a time in the life of his school when, considering the quality of the intake, there was little danger of the prospect, Thring warned his boys against the vanity of intellectualism.[48] Ford, at Harrow, wished above all, to turn out boys of character, and considered it wise not to train too highly the intellect of those of doubtful morality.[49] It is a truism that excellence can produce exaggerated self-esteem, but the athlete was more susceptible to this condition in the climate of the time than the intellectual. Explanations for the distaste with which headmasters viewed intellectually self-confident pupils may lie in the nature of the power structure of schools of the period, and in the emphasis on conformity that was so noticeable a feature. Nonconformist free-thinkers were troublesome. There was an indisputable attractiveness for many of these authoritarian headmasters in compliant, uncomplicated, not-too-well-read boys who would challenge neither the intellectual nor the moral authority of older men – at least not openly. The difficulty of dealing with the clever is that too often they have the confidence to think for themselves, the audacity to question established views and the fluency with which to defend their heresies.

While it cannot be the whole truth, A. H. Gilkes's description of Binnings at Stratton fits the personalities of several headmasters of the schools of this survey comfortably: 'So long as there was plenty of what he called public school spirit at Stratton, a warm interest in the sports and pursuits of the school . . . and a confident and courteous bearing among the boys; so long as the prefects were masterful and respected Binnings was satisfied.'[50] Such an attitude undoubtedly helped to create what was for many, a most attractive boy product – nicely mannered, straight-backed, clear-skinned. For all his defects so visible to the modern eye, for many of the period, the unintellectual games-playing public school boy was, in the words of Leslie Stephen, 'an animal of whom one finds it difficult not to be rather proud'.[51]

III

Inside the nineteenth-century public school classroom there was a blind belief in a classical prescription for all. Most found it irrelevant. It did nothing to train them for life; in consequence they had little use for school work. It was for this reason as much as any other that they became 'conscious Philistines'. It was said of these Philistines that 'they toil at games and play with books'.[52] As Stephen Marcus has observed of the relationship between Victorian prudery and pornography, it was a case of negative analogue – the greater the repression, the more intense was the desire to break free.[53] The aridity and narrowness of the academic syllabus exaggerated the attractiveness of first, the countryside, then, the games field.

The majority were certainly bored; but it was no different for the clever boy with little interest in semantic studies. The Harrovian, Augustus Hare, 'never learnt anything useful . . . Hours and hours were wasted daily on useless Latin verses, with sickening monotony.'[54] Similar criticisms span the generations. In 1900 an uncharitable reviewer in *The Spectator* noted of Howson and Warner's *Harrow School* that there were 31 pages devoted to cricket, 8 to bathing, 5 to football, 3 to racquets and 6 to the intellectual life of the school. He remarked acidly that this was about the right proportion in terms of the school's priorities – the allowance of intellect to athletics being rather like Falstaff's bread and sack – and concluded that if Latin and Greek had not been strained so far then the rebound in the direction of athletics would not have been so violent.[55]

Jack Hood's *Heart of a Schoolboy*, published in 1919, was a study of public school life intended to refute the accusations of excessive devotion to games, immorality and idleness contained in Alec Waugh's *The Loom of Youth*. In fact it merely reinforced Waugh's point about the games obsession but presented the manifestation in a kindlier light. Hood admitted that games came first with most of his contemporaries but considered that athletics would probably keep a boy straighter than too much book-worming. In case this standard argument might be wearing thin he added the honest rider that if some lived for athletics, it was simply because work was so dull. His fiercest castigations were reserved for classics.[56] *Punch*, always a close if irreverent observer of the public school scene, saw the bored public school boy as good-natured but quite unequivocal in his reaction to the curriculum of the time:

> By Jove and Jingo, old fellow, I say
> Don't I hate Latin and Greek![57]

Edward Lyttelton, as befitted a sober educationalist, considered the matter more seriously. He recognised that an interminable time was spent on abstract language work, and came to the conclusion that 'by making all brain exercise for boys bookish we have rendered athleticism a necessity'.[58] Lyttelton was greatly exercised by the problem and returned to it in his autobiography *Memories and Hopes* in which he recalled that at Eton in the 1880s, the teaching was 'tragic'. He echoed Hare's complaint that not only the less intelligent but all 'were made to groan and sweat at rudiments, utterly meaningless except as stepping stones to a literature which they never got to read'.[59]

Reform did come slowly; stimulated by men like T. H. Huxley, F. W. Farrar, Sir John Coleridge, H. E. Armstrong and L. C. Miall; promoted by official investigations such as the Public Schools and Schools Inquiry Commissions and the British Association committees of inquiry.[60] 'Modern sides' (offering subjects directly related to occupational futures) were instituted, science teaching was gradually introduced, the curriculum slowly widened; but classics remained the dominant classroom subject until well into the twentieth century.[61] Conservative staff and the matriculation demands of Oxford and Cambridge were the major reasons. The effects of both are well depicted by events at the Headmasters' Conference of 1890. J. E. C. Welldon informed those present that it was painful to read the biographies of distinguished men who, while they loved their school, found their years there intellectually wasteful 'because their attention was forcibly directed to subjects for which they had no aptitude'.[62] To reduce the amount of classics teaching he proposed recommending the abolition of Greek and Latin as compulsory subjects at Oxford and Cambridge. M. C. Glazebrook, the headmaster of Monmouth Grammar School, rallied to his support with the assertion that by the time the ordinary public school boy had journeyed towards a pass degree in Greek he had spent 3000 hours on the subject at school and university. They failed to win over a conference composed overwhelmingly of classicists.[63]

Consideration of a period analogy, providing an effect not unlike time-lapse photography, offers a remarkably clear insight into the role of games as an escape mechanism in the public schools. The analogous experience is that of the inmates of a German internment camp for the British at Ruhleben during the Great War.[64] At Ruhleben there occurred in a short space of time what was at the public schools a more lengthy and gradual process. Within the camp men from all walks of life sought for their psychological well-being a substitute world available to them all that would release them from the boredom and stress of captivity. They found it in organised games. These became their mental salvation: compensatory activities providing relief from the tedium of their predicament. The outcome was the construction of a complex system of tournaments and competitions, which permitted athlete, spectator and organiser to share in a common excitement. In turn, influence and respect became dependent on proficiency at games. And these became so important that they were ultimately dignified with impressive rituals and symbols.

The evolution of the rise to prominence of sport at Ruhleben is a microstudy on a collapsed time scale of striving for a meaningful existence based on common values within a 'total institution', which mirrors the straitjacket public school system of the nineteenth and early twentieth centuries.

IV

Before 1850, as noted earlier, the public school master was a distant figure to his boys and for the most part indifferent to their extracurricular pastimes. Cotton, Thring and Almond, in particular, created for him a new semblance. In their confident hands he changed from 'dry pedant' to 'perpetual schoolboy', terms admittedly describing 'ideal-types',[65] but containing a large element of truth.

It was not so much that a generation of schoolmasters simultaneously rediscovered the fascination of games or miraculously retained the physical exuberance, power and elasticity of youth in middle age. The introduction of games into the curriculum by the headmasters of Uppingham, Marlborough, Loretto and elsewhere largely determined their evolution. Games playing now became an expected part of the schoolmaster's role. Also important, however, was the self-assurance of Almond and Thring in throwing off patrician dignity and running, hitting and tackling on playing fields with their pupils. This, coupled with their power to select staff in their own image, meant that they could speedily establish a fresh identity for the public school master.[66]

Once games were an integral part of the curriculum and headmasters had set the example of playing themselves and required imitators and apostles, masters with new educational talents were sought, and were forthcoming. There was an influx of men of broadly three types: the talented all-rounder; the moderate all-rounder, who often sought in the obscure post of assistant master the security of the past; and the outstanding games player of moderate or mediocre intellectual ability, who cast an appraising eye over the games facilities and found they offered the opportunity of an attractive way of life.

The laurels – the headships – now often went to those with both academic and athletic talent.[67] But so important did athletic distinction become that some considered that skill at games rather than brilliance at classics counted for more when headships became available. Joseph Wood, appointed to Harrow in 1893, was greeted with the following 'Appreciation': 'Our headmaster's marked love for athletics has undoubtedly contributed to his success. To use a homely but expressive phrase, he is a sportsman.'[68] And the possibility of Edmond Warre becoming headmaster of Eton provoked an exchange of correspondence in *The Times* in 1884 because it was felt he owed his eligibility to the fact that he was 'the best rowing coach in England'. His intellectual capacity was considered quite unequal to that of his nearest rival, J. E. C. Welldon.[69] But it did not escape the notice of the observant that *both* were athletes, an attribute grudgingly admitted by this time to be indispensable.[70]

The second group of new recruits to public school masterships included an interesting body of 'faithful retainers'. These were men of reasonable wealth who might have led pleasant lives of leisure, but chose to teach. Evelyn Waugh, pondering on the impulse that took them into public school teaching, came close to the heart of the matter: 'Much of the strength and virtue of the public school system was drawn from unambitious men . . . men of moderate learning, often with private means, who found refreshment in the company of the young and were content to settle for a lifetime in the scene of their youth, preserving its continuity.'[71] Many were ingenuous idealists, who, like Percival in *The Twymans*, caught 'a glimpse behind the mere beauty of the young white figures shining so coolly in the slant evening sunshine, of the finely planned order and long-descended discipline they symbolised'.[72] Wealth, loyalty and idealism made these men indispensable adducts of the system, and notable contributors to the athletic life of the school.

The third group became necessary because they brought prestige through the favourable publicity that attended them, because they could control the lower forms and because they were popular housemasters attracting a constant supply of boys from admiring parents and name-dropping preparatory school headmasters. From their ranks came the games master, in time an instantly recognisable type in public school mythology. Ronald Gurner has supplied his standard *curriculum vitae*: college to university, back to college with a blue, junior form teaching and control of games.[73] And Alec Waugh has drawn an unforgettable portrait of the games master as hero in his depiction of Buller of Fernhurst:

> . . . He was indeed a splendid person. He wore a double-breasted coat, that on anyone else would have looked ridiculous, and even so was strikingly original. He had the strong face of one who had fought every inch of the way. It was a great sight to see 'the Bull', as he was called, take a game; he rushed up and down the field cursing and swearing. His voice thundered over the ground. It was the first game after the summer holidays, and everyone felt rather flabby. At half-time the great man burst out: 'I have played football for twenty-five years, I coached Oxford teams and Gloucestershire teams, led an English scrum, and for fifteen years I have taught footer here, but never saw I such a display! Shirking, the whole lot of you! Get your shoulders down and shove. Never saw anything like it. Awful!' The Bull said this to every team at least three times every season, but he was every bit as generous with his praise as with his blame when things went well, and he was a great man, a personality. Even a desultory Pick-Up woke into excitement when the shrill, piping voice of a full-back came in with, 'The Bull's coming.'[74]

Although popular with boys and parents, such men's single-minded appropriation of both facilities and assistants could arouse resentment. They frequently joined the staff attracted by the free amenities of nets, courts and fields and a constant stream of partners and opponents. For this they were openly condemned by their colleagues.[75]

The 'games master' is a phenomenon which has attracted considerable attention in studies of public school games.[76] The point is seldom made, however, that the games-playing master *as much as* the games master was the outcome of ideological fashion. Athleticism produced both. And it was the former who represented the ideal of the perfect master, personified by Arnold Hepburn who was described in the *Lancing College Magazine* as 'scholar, athlete and Christian'.[77] Such Christian all-rounders became commonplace in time: the Marlborough staff could turn out seven racquets pairs against the school in 1880.[78] The eventual extent of the involvement of very ordinary staff in their pupils' games is touchingly recorded in the diary of the wife of S. A. Haslam, a loyal and undistinguished Uppingham housemaster: 'Sam played hand fives from 12.15 till 1.15. After dinner he played football . . . Sam very tired.'[79] The diary is filled with details of house and school matches which preoccupied her husband. By the twentieth century Paul Ford could proudly assert: 'The pedagogue with academic mind and furrowed brow is not the schoolmaster of today, he is a warm creature of flesh and blood who loves exercise.'[80] Boyishness, Ford suggested, was an important new quality. A more sardonic view was expressed by G. G. Coulton. His Felsted masters 'were little more than grown up schoolboys to the end'.[81]

Valetes and obituaries leave the reader in no doubt as to the widespread existence and general popularity of the late Victorian and Edwardian schoolmaster ideal: the boylike pedagogue who loved games. At Uppingham valetes for departing staff frequently included the phrase 'will be greatly missed by us in our games'.[82] More personal tributes can be found: 'No housemaster ever took more interest in the cricket of his house' was the compliment paid to Uppingham's F. W. Weldon on his departure.[83] And the *Marlburian* recorded admiringly of Charles Henry Thursfield Wood, keen scholar and fine athlete, that 'he never ceased to be a boy'.[84]

Ultimately the public school world in the late nineteenth century looked so favourably on games-playing staff that many undergraduates played with the express purpose of getting employment. Correspondents to *The Times* in both the public school controversies of 1889 and 1903 laboured this point[85] and E. H. Culley, in the Headmasters' Conference of 1897, rebuked headmasters for attaching too much importance to athletic qualifications in the appointment of *general* staff. He claimed that of the 150 names on the School Agency list at Cambridge in a recent year, 130 had offered 'athletics' as an interest, and that 'athletics' had become such a vital professional credential that the mere scholar was treated with contempt.[86] The *Athenaeum* found his case against the schools 'miserably strong'[87] and in corroboration of his argument, the very next year the *Public School Magazine* included an article – 'Practical hints on varsity life' – by the philathlete, Eustace Miles, in which he urged students to keep up their games as good masterships went to

11 Edward Bowen,
Harrow housemaster and philathlete

12 G. M. Carey, Sherborne
housemaster and noted games coach

13   Edward Bowen celebrating a house victory at the Grove, Harrow, circa 1895

14   A. H. Beesly and a triumphant house team at Marlborough circa 1874

good games players. They might find themselves appointed to teach academic subjects yet, Miles suggested euphemistically, they would discover that 'football was something of importance'.[88] S. P. B. Mais discovered the truth of this claim when, on coming down from Oxford in 1909, he sought a public school post. On the strength of a 'double blue', and despite a third, he was in immediate demand.[89]

As games became the major constituent of public school life, the master who did not play something could find himself quite isolated.[90] Even more seriously, to stand aloof from games was to court failure in the classroom. The pressure to conform and be acceptable was therefore considerable. Even anchorite academics such as Harrow's Brooke Foss Westcott contended with the most active 'amid winter wind and rain',[91] and the gentle Father Hunter at Stonyhurst found it desirable to run up and down the pitch in imitation of the more capable staff.[92] Involvement had become necessary not only for selection and promotion, but as a badge of normality and as a form of practical insurance; yet it should not be forgotten that it also reflected devotion to a belief that to lead by example in these areas of school life was to properly emphasise their importance and value.[93]

Seeking to explain the spread of support for athleticism among public school masters, David Newsome favoured the thesis that pandering to popular demand and creating out of it virtuous precepts worth the teaching is a common temptation of the schoolmaster.[94] Not without truth, this is nevertheless another over-simplification. An adequate analysis of staff adherence would certainly include the opportunism of the popularist but also the realism of the pragmatist, the hedonism of the indulgent, the idealism of the moralistic – and the enthusiasm of the escapist. As regards this last point, games were as much a cultural surrogate for many masters as for most boys. Academic staff, disillusioned by disillusioned boys, found mornings teaching classics onerous and afternoons heaving in mauls or taking guard at the wicket refreshing.[95] Guy Kendall wrote feelingly that nothing could touch a man engaged in a good game of fives, 'not even the prospect of dragging recalcitrant forms of thirty through a sentence of Caesar's half a page long, the beginning of which is quite forgotten by the time we have got to the end!'[96]

In reality once the new model of the games-playing 'beak' was launched by Cotton and the other headmasters, popularism, pragmatism, egotism, idealism, escapism – all combined to ensure that athleticism received considerable participatory, organisational and financial support from staff. And it must never be overlooked that to a large extent it was the staff in the schools, who, for these various reasons, found funds for facilities, coached teams, judged, refereed, acted as treasurers of games accounts and secretaries of appeal funds as well as played, exhorted and supported.[97] The extent of their participation in the machinery of games could not fail to impress the boys with the 'sacredness' of an institution to which such effort was allotted.

The late-Victorian image of the schoolmaster cannot be better exemplified than in the person of Henry Hart – fine classicist, courageous footballer and intense Christian.[98] Hart spent the greater part of his life in the public school system as schoolboy, assistant master and headmaster. His teaching career spanned thirty-four years from 1866 to 1900. He was educated at Rugby under Temple, a zealous athlete who was reputed to be able to sprint, climb a tree or jump a brook with the best of his boys and who had a reputation for never stopping a scrummage 'short of manslaughter'. Temple was an inspirational model for Hart. His interests became Hart's interests. In their correspondence, we are told, 'the interest of master and boy in football comes out in every part'.[99] This love of football remained with Hart all his life, and although slight of build his 'force and fury, vigour and pluck' won him warm admiration at Haileybury where he went as assistant master in 1866. He moved to Harrow in 1873. No details of his Harrovian football exploits appear to exist, but his enthusiasm would have been well received in Bowen's world of manly gentlemen. When his talents were sufficiently widely known he sought and gained a headship. In 1880 he was appointed to a remote grammar school at Sedbergh in rural Yorkshire. It provided a marvellous opportunity for proselytism. Before his arrival no rugby was played, only occasional cricket and there was no running. Hart transformed this lethargic Arcadian school into an energetic Spartan public school. He was profoundly influenced by Almond's Loretto, adopting several Loretto customs as well as the school motto. He introduced rugby (like Thring seeking and procuring the pitches himself), systematised cricket and organised runs over the hills. In the best tradition of the new schoolmaster he inspired by example and played and ran with his boys until his fiftieth year. And always in his philathleticism he passionately pursued virility and simplicity, rebuking effeminacy and ostentation in the interest of the inculcation of Christian manliness.[100]

Hart is doubly interesting as one inspired and inspiring. Rugby was the birthplace of his enthusiasms; Haileybury, Harrow but especially Sedbergh provided him with the opportunity for their diffusion; Loretto transmuted them finally into moral passion.[101] He was the embodiment of a new school morality; the epitome of a pedagogic ideal; the model of an energetic agent of ideological innovation and diffusion.

6

Oxbridge fashions, complacent parents and imperialism

Until the Second World War public school masters, it appears, were recruited almost exclusively from Oxford and Cambridge.[1] For most of the preceding hundred years, these universities had been, in the words of Noel Annan, 'little more than finishing schools for public schoolboys'.[2] Firmly implanted habits and the security of personal wealth[3] meant that the enthusiasms and practices of schooldays were extended into student days, with the result that during this period games were uppermost in the minds of many.

In the wake of the introduction of organised games in the public schools – and as a direct consequence – the traditional university recreations of gambling, drinking and horses declined in popularity. A 'love of exercising their muscles and training their bodies to physical endurance' became a feature of the students' life.[4] The 'Greek worship of muscle' now took pride of place. Dons noted the transformation. A university witness declared to the Public Schools Commission of 1864, that a notable improvement in the moral character of the average undergraduate had recently occurred because of the introduction, chiefly due to the public schools, of new athletic amusements.[5] He observed that cricket had greatly increased; fives and racquets courts had been established; 'athletic sports' had been introduced and an excellent gymnasium drew substantial support. As a consequence hunting was much rarer, and idle driving and riding had greatly decreased. The happy result had been to discourage expensive habits and to remove temptation to immorality. Others delighted in the new ethos. In 1866 an anonymous contributor to *Blackwood's Magazine* thought 'the new gospel of athletics' at the universities a splendid thing: '. . . better to go to bed early tired out by cricket than to sit up drinking; better hours of relaxation on rivers than galloping a wretched hack along turnpikes or over fences for a bet.'[6] This sanguine journalist rejoiced in the availability of a new earthly paradise in which the talented might wander through England with the Zingari or win silver challenge cups in perpetual regattas.

Hippolyte Taine found much to please him in the healthy tone of the English universities of the time – the students exemplifying an extreme decency in their 'almost universal taste for bodily exercise'.[7] In this respect the universities, in his view, were merely an extension of the public schools. Low intellectual standards as well as plentiful exercise support this contention. Yet for all his admiration of the students Taine could not withhold the remark that English 'varsity life proved the soundness of the Platonic reflection that the lives of thinker and athlete were incompatible; much used muscle and large appetites precluded subtle philology and elevated philosophical speculation'.[8]

Those closer to university life came to the same conclusion. Mark Pattison, in particular, savaged the new 'barbarized athlete' at Oxford and yearned for the presence of learned and scientific men.[9] D. A. Winstanley has written pithily that the Cambridge of this period witnessed 'the demonstration of gross ignorance in a home of learning'.[10] A statistic and an anecdote jointly provide a glimpse of late-nineteenth-century academic standards at the universities. At Cambridge, according to Winstanley, 101 out of 200 students in a single year failed the Previous Examination taken in the Michaelmas Term of their second year in residence,[11] while at Oxford in the 1870s the former Lancing schoolboy, Thomas Pellatt, found that the most effective way to avoid idle friends was to purchase a library ticket for the Bodleian. There he was as safe from discovery as if Queen Victoria had given him a room at Frogmore.[12]

Other similarities to the public school existed. Loyalty to the college, for example, was often demanded as rigorously as once loyalty to the house had been. The belief has been expressed that at the universities, in contrast to the public schools, there was 'no compulsion or undue pressure put upon students by their fellows to play games'.[13] In fact, this was not so. Able performers were often obliged to support their college on field and river. Lord Ernle wrote of his student days at Balliol, 'It was the duty of all who had the necessary physique . . . to do service.'[14] Another ex-Marlburian, E. C. C. Firth, spent the afternoons of his first week at Oxford on the river 'learning the science of rowing' at the 'request' of senior members of Pembroke. He was relieved to find himself a feeble exponent; ability resulted in virtual compulsion.[15] His was a common experience.[16]

It was not only fellow students who demanded 'service'. Certain tutors were indistinguishable from housemasters in their energetic quest for institutional athletic fame and their enthusiasm for the muscular life. The most enthusiastic included Leslie Stephen, E. H. Morgan and H. A. Morgan at Cambridge and Charles Cloverly Price and William Ince at Oxford.[17] Culley's anonymous tutor, on whom he relied heavily for his picture of university life in his general attack upon athleticism at the Headmasters' Conference in 1897, claimed that in the atmosphere of an 'absolute supremacy of athlete interests' in the 1890s, it was hinted that both masterships and scholarships were given for athletic prominence.[18] That this assertion had substance is indicated by the fact that another observer found the Oxford heads of colleges of the 1890s substantially different in personality to those of thirty years before. The new men were men of physical activity and vitality – one was even a member of Vincent's (the students' club which caters exclusively for successful athletes).[19]

Memories of Oxford and Cambridge throughout the second half of Victoria's reign are predominantly those of 'idle years of cricket, fives, racquets and billiards',[20] when work weighed lightly on the conscience and the river and the games field engrossed many students. One disillusioned Uppingham scholar found Cambridge minds of the time 'not in reality much occupied with . . . lofty themes' and eyes of the time 'if open at all, were more likely to be fixed on some vision of Cam or Thames than on the deep flowing river of Thought'.[21] Lewis Farnell, a 'sympathetic watcher' of the early stages of athleticism at Oxford between 1874 and 1885 and conversant with its 'extravagances and absurdities', summed up its impact as follows:

> The ceaseless *exigeance* of the athletic claim expressed itself in various ways – by inroads in the proper time of study claimed by home and foreign matches; by the withdrawal of scholars and exhibitioners from intellectual work . . .; by attempts of headmasters to influence our scholarship elections by athletic testimonials; by the attempt to influence even elections to tutorial fellowships by athletic considerations.[22]

'The Reign of Athletics is at hand' an astonished undergraduate reported back to Stonyhurst in 1896.[23] Small wonder that in the same year *The Spectator* took the universities to task over the comparative insignificance of nominalism, idealism, realism and materialism in contrast to athleticism.[24] Contemporary university values were fairly expressed in an advertisement for *Isis* (the Oxford student magazine) in the *Public School Magazine* for June 1900. It announced Up-to-date Notes on Oxford Rowing, Oxford Football, Oxford Cricket, Oxford Sports, Golf and Hockey' in large type; less delectable items such as reports of university debates, music and drama merited a much smaller print. The difference in emphasis reflected an upsurge in organised physical activities demonstrated in table VI.

Table VI *First sports meetings between Oxford and Cambridge 1825–1925*

1825–50	1851–75		1876–1900		1901–25	
Cricket 1827	Racquets		Golf	1878	Gymnastics	1908
Boat race 1829	doubles	1855	Polo	1878	Epee	1913
	singles	1858	Cross country	1880	Winter	
	Tennis	1859	Lawn tennis	1881	sports	1922
	Steeple-		Hockey	1890	Table-	
	chasing	1863	Water polo	1891	tennis	1923
	Athletics	1864	Bandy	1895	Squash	1925
	Rugby	1872	Skating	1895	Fives	1925
	Soccer	1874	Boxing	1897		
	Bicycling	1874	Fencing	1897		
			Swimming	1892		
			Ice hockey	1900		
			Lacrosse	1900		

Source: H. M. Abrahams and J. B. Kerr, *Oxford versus Cambridge* (1931).

During the last quarter of the nineteenth century *Punch* systematically monitored the evolution of muscularity at the universities, and consistently shot small, sharp, verbal barbs in the direction of philathletic staff and students. An early volley in 1873 contained the suggestion that Corpus, a college with an old name, might acquire a new meaning in the light of recent Cambridge developments.[25] On occasion verse replaced prose as the satirical weapon:

> Carfax College was plunged in gloom,
> And a cloud hung over the Common room,
> For alas, the College no longer held
> The place that she did in the days of old.
> There had been a time when she used to shiver
> Unless she remained at the head of the river,

And Carfax men were wont to yield
To none in the cricket or football field.
But now the glory was all departed,
What wonder the College was broken-hearted?
Twas years since she'd boasted a bat of note
Or a single man in the Varsity boat.
Why, worse – well might the dons turn pale!
Last year – I shudder to tell the tale –
There happened that which appeared to portend
The fatal beginning that marked the end.
Last year – they did their best, no doubt,
To hush up the horror, but truth will out –
Last year, by some curious freak of the fates,
A Carfax man took a first in Greats.

This opening passage of 'Getting the Blues: a story founded on fact'[26] is followed by a description of how Carfax, due to the superb initiative of its master in rushing to meet the Sydney boat, obtained the services of the great Australian oarsman, 'Tom Brown', and thus transformed college defeat upon the river into success. Another sardonic jingle lamented the prevalent state of affairs in which the athlete proved to be a more efficacious college advertisement than the Senior Wrangler.[27] In prose and more sober vein, in 1908 the magazine even went so far as to call for the 'de-athletising' of the universities and the elimination from them of blues and 'bloods'.[28]

Over-simplification must, of course, be resisted. Student pursuit of the intellect did exist. The distinguished historian, G. M. Trevelyan, for one, has left a delightful picture of earnest, idealistic students, among them George Moore, Bertrand Russell and Alfred Whitehead, in serious discourse at Cambridge at the turn of the century.[29] Some studied; others studied and played; many simply played.

The significance for the spread of athleticism of the similarity of life style that enveloped public school and 'Oxbridge' was that a process of circular causality was set up. The successful games player at school flourished in the same capacity at the university and then returned to school as lauded assistant master to set another generation of devotees along the same route. Thus a cycle of 'schoolboy sportsman, university sportsman and schoolmaster sportsman was created'.[30] The universities were the matrix from which athletic young men spread through the public school system, carrying back into it an unadulterated enthusiasm for, and an often untainted belief in, games for physical and moral well-being. Certainty of conviction was safeguarded by insularity within a self-confident, high-status social structure comprising the schools and universities. There was, to quote Smelser's useful expression, a situation of 'structural conduciveness' which aided ideological consolidation and facilitated a closed ideological circle.[31]

A coterie of Cambridge zealots – C. C. Cotterill, S. A. Haslam and Henry Hart – perfectly exemplifies the relationship between matrix, structure and ideology. All were muscular Christians together at St John's College, Cambridge, in the 1860s where they fed on each other's enthusiasm. They all became public school masters, and remained in the protective cocoon of the public school system all their professional lives diffusing their athletocratic values throughout it, with certainty, energy and efficiency by both precept and example.

II

Those who opposed the excesses of the athleticism movement, J. H. Simpson noted, struggled not only with pupils but also with adults, inside *and* outside the schools.[32] Outsiders who sent the public schools their offspring, were cruelly flagellated, metaphorically, by the great Hellenist of nineteenth-century England, Matthew Arnold, for either licentious hedonism or an unreflective fixation with commerce and religiosity. On the one hand Arnold was contemptuous of the intellectual poverty of the aristocracy corrupted by 'those mighty and external seducers – pleasure, power, security and worldly splendour'; on the other he was equally disdainful of the middle classes 'drugged with business' and 'a narrow, unintelligent repulsive religion'.[33] Modern sociologists and psychologists are at pains to emphasise the marginal influence of the school, and the central role of the home in determining attitudes, values and behaviour.[34] If Arnold's strictures are correct, it should cause little surprise to present-day educationalists that the products of such backgrounds were, in the main, pronounced anti-intellectuals.

Arnold's opinions concerning the nineteenth-century aristocracy are upheld by the historian, E. Wingfield-Stratford. In his view, after the Georgian era the British nobility experienced a 'cultural slump': 'The bumpkin or booby squire was no longer, as in the days of Fielding, pilloried as an awful example; he was accorded a halo of romantic adoration as the finest type of old-fashioned Englishman, and all the finer for being half-educated . . . and a barely literate simpleton.'[35] The symbol of the new squirarchy was the shotgun rather than the book. The library was now 'dusty and generally locked. A set of Lever, a set of Surtees, a set of Thackeray and one of Dickens were placed on the few empty shelves that remained, and thereafter the master's activities were confined to the gunroom.'[36]

The sporting tradition of the English aristocracy has deep historical roots[37] however, which Georgian 'savants' failed to dig out, sever or cauterise. This tradition in fact coexisted with a literate eighteenth-century squirarchy and survived to bloom strongly in Victorian times. Its flower did not fade with the onset of Wesleyan revivalism or Victorian urbanisation. It enjoyed the advantageous climate of an Indian summer in the second half of the nineteenth century through the new wealth brought into the countryside by the industrial plutocracy as they took up residence in their newly acquired country seats. It was twentieth-century wars, successful economic rivalries and changing political and social ideals which eventually impoverished the sporting squires and scattered their packs of hounds and cheap rural labour force of beaters, gamekeepers and gardener–cricketers.[38]

While the old squirarchy mingled with the new on the grouse moors and in the hunt balls, on the outskirts of the spreading Victorian cities suburbs arose, which housed a growing middle class of lesser but reasonable income. Its members earned their living in expanding industrial and commercial operations and could now afford a public school education for their sons.[39] The public schools drew them as filings to a magnet. For the aristocracy a public school education was merely a continuation of a tradition which reinforced its social separateness and emphasised its subcultural homogeneity; for the 'nouveaux riches' it was a means of providing access to this subculture and of ensuring status for their children by the provision of a caste mark.[40] The proud parent of Etonian brothers perfectly expressed the feelings of the socially ambitious, when he wrote of the ultimate realisation of their aspirations – an Eton schooling – in these terms: 'To be brought up amid those historic fields, upon the banks of that famous and poetic river, under the shadow of the old seat of English royalty, appeared such a privileged fate as one would wish for every English boy.'[41] It was membership that was desired; the education provided was of secondary importance. Parents looked with benevolent contempt on the clerical masters with their esoteric degrees in classics;[42] but they fully perceived the value of inclusion. The Schools Inquiry Commission reported that at Eton, Rugby and Marlborough no matter what its shortcomings, the education provided had received whatever stamp of public approval could be considered given by overflowing numbers. It added that the attraction was the training provided by school life rather than the teaching.[43]

The fact that his son might spend a large part of his time playing games at his expensive school was probably not too shocking to the country magnate. Such a schooling after all, was not all that far removed from the life of the rural estate.[44] But the meek acceptance of this state of affairs by the businessman is less easy to understand. Perhaps it really was, as W. B. Gallie has suggested, that life was more than economic struggle and business plans for the self-made Victorian industrialist; that it did embrace disinterested sentiment, social myth and the pursuit of a heroic ideal.[45] The new urban rich, argued Gallie, drawing upon memories of his own childhood, held to the Wordsworthian belief that exercise in the open air was 'the best of all moral tonics'; displayed a simple-minded belief in the value of the games field for the production of 'captains of industry' as well as 'leaders of empire'; and being seldom heroes to themselves, their wives or their children, sought a heroic ideal if not for themselves, for their sons. For this reason above all others, he alleged, these sons went to public schools. There they learned the appurtenances of social, political and imperial leadership. If these were dependent on the games field – so be it.[46]

Explanations such as those offered by W. B. Gallie and 'the proud parent' above, fail to exhaust the possibilities. It was not merely complacency at securing a public school education for their sons and indifference to what went on in the classroom; nor an unsophisticated belief in the value of clear eyes, ruddy cheeks and strong limbs coupled with suspicion of the havoc books would wreak on these engaging physical attributes. Parents knew full well that there were direct occupational returns to be had from skill with bat, racket and ball. For the upper-class boy of the time, success at games was often a passport to worldly success.[47] Witness the person of Bill Furse, William Cory's nephew, with 'fine looks, high spirits, sociability . . . athletic, a crack tennis player and . . . a sportsman. Bound for a career . . .' who became in time Lieutenant-General Sir William Furse, K.C.B., K.C.M.G.[48] Calculation, as well as enthusiasm, ensured that parents preferred a school career to end as captain of games rather than head of school.[49]

A wider public than the English upper classes applauded the stress on games in public school education. English schooling was the admiration of continental idealists. Frenchmen such as Demogeot and Montucci in a survey of English (and Scottish) education in 1868, while critical even at that time of athletic excess, expressed respect for the games, freedom and independence of public school boys.[50] In 1876 the German, Ludwig Wiese, considered the conduct of English upper-class youth 'a pedagogic virtue' and praised the way in which 'the germ of manliness' was nurtured.[51] Edward Demolins asked *A quoi tient la supériorité des Anglo-Saxons*, in a book of that title published in 1897, and was quite certain the answer lay *inter alia* in the emphasis on ample physical exercise in their schools. That 'confirmed Anglomaniac',[52] Pierre de Coubertin, inspired by an Arnold who existed only in the imagination of Thomas Hughes, in *L'Education en Angleterre* (1888), testified to an absolute belief in the English boarding school system in which, 'L'éducation physique et l'éducation morale sont étroitement liées: l'une ne saurait marcher sans l'autre.'[53]

Demogeot and Montucci were reviewed in the English journals,[54] Wiese and Demolins were translated into English – Demolins ran to ten reprints in translation in the first year of publication. Coubertin wrote eulogistically for the English press.[55] Furthermore, even the praise of obscure foreign schoolboys and teachers was thought worthy of publication.[56] Continental accolades could even be found in school magazines. The *Marlburian*, for example, selected complimentary titbits for its readers from Max O'Reilly's *John Bull et son Ile: Moeurs anglaises contemporaines*.[57] And the *Harrovian* in 1899 reported modestly on a new French venture, Le Collège Normand, which proposed 'de former comme Harrow School des jeunes gens ayant développé toutes leurs aptitudes physiques, assoupli leurs membres à tous les exercises, conqui toute la vigueur dont le corps est capable pour le bien-être même de l'esprit'.[58] The Harrow School archives contain a fascinating letter from a Monsieur Pierre Janelle which duly found its way into the school magazine. It includes a French translation of Bowen's 'Forty Years On'. In the early years of the twentieth century Janelle's English teacher at his lycée used to make the pupils sing Bowen's song 'avec an élan d'idéalisme bien anglais'.

Such carefully publicised foreign admiration helped confirm the

wealthy John Bull in his belief in the soundness of his son's schooling. And there was also the British press. In late-Victorian and
Edwardian England both the national and local press, denied the
modern range of professional sporting 'superstars', glamorised
instead the athletic public school boy. It was written of a typical
Harrow game for example:

> How the papers seized the Tidings
> Heard by telegraph dispatch
> 'Land and Water', 'Field' and 'Bell's Life'
> 'Sporting Times' describe the match.[59]

Paterfamilias frequently basked in the reflected glory of his sons and
old school. It was stated at the Headmasters' Conference of 1873
that as long as the result of matches can be instantly flashed by
telegraph wire through the kingdom to fashionable society, and as
long as the boy who gets fifty at Lord's is regarded as a hero and the
winner of literary prizes is ignored, games will be thought the
serious part of life.[60]

A nostalgic romanticism also generated support. F. W. Farrar
once suggested to his pupils: '. . . perhaps as you faint on the arid
plains of India, perhaps as you toil in the dingy back streets of great
cities, amid haunts of poverty and crime – may come the memory
of sunny cricket grounds where once you played. Like a draught of
clear water in the desert – like that sparkling cup which his warriors
brought to David from the well which he had loved in boyhood –
you will drink of the innocent delights of these schooldays.'[61] In
many instances *Paterfamilias* also was haunted by an unfading vision
of slim white figures in an emerald lotus land where the 'sweet
music' was that of bat striking ball; a land he had once inhabited and
to which he longed to return. Like Kendall's 'typical father' when
speech day came around, he paid a morning visit to the housemaster
to learn of classroom misdemeanours but straightforward, alert
integrity in the house; walked with his son for the required delivery
of insincere clichés about the importance of working hard; lunched
in town, and afterwards strolled to that prettiest and most inspiring
of sights, a school match on the big ground, with everywhere white
flannels, bright sun and shady trees; the enthusiastic cheers of boys,
the happy chatter, the friendships, the lady visitors in summer
gowns – everything impressing the idea of how happy and healthy
was public school life and how lucky the fellow was, who was

privileged to enjoy it; evening brought the intense desire to have his time over again.[62]

The power of evocation must be acknowledged. City offices, mess halls, country seats and housemasters' studies were populated by 'nostalgiciens'[63] seeking a lost boyhood in an ideal landscape. They lived a schoolboy idyll which lasted a lifetime. Vachell's Mark in *Brothers*, who remembered of his schooldays only that he swam 'in Ducker . . . was taught to play cricket with a straight bat . . . lay upon the green slopes of the Sixth Form Ground and ate ices . . . spent his exeats at Randolph House in Belgrave Square, and witnessed the Lord's Match from the top of Lord Randolph's coach', was ubiquitous.[64] For many the past was the present; the words of the most famous of boating songs were prophetic:

> Nothing in life shall sever
> The chains that surround us now.[65]

There was also a familiar moral romanticism. Stimulated by the ideologues Charles Kingsley and Thomas Hughes, parents wished their sons to be brought up in the now well-explored image of Tom Brown.[66] As much as masters they subscribed to the ethical value of games as the source of good sense, noble traits, manly feelings, generous disposition, gentlemanly deportment, comradely loyalty.[67] It was all of a whole for, as one critic of athleticism remarked, upper-class parents, characterised by decent extroversion and a distaste for book-worming, mouthed moral formulas mostly in foreign tongues and were convinced that if little was learnt in schoolrooms, solid virtue was inculcated on games fields 'where the Honour of the School shines as a beacon in the sight of the humblest'.[68]

In ironic contrast to the moral romanticism of the fanciful there also existed the puritanical pragmatism of the realists who saw games 'as the greatest antidote to immorality'. Such parents smugly contrasted English and French boyhood, pitying French youth, sapped of its strength and France, robbed of its leaders, because of an educational system which allowed opportunity for 'idle thoughts to take the form of vicious desire'. English boys on English fields were safe from such depravity.[69]

Whatever the reasons for approval and support there is no lack of comment concerning the constancy of middle- and upper-class parents to the games of the public schools and their indifference to the classical curriculum. The Public Schools Commission found parents 'the greatest obstacle to progress'.[70] And Bernard Darwin has insisted that for the next sixty years, most parents were blind worshippers of the system, thought little of things of the intellect and were firm opponents of change.[71] Parental priorities noted by the Public Schools Commission – the making of gentlemen and the forming of great acquaintances – remained in vogue until well into the twentieth century. He who pays the piper calls the tune: what the parent wanted, he generally got. In consequence, by 1900, criticism of parents by reformers was unrestrained. Edward Lyttelton, for example, apportioned the blame for widespread laziness at school wholly to attitudes in the home. He set out the causal sequence for his readers: popularity meant useful friendships while a reputation for 'swotting' guaranteed unpopularity; parents therefore warned their offspring against getting over fond of books; in consequence boys went to school 'with a disposition framed for frivolity', and this frivolity led directly to the 'unruly growth' of an excessive interest in games.[72] His final comment is yet another analytical over-simplification but it does bring into prominence the fact that parents played a far from insignificant part in athleticism's rise to pre-eminence.

A. H. Gilkes, when headmaster of Dulwich, was equally outspoken. During the controversy in *The Times*, in January 1903, concerning the advantages and disadvantages of a classical schooling, he switched the direction of the debate from classics to idleness. First he attacked the unsatisfactory attitude to study which permeated the public schools and blamed values in the boys' homes.[73] Later he was more specific: parental assistance in outwitting the academic demands of the schoolmaster and over-indulgence in games were too common.[74] Gilkes had suffered patiently. He had made the same accusations in one of his novels of public school life published in 1894.[75]

The triangular relationship between anti-intellectualism, athleticism and parental attitudes was at the centre of yet another debate, this time in *The Times Educational Supplement* in October 1918.[76] Parents again bore the brunt of the attack: 'They had the English love of sport . . . were bitten by the prevailing mania for athletics and they impressed their ideals on their own boys . . . and so insensibly on the authorities.' These were the fiery words of a 'Veteran Assistant Master' who considered parental support for games had brought about the obvious decline in the intellectual standards of public schools over the years. In a subsequent letter he warned against 'writing him off' as an oddity; the great majority of public school masters, he asserted, would support his contentions.

Dailies, weeklies and quarterlies gave considerable space for the airing of opinion – much of it hostile – on the elevation of athleticism to pride of place among the various ideologies which struggled for supremacy in the public schools between the Franco-Prussian and Second World Wars. A most consistent critic of the parental role in the rise of athleticism was *The Spectator* which only ceased its campaign, begun in 1900, in 1934.[77]

Lyttelton, Gilkes and the 'Veteran Assistant Master' were more plain spoken than most school staff about parents and games, but several who served at the schools of this study did not hesitate to voice their opinions on the subject: Cyril Alington, in his memoirs, remarked tersely that athleticism and anti-intellectualism would only be understood if it were realised that schools reflected the average home;[78] Cyril Norwood wrote that 'fathers, mothers, brothers, sisters, cousins and aunts' were the source of boys' single-minded ambition to get a place in the eleven or fifteen;[79] Frank Fletcher, scourge of 'hearties' during his years at Marlborough, asked plaintively of the Headmasters' Conference at the end of the Great War, 'What can be done to remedy the exaltation of the athlete, to which all boys, many parents and some masters subscribe?';[80] Lionel Ford, an enthusiastic lover of games himself, complained that the parents of his Harrovians were more obsessed with games than their sons.[81] The fictional Lord Verniker, possessed of 'the athletic, unliterary air of the English gentleman', was culled from J. E. C. Welldon's Harrow experiences. His advice to his son on his first day at school nicely underlines Ford's point: 'You've not got to earn your living, you know, so you need not work your eyes out: I'd much rather you got into the eleven.'[82]

Alec Waugh was of the opinion that parents were the victims of a masters' conspiracy of silence, and so they failed to realise that schools 'made a god of games'.[83] A different impression is gained from the sources above. These cover a greater span of years, places and experiences and would seem therefore to provide more representative evidence. Contrary to Waugh's suggestion, parents appear to have been significant contributors to the rise and stability of athleticism.

III

A curious educational paradox in the nineteenth- and early twentieth-century public schools was the co-existence of two apparently irreconcilable systems of belief – Christian gentility and social Darwinism:[84] uncomfortable but actual ideological bed-fellows. As a result, while the 'ideal schoolboy' might be seen as possessing the virtues of a young Christian gentleman – honesty, modesty, honour and a foundation of true religion – the *Dublin Review* could express dismay at a too common reality – an irreligious, oaken-headed, oaken-hearted Englishman – and accurately ascribe the cause to a system in which the 'battle went to the strong'.[85] Public school life was frequently unChristian and ungentlemanly. The much applauded *esprit de corps* masked at un-relenting individual struggle, stimulated by the games system,[86] which was fully in accord with the cryptic and misleading Darwinian apothegm 'the survival of the fittest'. After 1850 this condition was not simply the consequence of adult indifference. On the contrary many adults saw it as necessary and laudable.

This statement of principle in defence of the rigours of public school life came appropriately close on the heels of the publication of the *Origin of Species*:

. . . constant reliance upon another for aid in difficulties . . . fatally weakens the fibre of the character. Boys, like nations, can only attain to the genuine stout self-reliance which is true manliness by battling for themselves against their difficulties, and forming their own characters by the light of their own blunders and their own troubles. It is the great benefit of our public schools that they help characters to grow . . . a benefit that would be wholly lost if their system were not based on a salutary neglect. The object of the public school is to introduce a boy early to the world, that he may be trained in due time for the struggle that lies before him.[87]

'Manliness', a substantive widely favoured by prelates on speech days and headmasters on Sundays, embraced antithetical values – success, aggression and ruthlessness, yet victory within the rules, courtesy in triumph, compassion for the defeated. The concept contained the substance not only of Spencerian functionalism but also the chivalric romanticism of an English Bayard: egotism co-existed uneasily with altruism.

This altruism owed as much to the Elizabethan, Richard Braith-waite, as to the Victorian, Thomas Arnold. Modesty, compassion, piety and an active life as a reflection of moral virtue were the qualities of Braithwaite's 'Christian gentleman'.[88] The Arnoldian ideal was the resuscitation of an Elizabethan aspiration rather than an Evangelical innovation. Arnold's 'Christian gentleman', however, was idiosyncratically guilt-ridden and sombre, and most unpalatable to Squire Brown. The Public School Commission publicised and sanctioned the ideal of the gentleman, but translated it into a more acceptable image: 'Love of healthy sport and exercise' and 'vigour and manliness of character' were substituted for religious fervour. The image, as Harold Perkins has remarked, now came closer to the feudal aristocratic tradition in which the gentleman's code had about as much to do with gentleness as serfdom had to do with villainy.[89]

In the years following the Public Schools Commission whatever lip-service was paid to the importance of the chapel in public school life, the character of the future gentleman was largely shaped by the allegedly moral lessons learnt on the games field; and that character represented not so much Christian virtuousness as a capacity for effective leadership.[90]

It was the new imperialism of late-Victorian Britain which produced the precarious fusion of Christian gentility and social Darwinism. Three sets of values became enmeshed: imperial Darwinism – the God-granted right of the white man to rule, civilise and baptise the inferior coloured races; institutional Darwinism – the cultivation of physical and psychological stamina at school in preparation for the rigours of imperial duty; the gentleman's education – the nurture of leadership qualities for military conquest abroad and political dominance at home. In this amalgam Christianity came out second best. The triad resulted in 'Darwinism misinterpreted as the survival of the most belligerent rather than the most adaptable'.[91] Bertrand Russell believed, with some justification, that he could discern the precise relationship between imperialism, Darwinism and the English gentleman. In the public schools, he declared, physical fitness, stoicism and a sense of mission were carefully nurtured, kindliness sacrificed for toughness, imagination for firmness, intellect for certainty; and sympathy was rejected because it might interfere with the governing of inferior races.[92]

If Russell's assertion was in general terms more polemical than exact, it was wholly correct in one thing. The need to prepare for imperial service was incessantly preached in the late-nineteenth-century public schools.[93] In upper-class society and its schools, traditional, social, intellectual and spiritual certainties may have been weakened in the wake of Clarendon, Darwin, Temple and Colenso. But fresh certainties sprang up to replace them. One was the imperial duty of the public school boy. *Empire Oblige*. The Uppingham master, Charles Byles wrote:

> Hark the Empire calls, and what we answer give?
> How to prove us worthy of the splendid trust?
> Lo! we serve the Empire by the lives we live;
> True in all our dealings, honest, brave and just,
> Training mind and body for the Empire's need.[94]

And others alerted the upper-class youth to his new destiny: 'Strive to be ready when the call shall come to whatever duty, at whatever sacrifice, in whatever part of Her Majesty's dominions . . . You shall conquer and rule others . . . you shall do your duty . . . Go forth and show yourselves worthy of this high mission.'[95]

Headmasters were intoxicated with the grandeur and nobility of the gubernatorial exercise. Welldon gloried in the solemnity of the responsibility of the British empire to elevate inferior races, and sedulously attempted to bring the imperial festivals before his Harrovians.[96] Thring considered the creation of a great empire a marvellous ambition, maintaining that the British flag should fly over 'every unoccupied land essential to our colonies'.[97] His history texts were Mommsen's *Rome*, Moltey's *United Netherlands* and Kaye's *Indian Officers*; a wholly logical selection, for, as one pupil recalled, 'The Great Romans, the Great Dutchmen, the type of Englishman that built our Indian Empire . . . were the types to mould our young Britons.'[98]

The enthusiasm and convictions of such men ensured that the exciting world of empire was systematically and frequently publicised in the school magazines by means of contributions from former pupils with seductive titles such as 'With the Frontier Light Horse in Zululand', 'On Life in Melanesia', 'A Kangaroo Drive', 'Pig-Sticking in Bombay', 'Elk Hunting in Ceylon', 'A Week among the Maoris', 'My First Shot at a Tiger', 'An Old Boy in the Bush' and 'On the Warpath in Manipur'. To a considerable extent it was the games field which prepared boys for these imperial adventures. As E. C. Mack acknowledged, the rise of imperialism put a premium on authority, discipline and team spirit allegedly learnt in these arenas.[99] To the moral argument was added the physical: 'If asked what our muscular Christianity has done, we point to the British Empire. Our Empire would never have been built up by a nation of idealists and logicians. Physical vigour is as necessary for the maintenance of our Empire as mental vigour.'[100] A bizarre use of physical vigour in imperial service occurred at the siege of Lucknow. A Captain Brick and a Captain Wilson were each determined to be the last to leave the Residency. Brick won. Wilson 'could not stand the trick of a shoulder to shoulder, learnt on the Harrow football fields'.[101] Of course it mattered little whether or not the hours spent on Harrow football fields had a beneficial moral or physical effect. What was important was that those of the time believed they did. A belief many held with unshakable tenacity.[102]

For many Victorians and Edwardians there was an obvious link between the development of endurance, toughness and courage on English playing fields and pioneering in Australia, preaching in Africa and soldiering in Burma.[103] And though the association between playing field and battle field may have been too tightly made, it did make some sense. The ferocity of keenly-contested house matches helped create a hardened imperial officer class naively eager for colonial wars. With Britain's vast empire offering as James Morris has observed, 'a more or less perpetual battlefield',[104] the public schools with superogatory zeal, sent forth a constant flow of athletic, young warriors. By the end of the nineteenth century, as a youthful poet in the *Cheltonian* acknowledged, English playing fields were recognised training grounds for imperial battlefields:

> How many a charge through the ranks of the foe
> Have been made by a warrior, who years ago,
> Hurried the leather from hand to hand
> And 'gainst heavy odds made sturdy stand?
> 'Neath old England's banner in every land
> Our football players to guard it, stand.[105]

Newbolt is the more familiar poet of Victorian imperial wars. And his schoolboy world of 'hazardous pitch', 'distant tape' and 'immortal games' was simply preparation for the eventual desert square. In his various descriptions of the public school boy at war from Afghanistan to Matabeleland, the ethnocentric, unashamed social Darwinist stands defiant; but nowhere more typically than in these ringing phrases from 'Clifton Chapel' – 'to count the life of battle good'; 'to honour as you strike him down the foe that comes with fearless eye'.[106]

The pragmatism explicit in the public school cultivation of the physical had a more than military advantage. It also embodied 'the code of the frontiersman' with its stress on the pioneering virtues of stamina and resolution.[107] This additional dimension of athleticism was fully understood by those of the time. Inspired by Ruskin, Tennyson, Dilke, Parkin, Seeley and a host of minor figures on speech days, many public school boys of limited academic ability, whose compensatory delight was muscle,[108] became colonial farmers, ranchers and planters. Service's 'stalwart younger sons' went in their thousands direct from school to build 'Britain's greatness o'er the foam'.[109] In imitation of *Punch's* schoolboy dunce, they took their ample brawn to Canada, Australia, New Zealand and more exotic places.[110] The empire was in fact as well as in phrase 'a vast system of outdoor relief for the upper classes'. Doubtless few could match a certain Richard Burton (Eton, Sandhurst and College of Agriculture, Cheltenham), a colonial wanderer with the soundest credentials: 'a crack shot, a fine boxer . . . afraid of nothing that either walked, flew or swam';[111] but letters and articles from old boys in the school magazines constantly warned of the need for physical skills and toughness. A Lorettonian in Australia stated the general position when he described physical effort as the essence of colonial life.[112]

Missionary work also could be severely arduous in demanding climates and harsh landscapes with few roads and inadequate transport 'up country'. A state of affairs well described in the diary of Bishop Selwyn: 'My last pair of shoes being worn out, and my feet much blistered with walking . . . I borrowed a horse from the native teacher, and started out at four a.m. to go twelve miles to Mr. Hamilton's Mission station at Manukar harbour . . . I sailed in Mr. Hamilton's boat ten miles across Manukar Bay . . . and my last remaining pair of shoes . . . were strong enough for the light and sandy walk of six miles . . . to Auckland.'[113] Where missionary life was more settled, the imported values of Christian manliness ensured that public school habits became valuable as part of an education geared to producing African, Indian and Antipodian copies of the English public school boy.[114]

In total, the various obligations and opportunities of empire served the games field well.

IV

Walter Houghton has ascribed to the Victorian upper classes the idolatrous worship of physical strength.[115] To this truth, the last two chapters bear solid witness. The Victorians possessed a curious doctrinal concoction of harsh Darwinism blended with pious Christianity, which in general, effectively promoted comfortable complacency and successfully checked subversive reflections in favoured households on such disharmonious topics as social exploitation, injustice and inequality.

Think little, read less and do the instinctual things, Kingsley urged his wife. Squirarchical habits or pretensions, factory or office preoccupations, disturbing social, intellectual and spiritual radicalism ensured that many upper-class parents did just that.[116] Their schoolboy sons, created in the same restricted image, had the further incentives of an indigestible academic fare unappetisingly served up well into their early manhood, daily proximity to pedagogic heroes who epitomised the attractive masculinity of the playing fields and a scarcity of alternative enthusiasms. And to tip the balance towards athleticism irredeemably, there were the demands of imperial destiny which allegedly only the hardy could adequately meet.

Furthermore, a decaying feudalism made the late-Victorian and Edwardian upper-class youth frenetic, perhaps unconsciously, in his muscular interests. For in fact, his was a last fling of buttressed privilege more widely extended than ever before by the freely-given wealth of self-made magnates, entrepreneurs and landowners of a prosperous industrial Britain, which was to be steadily eroded by the acid of proletarian anger translated into political action and increasingly usurped by growing numbers of ambitious and talented state-educated youth.

This last fling was cheered by *Paterfamilias*, flattered by the admiring noises of foreigners and journalists; insulated by sufficient wealth or influence from much anxiety over filial careers, or calculatedly realistic about the relative occupational value of colours and classics; frequently intoxicated by an addictive nostalgia for times past; sometimes obsessed with the licence that supposedly tempted the idle and enfeebled the manly.

Nor was this all. Within the schools the worship of muscle became steadily encrusted with symbols and rituals of prostration and power which exalted the athletic, excited the devout and stigmatised the heretical. The next two chapters examine the nature and extent of this protective, sustaining and crushing symbolism.

7

Fez, 'blood' and hunting crop: the symbols and rituals of a spartan culture

In John Bunyan's lesser allegory *The Holy War* the fortified city of Mansoul had five gates: Eyegate, Eargate, Mouthgate, Nosegate and Feelgate. The captains of Immanuel in their efforts to overwhelm the occupier Diabolus, marshalled their forces first against the Eargate, then the Eyegate.[1] It was a strategy public school symbolists of the past would have readily appreciated:

When the miscreant arrives – the tradition is that he should be called up by the captain of the school shouting 'Underschool' from the window, and sending for him – he must knock . . ., come in and stand immediately in front of the door. *These particulars must be insisted upon* [emphasis added]. The captain of the school says, 'come in' and corrects errors in behaviour. The official having the fellow up says, 'you are going to be licked for . . .'[2]

This heavily ritualised preliminary to a beating at Lancing is a forceful attack upon the auditory and visual senses as well as a skilful exercise in impression management, creating, as it undoubtedly did, and was intended to do, anticipatory fear, a sense of public shame, personal insignificance on the part of the culprit and an impression of awesome power in the hands of the prefectorial authorities. It reveals a sensitive awareness of the social and psychological power of symbolism on the part of the Lancing monitors. These monitors and others – Bryant's description of Harrow beatings has certain similarities[3] – clearly understood the role of ritualistic activities and symbolic objects in the lives of public school boys. Through a single punishment ritual they defined social position, emphasised the location of power and moulded group behaviour.

The *Shorter Oxford English Dictionary* defines symbolism as 'the practice of representing things by symbols or giving a symbolic character to objects and acts'. In this chapter on the symbolism of athleticism we consider first the acts, and then the objects.

Symbolic acts are generally described as rituals.[4] However, a

141

helpful reminder has been issued to the effect that although students of society too often discuss ritual having in mind behaviour of a non-verbal kind, speech is often a form of ritual and non-verbal ritual merely a signal system of a less specialised kind.[5] The point is taken and the verbal liturgy of athleticism will receive attention in chapter 8. Our concern below is with symbolism of a non-verbal nature.

To define ritual is not a simple task. Social scientists have many definitions and diverse opinions.[6] Rituals have been defined as formal behaviour patterns necessary for the establishment of ordered social relations.[7] This definition adequately explains *in nuce* the purpose of traditional public school rites and ceremonies but this purpose has been described elsewhere more fully and particularly well: 'the symbolic function of ritual is to relate the individual through ritualistic acts to a social order, to heighten respect for that order . . . and, in particular, to deepen acceptance of the procedures used to maintain continuity, order and boundary'.[8]

In short, in the schools symbolism acted as an instrument of segregation, of power, of control and as a transmitter of cultural heritage. There was nothing original in this. These are basic contributions to order observed in other cultural contexts: 'Among the various qualities and values . . . shown to be symbolised in ritual, are differences in social status . . . the need to keep separate things which there is a danger of confusing, such as different lineages, generations and sexes . . . as well as the social order itself. Thus ritual can provide a means to the expression of many different cultural values . . .'[9] Expression of cultural values has been singled out as the defining characteristic of ritual in education.[10] But this is to put the cart before the horse. Ritual has the even more fundamental role of creating and sustaining cohesion: it is the idiom of conformity.[11] And the public schools of this study evolved an elaborate symbol system both to promote this conformity and to express unifying cultural values and the consequent relationships between objects and those things they symbolised. Games, games players and games fields held a central position in this system. If this fact has attracted little analytical attention until now it is possibly because of our continued tendency to equate ritual with preliterate cultures, and because of a selective interpretation of games as a 'trivial' aspect of social life in general and the social system in particular.[12] In promoting conformity, symbolism had at least three specific roles: as a focusing mechanism creating a frame for experience which assisted concentration and minimised distractions; as a mnemonic agent reinforcing memory by making vivid what was dim and recalling what was forgotten; as a filter of social experience determining the nature of social reality by surrounding certain relationships with powerful emotional feelings.[13]

The argument has been put forward that whatever the historical or ideological creative impulse, survival became the eventual goal of the public school and unquestioning loyalty the mechanism by which that goal was realised. The institution became more revered than its purpose and the moral imperative to be loyal took on a greater importance than any evaluation of the object of loyalty however sincere.[14] There is considerable truth in this observation.[15] Powerful rites of intensification were fostered to this end. These consensual rituals bound together the whole group as a moral community. They were cohesive agents and as such operated at two levels. There were those concerned with the school as a whole, and those concerned with sections of the school. The latter were by far the more important and paradoxically, since they were also 'differentiating' rituals segregating bodies of pupils, the most effective means of ensuring allegiance, affection and unity, as will be seen shortly. The former, however, were not without power.

Harrow provides probably the finest example in the form of the annual Lord's Match against Eton – a focusing mechanism, mnemonic agent and value filter *par excellence*. It was, as one Harrovian described it, 'the supreme rite when one identified oneself with every member of the side, suffered in their failures, exalted in their triumphs'.[16] Another recalled that any Harrow boy who absented himself from it was a traitor and sterner spirits even thought it base to be out of one's seat during even a moment of play.[17] The pressure on deviants to support this solidarity ritual is well depicted by the experience of C. C. Martindale, a religious introvert, whose real but secret love at Harrow was for *objets de piété* and High Anglican rites. On confessing to his housemaster his traitorous desire to absent himself from the annual conflict, he was curtly informed that he would 'lose caste' if he failed to attend. He was miserable as well as bored – his top hat gave him a headache and his buttonhole made him sick – but he watched![18]

The support this annual confrontation generated was remarkable. As early as 1866 the *Pall Mall Gazette* recorded 10,000 spectators[19] and a writer in *Blackwood's Magazine* could state that of the MCC's income for 1866 totalling about £17,000, £2778 were the proceeds of the University and Eton v. Harrow matches, and this despite elections for parliament in the same week.[20] In 1910 there were 15,000 present. This was the year of a great Eton victory. An Eton pen recorded the exuberance of the winners '. . . a Cabinet Minister weeping, laughing and dancing on a Harrovian flag; portly citizens in Bond Street yelling the news to strangers with the light blue ribbon on them who had quitted the ground in despair an hour before. Such were the English just before the Great War.'[21] While distinguished politicians in middle age occasionally performed exuberant dances on the standard of the defeated, waving elegant symbols of devotion – large silk handkerchiefs of dark and light blue respectively – the younger supporters would clash regularly in front of the pavilion at the end of the match in a free-for-all that in a modern football ground would attract the opprobium of a scandalised public. In those more robust times this exhibition of upper-class virility was tolerated as a manly gesture of loyalty. Support for the Lord's Match is a useful barometer of the climate of opinion surrounding athleticism. This is illustrated by the figures for attendance between 1871 and 1886 and between 1936 and 1972 in table VII on p. 145.

'St Andrew's Day sums it all up,' Eric Parker declared of the Eton Wall game, 'and sums up more than mere football. Those who have watched the College team leave the field after winning on St Andrew's Day know that they have watched more than the winning of a game . . . It belongs to more days than that one day, and to more than that one match; to more than any playing of games . . . they have stood in the old ways.'[22] What was true of the Wall game was equally true of the Lord's Match. And Lancing, Marlborough, Uppingham, Stonyhurst and Loretto had their equivalent athletic rituals of solidarity and permanence, although of unquestionably lesser status: Marlborough v. Rugby also at Lord's; Lancing v. Brighton at the Sussex County Ground; Uppingham v. Rugby on the Upper; Stonyhurst v. Beaumont on the Higher Line Oval; and Loretto v. Fettes on Pinkie.

In addition the schools had their old boys' matches and sports clubs. If, as has been claimed, a main objective of the old boys' clubs was 'to enjoy the pleasure and pathos of retrospect',[23] then memories of matches lost and won in boyhood would figure prominently in conversation in a world where games counted for so much. For the young and energetic the logical step was the actual continuation of these past experiences through the creation of teams of former

Table VII *Public attendance at the Eton versus Harrow matches at Lord's 1871–1972 (at three-year intervals)*

1871–86	(total for two days)		
1871	24,626	1880	15,047
1874	15,364	1883	12,289
1877	13,416	1886	11,744

Source: Wisden 1887.

1936–72			
1936	20,489	1960	8,577
1939	19,174	1963	5,836
1948	18,806	1966	7,219
1951	17,864	1969	3,247
1954	14,845	1972	2,466
1957	12,025		

Source: MCC archives.

Note: These figures cover gate entries only and do not include members of the Marylebone Cricket Club. 1871 was the first year records were kept of turnstile entrants. Figures are given at three-year intervals to indicate a trend. Details between 1887 and 1936 are unfortunately not available. The writer acknowledges his debt to Mr Stephen Green, curator of the MCC, for help in computing these figures.

schoolfellows. Thus a common feature of the schools was the old boys' cricket and football teams, providing 'permanence amidst change . . . unity amidst succession'.[24]

Of the nineteenth-century public school boy it is alleged that once his capacity for loyalty had been developed by the school he was expected to transfer that loyalty to his adult group: the regiment, the trading company, the Foreign Office or whatever.[25] More to the point, what the public school boy did was to take his school world and its symbolic actions and trappings *with him* into the outside world. The Uppingham archives contain an excellent example of this process at work. In 1910, enterprising and nostalgic Uppinghamians in India formed an Old Boys' Club. In a booklet entitled *Old Uppingham in India*[26] they described its objectives. They aimed simply to ensure that Uppinghamians on the sub-continent kept in touch with their old school. To this end they played their former games and replicated the entire sporting outfit of their *alma mater*. A blazer of dark blue cloth with blue buttons and the school crest on the pocket was designed, and it was arranged that C. Baldwin of Uppingham, the school outfitter, would supply long knitted silk (motor) scarves, silk scarves (to wear round the waist), silk diagonal ties, cricket caps and hat ribbons of varying width in the school colours.

Ritual activities and symbolic garments provided these former pupils with a familiar identity. They maintained an expressive link with their old school across the seas, which was projected into the past and into the future. As it has been written, '. . . being . . . a community which could exercise an emotional hold not only during schooldays but for after life, the public school became an alternative to the Victorian family'.[27]

The rival matches at Lord's and elsewhere, the old boy reunions and the old boy club games helped effect this transfer as well as helping to promote solidarity and permanence of identity. At the same time, while it is important to emphasise the expressive value of public school symbolism, its instrumental functions should not be overlooked: old boys might have sported the old school tie less readily had it not been a means of identifying the high-status phenomenon of the period – the ex-public school boy.

II

While some athletic rituals of unity and identity embraced the whole body of the school, curiously, communal solidarity was achieved by deliberately created internal diversity so that opposing groups of pupils met frequently on playing fields throughout the year. The instrument of this calculated segregation was the house system with its repetitious, fiercely contested house matches. House matches were first played at Harrow in the 1830s and at Marlborough, Lancing and Uppingham in the 1850s, but an organised system of inter-house competitions generating intense chauvinism took a while to develop. By 1870 the system was widely established. Stonyhurst and Loretto, however, prove interesting exceptions.

Stonyhurst never possessed a house system. Pupils were organised on the principle of competition both in physical and academic activities, but there were important differences in approach from the Protestant public schools, which helped ensure that the symbolism of athleticism which flourished elsewhere was there still-born.

There were two main reasons for this: the centralisation of authority discussed earlier in this study, which in practical terms meant constant control and supervision by a small official body of staff so that the boys had less freedom than elsewhere to generate the hysteria and devise the insignia that were associated with houses at other schools; and also horizontal segregation of pupils by age which was an effective bar to domination by senior boys and the establishment of the hierarchical boy culture based on games ability that was so often a feature where the house system flourished.

Whatever the theoretical definition of a public school the Jesuits kept power firmly in their own hands.[28] Character training by delegation of responsibility was not their method. They were conscious of the propensity for evil of the young if left to themselves, especially in idle moments. For leisure activities the pupils were highly organised and divided into horizontal groupings by means of a 'playroom' system within the framework of a bilateral segregation into Higher and Lower Lines. For many years there were three playrooms.[29] Each had its own games areas and indoor facilities for wet weather activities and a prefect continually in charge, who supervised, organised and played with the boys. There was to be no major change in this pattern of close supervision by staff until well after the Great War. And the organisational principles of centralisation of authority and horizontal as distinct from vertical grouping in the decades in which athleticism had a powerful influence elsewhere, ensured at Stonyhurst minimum preoccupation with games and their associated rituals and symbols.

At Loretto Almond tolerated no house system. He desired too strongly that his pupils be moulded in his own image for it to be otherwise. He would not countenance the rejection or even the modification of his own ideals through independent, strong-minded housemasters pursuing their own ends, and demanding loyalty to house at the expense of loyalty to Almond.[30] He had, therefore, no houses and no rituals and symbols of house allegiance and status, but their absence failed to have the same significance as at Stonyhurst. The plain fact is that during Almond's headship the school was in effect little more than a large 'house'[31] with one dominant, paternalistic 'housemaster' in the person of Almond himself and with its own idiosyncratic symbols of athleticism – a point which will be dealt with more fully later in this chapter.

The part played by the house system in the development of athleticism, underlined by the significant exceptions of Stonyhurst

and Loretto, was considerable. In the first instance it passed power to the pupils. The orthodox public schools' unshakable belief in the virtues of 'pupil power' is perfectly illustrated by one housemaster zealot who once declared: 'A boy who, at nineteen, can rule a house at a public school, at fifty can rule a nation. The two tasks are equally easy, equally difficult. They demand the same gifts and the same qualities.'[32]

The wisdom of such a firm belief in the delegation of widespread powers to pupils was certainly questionable. The 'boy culture' in which, in general, the oldest and biggest had considerable power, was not always dutiful, responsible or honourable.[33] The ideal of self-government offered the possibility of considerable abuse and the offer was certainly accepted.[34] It made possible, *inter alia*, an excessive veneration of games. How widespread the abuse was at any particular time is impossible to say. Whenever there was public complaint, the excuse was 'a bad lot, in a bad house, at a bad time'. Stoicism was the admired practice and silence the norm.[35]

From the point of view of the headmaster, however, self-government was excellent in two practical ways. Firstly it was a valuable asset in the recruitment and retention of staff. The practice of delegating authority to prefects made the housemaster's task so much easier; it allowed him, if he wished, to remain securely behind 'the traditional green baize door'[36] in undisturbed tranquillity, leaving his prefects to maintain control in their own way. It was said, for example, of Thomas Henry Steel,[37] housemaster at the Grove, Harrow, from 1855 to 1881, that he had never been seen on the boys' side of it. It is interesting to read Fitzgerald's description of the 'toilsome life' of the three prefects in charge of the boys' leisure at Stonyhurst,[38] who had little or no support from the rest of staff and no boy helpers. It is tempting to believe that only the celibate vocationalist, married to the institution and with few external interests, could have coped. Self-government also meant, as already touched upon earlier, that the prefectorial system with its associated privileges divided the boys and lured the most powerful to the side of the masters. The truth of the matter would seem to be that self-government was as much an instrument of staff convenience and pupil control, as a means of training character.

An even more potent factor in the recruitment of staff was the fact that until the twentieth century houses were owned and run for profit by the housemasters. The Moral Rearmament campaigner, Stephen Foot, was one of the first to advocate and introduce school

control of the finances of the houses. He lectured widely throughout the public school system in the 1920s recommending the adoption of his ideas because he believed that the old house system was
thoroughly bad and that boys' interests were neglected by avari-
cious housemasters seeking high profits.[39] By the Second World
War the principle of the house as a speculation in which the housemaster invested his money was ended.

Until then, however, the possession of a successful house in a
popular school could mean substantial monetary reward and headmasters were well aware of the need for the availability of this
source of revenue when seeking desirable recruits. In 1897, for
example, A. J. Wilson, headmaster of Lancing, wrote a report to
the provost[40] in which he expressed concern that due to a marked
decline in numbers the house system would fail to provide sufficient inducement to attract able staff. Mistakes at Marlborough
underline the drawing power of the possession of a house. The
college founders took a calculated risk in launching their enterprise
without a house system. It was their intention to save parents the
profits that went into housemasters' pockets. They foundered on
the rocks of self-interest. According to the official history they had
to reverse their decision because 'they overlooked . . . the fact that a
large income of a boarding house was one of the chief financial
inducements to men of first-rate ability'.[41] The important point for
this study is that, in time, the definition of first-rate ability came to
mean in many cases games ability or at least enthusiasm. This,
coupled with the fact that the financially independent housemaster
was virtually autonomous in all matters regarding his house, had
important consequences for athleticism which will be explored
more fully in due course.

Yet a further reason why the house system was important for the
growth of athleticism was simply that its main structural feature, a
relatively small number of pupils under the control of a housemaster, house tutor and the older boys, enabled the public school
boy to be supervised, controlled and manipulated more efficiently
than previously. In this way the small unit of the house was a
powerful means of conditioning the inmates. It provided an intensive ritualistic 'frame' inside which the boys learnt to respond
correctly to the stimuli of conventional values. Through the constant repetition of house activities, especially games, a value system
was assimilated, emotions were stimulated and for many pleasant
experience accumulated. The house system, therefore, was a

method of 'system maintenance' stressing dominant values, reducing discontent, promoting acceptance of school life and providing delightful reminiscences in adulthood, which guaranteed a steady supply of recruits to the public schools. 'You were at Harrow were you?' wrote E. M. Venables of a typical chance meeting of old boys in after life. 'Which House? Behind this question . . . lies a little world of loyalties stored with memories.'[42] Of course it was a world in which success in games was the Everest of achievement and a world inhabited by many former pupils for a lifetime. J. E. C. Welldon once wrote, 'It would need the pen of a Thucydides to convey the emotions and involvement of partisans at House Matches. There are elderly gentlemen leading quiet, respectable lives in remote parts of the country who cannot now meet after fifty years without exchanging words like these: "You remember that catch, my dear fellow, why did you let that ball go through your legs?"'[43]

The house system was, in fact, a brilliantly successful piece of social engineering whereby large numbers of boys could be herded together away from home and its comforts and be adequately controlled and emotionally sustained, while at the same time the life of the virtually autonomous supervisor was tolerable and even attractive. At another level of analysis, from the point of view of ideological indoctrination, the house system was a *memoria technica* providing both an instrumental and expressive frame inside which individuals enacted continually, and in this way learnt, licensed group responses to the demands of the institution and their social class.[44] In short, the house was a symbolic crucible in which individuality was melted down into conformity.

The evolution of the house system varied in detail among the four schools but in one important aspect Laborde's neat summary of developments at Harrow is relevant to them all:

Between 1820 and 1850 the character of the boarding-houses underwent considerable modification. The houses ceased to be merely places where the 'foreigners' boarded and became integral parts of the organisation of the school. Each house developed into a community with its place in the wider community of the school. As games became organised, the houses . . . became the basis of their organisation.[45]

The point to note is the close association between games and the house system. In the history of the public school after 1850 these two are as inseparable as Tweedledum and Tweedledee. The Lancing historian, B. W. T. Handford, has attributed the rise of Lancing as a public school to the simultaneous construction of houses and a games field. In 1857 after the college moved from Shoreham, in Handford's words, '[it] began to turn into a public school. The boys were divided into Houses, the Headmaster's, the Second Master's and the School House. A playing field was made on the only piece of flat land on the College estate – the Dyke Field.'[46]

These twin factors more than any other ensured the success and popularity of the public school system with the boys. In harness they seduced the clientele. They were anoetic focuses for emotional attachment, the one reinforcing the other. Together they were responsible for a wall of emotion that shielded the loyal from the attacks of the cynical and disillusioned. They were hugely successful filters of experience. Homeric deeds in house matches remained vivid in the memory. 'In truth I was an indifferent athlete and more at home with books than with games', declared a Harrovian in old age, yet he recalled with 'telescopic accuracy' the fierce battle between Druries and Stogdons which stood between Druries and the Cock House award for the third successive year, and in which to the accompaniment of wild cheering, in front of the greater part of the school, he scored the winning base.[47]

Professor Honey has argued that the private insular world of the nineteenth-century public school possessed in athleticism and communal songs, powerful means of generating ideals, attitudes and emotions and above all, loyalty to the school.[48] He might have gone further and drawn attention to the fact that the relationship between communal songs and athleticism was itself very close. More often than not the school songs glorified and mythologised athletic deeds and doers. Events on the playing field were often the inspiration of the songs in the concert room. Songs and games were instruments of solidarity which were inseparably linked. The one inspired the other: the one reinforced the other. This common role and frequent juxtaposition is demonstrated by the Harrow Founder's Day order of events before the Great War:

Order of day
1. Two football matches in the afternoon between the first and second Harrow elevens, and two elevens of Old Harrovians.
2. Service in chapel.
3. Dinner in the head's house followed by reception in the Vaughan Library.
4. Old Harrovian singing of school songs.[49]

But while loyalty to the school was undoubtedly generated on the school playing fields and through communal singing of the school songs as Honey claims, where the house system was well developed it was loyalty largely but not exclusively *refracted* through house playing fields. What J. M. Broughton claimed for Harrow, namely that no boy could leave without being inspired, 'with a true spirit of loyalty, while taking part in or even while watching the ebbs and flows of a Football House match',[50] would go undisputed by old boys of the other schools of the study with a similar house system. For the most part it was the house match not the school match which produced exhilaration in victory, dejection in defeat, a fact clearly recognised by the anonymous author of an article on 'Unity' in the *Harrovian* in 1870 who decried the rise of the house spirit in games to the detriment of the school spirit.[51]

The student of ritual has been warned against an over-optimistic belief in the efficacy of the consensual rituals of 'total institutions'. Goffman has remarked that it is a nice question if any solidarity is achieved by them.[52] Sensible if over-cautious words. Apart from the matches against notable rivals, even in the heyday of athleticism, school matches were often less than enthusiastically watched. Sometimes strong measures had to be taken to encourage support. Selwyn of Uppingham, a revered exponent of the simple philosophy of 'fear God; speak the truth and shoot straight', used to walk up and down the side lines of the Leicester ground 'using his gold-headed stick on any part of their [the boys'] lower anatomies and exhorting them to shout'.[53] As he did so he would drive the boys over the touch line to be driven back by the hunting crops of the praepostors. The latter also exerted their influence. In his autobiography one former pupil recalled being 'tanned' by a praepostor for not shouting loudly enough at a rugger match, and added that to that day he could still remember the sounds the whips made on the overcoats of the spectators.[54]

Desmond Coke's description of Shrewsbury will serve admirably to represent a general discrepancy between 'foreign' matches and the internecine matches for the Cock House Cup. At 'the school footer matches,' he wrote, excepting those against 'beastly rival schools' such as Malvern or Repton,

you stood and shivered, even on a warm day, along one side of the field, and every now and then a long-drawn 'Play up-schoo-oo-ools' went calmly along the row, like some wave breaking down a rocky coast . . . the real thing was the House matches . . . you kept pushing forward to the linesman's anger so as to miss nothing, shouting and jumping, drowning the cries of the other Houses and even running up and down the line. Cheering and excitement kept you warm. And when your House was in the final – Yes, the House was certainly the thing![55]

A series of Marlborough vignettes down the decades provides linked images of the continuous power of the house match to stir emotions and generate loyalty. A *Marlburian* editorial of 1865 stated, 'On the day of a House Match the greatest possible excitement is created in the Houses. The elevens are put on their best mettle. The school flocks to witness the exhibition of play and to watch the result of the battle.'[56] In 1889 a Marlborough versifier wrote:

> Our hearts are throbbing – as Homer would say
> They are kicking our bosoms, 'tis House match today,
> And an icy fear is ingested in our hearts
> For such are the tremors that the House match imparts.[57]

E. F. Benson, in the opening years of the twentieth century, described in *David Blaize* the tensions that produced these tremors: 'Everybody was utterly absorbed in what was going on at the wickets. The whole school and the whole staff were there watching to the end of the final tie in house matches in absolute tense silence.'[58] And Gerald Murray has written of Marlborough before the Second World War: 'The housemaster, maybe his wife, matron, house tutor and boys would crowd the line, the junior boys to cheer the 'House Heroes' in their resplendent jerseys. While the headmaster attended the lot.'[59]

Roger Ellis, the present headmaster of Marlborough, writing of public school house games, has stated that the comparatively small size of the houses meant that almost everyone had to play in house matches at various levels with the result that day after day the good performer was exalted and the poor one abased. As a consequence, he has argued, it was above all through the house that athleticism grew and flourished.[60] This is a point of the utmost significance. House games were unavoidable participatory rituals. All members were involved in these internal battles: they were either spectators or players depending on the occasion. All were in their different ways symbols of compulsory institutional patriotism which brought the chance of personal glory or disgrace in those things that for the majority mattered most. Edward Lyttelton warned his readers that the extent to which athleticism went and how far it dominated the public school boy view of life could not be gauged without reckoning the rivalry of the houses with regard to games. In his experience house spirit fostered violent partisanship and even those of broad and tolerant disposition were swept away by it.[61] In this atmosphere heroes were easily made and scapegoats chosen. But, more importantly, in this way unity was effected out of diversity and retrospective affection out of immediate hostility.

III

Athletic glory or disgrace could be accentuated or mitigated by a famous symbol of the house system: the housemaster. This pillar of the public school system was for many a father figure whose influence could be considerable long after the celebration tea in his drawing room or the exhortations on the touchline were past:

Just as the sun never sets on the British Empire, so it never sets upon all the Old Boys of a great public school at once. They are gone out into all lands: they are upholding the honour of the School all the world over. And wherever they are – London, Simla, Johannesburg, Nairobi or Little Pedlington Vicarage – they never lose touch with their old Housemaster. His correspondence is enormous; it weighs him down; but he would not relinquish a single picture postcard of it. He knows that whenever two or three of his Old Boys are gathered together, be it in Bangalore or Bulawayo, the talk will always drift round in time to the Old School and the Old House.[62]

Such was the claim of the writer Ian Hay in a purple passage which would seem, for all that, a remarkably accurate observation. Three real-life examples might be cited. At Harrow Edward Bowen kept up correspondence with many of his pupils after they left and advised them as the occasion arose, while a current Harrow housemaster not only corresponds with former members of his house but is often sought out for advice by their parents. At Marlborough, by the time of his death, T. C. G. Sandford had several trunks full of correspondence from former members of his house.

Housemasters could be, and sometimes were, a thorn in the flesh of the headmaster. Chowdler in *The Lanchester Tradition* had his equivalents in reality. The power to stand up to the headmaster, a power notably denied to the more professionally emasculated colleague, the assistant master, came from the substantial independence of owning his own house. The situation at Harrow was, to a considerable extent, general:

Once a master had assumed charge of a house . . . he was in complete control of it and did not recognise the right of the Headmaster to intervene in his domestic affairs. In fact during the latter half of the nineteenth century and the first twenty-five years of the twentieth, the School was governed by a kind of federal system in which the several houses were the states of the union, while the housemasters exercised an influence so great as to make the Headmaster's position one of 'primus inter pares' among his senior colleagues.[63]

And it was virtually impossible to remove them. Loyalty, gratitude for past services, reluctance to cause embarrassment kept men in positions of responsibility which mentally and physically they were unfit to administer. The novelist H. A. Vachell wrote, 'It is almost as difficult to turn an Eton or Harrow master out of his house, as to turn a person of the Church of England out of his pulpit.'[64] In the nineteenth-century public school the house in fact constituted 'a state within a state'.

Thring's bitter conflicts with several of his housemasters recorded both in his diary and by his biographer, G. R. Parkin, illustrate this point nicely. The source of the trouble was Thring's desire to be an absolute monarch. He was strongly resisted. In turn, he was adamant. 'You spoke to me of your claim because you built', he wrote to one housemaster. 'You have no claims . . . To bring this to a clear issue, I utterly deny any claims.'[65] To another he wrote, 'I am not a constitutional monarch . . . You *cannot* share the main responsibility of the school . . . My position is far more that of a military commander who must act on his own responsibility, however much he may listen to advice.'[66] Parkin includes an extract from Thring's diary to the effect that a headmaster would put up with almost anything rather than risk a clash with a housemaster, which reveals that while Thring attempted to lay down the manner in which the houses should be run, he fully appreciated the power of the master in charge. Although Parkin attributes Thring's failure to carry out his principles of control and dismissal of staff as vigorously as he expressed them in theory to his kindheartedness, there is at least one other explanation – that the resistance of housemasters was up to a point successful even against his strong-minded opposition.

The ruler of the little sovereignty of the house, therefore, could determine the life-style of its members. The headmaster might stand before the curtain, but the housemaster issued stage directions to the cast from the wings. *Punch* understood his covert power:

> He served three Heads with equal zeal
> And equal absence of ambition;
> He knew his power, and did not feel
> The least desire for recognition;
> But shrewd observers, who could trace
> Back to their source results far-reaching,
> Saw the true Genius of the Place
> Embodied in his life and teaching.[67]

This power often ensured that the passions of his life and teaching were personified in his boys – animated marionettes responding to his touch, mostly enthusiastically; for his passions themselves were often predominantly youthful.

Support in *The Spectator* in 1913 for R.C.T.'s *A Housemaster's Letters*, a book concerned to justify the freely admitted preoccupation with games in the house system of the public schools, suggests the truth of this assertion. A 'Long-Serving Housemaster' wrote that housemasters were honest men; they would readily admit if the point was put fairly and squarely to them that the promotion of athletic distinction took deliberate precedence over the encouragement of active-minded boys, and it was a matter of comparative unimportance to them if a boy's mind was not being trained at this time of life.[68] It was written of one Harrow housemaster of the time, for example, that what he desired most and what he got was 'a set of good, clean fellows playing the game'. This ambition was widely shared.[69]

Harrow, Marlborough, Uppingham and Lancing all have factual records and supportive myths of housemasters who were legendary lovers of games and whose houses in consequence reflected their enthusiasms. These actors were human value filters, focusing mechanisms and mnemonic agents. In the history of athleticism such men are archetypal symbols of ideological purity. Edward Bowen is probably the most famous.

Bowen was assistant master at Harrow from 1859 to 1901. He was 'an untiring athlete and admirer of feats of endurance'. His own feats of endurance have become legends. As an undergraduate he apparently thought little of walking from Cambridge to London and once walked from London to Oxford in twenty-six consecutive hours.[70] In later life he was reputed to have walked round the whole coastline of England and Wales. 'His influence on athleticism at Harrow,' declared his nephew, 'though not supreme, was at any rate considerable.'[71] This odd comment, was perhaps dictated by modesty, possibly by a diplomatic desire to spare the feelings of the friends of Robert Grimston and the Earl of Bessborough, the two devoted amateur coaches of generations of Harrow cricketers. In fact he has no close rival in this sphere. So extensive was his influence over such a long period of time that the *Harrovian* rightly asserted on his death, that 'few things would be more difficult to convey to a stranger than an idea of Bowen's influence upon athletics'.[72]

He was unique as performer, organiser and inspirationalist. Literally 'the playmate of youth to the last' he played football at the age of sixty-five within weeks of his death.[73] He contributed hugely to the systematic organisation of Harrow games. He was responsible for the 'Cricket Ground Bill' which shifted the traditional afternoon roll-call from the 'Bill Yard' to the cricket fields and so saved the players considerable time as well as the effort of trudging up the hill. He created the 'Torpids' (junior house matches), the 'Ones' (house ties between single football players), the 'Infants' cricket match for junior boys and the ritual of the 'Tree Planting Ceremony' on the Philathletic Field for cricketers who scored fifty runs excluding boundaries in a school match. The potency of his school and house songs which 'cast the mantle of poetry round daily struggle with bat and ball'[74] has been recorded by many Old Harrovians. Even his discipline was imbued with physical concern. To him lines meant 'fugging' indoors and so instead he would hide objects several miles from school and send defaulters to find them, or send them on a run to Pinner or another neighbouring village to count the palings round a whitewashed cottage.[75]

In the wider world his contribution to physical activity was also considerable. He was one of the founders of Association Football and played for the famous 'Wanderers FC' which won the Football Association Challenge Cup outright. He organised cricket tours and football matches for Harrovians including the 'office hours' match each Christmas in London, played continuously from ten o'clock in the morning until four in the afternoon. While others stole short rests, Bowen normally contrived to survive the six hours without any cessation of activity. In 1877 he recommended to the Civil Service Commission investigating the examination system for the Army and the Indian Civil Service an examination of speed, strength and endurance which was accepted in modified form.

His interest in the match at Lord's 'was unsurpassed by boy or colleague' and his verses celebrating famous matches – 'A Gentleman A-Bowling', 'Lord's 1873', 'Lord's 1878' and 'Lord's 1900' – are major contributions to Harrow folklore and to the mythology of athleticism. It was in one of these verses celebrating a tense moment in the annual meeting that he revealed much of his philosophy and that of many pupils of his era:

> What is it? Forty, thirty more?
> You in the trousers white,

What did you come to Harrow for
If we lose the match tonight?[76]

A more expansive outline of his philosophy is to be found in the
essay entitled simply 'Games' which he wrote for the small coterie
of public school masters called 'The United Ushers' who met
regularly in London to discuss educational matters. A typical extract reads: 'I offer as my deliberate opinion, that the best boys are
on the whole the players of games. I had rather regenerate England
with the football elevens than the average Member of Parliament
. . . When I reflect on the vices to which games are a permanent
corrective – laziness, foppery, man-of-the-worldness – I am not
surprised at being led to the verdict which I have just delivered.'[77]
Of this paper Bowen's biographer wrote, 'Beneath all the levity
there runs a steady purpose – the advocacy of athleticism as the
most important and valuable of all factors making up our educational system.'[78]

In 1882 Bowen became housemaster of one of the large Harrow
houses, the Grove, and, wrote his biographer, 'It need not be said
that Edward Bowen's interest in athletics showed itself very
strongly in connection with his House.'[79] He was now at the apogee
of his power and encouraged *con fuenco* all activities that strengthened a healthy, manly, unselfish, corporated life. He enthusiastically embraced the Coubertin aphorism 'to strengthen the mind
you must harden the muscles', maintaining that he would 'a hundred times cut two schools rather than one house match'.[80] He had
no time, therefore, for the individualistic activities such as racquets,
fives and gymnastics. In addition he was an apostle of simple
vigorous, hardy living. He would tolerate no armchairs, warm
baths, daintily furnished rooms or early fires. In his chilly, bleakly-
furnished house the boys were expected to endure without
complaint. The only permitted luxury was his 'glorification' or
'consolation' cake (depending on the result) for house games teams
eaten in his unpretentious drawing-room.

In Bowen an ethos and a society are splendidly epitomised in a
single man. But there were other less famous but equally committed figures, singled out by obituarists, historians and biographers.
These merit a definite, if less ostentatious place in the pantheon of
athleticism. At Harrow, M. C. Kemp (housemaster of Moreton's
1904–21) was 'before all else a games-player'. He established a
strong games-playing tradition at Moreton's and 'games always

came first'. This tradition lived on long after his retirement. 'For many years,' the *Harrovian* recorded, 'until the pressure of modern examinations and rising standards, Moreton's was exclusively a games-playing house where 'grouse' [swot] was a violent reproach.'[81] At Elmfield Cyril Browne (1933–48), 'a great House Master of the old school', carefully built up the character of his boys through the playing of games.[82]

At Marlborough there was John Babington (C3 1869–75) who under his pseudonym 'Trebla' wrote euphuistic pieces in the *Marlburian* in support of the moral qualities of games.[83] There was also W. J. Ford (C1 1877–86) who went to be principal of Nelson College, New Zealand. He displayed 'extraordinary prowess at games' and was a noted cricket writer whose work included histories of Middlesex CC and Cambridge University CC and a biography of W. G. Grace. Another Marlborough games enthusiast was A. H. Beesly (C2 1865–75, Summerfield 1875–85). In the words of J.B., a Marlburian poet, 'of boy-like zest in games of strength and skill', Beesly was considered by some to be too deeply absorbed in athletics, to make too much of games and to lead boys to attach undue importance to them.[84] He wrote poems of schoolboy nostalgia typical of the period. It was in one of them, 'The Old School Gate', that he visualised the Old Marlburian out in the empire recalling wistfully,

> The caps and vestures of infinite hue
> That gleam in the strife of the Red and Blue.[85]

Uppingham housemasters who have won a minor place in posterity for their games enthusiasm include W. J. Earle (Brooklands 1861–80), A. C. Taylor (West Deyne 1899–1927) and F. W. Weldon (Lorne 1895–1919). Earle, in his time as master, played for his house, the school and Uppingham Rovers, and in his later years in retirement in his Essex rectory 'would delight in welcoming his old boys and talking over with them, the good old days when his boys were captains of the School Eleven, and when his house held the champion cup'.[86] Taylor rebuilt the sporting tradition of West Deyne after it had lapsed for some years, and due to his encouragement the school year 1905–6 saw his house win seven first fifteen colours and four first eleven colours.[87] The historians of Lorne House have written of Weldon that he 'was not one to miss the chance of a game, and in his time the House entered upon an era of athletic success especially cricket'.[88] The peak was reached in the decade 1897–1907 when Lorne House recorded an unprecedented run of five consecutive victories in the 'Overs', the house cricket competition.

In the Bowen mould at Lancing was T. D. Cook (Seconds House 1895–1911) an old boy of the school who continued to play football into his fifties.[89] Cook was yet another orthodox muscular Christian of the period. On one occasion he recorded in his diary, 'Rode to Thakenham Rectory for our clerical meeting. Briscoe, our host, is quite a good chap and read a high-toned paper on the Clergy and Sports and Games . . .'[90] Another celebrated housemaster at Lancing was A. C. Wilson (Seconds House 1859–70), who, as we have seen, was dedicated to making his house successful at games; between 1858 and 1868 its cricket team remained unbeaten. W. B. Harris (Head's House tutor 1916–19, Gibbs housemaster 1919–26), one-time captain of England's amateur football team, was another who strongly influenced Lancing house games. He is reputed to have lived for football and among his contributions was the creation of house leagues.[91]

Some of these men, while inspirational on the games field, were 'muscular' by propensity, *borné* by virtue of their early conditioning and their successes, but it would be naive to press them all into the same mould. For example, Edward Bowen was in the view of one admirer 'the most brilliant, original and liberal-minded of teachers' and a thoughtful religious, political and educational radical in a highly conservative school.[92] A. H. Beesly was a writer of repute and author of several books of poetry and history[93], A. C. Taylor 'a scholar, athlete and cricketer' in that order.[94] What they all shared, however, was a belief, firmly held and energetically put into practice, in the central role of team games in school life. It was written of the Eton masters, Mitchell and Dupuis, that: 'Their conception of duty was to sacrifice themselves in all their available time to coaching, and to expect the boys to do the same . . . They far outdid the juveniles in their worship of the game and the influence of these magnificent exponents of the art of hitting and kicking balls . . . actualising a boyish ideal of life, was, of course, boundlessly potent.'[95] This eulogy is essentially a description of all the sporting housemasters of the English public school. They personified 'the boyish ideal of life': their passion inspired passion; their effort stimulated effort. As 'magnificent exponents' and in consequence as inspirational symbols, buttressed by the independence of their position and supported by upper-class society in general, they were able to act out their philosophy of education, indulge in their physical obsessions and insist that their way was the way of those under their tutelage and roof. Secure in their autonomy and popularity they played a large part in ensuring the popularity of athleticism.

IV

Rupert Wilkinson has argued that public school inculcation of loyalty amounted to education by symbol.[96] His statement constitutes half the truth. There was symbolic inculcation not only of loyalty but of obeisance. Participants in the sporting rituals of the public schools created for themselves dazzling symbolic trappings of *both* fealty and dominance: caps, badges, ties, belts, hatbands, blazers, buttons, stockings, scarves, tassels and shirts all acted as vivid mnemonic agents. In classroom and chapel, to and from games fields, the warring factions were labelled and the famous were garlanded. In the Golden Age of the public schools and athleticism between approximately 1860 annd 1914 when economies were virtually unknown and indulgence accepted, these sporting symbols of identity and success were numerous and gorgeous. The good games player was the proud owner of a colourful athletic wardrobe that made him 'a cynosure of the vulgar and an object of complacent admiration to himself'.[97] Schoolboy imaginations were not squandered on textbook images of Homeric heroes voyaging through the Aegean but were exercised in the creation of emblems of local patriotism.

Of Harrow in the 1860s it was written:

No sight could have been more picturesque than that of the boys going down to 'footer'. The Middlemites wore their dark blue coats and blue stockings, the Tommyites (Steele's not Bowen's) their scarlet coats and red stockings, the 'Monkeyites' their carnation striped coats, the Bradbyites their purple striped coats, while we Butlerites were content to play in our pink and white shirts. It was not considered good form in a Butlerite to wear a coat 'down to footer' and then you might swathe in magenta . . . I will not attempt to describe the gorgeous plumage of the 'Billyites' the 'Harrisites' and the young 'Vaughanites'.[98]

Representatives of the school could scarcely be less flamboyant. And the Uppingham fifteen eventually went to their home matches on the Leicester Field dressed in blue silk sashes and ornamental caps of black velvet with the school crest embroidered in silver thread, bindings of silver braid and silk tassels. Their regalia included hunting crops which were handed to the 'Pollies' (praepostors) who used them for keeping order during the game.[99] And emblems of success were designed for other heroes than representatives of school and house. At Uppingham, for example, all the school was divided into 'games' for rugby, hockey and cricket. The skilful were promoted from one 'game' to the next and so on. This distinction was known as 'winning one's "land"' and was signified by a star. Each 'game' had its own distinctive star and thus the successful proudly displayed an impressive row of stars on their chests.[100] A bizarre and melancholy occurrence concerning one Harrovian provides some insight into the great importance public schools attached to 'colours'. In 1871 G. C. Cottrell was tragically killed on the Sixth Form Ground a short time before the Lord's Match in which he was certain to have played. The 'cap' he would have won was sent to his mother by the captain of the eleven and solemnly buried with him.[101]

Such extreme reverence inevitably produced its Sadducee – G. W. S. Howson. Howson took up the headship of Gresham's School, at that time an insignificant grammar school in Norfolk, in 1900. Prior to this he had been an assistant master at Uppingham for fourteen years (1886–1900) and there he had become completely disillusioned with the whole business of the adulation of the athlete. He was a double misfit – a scientist in a classical school and a non-athlete 'in a school where athletics counted for so much'.[102] At Gresham's in consequence, he had 'the most salutary contempt for the athletic grandee' and was a bitter foe of athleticism. He expressed his opposition strongly, frequently and calculatedly in words and actions. On one occasion even his loyal biographer, J. H. Simpson, a master at Gresham's between 1908 and 1910, was somewhat shocked when Howson called a boy off the pitch to his study during an important house match. There were no cups or athletic trophies, no matches against other schools and colours were reduced to a minimum – Howson had little taste for athletic millinery.

Almond shared Howson's dislike of the sartorial trappings of athletic success.[103] In taking this attitude, as in his rejection of the house system, he again emphasised the individual nature of his own ideals and the position of his school outside the mainstream culture of the public school system. However, while it is possible because of Almond's many sensible ideas to agree with the conclusion of a recent commentator that Almond was an educator of considerable stature, it is not easy to see how the same writer could conclude that throughout his forty years at Loretto Almond attempted to nullify the tendency to conformity, prevalent in the English public schools of the period.[104] Certainly Almond neither admired nor emulated some of the excesses of athleticism, including dress, that characterised the upper-class boarding schools of the south. He opposed vehemently the award of colours, blazers or caps for games because of the individualism they underlined.[105] And as there was no house system at Loretto there were no house symbols of identity and prestige. Certainly he was the plain Methodist of the games field when set alongside the High Anglican of the Philathletic, the Upper or the Dyke Field; but Loretto had its own corporate symbols of being: the open neck, the flannel shorts, the boots, the bare heads, the coatless backs. These were Almond's symbols of institutional conformity, of Lorettonianism or Rationality – an extreme, if in some ways more sensible, manifestation of the games movement. In fact, both Lorettonianism and mainstream conformity were hostages of athleticism. Both elevated the athletic in their different ways. Ironically, Howson and Almond, while sharing some antipathies, did not exert the same influence.

The Jesuits did not escape pressure to conform to the general public school image. By the 1890s the geographical and social isolation of Stonyhurst was being somewhat reduced. Access to Oxford and Cambridge was now possible. Contact with other schools for both football and cricket matches had been established for several years and the boys were becoming more conscious of their social similarities to other public school boys and less conscious of their religious dissimilarity which had meant a traditional ostracism. The editors of the school magazine considered this progressive breakdown of isolation was nowhere more pronounced than in organised games; masters and boys observed their Protestant contemporaries and found some of their ways attractive. The *Stonyhurst Football Journal* records that in 1890 Father James Robinson set up an inter-class football league on the lines of a Cock-House competition after reading an account of house matches in the *Rossallian*.[106] It is not surprising therefore to find in 1894 a letter in the magazine requesting college colours, and by 1896 we learn that it had become the fashion of the cricket eleven to wear white blazers trimmed with blue. One correspondent even wrote of the need for a realisation that the status of the college in the public school system was dependent on its cricket. Another complained about apathetic attitudes and poor attendances at school matches and proposed that consideration be given to several reforms to ensure that members of the eleven felt it to be a distinction to be chosen for the school team. Among the necessary reforms listed were a colours presentation 'with solemnity', privileges for 'old blues' and a greater number of regular matches.[107] These proposals show yet again just how far from the norm Stonyhurst stood and just how carelessly officialdom treated the athletic hero. This was deliberate. The authorities had become concerned about the too great enthusiasm expressed for games and a senior member of the staff had been set the task of curbing it.[108]

But Stonyhurst was a school for upper-class boys proud of its public school status and despite official concern could carry its individualism only so far. If the symbols and rituals of athleticism were an integral part of public school life, then to ignore them completely was to emphasise difference, perpetuate suspicion and prolong the school's long history of social insecurity which deliberate effort over the decades had tended to lessen. The emulators had their way: the indigenous Stonyhurst football and cricket were played less and 'London' cricket became firmly institutionalised; a set of permanent cups were awarded for athletics[109] and in 1907 colours for school teams were introduced – a green and white blazer, hatband, tie, cap and sash.[110] This conscious move towards integration grew in strength over the subsequent decades. It is symbolised by the request in the magazine in 1917 for the introduction of rugby football, in the view of its protagonist, the public school game *par excellence*.[111]

However the continued absence of a house system, school discipline firmly in the hands of the priests and the Jesuit tradition of strenuous intellectual endeavour ensured that the values of the athletocrat remained subservient to those of the Order. Philip Bell, an articulate Stonyhurst pupil, reflecting on *The Loom of Youth* in a book of essays, *Idols and Idylls* published in 1917, thought that Stonyhurst provided a better education, achieved better academic results and turned out better men than Fernhurst – because of religion. But he considered the college was not without faults. More authority should be in the boys' hands.[112] In particular they were not given enough say in the control of games.

There can be little doubt that the bitterness of Howson, the independence of Almond, the constraints of the Jesuits, were justified. One indication of eventual over-enthusiasm for games is that house colours ultimately preoccupied many masters and boys to a ridiculous degree.

At Harrow, by 1891 the house fez (football cap) was in general use in all houses and most houses had three. At Druries, for example, there was an 'ordinary fez' of red and black stripes with a black tassel, the 'cap fez' with no tassel and the 'match fez' of black velvet with a red tassel. The latter was to be worn only for house matches while the distinction between the other two has been lost in history.[113] Butler's in the previous decade provided even more exotic headgear. There were three fezzes: all pink (the house match fez), pink sides and tassel with white top ('the wedding cake'), pink and white check with a pink and white tassel.[114]

In 1896 a correspondent of the Uppingham magazine with a predilection for both symmetry and the aesthetic urged the extension of the house 'colour' system of caps, ribands and belts to ordinary cricket matches on the Upper, Middle and Lower Ground pitches, so that each ground would have its characteristic cap and belt.[115]

An inspection of the 1921 report book of the Lancing College Games Committee, which consisted of both staff and pupils, reveals that they spent much of their time, even at this late date, discussing the problem of house and school 'colour' awards, patterns and designs. Among the issues debated – sometimes sharply – were the right to 'colours' of boxers, athletes, rugby, fives and tennis players, the possibility of replacing college caps with college stockings and the design of blazer badges for the school elevens. For the prominent house athlete, the report book further reveals, a house cap, tie, square and scarf were the commonplace adornments of success. There were, in addition, house sweaters for soccer and cricket. If this was not sufficient by way of decoration, one of the early meetings dealt with a complaint about brass buttons on blazers, irregular hat bands and spurious colours of all kinds worn by envious and less successful members of the school.[116]

Watchdogs of the system who kept guard over the raiment of the athletocracy fell into two categories. There were the jealous guardians of privileges and respecters of tradition, such as the Lancing Games Committee above, the Harrow Philathletic Club, the Uppingham Committee of Five and the Marlborough Dress Committee. They were responsible for drawing up rules and regulations concerning games apparel. A Harrovian 'ukase' for 1914, for example, read: 'Scarves: No coloured scarves or mufflers should be

15   Harrow eleven 1863: the informality of the group pose and the less than immaculate attire reflect the relatively casual and unorganised approach to games of this early period.

16   Harrow eleven 1877: there is still an air of casualness and the equipment is far from clean. It might almost be a village team.

EVOLUTION OF DRESS, HARROW ELEVEN 1863–1912

17   Harrow eleven 1889: the eleven is now both more dignified in pose and more neatly dressed but still lacks the full range of elegant sartorial symbols that ultimately distinguished the 'blood' from his inferiors.

18   Harrow eleven 1912: immaculately and expensively attired, these 'bloods' pose in the full glory of caps, scarves, blazers and spotless flannels symbolising the high point of ante-bellum athleticism.

worn by any boy who is not a member of the School Elevens or Eights. If scarves are worn at all, they must be either plain white ones or the recognised sashes of the School Cricket Eleven, the School Football Eleven, the Gymnastics Eight, the School Shooting Eight or Each House.'[117]

The second category of watchdogs were those headmasters and assistant masters who were not at all happy with the lavish expenditure on games dress and trophies. Montagu Butler attracted a most irreverent set of verses for his attempts to reduce the athletics finery at Harrow by abolishing games 'blazers' and house stockings in 1874. Two less offensive stanzas read:

> By each useless harmful rule,
> That o'erhangs this ancient school,
> By each antiquated law,
> That should burden us no more,
> Why should I at footer wear,
> No blue coat or stockings fair?
>
> By the numerous matches lost
> Since thy form this threshold crossed,
> By the myriad parents bated,
> By the superannuated
> Oh! thou interfering scum
> Wherefore didst thou ever come?[118]

At various times schools attempted to limit clothing excesses. One issue of the Harrow handbook *Existing Customs* contained the following rules of dress: 'The Fez or Fez Cap (at the Housemaster's discretion) is to be the only distinction between the Eleven and the rest of the House. No distinctive coats, belts, comforters are allowed except in the case of the School Eleven . . . No badges for games may be instituted without the Headmaster's sanction. House racquets badges are not allowed.'[119] These endeavours do not appear to have met with much success. The problem of games clothing eventually became serious enough to concern the members of the Headmasters' Conference. 'I think there has been a great deal of unnecessary expenditure on athletics in the schools . . . An enormous amount of money has been spent of late years, and is still being spent, by the school, on the upkeep of grounds and upon athletics generally and by parents, on what I may call athletic drapery . . . When I was a boy at Rugby there was quite enough spent; but since then there has been a change for the worse in every way', declared W. Vaughan, headmaster of Rugby school, to the assembled members in 1914.[120] Vaughan used the excuse of desirable war economies to curtail expenditure and in 1916 the War Economies Sub-committee reported that at schools associated with the Conference team caps, blazers, jerseys, and scarves were being discontinued.

The Great War was seen by some as a watershed in the history of public school games. J. P. Graham, the Uppingham master, with others, considered that the old world of security, stability and order had gone forever.[121] He noted that virtually no foreign matches and competitions took place after a while and the abolition of the periodic days of festivity and reunion, hallowed by long established custom inevitably broke cherished traditions. If the old certainties were gone, and old traditions lost, the war economies were not permanent, and while it would seem that the eventual austerities of the 1930s,[122] the ever widening choice of activity in schools and the increasing academic emphasis together ensured that the lavish spectacles of pre-war years were no longer the norm, the house system and the school teams remained and the symbols associated with them, although muted and perhaps increasingly less symbolic of loyalty and status, also remained.[123] It was only after the Second World War, for example, that the status of the Harrow athlete and the associated symbols declined in number and importance. Even as late as 1950 it was recorded: 'Those who have won distinction at school sport wear different coloured scarves, blue for cricket, blue and grey for rugger, blue and white for footer . . . and many others which make up a dazzling array of colours together. Anyone who knows the significance of every scarf has learnt a lot.'[124]

The daily acts of worship which were once a feature of the education of Christian gentlemen in the English public school were one effective means of emphasising and identifying hierarchical levels in the school – through difference in dress, seating, order of arrival and departure, duties and responsibilities.[125] The systematic reiteration of social position involved in daily chapel attendances are a fascinating aspect of status differentiation to the student of the social role of symbolism. Yet there exists a detailed record at Harrow of an even more elaborate and intensive system of segregation by symbolism (which in less sophisticated form existed in all the schools) associated particularly with the house, and by means of which the pre-eminent status of the athlete received due emphasis. Arnold Lunn has asserted that Edwardian Harrow 'was a society intensely occupied with trivial interests to the entire exclusion of all intellectual appeals, and all absurdly serious about their own rights of precedence over each other. The various claims of time in the school, athletic prowess and even official school rank were graded with meticulous accuracy'.[126] Lunn's house was the Knoll and the house rule books for the period 1909–42,[127] still happily extant, reveal that things changed little after his departure.

All the large Harrow houses evolved similar rules governing the dress and behaviour of their members and those of the Knoll are typical statements about relationships between pupils and the nature of the boy society. What these books, 'instruments of semi-legalised tyranny',[128] symbolised, was a caste society in which position was precisely defined and the athletes were the Brahmins.

In his *English Saga 1840–1940* the historian, Sir Arthur Bryant, recorded that 'the ritual . . . of a great public school was as intricate and finely woven as a Beethoven sonata'.[129] He drew his experience first hand from the Knoll where he resided after Arnold Lunn. He did not exaggerate. An incredible array of ritual observances associated with hierarchical positions are set out in the rule books, dealing with such activities as dressing, fagging, praying and cooking; and with areas such as the garden, the library and the house steps. The principle of organisation was simple. It involved what Stephen Foot labelled 'keeping under', and what is more colloquially referred to as the pecking order. House members were stratified by age, by prefectorial responsibilities and by athletic accomplishment.

As with the rhetoric of cohesion, identity, patriotism, and morality to be considered in chapter 8 these symbols of status call for detailed examination. Only in this way can the elaborate nature of the system be fully appreciated. Bluer[130] buttons illustrate the principle of 'keeping under'. The Knoll rule book states: 'It is a one year priv. [privilege] to have the bottom button of one's bluer undone [and] a three summer priv. to have all the buttons of one's bluer undone.' In such small but significant ways the caste system was regulated. Obeisance to the fashions of dominance and subservience was enforced by beatings.

The privileges at the apex of the hierarchy where the athlete resided were of two kinds: those of status and comfort. The first category included: 'It is a fez [holder of a football cap] priv. to wear an anklet showing for football, to wear a white scarf, to wear a white lacer for footer.' In the second category there occurred: 'It is a fez priv. to wear brown shoes for "exercise changed", not to wear garters of some sort for games, to wear a sweater for footer.' Of course there was overlap of function. This was often more apparent in other privileges. For example, it was a fez privilege to leave books on, or to sit on the fez bench outside the house or to have one's hands in one's pockets when in footer clothes. Naturally the house member of the Philathletic Club took precedence over the house games players, his position isolated by further rights. He was permitted, for example, to wear the collar of his bluer up when going up to school, except in the case of rain or when wearing a scarf, to wear a white shirt at 'exercise changed' and to carry a sweater up from house games. The most elevated status of all was given to the house member of the school cricket eleven. Instantly recognisable in his speckled straw hat, and 'manifestly a person of very considerable importance', a boy who had won his 'flannels' at Harrow, it has been reliably suggested, probably never possessed such power again.[131]

V

Not merely Harrovian cricketers but all the athletocrats of the period were, in fact, persons of considerable importance and enjoyed not only official privileges but also unofficial ones of their own making. 'In my house,' Lunn recalled, 'the Homeric heroes who led our cohorts into battle on the playing fields of Harrow disported themselves at ease during the hours set aside for homework, while the local intelligentsia did their homework for them.'[132] One of these heroes, Cadby, used to raffle his preparation for a week every Saturday evening.

Lunn's Cadby in the idiom of the time was a 'blood', a member of the games aristocracy. Such were 'the lords of creation'.[133] It was written of the Uppingham captain of games:

> Groundsmen will tremble at your slightest nod:
> Masters you'll treat with kind but lofty scorn:
> Fags will wish, writhing neath your iron rod,
> They'd never been born.[134]

With its usual sharp eye for the absurdities of life in 1887 *Punch* published a cartoon depicting a small public school boy urgently imploring his grandfather, 'General Sir George G.C.B., G.S.I., V.C., etc. etc. etc.', to put his hat a little straighter at the approach of a supercilious youth – captain of the eleven – complete with boater, cigarette and walking stick (see p. 90 above).

'Jerry' in the famous Harrow song was, according to the Old Harrovian S. W. Gore, more than an aristocrat; he was a monarch by virtue of his skill at games:[135]

> Champion at racquets and fives –
> Cricketers youthful and old
> Watching his 'cuts' and his 'drives'
> Football associates vow
> Jerry is worthy of praise –
> Verily Jerry is now
> Monarch of all he surveys.

In the photographs of the members of the Philathletic Club between 1885 and 1922[136] bow-tied, boatered, often moustached 'monarchs' sprawl about, arrogant and assured; laurel branches dangle from limp hands or are draped around strong necks and boaters are tilted in self-conscious affectation.

These complacent adolescents, the artless verse of Gore, the pointed humour of *Punch* and the envious quatrain from Uppingham stand historical guardians of a simple truth. After the fashion of the Calvinists there was a clear division in the public schools between the elect and the world. The distinction in this instance lay between 'bloods' and non-bloods.

> Before his face of haughty grace
> The ordinary mortal cowers
> A 'forty cap' has put the chap
> Into another world from ours.[137]

As suggested in these lines by Sorley on the Marlborough 'blood', it was a division between arrogance and deference, power and powerlessness, fame and insignificance. Those who possessed the virtues of physical courage and athletic talent were often themselves above the law and *de facto* if not *de jure* the instruments of that law.[138] In his verse biography *Summoned by Bells* John Betjeman recalled that in Marlborough's Upper School, 'Four captains ruled selected for their bravery and skill at games.'[139] A less well-known but more unflattering poetic description of the same 'bloods' goes:

> Alas for them, that wrapped in swaddling clothes
> Are A House's special care,
> Who dread the 'bloods' that turn their collars up,
> Wear coloured socks and paste their hair.
>
> Alas for them, I say, when plunged from thence
> To pan barbaric Upper School,

> Whose aspect grim within is not denied
> Where hardy, stubborn athletes rule.[140]

The discussion in *The Loom of Youth* concerning the respective merits of Meredith, the 'blood', and Daneham, the intellectual, throws light on the reason for this latitude. It was quite simple. Meredith was indispensable to the house by virtue of his splendid athletic gifts exemplified in his saving tackle on Freeman in Two Cock, and so was permitted considerable licence. Daneham, on the other hand, poor at games and enthusiastic only about fossils served no useful purpose[141] and thus merited no indulgence.

For Meredith and his fellow 'bloods' in other schools it was often the case that school rules ceased to exist. Fox ingenuously commented of Harrow in his *Public School Life: Harrow* that a fez guaranteed more freedom of action.[142] An indication of the extent of this freedom is given by Lunn: 'A head of house, if he was not himself a member of the athletocracy, was expected to content himself with the appearance of power and the control of the house.' Like his autobiographical hero Peter O'Connel in *The Harrovians*, Lunn was the exception to the rule and successfully defied tradition.[143] One of Howson's cheerful songs, however, told of the more common inspirational fantasy and for the few, the ultimate reality:

> And as fury grows prophetic
> I anticipate the hour
> When I soar by feats athletic
> To the shining ranks of power.[144]

One Harrovian sufferer pleading for a change in school values in which, compared to 'the triple blood', the scholar's name 'was simply mud' succinctly summed up the source of the anguish and the exaltation of generations:

> In corpore sano seems to us
> The essence of the syllabus.[145]

The power of the 'blood' was revealed in unusual ways. It was alleged, for example, that he could even overcome social class barriers. In 1912 in an article entitled 'Snobbishness in schools', *The Spectator* claimed that the snobbery in the public schools was one of athletic prowess not social rank and pointed to the popularity of Hornung's 'Jan' in *Fathers of Men* who, as a working-class boy, had won his place in the sun because he turned out to be a superb left-handed bowler.[146] Unfortunately a living as distinct from a fictional example could not be cited!

The 'blood's' approval, it seems, could even guarantee the success of unpopular innovations. C. H. P. Mayo, the Harrow master, once recounted how the school cadet corps languished on its introduction until the 'bloods' joined, and the corps came into its own.[147] His support could also ensure smooth classroom discipline. The First World War saw the unusual phenomenon of a lady teacher at Harrow, who, in later years, confessed that in class the chivalrous members of the eleven were the custodians of her authority. Not until their absence for matches did she note their dominance.[148]

The 'bloods' dominance was further underlined by the occasional success of his inferiors. The writer, Walter Sichel, was astonished when, having succeeded in the Balliol scholarship examination in 1872, he found himself clapped down the steps at Harrow. He could recall no other occasion when the school had accorded such an honour except for success in games and athletics.[149] And on the premature death of the captain of the school at Uppingham in 1902, a friend commented that he had raised the tone of the school wonderfully which seemed marvellous, for he was no cricketer.[150]

Finally, for the 'blood' academic ineptitude need be no obstacle to entry to the universities. At Edwardian Lancing, a rather clever pupil was somewhat surprised to find himself, a new boy, sitting in the fifth form next to the captain of the eleven who had already passed for Oxford. He quickly appreciated that little exertion was called for from him for the next few years.[151]

In two ostentatious ways – dress and walk – the 'bloods' publicised and symbolised their authority. At Harrow it was a 'blood's priv.' to sport fancy waistcoats, to display more than eight inches of shirt front and to walk in the middle of the high street. Such was his standing that even the captain of the school would never have dared to appear in a fancy waistcoat or walk down the middle of the road, reserved for the athletic heroes, unless he had achieved some distinction as a games player.[152] The predilection for coloured waistcoats and other things besides was also in evidence at Marlborough:

> If I were a school blood, sir,
> And you a wretched worm
> I'd strut by you, my fellow
> With boots of blazing yellow,
> With waistcoat, diamond stud, sir
> While you with awe would squirm.[153]

At Uppingham the 'bloods' walked arm in arm in fours and fives down the street, distinguished by their colourful clothing, scarf of red and blue and rolling haughty gait.[154]

A 'rolling haughty gait' was a distinctive feature of display; it was described by a cynical Marlburian as symptomatic of a disease contracted by the early winning of a school cap.[155] However, the conventional and successful took such mannerisms very seriously. The arrogant demeanour, the distinctive clothes, the affected walk were part of a general behaviour pattern referred to as 'swagger' or 'roll' and were established symbols of differentiation which allegedly created a sense of tradition and hierarchy. 'Swagger', pontificated a Harrovian editorial on one occasion, 'is a blessing when used by bigger fellows to strengthen their position. Gradation is a good thing. Small boys should be taught their place.'[156] To 'swagger' or 'roll' was a closely protected privilege. One Old Uppinghamian recalled that in his time a junior who put on 'roll' was merely chastised but for an older pupil who assumed the privileges of the 'blood' without due warrant 'real sanguinaries' lay in wait.[157] These involved the punishment known as 'Over the railings'. The railings in question were on the east side of a steep rise on the way to the Hill houses above the main school. The procedure as carried out for one such 'execution' has been described by Rome:

Shortly before the luncheon hour some two hundred boys . . . waited in a silent throng . . . close to the place of punishment. Slightly apart from them stood a small knot of praepostors and 'bloods'. Every eye of the crowd was fixed on an empty Scale Hill. Suddenly a single boy appeared walking slowly towards the waiting crowd. As he reached the spot, a small group of executioners moved forward in complete silence, lifted him unresistingly by his shoulders and legs and dropped him over the railings onto the steep slope below. Without a word the onlookers dispersed to their various houses leaving the victim to look after himself. He had been guilty of a degree of roll which his peers considered unbecoming on his part.[158]

The isolation, humiliation and helplessness of the offender in the face of the school heroes and their camp followers is well depicted in Rome's description. The ritual must have been a singularly effective means of control.

The ostentatiously vaunted status of the athlete was balanced by the public stigma of the notoriously unathletic.[159] One brave group of pupils in the unenviable position of the stigmatised inverted the symbol system of athleticism in a pitiful attempt to lay the spirit of Sparta. Insulated by their irreversible alienation they became reckless exhibitionists flaunting stigma symbols to the exasperation of the conventional. These were the famous Marlborough aesthetes, among them John Betjeman, Anthony Blunt and Louis MacNeice,[160] who dangled colourful silk handkerchiefs as they walked down the aisle in chapel and played 'catch' with bright coloured balls through the traditional games of their well-adjusted and fully-assimilated colleagues. They suffered; but at least made a small gesture of defiance.[161]

A major reason why the 'blood' achieved such pre-eminence and was permitted to create and adopt such a wide range of symbolic trappings of high status was that he *himself* was a symbol. In this role he became one of Mead's 'significant others' who provided lesser schoolboys with the means of perceiving and defining the world. They took their standards from him. He was aided by the twin forces of idealism and romanticism. The bombardment of symbolic imagery to which the public school boy was subjected left no doubt that while some types of behaviour revealed moral adequacy – the clean break for the line, the chanceless century, others displayed, for all to see, moral inadequacy – the funked tackle and the consistent duck. 'It is a mistake to think that boys worship the athletic hero because of his athletics; it is because of those qualities that go into the making of a good athlete,' claimed the Dean of Bristol in a eulogistic speech on the virtues of the public school boy to the Marlborough boys during the Great War.[162] Many examples have been quoted in this study of the alleged qualities believed inherent in the athlete and reiterated time and again by bishops, headmasters, field marshals and similar establishment figures.

The simple-minded, well-meaning romanticism of the boys' literature of the time was also a potent means of image dissemination. *Union Jack, Chums, Boys' Own, The Rover*, each depicted the 'blood' as the apotheosis of manly virtue. One typical example suffices for them all: Albert Mayne in *The Union Jack* tale of Rawdon School.[163] Here physical power and moral soundness are inseparable. Albert was strong, athletic, broad-shouldered, with honest brown eyes and fine open forehead. Throughout the story he displays, 'coolness, science and dash' in his defeats of other schools, but also moral courage in adversity, compassion in supremacy and modesty in success. *Suaviter in modo, fortiter in re*[164] was the standard motto of such heroes.

Yet in the schools harassed liliputians of the lower forms often saw the 'blood' in a less noble light:

Der Scheinkönig

Hush'd all is hush'd. No solemn trump resounds
To mete the footfalls of his proud advance.
Stately he struts; his grandeur knows no bounds
As on some worshipper he casts his glance.

Ye gods and little fishes, bow your heads!
For here comes one far mightier than a god.
Observe his waistcoat flashing blues and reds:
Notice his azure cuff exposed to view.

'Why walks he thus?' I really cannot tell.
'Why is he haughty?' Ask me no such thing.
I know not: only this I know full well.
I'd rather die, than ape a pseudo-king. [165]

An injection of reality is also provided by a statement of considerable frankness by an American physical educationalist who toured the public schools in the 1920s. He suggested that perhaps the nearest equivalent for 'blood' in American slang was 'bully'. He considered that certainly the 'blood's' aim at school was 'to dominate, if not domineer', an objective he achieved by a mixture of brute force, physical power and a reputation for dissipation. He concluded that he was not a pleasant type of schoolboy to contemplate. [166]

VI

Foreign matches, old boys' teams and the Cock House Cup, model housemasters, colours and 'bloods' add up to an elaborate, extensive and dominant symbol system in support of ideological fashion, which demonstrated success, moulded aspirations and inspired imitation. By means of this system the public school boy focused on and remembered essential values, filtering out the inessential.

Self-government within the house system was the fertile source of symbolism. For the definition of reality was tightly controlled by those whose values were athletic. Power was given to the boys for realistic and idealistic reasons – it was sanctioned by a political acumen which appreciated the need to divide to rule, by a very human desire to enjoy the reduced labour ensuing from delegation and by a sometimes sincere belief that externals mirror inner virtue.

And where power was not given it was often taken. In the hands of the boys, aided and abetted by sympathetic or indifferent masters, sporting symbols and ceremonial proliferated. In this way a favoured ideology was sustained by an incredible assortment of concrete actions and objects, animate and inanimate.

8

Play up and play the game: the rhetoric of cohesion, identity, patriotism and morality

At the Harrow speech day of 1907 Dr Wood, the headmaster, ended a self-congratulatory eulogy on the public schools with the statement that their motto was 'Run straight and play the game'.[1] This and similar expressions, 'Keep a straight bat' and 'It's not cricket', were common catch phrases of the public school culture of the late nineteenth and early twentieth centuries. And they were part of a wider vocabulary which drew on the games field for analogy, experience and truth.

Sporting prosody was a noticeable feature of Victorian and Edwardian upper-class Britain, so much so that P. G. Wodehouse once claimed the distinction of being the only literate male in the United Kingdom who had never written a song about football, rhyming 'leather' with 'weather';[2] and Siegfried Sassoon's first published poem, while a schoolboy at Marlborough, was a cricketing poem, 'The Extra Inch', in the magazine *Cricket*.[3] Typical examples of the genre are Alan R. Haig-Brown's[4] *Sporting Sonnets and Other Verses* (1903), Norman Gale's *Cricket Songs* (1894) and *More Cricket Songs* (1905) and Hedley Peek's *The Poetry of Sport* (1902). *Punch* too, at this time, was fond of sporting doggerel, albeit of a whimsical nature. In a single month (September 1894), for example, it included such verses as 'Wet Willow', 'On a Clumsy Cricketer', 'A Song for a Slogger' and 'Bowl Me No More'.

The literary critic would consider most of this verse execrable. G. F. Bradby's 'Song of Chiltern' in *The Lanchester Tradition*, which without 'lapsing into poetry' maintained 'a fair rhythm and a high level of imbecility', is a marvellous caricature that cruelly exposes the frailties of many a sincere creation:

179

John Buss was a farrier bold,
And he turned his sweat into drops of gold;
He fought hard battles, and when he died,
He left a school for his country's pride,
The best of schools, that has won renown
From Chiltern chimes to the frontier town.

Chorus: John Buss, John of Us,
            Played good cricket and made no fuss.[5]

While the literary quality of such rhyming is irrelevant to this study of athleticism, the verse itself is of considerable significance. Its primary purpose was to provide assertions, paeans and exhortations for the propagation of the ideology. The doggerel constituted a communal symbolism which maintained a belief system.[6] J. E. C. Welldon once wrote, 'If anyone who was a stranger to Harrow, would fain learn what is the essential character of this famous school, it is . . . to the school songs I would refer him.'[7] Most of these songs, as we have already discovered, were written by Edward Bowen, and many were devoted to the nobility of physical activity. Of forty-one songs in Bowen's biography by his nephew, twenty-six were devoted wholly or largely to games. Welldon saw Bowen's verse, which represented in Julian Amery's words 'a simple, straightforward philosophy of the strenuous life', as representative of an upper-class philosophy of education. Such was the value of this symbolism that one of Welldon's early actions as headmaster was to give Bowen 'three days special leave' to compose a memorial to F. S. Jackson, the Harrovian, who in the Lord's Match of 1888 took eleven wickets and scored twenty-one and fifty-nine. The result was 'A Gentleman's-a-Bowling'.[8]

Winston Churchill, Arthur Bryant, H. A. Vachell and many other Harrovians have written in the same vein as Welldon of their school songs.[9] 'Harrow songs,' Vachell asserted, 'make for something greater than entertainment. They are redolent with the public school spirit, a clarion call to strenuous endeavour, an injunction to work and play with faith and courage, to fight against the odds . . . to sacrifice self, if need be, to the common end.'[10] Bowen was, in fact, a spokesman for an era. His values are those of a whole culture but most of the parochial literature which symbolised this culture lies unsifted and forgotten in school magazines. Their pages, often discoloured with age, contain a strangely touching dogmatism and moral fervour linked to games quite alien to educationalists of the second half of the twentieth century. Consideration of the rhetoric of this certainty and zeal is indispensable if we wish to understand the unique mixture of emotionalism, innocence, myopia and rigidity that once characterised a now ridiculed and despised ideology, if we wish to expose the depth of feeling and the strength of belief embedded in the works of poets such as Bowen, and if we wish to explore the close relationship between action and language.

It is now a familiar argument that the 'speech'[11] of a culture, namely all forms of its language including poetry, song and prose, orders the experience of its members, shapes their view of reality and determines their actions. Some fifty years ago, Edward Sapir, the distinguished American anthropologist, drew attention to the interaction of language and life style. 'The real world,' he claimed, 'is to a large extent built upon the language habits of the group . . . We see and hear and . . . experience very largely . . . because the language habits of our community pre-dispose certain choices of interpretation.'[12] More recently the sociologist, Basil Bernstein, has written that language is a major process in the transmission of social genes and in this way determines and reflects collective values, ways of acting and the social structure itself.[13] Such an insight, of course, is not restricted to the social scientist. It is a truth equally well appreciated by the man of letters. 'Words have power,' wrote Aldous Huxley, 'to mould men's thinking, to canalise their feelings, to direct their willing and acting.'[14] The nineteenth-century poet William Cory urged his readers to doubt whether in human experience an idea becomes complete until it has found words in which to embody itself, adding the useful caveat that not to appreciate this fact is to indulge in a 'peculiarly idle form of intellectual self-deceit'.[15]

What is attempted then in the following pages is a portrayal of the rhetoric of a specific but now defunct ideology,[16] together with an analysis of its role in determining reality, values and behaviour.[17]

For approximately seventy years between 1860 and 1930 at Harrow, Lancing, Loretto, Marlborough, Stonyhurst and Uppingham, an assortment of headmasters, masters, old boys and pupils wove around their games and playing fields a sometimes attractive, frequently naive, and occasionally ridiculous web of romance and chivalry through both published prose and verse,[18] and articles and songs in school magazines. The schools vary in the amount of effort devoted to the subject. As in other matters they display individuality. Stonyhurst predictably provides very little 'literary' material on athleticism, particularly of a 'poetic' nature. This is, in itself, a revealing aspect of alternative ideological commitment – for the unique feature of Stonyhurst verse is its religious theme. Instead of such verses as 'Dropped from the Team', 'He did his Best' and 'Roundel on Tackling', we find 'Pentecost', 'The Garments of God' and 'The Ballad of our Lady's Mantle'. Loretto on the other hand is especially rich in sporting verse.

The verbal symbols of ideological commitment to be found in the various sources fall into four major categories: the rhetoric of cohesion, of sexual identity, of patriotism and above all, of morality. Messages of loyalty, masculinity, chauvinism and decency occur and recur. They constitute an unmistakable and unequivocal blueprint for action. Reproduction of the actual verse and prose of the period would seem to be the perfect way in which the unique nature of these messages can be captured and thrust before the perhaps startled and incredulous inhabitants of an age so far removed in preoccupation. For this reason illustrative lines and passages are liberally presented below.

II

Creators of the famous quality of *esprit de corps*, allegedly instilled by the public school system in its Golden Age, developed an extensive battery of literary symbols of an athletic nature emphasising unity. At Uppingham, Loretto and Harrow, headmasters and assistant masters put pen to paper to catch the spirit of those intense feelings of solidarity generated by energetic or skilful happenings on the Upper, Pinkie or the Upper Sixth.[19]

In the early years of Uppingham school, Edward Thring produced five school songs: 'The Cricket Song', 'The Fives Song', 'The Rockingham Match', 'The Uppingham Chorus', and 'Echoes of Uppingham'.[20] The first three joyfully describe the pleasures of bodily exercise, and all five were designed to create a corporate identity for the school. In his 'Rockingham Match', which celebrated an annual cricket fixture with a local team attended by the whole school, Thring embraced his pupil–players and spectators metaphorically with a proud paternal gesture of ownership:

> Blue caps, where are my blue caps?
> They marshall fair
> On yon green hill.

It was a conscious and calculated attempt to form a community. Thring noted in his diary: 'I trust very much to our literature in days to come keeping the school true to high principles and giving them *esprit de corps*'[21] and, in an edition of the *School Songs* published in 1858, he praised the songs as being a 'genial solvent' breaking down barriers and promoting integration.[22]

At Loretto, an enthusiastic promotor of *esprit de corps* was the rugby blue and international, H. B. Tristram, initially assistant master, later vice-gerant (acting head) and eventually headmaster on Almond's death. The traditional school song, 'The Old Red Coat',[23] 'Going Strong' and 'Go Like Blazes' are typical products of his desire to propagate the virtues of loyalty and fellowship through the medium of the sporting lyric. In 'The Old Red Coat' he attempted to rouse institutional patriotism with the familiar technique of symbolic reiteration of symbolism:

> There are plenty of colours for others to wear
> But never a one with the Red can compare,
> Whether faded or fresh it gladdens the sight
> For we all give our hearts for the Old Red and White[24]

and the chorus reinforced both unity and uniqueness:

> To the Old Red Coat, and the open throat
> And the School where we can wear it,
> And we always shall bless the free jolly dress
> And be glad that we still can share it.

Tristram attempted to fuse the emotions of pupils at school; in his famous 'Forty Years On' Edward Bowen caught a dimension of public school solidarity which was far from exclusive to Harrow – the fusion of past and present. A fusion developed through the games field more than anywhere else:

> Routs and discomfitures, rushes and rallies,
> Bases attempted, and rescued and won,
> Strife without anger, and art without malice,
> How will it seem to you, forty years on?
> Then, you will say, not a feverish minute
> Strained the weak heart and the wavering knee,
> Never the battle raged hottest, but in it,
> Neither the last nor the faintest were we![25]

'Echoes of dreamland' and 'visions of boyhood' linked many old alumni with their school. Through their nostalgic verses they immortalised the strenuous activities of former generations, and sanctioned those of the new with their reiteration of a belief in the delight and soundness of their own boyhood experiences. For these traditionalists the passage of time was unwanted and its attempted annulment resulted in the symbolism of renewal and recreation:[26]

> Oh give me back that golden time again
> When youth ran riot through the heart and brain.
> Even now I seem to hear the rival cheers
> That tell our House match days of hopes and fears.
> The gathering tramp of forwards sweeping on,
> The net's exultant hiss which shows our goal is won.[27]

> When we see the Lorettonian, we are boys and young once more,
> And our thoughts fly back to Scotland from some far Pacific shore,
> From the neighbouring green island
> Or some distant frontier highland
> And we long to see again the red jersey once we wore.[28]

> Forgotten cheers are in our ears,
> Again we play our matches,
> And memory swells with wizard spells
> Our bygone scores and catches;
> Again we rush across the slush –
> A pack of breathless faces –
> And charge and fall, and see the ball
> Fly whizzing through the bases.[29]

Unsurprisingly, former pupils proved to be zealous guardians of tradition and fierce, if, on occasion, unsuccessful upholders of hallowed manliness. The introduction of rugby football at Stonyhurst inspired one old boy to write 'The Game of our Fathers' – a poem extolling the virtues of a hardy and idiosyncratic form of football. It was a passionate attempt to sustain tradition and to continue the past into the future in the face of a desire in the school to ape the southern schools and the Protestant elite. Ejaculations of dismay are mixed with impassioned appeals for a change of heart:

> Your hands are in your pockets boys,
> Your legs are lazy now.
> . . . .
> Avaunt your soccer's mincing grace
> Your rugger's rigid commonplace
> Line out my splendid Stonyhurst,
> Line out there for the game.[30]

In other cases intense memories and the resigned acceptance of the passing of time are to be found, in conjunction with a desire to return to the womb of Alma Mater:

> In city streets
> In desert heat
> Or beneath the Aurora's flame
> Quite an ordinary game
> On Rutland fields, lying cold and wet
> Some there shall be who will never forget
> Never forget – Never forget.[31]

Few, it seems, grew old without a nostalgic yearning for the years of youth on green or muddy games fields. But summer days appear to have had an especially evocative quality and stimulated attempts through 'womb-regressive imagery' to close the widening gap of the years and to recapture the sweetness of the crack of the cricket bat:

> Or even the month of June has passed
> Old Boys think of the days that have been.
> Summer by summer their thoughts are cast
> Over the years and the miles between,
> Back to the Upper and scented limes
> To matches lost and matches won,
> Boundaries hit in far off times,
> To carefree days in the summer sun.[32]

Thring, in his song, 'The Old Boys' Match', composed in his later years, portrays a carefully depicted idyll of adolescence sanctified by the old boy in maturity. It is always sunshine 'for the match of matches' and the days are splendid with 'sunny hits and sunny catches' through the 'sunny hours' of the 'sunny game'. The repetition might be tedious but it is not ineffectual in creating simple images of delight for unsophisticated boys of all ages.

The Uppingham Rovers Cricket Club was created in 1863. Membership was restricted to those chosen from the school eleven and from old boys of outstanding cricketing ability. Its annual dinner was an opportunity for a ritualistic indulgence in topical sporting lyrics composed for the occasion, celebrating Uppingham heroes and heroic incidents of the playing fields. It lies with the Uppingham Rovers to sum up the cohesive role of the verbal symbolism associated with these playing fields in a short verse entitled 'The Same Old Game' in which projection of present into future is well depicted:

The same old game
The same old game
To forget or forgo it were a shame.
When we are past and gone
The young ones coming on
Will carry on the same old game.[33]

III

As a schoolboy at Winchester, the poet Lionel Johnson played the role of wan aesthete to perfection; he was reputed to have read all the books in the school library, embraced Buddhism and drunk eau de cologne for his amusement.[34] In later years, his schooldays conjured up pre-Raphaelite visions of 'cloisters touched with white moonlight'. For those more prosaic, but in their own way equally intense, schooldays were often associated with a less exotic hedonism which carried the added attraction of an acceptable and secure sexual identity, closely linked with enthusiasm for games and defined in the imagery of 'manliness' used assertively by juvenile versifiers, schoolmaster songsters and headmaster preachers.

The elements of sexual identity and legitimate sensuality are inseparable from the worship of games during the period under discussion.[35] To be manly was a condition that exuded the physical, but, at the same time, it was an asexual 'physicality' extended into early manhood, in which sexual knowledge and experience were taboo. The rationale for this is provided by the public school master who argued for games instead of girls:

I believe that in England we have groped our way unconsciously to a great truth in man's development; it is that 'slow growth is the best', and the splendid products of our Public Schools and Universities in the past have been due, I suggest, primarily to the fact that the period of boyhood pastimes has been prolonged for as long as possible. If this is true, and I know I am not alone in my opinion, then aping the man is a tendency which in a schoolboy should be sternly checked.[36]

The Old Harrovian prime minister, Stanley Baldwin, delighted in this simple tenet extending it to embrace intellectual development. 'Thanks be to Heaven,' he declared at the 1923 annual dinner of the Harrow Association, 'there is in every English boy an unconscious but impregnable resistance to every form of pressure made by any schoolmaster who works him too hard or tries to put too much inside him . . . It is to this that Englishmen owe so largely the careful cultivation of their physical growth. They let the body grow, undisturbed by mental storm until they get into their early twenties, and then they go into the world able to graft the sane mind on to the sane body.'[37] It is certainly an interesting theory, but perhaps an obscure critic of the public school came closer to the truth when he suggested that the chief weakness of the system lay in the fact that it did not so much help as retard growth: it related prestige to physique[38] rather than intellect. Furthermore while the 'slow growth' theory encapsulated a puritanical ideal, the reality could be quite different.[39]

Ironically sensuality was not only permitted, it was demanded; but it was a sensuality in which physical contact was channelled into football mauls, and emotional feelings into hero worship of the athletic 'blood'. No one better than Edward Thring, muscular Christian *par excellence*, caught the ethos of circumscribed Christian hedonism that was the expected life style of the cloistered young man of the English public school. He also added the interesting ingredients of pain and sublimation. The three motifs, masculinity, sensuality and pain, are found in the first verse of his 'Fives Song' in which the vitality and the exuberance of the muscular Christian are beautifully portrayed:

> Oh the spirit in the ball
> Dancing round about the wall
> In your eye and out again
> Ere there's time to feel the pain
> Hands and fingers all alive
> Doing duty each for five.[40]

Thring returned to the theme of pain and masculinity in his published sermons, but his interest was not idiosyncratic. Almond too, thought pain a necessary initiation into manhood; Edward Lyttelton bemoaned the removal of the element of pain in cricket, due to the development of smooth pitches which made the game 'comparatively worthless'. F. B. Malim considered golf and lawn tennis undesirable school games because they were insufficiently painful.[41] And then in the second verse of Thring's 'Fives Song' occur the curious lines which suggest a powerful subliminatory urge quite in keeping with the Pauline ambivalence to the flesh of the intense Victorian Christian:

> Bodies, bodies are no more
> All is hit and spring and score.[42]

The various themes recur in Thring's 'Football Song' in which the heavy, daily load of sobriety and responsibility are lost in an amnesia of physical effort:

> See the madness surge and rise,
> Tries twice sixty hit the skies
> Shrieks of triumph, shrieks of woe
> Heads like nuts together go.
> Cowards staring, cracking shins,
> Rubbing hands and no-one wins;
> Heels are flying into air
> Head and shoulders anywhere
> Now the charm is working free
> Brad-awl paint, and mad ball glee.[43]

The song contains an important reminder to the Victorian and Edwardian schoolboy, namely, cowards merely stare, heroes act. That such corybantic activity as Thring describes might cause the imaginative and less robust to stare in amazement and sensibly refrain is a quite unacceptable viewpoint, and we are back once again to that simple linear relationship between physical courage and moral worth – a relationship that represented essential masculinity to the initiated, the moral overtones of which will be considered more closely later in this chapter.

Bowen's 'Tom' contains a further illuminating set of images which starkly depict the upper-class Englishman's equivalent of Latin American *machismo*:

> Base is the player who stops
> Fight, till the fighting is o'er;
> Who follows up till he drops,
> Panting and limping and sore?
> Tom![44]

On the field, Tom, uncomplicated in action and aspiration, crashes through the opposition with force and fury, and off the field his noblest ambition is to develop an 'eleven of Toms' to win glory for his house.

Investigators of the literature of public school life will look in vain for the hero as intellectual, dilettante or cosmopolitan. The heroes of the time were, in Kipling's words, 'Gentlemen of England, cleanly bred'. Their pleasures were wonderfully stoical, their virtues grounded in the physical:

> And here's to the team with the old fashioned pluck
> Not wild in good fortune, nor beat by ill luck
> Three cheers for Lancing that turns out such men
> They've done it before and they'll do it again![45]

'Thank God for sport,' carolled the public school master R. C. Taylor in *A Housemaster's Letters*, 'when you see the average public school boy leave the University with his fine physique, clear skin and eyes and a sense of discipline,' which is not 'such a bad outfit for a life voyage'.[46] Such a boy had his limitations, he acknowledged, but demanded that contempt be reserved for those who spent their days 'in a maze of fancy waistcoats, sporting papers, coloured socks, actresses' photographs, theatre programmes, action bridge, billiards, motor cars, race meetings, visits to town, stern notes from College deans, general vacuity – and an occasional lecture'. In the *Dark Blue*, in 1872, W. Turley, urging support for muscularity, argued that 'a nation of effeminate, enfeebled bookworms scarcely forms the most effective bulwark of a nation's liberties'.[47] Some years later Norman Gale inquired:

> What in the world is the use of a creature
> All flabbily bent on avoiding the Pitch,
> Who wanders about, with a sob in each feature
> Devising a headache, inventing a stitch?
> There surely would be a quick end to my joy
> If possessed of that monster – a feminine boy.[48]

Punch, however, took a refreshingly sly poke at the simple, muscular idealism exemplified by Taylor, Turley and Gale, while acknowledging its existence at the 'varsities' among both students *and* dons:

> Who cares a hang for a first in Greats
> And Academic glory,
> Dull bookworm, come and see the sights
> And shut *de Oratore*!
> Learn what a thing a man might be
> And think to win a pewter
> More splendid than a first, like me your Tutor.[49]

An Uppingham song from the period in similar vein, but wholly conventional in approval, goes:

> A pound of weight
> With an empty pate
> Is far more gain
> Than a pound of brain
> It tells in scrum
> And makes things hum:
> Can heel and screw
> Which Greek can't do.

No sterner a defender of the games field as a creator of that curious paradox, asexual masculinity, could be found than the Clifton headmaster, J. M. Wilson. In his much-publicised essay *Morality in Public Schools and its Relation to Religion* he sadly asserted that parents who kept their boys off the playing field would ask themselves in regret why they had become poor, strutting creatures.[50] He urged co-operation with the schoolmaster in enforcing games. If parents did not provide support, they would be exposing their sons to risks a thousand times worse than getting their shins kicked. He followed up this advice with an unconsciously amusing, but, considering the frenetic prudery of the period, entirely logical defence of the conversational shortcomings of public school clientele: 'Did you ever think what a priceless boon is the innocence of school games as a subject of conversation? You are perhaps bored by the incessant talk about matches and runs, and place kicks, and scrummages; you think games occupy a disproportionate share of the boy's mind. You may be thankful this is so. What do French boys talk about?'[51] His stern conviction was appreciated. In his obituary it was stated that boys admired his enthusiasm for games, and parents felt secure in 'his moral earnestness'.[52]

Loretto verse is replete with images of robust masculinity. 'J.M.', for example, in a verse entitled 'Floreat Loretto' celebrating the school's success at producing university blues with adequate degrees specified that it was done 'without unwholesome cram'. At Loretto, he emphasised, there was one type that would never be tolerated, namely:

> The scholar without chest or limbs
> Who can do nought but read.[53]

The same point was reiterated in the *Lorettonian* in the following year:

> Puny students burn the oil of midnight lamps and strain
> Their addled senses till they swim, and every thought is pain,
> But give to me the healthy frame, the brain from cobwebs free,
> The struggles of the playing field, the drive from off the tee;
> The *sano mens* without the rest must be a rope of sand
> For Health and Education must still go hand in hand.[54]

Boys at Loretto were reminded that to 'Go Like Blazes' was suitably representative of the manly breed, that 'to be always on the ball', 'to carry every maul' and always 'go strong from first to last' was the expected behaviour of Lorettonians down Pinkie Hill and in life. The ongoing nature of the proud tradition was stipulated in the last verse of Tristram's exhortation:

> Here's to the gallant souls, who've worn the jersey red,
> Here's to all the captains who the School Fifteen have led,
> Here's to all who've got their pluck, and in their footsteps tread![55]

In short, the perfect representative of public school masculinity during the period of athleticism was aggressive, brave, decent in thought and deed, and intellectually unostentatious. The ideal emulated by pupils and admired by many staff was Bowen's 'Jack' who:

> Dines in pads for the practice sake
> Goes with a bat to bed.[56]

The stereotype is unsubtle; but the couplet is scarcely hyperbolic. The image is depicted time and again over the decades. The dogmatism of the language is total; the imagery is equally inflexible. In time, this extremism ensured reaction and revulsion, but it would scarcely be audacious to suggest that it structured the reality of the simple-minded, the unreflective and the conformist to a considerable degree. 'The Man to Look For' typifying the public school ideal of manhood of the time, which many strove to achieve, has been well described in this verse by W. E. Remisol:

> He mayn't be good at Latin, he mayn't be good at Greek
> But he's every bit a sportsman, and not a bit a sneak,
> For he's the man of Scotland, and England, Ireland, Wales;
> He's the man who weighs the weight in the Empire's mighty scales.
> He'll play a game of rugger in the spirit all should have;
> He'll make a duck at cricket, and come smiling to the pav.,
> Now he's the man to look for, he's sturdy through and through;
> He'll come to call of country and he'll come the first man too.[57]

IV

Throughout the years of imperial expansion, dominance and defence, the Lacedaemonians of the public schools were continually reminded of their patriotic martial duty, of their role as military leaders and of the close relationship between games and war:

> If you should ask me why 'tis that in England
> Schoolboys are taught the king of games to play,
> As well as learning French and mathematics
> ('A beastly waste of time' perchance you'll say).

> Not so, not so, my gentle reader, listen!
> Turn for a time, and give it sober thought;
> That war out of which we came victorious
> Was largely won upon the fields of sport.
>
> Could our young men have turned out so quickly;
> Well trained for all the hardships of the front,
> Had they not become quite well accustomed
> Of hard and nasty knocks to bear the brunt?
>
> No, they could not, gentle, thoughtless reader,
> Study's necessary in its way,
> But not more so than are games like cricket,
> To keep old England where she is today.[58]

Humble verse in school magazines and national journals, sermons, biographies, novels and letters to the press, down the years, all stressed the similarity of endeavour involved in battle and match. The catastrophes of the army in the Crimea were attributed in part by 'A Templar' to defects in the cricket system at Eton. Improve one and you would remedy the other.[59] By the end of the century, Norman Gale was inclined to believe the reform of public school cricket had been successful, and the consequences for British arms improved:

> See in bronzing sunshine
> Thousands of good fellows,
> Such as roll the world along,
> Such as cricket mellows!
> These shall keep the Motherland
> Safe amid her quarrels;
> Lucky lads, plucky lads,
> Trained to snatch at laurels![60]

Football, too, was a direct form of military education. Harrow boys were compelled to play football so that they would make good warriors observed a latter-day Herodotus recording the school's mores in 1879.[61] A similar point of view was expressed in the *Lorettonian*: 'Football brings out all the qualities that ought to be innate in a brave soldier', it asserted with confidence.[62] And one Lancing master wrote of 'The Football Player':

> . . . the use on peaceful playing fields
> Of supple limbs and ever-quickening eye
> Win for him laurels in a sterner game
> Giving resource and strength that never yields,
> Making him such that he would rather die
> Than soil the honour of his country's name.[63]

Both footballers and cricketers were celebrated in this Marl-borough College song:

> Vivat vis pedariorum!
> Vivat Undecimvirorum!
> Folle, pila, seu tormento,
> Civitati propugnanto.[64]

Inexperienced youth learnt their lessons on school fields and bravely and innocently went off to fight. On the outbreak of the Boer War, the *Lorettonian* printed a poem 'To Loretto from her Volunteers' in which the young heroes on the veld assured the school that though the colours might be changed from red to khaki:

> For the bowling we are ready
> And will keep the right foot steady
> And try not to flinch as they hum past our head.[65]

Those at home were reassured that their sons possessed the neces-sary stoicism and courage, that it was not forgotten that even when the scrums got roughish and the hacks freely distributed, Loretto boys never whined, always led the charge and appreciated their expendability for the good of the side. The Stonyhurst magazine appealed to a similar breed of volunteers of a later era for the same response, when it informed Old Stonyhurstians of Kitchener's army that,

> The ancient trust is yours to keep or break
> And in your hands by old tradition set,
> The name of English sportsmen lies at stake.[66]

The ingenuous talent of authors and poets of the Great War period for linking symbols of summer afternoons with the bloody agonies of trench warfare startles the modern reader familiar with the bitter honesty and savage cynicism of Sassoon, Graves, Owen and Sorley. Shortly after the Great War, the Old Uppinghamian E. W. Hornung published a small book of war poetry which con-tained a marvellously pure example of such ingenuousness, a poem entitled 'Lord's Leave 1915' in which the symbols of school games were extensively used to depict the face of war. The first two verses offer a flavour of the whole:

> No Lord's this year: no silken lawn on which
> A dignified and dainty throng meanders.
> The Schools take guard upon a fiercer pitch
> Somewhere in Flanders.

> Bigger the cricket here: yet some who tried
> In vain to earn a colour while at Eton,
> Have found a place upon an England side
> That can't be beaten.[67]

The poem is saturated with cricketing parlance. The public school boy faces the Hun demon bowler, his field gun trained upon the stumps pumping Krupp's shells from 'a concrete grandstand far beyond the boundary'. The stars blink down from the pavilion and the conditions are atrocious – 'no screen and too much mud for cricket lovers'; but there is no appealing against the light in this match.

It was on the eve of the First World War, with a strong premonition of coming events, that Hornung provided another pure nugget from his unique vein of war-as-games literature:

For here now 'we see through a glass darkly', so darkly that try as we will, we cannot see the score; so darkly that we can hardly see to play the game; but not so darkly that we are going to appeal against the light – nor so darkly that we cannot be sportsmen and glory in the difficulties we have to overcome. Who wants an easy victory? Who wants a life of full-pitches to leg? Do you think the Great Scorer is going to give you four runs every time for those? I believe with all my heart and soul that in this splendidly difficult Game of Life it is just the cheap and easy triumph which will be written in water on the score-sheet. And the way we played for our side, in the bad light, on the difficult pitch: the way we backed up and ran the other man's runs; . . . surely, surely it is these things above all that will count, when the innings is over, in the Pavilion of Heaven.[68]

The simple and foolish image of public school boys as sportsmen–soldiers is a recurring one in the literature of the schools. Another Old Uppinghamian, Charles Byles, for example, wrote of the young officers of the Great War in a farcical attempt to depict heroism:

> They fronted the storm and the flame
> They laughed in Death's face as they fell
> They rejoiced in red strife as a game:
> They sang as they strode into Hell.[69]

More soberly and sorrowfully, 'J.B.', the Marlborough master, sang in a poetic obituary of a former pupil, killed at the front:

> And now you've played your noblest game,
> And now you've won your grandest Blue,
> And Marlboro' lads shall read your name
> Upon the wall and honour you.[70]

Fed on a diet of the impossible romanticism of such as Hornung,

Byles and 'J.B.', it is little wonder, as Ronald Gurner wrote of Marlborough boys at the onset of the war, that they thought of it as 'a glorified football match in which, if peace did not come, they might take their places in the English team'.[71] How many subsequently reacted like Sheriff's Dennis Stanhope,[72] the perfect public school boy who under the strain of war became an alcoholic, will never be known. Gurner's statement sheds some light on the impact of the chauvinist vocabularies of motive associated with games, but of course, the extent of their influence is impossible to gauge with precision.

Those who wrote the verse and prose were undoubtedly sincere and ardent believers in the efficacy of games for soldiering, and the value of the games analogy for imprinting qualities of bravery, steadfastness and perseverance. And up to a point, no doubt, the fitness and willpower developed through activities demanding severe respiratory and muscular effort were useful, but it is interesting that when the 'war to end wars' came, the games fields of the public schools were emptied and the parade grounds filled. For as Cyril Alington wrote, 'whether Waterloo was or was not won on the playing fields of Eton, Armageddon will certainly not be decided on the cinder track'.[73] The bravery of the public school officer in the First World War cannot be questioned,[74] but the role of the playing field in its development cannot be evaluated with any exactness. Equally the influence of the motivating verse of Hornung and others cannot be exactly measured. It can only be recorded as an attempt at producing a simple patriotism through the medium of the written word.

The contribution that the internecine house struggles and the 'foreign' matches made to military prowess continued to be expounded throughout the Great War with simple certainty by soldier, teacher and pupil. One illustration from each will suffice. At the Harrow School War Memorial meeting at Merchant Taylors' Hall, Threadneedle Street, in May 1917, General Sir Horace Smith-Dorrien declared: 'What struck me . . . all the time I was out at the Front was the magnificent public school spirit, and the fact that the best material for leading troops came from those who had public school training, of which such an important part consists of games and sports.'[75] In the same year F. B. Malim, at one time assistant master at Marlborough and subsequently headmaster at several public schools, wrote: 'What virtues can we reasonably suppose to be developed by games? First I should put physical courage . . . for the security of the nation courage in her young men is indispensable. That it has been bred in the sons of England is attested by the fields of Flanders and the beaches of Gallipoli. We shall therefore give no heed to those who decry the danger of some schoolboy games . . .'[76]

The third example is perhaps the most significant as well as the most poignant. It sheds a particularly intense light on the influence of both the literature and practices of public schools before the Great War, being the statement of a public school boy, Paul Jones, who was himself a victim of the holocaust. Jones was at Dulwich before the First World War. He was no insensitive 'hearty'. He was the first Dulwich boy to win the Brackenbury Scholarship to Balliol as well as being captain of the fifteen, and he saw clearly the contribution of public school games to the war:

Nothing but athletics has succeeded in doing this sort of work [developing team spirit] in England. Religion has failed, intellect has failed, art has failed, science has failed. It is clear why: because each of these has laid emphasis on man's *selfish side*; the saving of his *own soul*, the cultivation of his *own mind*, the pleasing of his *own senses*. But your sportsman joins the Colours because in his games he has felt the real spirit of unselfishness, and has become accustomed to give all for a body to whose service he is sworn. Besides this, he has acquired the physical fitness necessary for a campaign. These facts explain the great part played by sport in this War . . . we suggest that this War has shown the training of the playing-fields of the public schools and the 'Varsities to be quite as good as that of the classroom; nay, as good? Why far better, if training for the path of Duty is the ideal end of education.[77]

His book contains a further moving example of the period language of patriotism by another Dulwich schoolboy also killed in the trenches, R. E. Vernede; the expected transition from athlete to warrior is quite explicit:

> Lad, with the merry smile and eyes
> Quick as the hawk's and clear as the day,
> You, who have counted the game the prize,
> Here is the game of games to play.
> Never a goal – the captains say –
> Matches the one that's needed now;
> Put the old blazer and cap away –
> England's colours await your brow.[78]

V

In March 1883, the *Lorettonian* contained an extract from a poem entitled 'Off-side' first published in the *Union Jack* earlier in the year:

> I know what 'off-side' means, to this very day
> When a trick upon me has been tried,
> I put the man down as a sneak, and I say
> 'He's been playing a bit of off-side'.
> If you notice a chap always up to that game
> You may safely be sure that in life
> He'll funk all the hacks, and the knocks and the dirt,
> And will sneak around the edge of the strife.
> But you – no, not you! You go into the thick,
> And enjoy all the fun of the maul;
> For sooner or later you know there's a chance
> Of getting a feel of the ball.
> And if you act up to your old football rule
> When you're launched on the world's busy tide,
> You'll find a much greater honour to lose,
> Than to win by the game of 'off-side'.[79]

'Off-side' may lack the balance, regular metre and comprehensiveness of moral precept of Kipling's 'If';[80] but it was equally serious in intention and spelled out an elementary moral code and collective orthodoxy with simple clarity. Football metaphors ingenuously proclaimed moral imperatives to the Celtic and northern English Tom Browns lodged at Loretto, the Musselburgh annexe of the English public school system.

The initiated in the system held firmly to the belief that robustness not only symbolised masculinity but also equalled rectitude; hearty pushing in 'squash' or 'maul' bulked not only muscle but moral fibre. Edward Bowen's Tom, valiant sportsman and the housemaster's *beau idéal*, personified the credo and demonstrated the validity of the equation:

> Rules that you make you obey;
> Courage to Honour is true;
> Who is the fairest in play
> Best and good temperedest, who?
> Tom![81]

Those acquainted with public school verse and stories will recognise familiar values clustering around this concrete symbol who was created as a model for his peers. Tom is the hero of a Harrow romance of nineteenth-century knighthood, a youthful public school Arthur, Lancelot and Galahad rolled into one. The 'Harrow grass' is his Chapel Perilous and Fair-Play his Holy Grail. And other schools also have their heroes and romances of the sporting ethic. There is Jan Rutter in E. W. Hornung's novel of Uppingham, *Fathers of Men*, Reginald Owen in R. M. Freeman's novel of Loretto, *Steady and Strong*, and to a lesser extent David Blaize in the Marlborough novel of that name by E. F. Benson.

The literature of cohesion, sexuality and patriotism was a symbolism of expedience; that of morality was one of principle. The former was essentially an attempt to ensure survival; the latter an attempt to promote nobility. Loyalty, masculinity and patriotism paid homage to morality and like Tom 'to honour were true'. Tom, in fact, embodied a simple mythology of morality delineated in verse and prose and woven into the public school culture thus dictating belief and behaviour.[82] The mythology depicted the essence of moral conduct; in turn moral conduct was the essence of communality; and linguistic symbolism was an important means by which the schools transmitted both. For reader and writer the symbolism was unitive.

Since moral lessons were taught through the language of games, it is to be expected that it was a popular activity of magazine moralists to draw a parallel not only between the games field and battle field, but between the games field and life in general. A delightful but somewhat atypical example is this gentle and elegant Stonyhurst sonnet:

> The warm green grass lies open to the sun,
> And cool white figures move about its face
> Time has stood still, and in this golden space
> Slowly my fancies gather one by one.
> Backward and forward slender figures run:
> A pause: a bowler springs with sinuous grace,
> Then hurls his bolt: the batsman moves a pace
> Forward . . . Fate cuts the thread that he has spun.
>
> Nor otherwise the pattern of our life
> Is woven, all of loveliness and strength,
> Struggle and pride and laughter and defeat,
> The skill that counters skill, courage to meet,
> The blows and runs of Fortune – till at length
> Darkness and death shall close our little strife.[83]

More typically, this jaunty Loretto song called attention to the preparation for manhood that took place on the public school turf:

> On cricket or on football fields,
> Begins our schoolboy life,

We fill our years with health and strength,
For life's long earnest strife.
Oh time to teach – oh time to prove,
Each lesson stern and true,
And come down hard on the fastest ball,
Time's changing hand shall bowl to you.[84]

Edward Bowen shared an enthusiasm for composing this type of verse with a surprisingly large number of masters in the public schools. E. W. Howson, a colleague at Harrow, took up the train-ing-for-life refrain:

They tell us the world is a scrimmage,
And life is a difficult run,
Where often a brother shall finish
A victory that we have begun.
What matter, we learnt it at Harrow
And that was the way that we won.[85]

And even busy headmasters found time to pen 'poetic' messages of moral exhortation in an athletic idiom. Cyril Norwood, when headmaster of Marlborough, was responsible for a 'Song of Rug-ger' which advocated 'going hard at the start, going hard at the end' as a suitable axiom for life as well as rugby football. Later, when headmaster of Harrow, he wrote the 'Song of the Forwards', the chorus of which went:

On, On, On, On
Take strength and good-temper and courage and speed
On, On, On, On
They're not a bad outfit for life and its need.[86]

On the subject of games as preparation for life even *Punch*, the nineteenth-century literary voyeur of the social manners of the upper classes, could be momentarily serious and admonish its readers for paying too much attention to the sneers of such as Wilkie Collins and his hysterical attack on athleticism in the novel *Man and Wife*. The villain of the book was the grotesquely overdrawn Geoffrey Delamayn, aristocrat and Oxbridge blue, 'deep in chest, thin in the flanks . . . a magnificent human animal'. Of Anglo-Saxon beauty, his looks were perfectly regular and perfectly un-intelligent. To complete the caricature, no one had seen him read anything but a newspaper or known him to be backward in settling a debt. According to Collins, Delamayn, with his mere muscular qualities, was the model of the young Briton of the time.[87]

Punch itself showed scant sympathy for Collins's furious riding of his hobby-horse. 'All is well with John Bull' was its reassuring message after the 1871 Boat Race, 'when pluck and gameness are so well exhibited', and it added that if the universities provided the opportunity for their exhibition, it was in the public schools that such important virtues necessary for the game of life were inculcated. These virtues were then listed in the fashionable literary mode of the period:

> There are worse schools than an eight oar
> With its discipline and training
> And its practical instruction in obeying and abstaining.
> There are worse lessons than this race suggests to the
>   reflecting
> To make our victors modest and our vanquished self-
>   respecting.[88]

The Spectator also expressed admiration for muscular youth, and contempt for the evangelistic Wilkie Collins. In an article entitled 'Softs' in 1889, it claimed that the reaction against athleticism, of which Collins was the self-appointed prophet, had spent itself. More men played games than ever before; the incidence of 'Softs' had not increased. They were in fact a little fewer and 'a great deal more unhappy!' There was a new virility, health and self-confidence in the young man of the day.[89]

Such sensible sermonising could elevate even the lowly to eminence. Uppingham's celebrated cricket professional H. H. Stevenson won a standing in the school far higher than a mere games coach normally achieved. One explanation lay in his personal qualities of dignity and intelligence, but another lay in the fact that he imbued his instruction with moral purpose, continually relating performance in everyday life to performance with those symbolic 'bats of the whitest grain'.[90] On one such typical occasion, a Stevenson spread, the professional gave the following reply to a toast to his health: 'Gentlemen, thank you; I will give you a piece of advice. I am near the end of my innings but I hope that you will do what I have tried to do – keep a straight bat to the end!'[91]

In the literature of the public schools, by far the most popular moralistic exhortation was 'play the game'. It was a refrain taken up again and again. Montagu Butler, at a dinner given by Old Harrovians to celebrate his eightieth birthday, beseeched his listeners in a wholly typical appeal: 'whether it be a matter of cricket . . . or politics or professional engagements, there is hardly any motto which I would more confidently commend . . . than "Play the

Game"! Remember your school and "Play the Game".[92] Shortly after Butler's appeal, Harrovians, old and young, were once more urged to:

> Play the Game! Play the Game!
> Boys of Harrow, Men of Harrow,
>   Play the Game.
> End each Match as just beginning,
> Bowl and field as sure of winning!
> Meet your Fate, but meet it grinning
>   Play the Game.[93]

At best this meant to act with decency, modesty and dignity; to hate what was mean, fraudulent and disingenuous.[94] At worst, it represented conformity to a rigid code of behaviour in which stoicism was the ideal, imagination was discouraged, and emotion was proscribed.[95]

Learning to 'play the game' on green and pleasant playing fields would appear to have been a universal feature of the English public school for many generations. With some perspicacity, and not a little idealism, Frank Ellis wrote in the *Boys' Own Annual* just before the Great War:

> The playing fields of England
> All up and down the land,
> Where English boys play English games,
> How bright and fair they stand!
> 'Tis there in a friendly rivalry
> School meets with neighbouring school
> And English boys all 'play the game'
> And learn to keep the rule.
> There each one plays for side, not self,
> And strength and skills employs,
> On the playing-fields of England,
> The Pride of English Boys.[96]

Some years earlier a Lancing College reviewer of Newbolt's *Collected Poems* had self-confidently asserted that 'the one great lesson the English public school life, the one lesson that cannot be learnt, or at any rate well-learnt anywhere else in the world, is splendidly summed up in the verse . . .'.[97] Then followed inevitably the last verse of 'Vitaï Lampada' with its ringing ultimate line which every latter-day admirer of Lytton Strachey, bored with the onerous virtuousness of such aspirations, now booms with gleeful malice, 'Play up! play up! and play the game'.

In the adult world the public school admonition to 'play the game' reverberated through the pages of journals in which secular and clerical missionaries either sought to set the world to right, or strove to maintain its rightness, through the simple expedient of propagating the public school ethic of playing the game.

It had its contribution to make to welfare, commerce and local, national and imperial government. In 1914, for example, S. P. Grundy, general secretary of the Manchester League of Help, used the pages of *Hibbert's Journal* to call on the public school boy to bring his famed spirit into the industrial chaos that reigned outside 'the charmed educational area' and 'play the game' in city slums.[98] And in commerce the precept was appreciated. 'We find,' said one businessman, 'that working class children are quite as good if not better in mental capacity . . . (but) they have not got the same sense of playing the game and working for the need of all instead of for themselves only.'[99] J. E. C. Welldon was in no doubt about its relevance for the export trade: English businessmen, he remarked, in one of his more foolish assertions, might not be the equal of the Japanese and Germans in effort, ingenuity and advertising, but 'the lesson of fair play in sport' guaranteed trustworthy manufacture even if the products were obsolete.[100]

Some were wholly convinced that local and national affairs suffered when left to those without a public school training. One disillusioned headmaster at the 1923 Headmasters' Conference drew attention to the difference in quality between the enlightened, civilised boards of governors of the public schools and people in charge of local education authorities, and regretted that more public school boys trained to 'play the game' did not take a greater part in local government.[101] And Welldon, who will be recognised by now as a noted apologist of games as an instrument of character formation, lectured the Labour Party in *Contemporary Review* in 1927 on the virtues of the public school tradition of pulling together for the good of the whole. His article was, in fact, a diatribe against strikes as a political weapon, in which he hectored the uninitiated into his own image: 'it might well be wished that all persons who take part in public life would learn the lesson of "playing the game". It is a lesson which has been regularly taught upon the playing fields of our public schools.'[102]

The practical virtue of 'playing the game' was extended beyond national welfare, economics and politics to imperial administration which owed its integrity, according to Sir Geoffrey Lagden in the *Nineteenth Century*, to those from Britain to whom 'It isn't cricket;

it isn't playing the game' was a moral axiom dictating colonial action.[103] His article is, in fact, a eulogy to the secular trinity – Games, Corps and Empire, and ends appropriately with the second verse of Newbolt's 'Clifton Chapel'. A eulogy to imperial manhood of another kind is this piece of breezy manliness from the hero of Mafeking, Baden-Powell: 'Don't be disgraced like the young Romans, who lost the Empire of their forefathers by being wishy-washy slackers without any go or patriotism in them. Play up. Each man in his place and play the game. Your forefathers worked hard, fought hard and died hard to make the Empire for you. Don't let them look down from heaven and see you loafing about with your hands in your pockets, doing nothing to keep it up.'[104]

The public schools' preoccupation with games instilled morality and produced a curious breed of early twentieth-century authors given to an analysis of the moral superiority of the Anglo-Saxon. One such writer was the physical fitness enthusiast and dietician Eustace Miles.[105] In 1904 he published *Let's Play the Game: Or the Anglo-Saxon Sportsmanlike Spirit*. It was replete with the fashionable sporting platitudes of the time. Moral admonition was by means of cricketing analogy. Human weaknesses were 'the balls that bowl most of us in daily life', an inability to remain free from sin was because 'we have taken our eye off the ball'. 'Playing the game' was, in his view, a source of justifiable pride to the Englishman. It was his exclusive heritage. Miles informed his readers that they were fortunate to be Anglo-Saxon: where two or three were gathered together, there was the sportsmanlike spirit in the midst. Like Sir Geoffrey Lagden, Miles reserved his strongest expressions of self-satisfaction for imperial rule because unlike some nations the English tried 'to play the game' with the natives.

Sir Theodore Cook was cast in the same ethnocentric, sporting mould as Miles. In *Character and Sportsmanship* published in 1927, he attempted an analysis of Anglo-Saxon superiority as a consequence of games enthusiasm. In Cook's treatise, all the familiar hallmarks of the sterling public school boy are recorded and applauded; games, fair play, loyalty and courage are inseparably enmeshed. '. . . We must be worthy of our heritage. We shall keep it by that sense of fair-play which is bred in our bones and courses through our blood, which makes a boy play the game . . .'[106] is typical of the many statements of patriotic self-pride in noble muscularity which permeate the pages.

The next year saw the publication of an equally effusive work on

English games entitled *Fair Play* by a German Anglophile, Rudolph Kircher.[107] It was his ambition to place the sporting terminology of the English public school in a comparative moralistic perspective and measure its influence. His pen was adulatory and unrestrained. Only for the English, he wrote, the censorious imperative 'That's not cricket', the classic postulate 'fair play' and the noble phrase 'playing the game' had moral significance. The simple expressions of the playing field were to be found 'engraved upon the English-man's table of commandments with a chisel of steel'. For the Anglo-Saxon, 'playing the game', he advised the literal Teuton, did not mean what it seemed to mean, but stood for playing with honour, dignity and according to the rules.

The use of the language of games to transmit simple moral messages to the English public school boy is nowhere more per-fectly illustrated than in the delightful, anonymous allegory *Bax-ter's Second Innings*.[108] It will serve to bring this section to a conclu-sion. If 'Tom' was a minor Arthurian romance of the nineteenth century, then *Baxter's Second Innings* is the equivalent of the public school boy's *Pilgrim's Progress*. The story opens with Baxter, our timid hero, reclining on a couch after the unfortunate experience of being knocked out in his very first innings by a demon fast bowler. Baxter's captain sitting beside him, advises the boy on how to play the cause of his injury in the future: ' "I shall begin by telling you his name," said the Captain. "It is Temptation." "Tim who?" said the boy. "Temptation," repeated the Captain. "Oh," said the boy. "I hope you are not going to be religious. I thought we were talking about games." "So we are," replied the Captain cheerily. "We are talking about the game of life . . . life is simply a cricket match – with Temptation as the Bowler." '[109]

After this stimulating introduction, his captain warns Baxter that every boy has three wickets to defend – Truth, Honour and Purity. To attack these wickets, the Demon Bowler uses three techniques – swifts, slows and screws. In short, temptation may come swiftly, slowly or spun as a cricket ball. Baxter, quick to take the point offered in these graphic terms, remarks innocently that if he defends his three wickets, then all will be well. He is speedily admonished.

He had overlooked the bails. His captain had been out several times with his wickets standing but 'one miserable inch of bail off!' He exhorts the boy to 'play the whole game', for sometimes Temp-tation does nothing but bowl at bails! For good measure, he adds the rider that the bowler employs further variations of delivery, including 'sneaks' and 'mixtures'. In view of the bowler's caddish-ness, Baxter asks sensibly why he is allowed to play. The reply is devastating in its logical simplicity – 'How could you score if there was no bowler?'

Baxter, depression creeping swiftly upon him, confesses that he is often bowled in private but, of course, no one knows. His self-delusion is ruthlessly exposed. He is informed curtly that all is written down in the score-sheet – his character. Depression now overtakes him at this news and he cries out that he can never win. But his captain is formidably persuasive. Baxter takes guard in his second innings, and despite all the wiles of the bowler, plays 'most carefully and brilliantly'.

The widespread impression today is that athleticism crushed the weak and inoffensive, elevated the strong and the callous, placed the aesthete and intellectual beneath the studded heel of the hearty's football and cricket boot. There is much truth in this; but the danger is that it is seen as the whole truth. The reality was, of course, more subtle. Many adherents of the ideology were insensitive in their enthusiasm, *simpliste* in their devotion, foolish in their claims for 'transfer', insufficiently critical in their passion, exaggerated in their symbolism. But there was virtue as well as vice in the ideology. There was, at times, decency, sense and soundness in the enunci-ation of moral principle. There was visionary idealism as well as myopic naivety in the exhortations of the committed, the aspi-rations of the innocent and the preaching of millenarians such as Almond. As a long-serving public school master has written: 'The general citizen of the pre-war public schools had an ideal of himself which he tended to live up to . . . we couldn't in these days stand up and sing some of the songs of the past seriously – but they did, and they did it without their tongue in their cheek, as I think a lot of modern people suspect.'[110]

'Off-side', Bowen's archetype, the simplistic claims of Welldon, Miles and Cook, Kircher's less well known obeisance *Fair Play* and the sweetly ingenuous *Baxter's Second Innings* provide period illus-trations of a naive, narrow and muscular but not ignoble rhetoric of morality. It may now be time to acknowledge its virtues rather than to continue to mock its shortcomings.

VI

Above, the voices of a past age have been allowed to speak for themselves in an effort to recreate a unique atmosphere and a simple faith; through their rhetoric of cohesion, identity, patriotism and morality which drew so extensively on the playing field for its inspiration, a frame of reference and a rationale for action were constructed for generations of public school boys; through repetitious trope, colourful epithet and hortatory cliché, desirable ways of thinking about the world and a desirable pattern of behaviour were delineated. Metaphor, manners and myth went hand in hand.

The literature of motive, enthusiasm and nostalgia with its rigid moral formulae and restricted imagery specified acceptable activities and instilled discriminatory perception. By means of parochial verbal symbolism, schoolboys developed an awareness of corporate values. Cultural imperatives were established which came to have their own momentum and increasingly determined behaviour.

It is impossible to measure the impact of the verbal symbolism of athleticism, and of course symbols can be contradictory of an actual state of affairs, but those of athleticism, it is suggested, both in the schools and in society, served to a greater rather than to a lesser extent as successful agents of socialisation, of social control and of social cohesion. In this way, they assisted in the development and reinforcement of individual role, collective habits and the institutional value system: they both created and reflected an ethos. They constituted, in short, a set of symbols for believing and acting.

Epilogue

The Great War may be conveniently taken as a divide – political, social, economic and educational:[1] new political principles, creeping embourgeoisement, declining national prosperity and a reformulation of educational ideals increasingly characterised the next fifty years. The eventual effect on the public schools was pronounced, but typically there was no charge to a liberal vanguard, nor an immediate recantation of firmly-held beliefs. The pressures for change were inexorable in nature but gradual in effect. And they were differently experienced. With memoirs unwritten and school archives as yet unfilled, it is impossible to determine at this close proximity in time either their order of importance or their relative influence with any certainty. Thus a detailed survey of the demise of athleticism is not the purpose of this study. Yet in the interests of completeness it might be useful – briefly and tentatively – to attempt to locate the major forces, which destroyed a powerful belief system and widespread practice.

Those, within the schools, who had a knowledge of the real world, possessed a sense of proportion, took pleasure in the intellect, and perhaps felt a Calvinistic urge to work, waged a long war against an extreme belief in the educational value of the games field, and what they saw as the licence permitted public school boys under cover of a wide-flung cloak of moral texture. A line of Marlborough headmasters extending back in time to the birth of athleticism stand witness to a constant unease at the muscular libertinism they thought too prevalent in the school.

As early as 1868 F. W. Farrar (headmaster 1871–6) complained to the members of the Royal Institute of an 'extravagant athleticism' in the public schools and looked back with something of utopianism to the seventeenth century, when, in his view, students left the ancient halls of Cambridge beautiful and strong *and* learned.[2] In the frequently irritating atmosphere of the classroom, we are told, Farrar was more realistic, and would quietly criticise the idle games zealot to his face. His ultimate limit in benevolent sarcasm was to refer to a pupil as 'a case hardened victim of Circe that ever conceived the world to be formed in the image of a cricket ball'.[3] From the chapel pulpit he continually pleaded with his young congregation for reasonableness, moderation and a little more intellectual effort.[4] Farrar's successor, G. C. Bell (1876–1903), as he approached the security of retirement, evinced an unrestrained exasperation with the games ethos, and in his last few prize day speeches was decidedly antagonistic towards the athlete. In retirement he donated an academic challenge cup to the school, and in 1906, as guest speaker on prize day, he vigorously attacked the balance in the school between body and mind.[5] In turn, Frank Fletcher (1903–11) was equally hostile to the established idolatry,[6] and was determined to loosen the grip of the athlete on school life.[7]

The concept of 'service' obsessed Cyril Norwood[8] (1916–26), and he harnessed games to the educational yoke in pursuit of his ideal: 'What is the justification of the games we play so much here save this ideal of service? . . . team games are played in order that you may learn to serve your side, to combine and avoid selfishness; in proportion as games lead to purely individual glorification they cease to be of value . . . You are not learning to win Olympic championships on the Marlborough playing fields. You are learning to serve.'[9] He was, therefore, less openly critical of the athlete than Farrar, Bell and Fletcher. At the same time he was a stern academic taskmaster. An advocate of twentieth-century knowledge, he modernised the entire school curriculum and introduced the School Certificate as a screening device for entry into the upper school. By these actions he put athleticism in its place: a junior partner in the business of education. His modernity contributed to its decline.

Norwood was followed by G. C. Turner (1926–39) – the 'Apollyon' of Marlborough athleticism.[10] The tone of his headship was set in his first school sermon when he confessed that at house matches his eyes wandered 'to the sunset dying over the Kennet' for the excellent reason that the sight lingered in his memory long after the cheers of victory. It was a statement of considerable courage in the atmosphere of the time;[11] it was equally a statement of firm conviction – under his regime the aesthetic and liberal arts were to be fostered.

Lord's CC Ground.

RUGBY v. MARLBOROUGH.

WEDNESDAY & THURSDAY, JULY 29, 30, 1908. (2-day Match.)

MARLBOROUGH.

		First Innings.		Second Innings.	
1	A. D. Womersley ... (Capt.)	b Symonds	1	c M.-Hallett, b Symonds	20
2	E. A. Shaw	b J. A. Cunningham	29	b Charles	27
3	G. H. Atkinson	run out	18	c King, b R. Cunningham	18
4	J. B. Brooks	lbw, b J. A. Cunningham	5	b J. A. Cunningham	1
5	R. O. Lagden	b Symonds	4	c and b R. Cunningham.	84
6	H. S. Scott	c J. Cunningham, b Charles	38	c Hallett, b R. Cunningham	31
7	G. S. Leventhorpe	c King, b Charles	49	c Hallett, b J. Cunningham	39
8	A. C. Wolfson	b R. Cunningham	24	st King, b Charles	13
9	C. L. Norman	c J. Cunningham, b Charles	2	not out	2
10	R. G. W. Knight	b Charles	27	c King, b R. Cunningham	21
11	L. D. Womersley	not out	25	c J., b R. Cunningham	13
		B 10, l-b 10, w 3, n-b	23	B 8, l-b 6, w 2, n-b 1,	17
		Total	245	Total	286

FALL OF THE WICKETS

1 2	2 57	3 57	4 63	5 65	6 143	7 169	8 171	9 193	10 245
1 33	2 67	3 85	4 153	5 158	6 202	7 228	8 271	9 275	10 286

ANALYSIS OF BOWLING

	1st Innings.					2nd Innings				
Name.	O.	M.	R.	W.	Wd.	N-b.	O.	M.	R.	W.	Wd.	N-b.
Symonds	18	3	67	2	...	...	15	2	69	1	...	1
R. Cunningham	12	3	23	1	1	...	19.4	5	56	5	...	...
Charles	15.4	2	63	4	1	...	15	2	61	2	1	...
J. A. Cunningham	14	2	43	2	...	...	18	0	83	2	1	...
Fraser	2	0	15	0	1	...	...	...	...	...	...	...

RUGBY.

		First Innings.		Second Innings.	
1	G. D. Forrester	c Shaw, b Wolfson	17	c Knight, b Wolfson	4
2	R. S. Rait-Kerr	c Wolfson, b Knight	7	not out	54
3	S. A. Miller-Hallett	st Shaw, b Knight	30	b Wolfson	13
4	R. Cunningham (Capt.)	c A. D., b L. D. Womersley	33	b Wolfson	0
5	R. W. Poulton	b Norman	14	b Knight	4
6	H. S. Sharp	not out	50	b Wolfson	17
7	P. S. Fraser	c Shaw, b Knight	0	b Wolfson	0
8	N. H. H. Charles	b Knight	3	b Wolfson	4
9	W. R. King	b Wolfson	4	b Wolfson	0
10	J. A. Cunningham	b Wolfson	6	c A. Womersley, b Wolfson	34
11	J. C. Symonds	b Lagden	3	c Laventhorpe, b Wolfson	7
		B 11, l-b 5, w 1, n-b 1,	18	B 5, l-b 3, w 1, n-b ,	9
		Total	185	Total	146

FALL OF THE WICKETS

1 22	2 30	3 72	4 95	5 120	6 120	7 125	8 134	9 153	10 185
1 14	2 29	3 33	4 38	5 55	6 55	7 61	8 61	9 125	10 146

ANALYSIS OF BOWLING.

	1st Innings					2nd Innings.				
Name.	O.	M.	R.	W.	Wd.	N-b.	O.	M.	R.	W.	Wd.	N-b.
Lagden	10	2	26	1	...	...	5	2	11	0	...	...
Knight	16	3	54	4	1	...	15	2	42	1	...	...
Wolfson	17	3	49	3	...	...	23.5	8	68	9	1	...
L. D. Womersley	3	0	15	1	...	...	...	...	...	...	...	...
Norman	4	2	15	1	...	1	3	0	16	0	...	...
A. D. Womersley	2	0	8	0	...	1	...	...	...	...	...	...

Umpires — Pougher and Richardson. Scorers — G. G. Hearne and Whiteside.

Play commence each day at 11

. The figures on the Scoring Board show the Batsmen in.

ONE PENNY.

Luncheon 1.30 p.m. Stumps drawn at 6.30 p.m.

19 Symbols of status and allegiance: the annual Eton versus Harrow match at Lord's had its imitators as this match card illustrates. R. O. Lagden, Marlborough's outstanding player in this match, was a brilliant games player, eventually representing Oxford at rugby, cricket and hockey and playing rugby for England. He was killed in the Great War and John Bain, the Marlborough master, wrote a poignant verse obituary celebrating his athletic skill. Several of Bain's war obituaries in memory of the school's athletic heroes are included in appendix VI.

20   F. W. Farrar (1871–76)   21   G. C. Bell (1876–1903)

22   F. Fletcher (1903–11)   23   G. C. Turner (1926–39)

Critics of athleticism: these four Marlborough headmasters were all determined opponents of the extreme manifestations of athleticism. Turner's reign saw the decline of the power of the athlete at the school.

Over the years constant internal criticism, demonstrated in word and action, of the self-confident athlete, in conjunction with a similarly persistent hostility expressed in the wider world of the novelist, social commentator, biographer and autobiographer,[12] undoubtedly played its part in dispossessing him of the certainty of his supremacy; but only in association with other forces which made the articulate and often sensitive critics appear less than neurotic and, in fact, remarkably level-headed.

By the end of the Victorian era, the Boer War, the Liberal and Conservative populist scramble for the votes of the enfranchised proletariat, concern over foreign commercial competition, the rise of German power and scientific and technological advances had created 'a consensus for educational reform'.[13] The resulting Balfour Education Act of 1902, with the subsequent systematisation and expansion of state secondary education, gradually increased the academic and occupational pressures on the public school boy. And middle-class parents were not impervious to the new state of affairs. In any case, headmasters were quick to sense the consequences of change and issued stern warnings on speech days. It would seem scarcely fortuitous, for example, that in the same year as the Balfour Act became law, Selwyn, at Uppingham, warned parents of the consequent disaster if boys in the public schools found themselves left behind by the growing numbers who took advantage of the opportunities offered by the expanding provincial colleges and universities. In 1903 the public schools introduced the Common Entrance Examination. A few years later, at the time of the Free Place Regulations of 1907,[14] G. A. N. Lowndes and his fellow pupils at their expensive preparatory school were given a grave lecture by the headmaster on the serious threat of increased competition from the state schools 'where boys did such an unfair amount of work'.[15] The pressure for 'a widening of the rungs of the educational ladder' exerted by socialism and new liberalism grew more severe: in 1917 the Board of Education allocated special grants for sixth-form courses, in 1918 the Fisher Education Act was passed, with its aim of establishing a national system of education for all capable of taking advantage of it, and in 1920 state scholarships were introduced. These thrusts towards fairer educational provision for all classes jolted the public schools out of their academic complacency.

But, of course, it was not only increasing state competition which led to an improvement in standards. In the wake of scientific

and technological developments there was also the growing demand for specialised skilled professionals of many kinds.[16] Parents,
while still ostensibly unintellectual, were always firmly practical
and quickly adapted to a new reality. In March 1928 *The Spectator*
declared, 'Not one parent in ten cares how much his son acquires in
the way of book-learning, provided that the school brings him to
the point of passing such exams as are necessary for his career.'[17] By
the end of the 1920s in consequence, the School Certificate, introduced in 1917, had established its hold over the public schools and
had raised the standard of performance.[18] Boys were working
harder – even at Harrow muscle became 'slightly discredited'.[19] The
halcyon days of leisurely ease and subscription to an appropriate
educational rationale were drawing to a close. The public school
boy was being compelled to learn new values.[20]

If the results of continual, albeit erratic, reform in state education
were disappointing,[21] it is still true that the state-educated were
gaining more frequent access to universities and better occupational
qualifications.[22] And in any case the threat they posed seemed more
potent in its effect than the reality they achieved. Thus, for example, at Uppingham in 1935, the headmaster John Wolfenden
presented parents with a 'New Deal' – essentially an emphasis on
the School Certificate – to ensure *their* sons were sufficiently well
qualified to win the posts in offices, businesses and factories.[23] At
Loretto, a major concern of the headmaster D. Forbes McIntosh
throughout the 1950s was to make the boys appreciate that examinations mattered as never before.[24] By 1947 R. W. Moore, the
headmaster of Harrow, could declare on speech day, with some
truth: 'The age of assumed and assured privilege is over. The public
schools are no longer a royal road or a short cut to eminence.'[25]
Later he expressed regret that the versatile commoner should be
squeezed out of Oxford and Cambridge by the 'subsidised and
specialised second rate'.[26]

Unaware of the resentment they engendered, these 'subsidised
and specialised second rate' had helped bring about a change of
lifestyle in the public school system. As the *Uppingham School
Magazine* stated in 1950: 'Much has changed . . . we are becoming
used to more work and less games and the passing of exams has
become the aim of many.'[27]

II

The Board of Education Regulations for Secondary Schools (1906) introduced the possibility of schools, not eligible or applying for grants, being recognised as efficient. In consequence, in the years before the Second World War, Harrow (1911, 1920, 1931), Lancing (1926, 1936) and Marlborough (1924, 1934, 1937) were all fully inspected.[28] Educational progress, it has been observed, is achieved by the illumination of genius, fertilised by the imitative power of the enthusiast and disseminated by the missionary efforts of inspectors.[29] Those inspectors who visited Harrow, Lancing and Marlborough were forceful emissaries of change. They urged the introduction of 'Swedish Drill' – first used in Britain in 1902 at the Royal Naval Physical Training School[30] – and recommended the appointment of qualified teachers trained in the principles of physical training. So successful was their pleading, not only at Harrow and Marlborough but throughout the public school system, that in 1924 the Headmasters' Conference produced *The Practice of Health*, a booklet which dealt with the virtues of the Swedish system.[31] And in 1930 the Conference proposed the foundation of a Physical Training College. As a direct result Carnegie College was established in 1933 and courses started at Loughborough in 1935 and at Goldsmith's in 1937. Nor was this all. In 1942 the Conference, in its *Memorandum of Evidence to the Norwood Committee* recommended that the public schools appoint directors of physical education. This gradually became the practice over the next thirty years and the image and status of the subject, hitherto taught by ex-army PTIs of little education and definite social inferiority, slowly improved.

In many cases the scope of physical education had already widened in the years between the wars to embrace camping, trekking, sailing and similar outdoor activities. Instrumental in these developments were men like Cecil Reddie at Abbotsholme, J. H. Bradley at Bedales, John Ford at Bootham and Kurt Hahn at Gordonstoun. All demonstrated a more rational, liberal and flexible approach to adolescent physical health and leisure than the more traditional public school headmasters. The organisations of the Boys' Brigade and the Boy Scouts also played their part in the spread of outdoor activities throughout the middle classes.[32] So too did the Youth Hostel Association established in 1930.

Among the recommendations on physical education, made to

the Norwood Committee by the 1942 Headmasters' Conference
mentioned earlier, was the establishment in the schools of 'a sound
and full system of Physical Education . . . including remedial treatment for remedial defects'.[33] Similar recommendations had been
made as early as 1907 when the School Medical Service was established. This body advised educational gymnastics for prophylactic
and remedial health purposes. In time a powerful corpus of medical
experts argued the case for a broad conception of physical education
to include these activities. And in 1935 the British Medical Association set up a committee to assess the physical efficiency of the
nation. Among other things it pointed to the inadequacy of physical
education in the public schools, and to an undue emphasis on
games. Simultaneously a few dedicated physical educationalists,
R. E. Roper and his disciples, G. W. Hedley and G. Murray,[34] set
about devising and implementing an adequate programme for use
in the public school system.

These various influences – the Inspectorate, the Headmasters'
Conference, liberal headmasters, medical experts and dedicated
teachers – helped to change the nature of physical exercise in the
public schools. They gradually widened the range of activities to
cater for the aptitudes and interests of as many boys as possible.
They substituted an individualistic argument for a corporate one,
and so weakened the moral basis of athleticism. At the same time
they provided a well-structured and effective practical alternative.

III

The individualistic emphasis of the new physical education har-
monised with the general social, philosophical and educational
fashions of the time. From the 1920s onwards, it has been argued,
the consensus of opinion in English education was on the side of
individualism.[35] Perhaps this reflected in part the increasing influence of Pestalozzi, Montessori and Froebel as revealed, for example, in the writings of Norman MacMunn, Caldwell Cook,
A. N. Whitehead and Bertrand Russell. It may also have reflected
the gradual dissemination of the psychological work of Freud,
McDougall and Ellis. In the specific context of the public schools,
possibly the arguments of new visionaries such as J. F. Roxburgh
played an important part. Certainly Roxburgh's *beau idéal* of the
public school boy, propounded in his *Eleutheros* and encouraged at
Stowe, was a creature of individuality, morality and intellect.[36] The

growing belief in individualism was certainly a consequence of reaction to an overlong emphasis on procrustean conformity: 'When I became a Headmaster I found myself unconsciously, and then consciously reacting against pre-war Marlboro': I had been disqualified myself from ever developing much in the way of artistic insight or imagination. I was perhaps a natural "converger" . . . but the tendency had been strongly encouraged and I found myself trying to create a situation where individuals could discover and express themselves.'[37]

Whatever the causes of the ascendancy of individualism, developments in the schools of this study firmly support general assertions that it occurred. It was nowhere more apparent than in physical activities. Lord Gornell wrote of Harrow in 1938 with pleasure and some disbelief:

There is (now) predominantly the sense of variety which is impressed upon me with vividness every visit I pay to the school. Forty years ago a boy was an individual only if his idiosyncracies were unusually pronounced – at all events individuality was not encouraged. All boys played games, the same games, cricket in the summer, Harrow football in the winter and spring . . . practically nobody specialised in work – they were classical or 'modern side' . . . Now the pendulum has swung to the other extreme . . . and every boy's individual tastes are developed.[38]

At Uppingham Malcolm Lloyd, headmaster from 1944 to 1965, was remembered warmly on his departure for his recognition of games other than the traditional, for the introduction of free afternoons, for his encouragement of mountaineering, pot-holing, golf and fishing and for the 'decompulsorisation' of senior cricket.[39] At Loretto, Sparta, the traditional inspirational ideal, was eventually redefined to suit the new fashion. Curiously it came to be regarded not primarily as a place of physical toughness as formerly, but as a community in which every member was important for himself.[40]

Of course it was not only in games that there was a move towards greater personal choice. It was apparent in the widening of the curriculum and, more particularly, in the huge increase in extra-curricular hobbies and enthusiasms. And reform was praised, encouraged and legitimated by public school staff in such books as Donald Hughes's *The Public Schools and the Future*, George Snow's *The Public School in the New Age* and J. F. Wolfenden's *The Public Schools Today*.

Headmasters now made a practice on speech day of requesting respect for personal inclination.[41] The shibboleths of solidarity were redundant. With unconscious irony however, speech day reports alternated between a defence of the nourishment of the inviolable self, and warnings about failing to appreciate the need to sacrifice this nourishment to the consuming demands of the School Certificate!

IV

The years after the Great War mirrored the violence of war and the violence of reaction to war.[42] They represented an era in which morals and manners were created anew, sometimes in reactionary frivolity, self-indulgence and cynicism.

Lytton Strachey's *Eminent Victorians* published in 1918, with its witty, acidulous irreverence for things and persons previously honoured, set a trend that surprisingly found ready imitators in the public schools. Where talent and the censor permitted, mockery became an instrument of attack on former values. By means of a curious time lag, the Aesthete Movement of the 1880s seemed to experience a delayed efflorescence in the freshly-turned school soil of the 1920s. A pre-Raphaelite whimsy took hold of some pupils. The words of *Punch* of the earlier era were singularly appropriate to these latter-day Bunghornes:

> I built myself a lordly place
> Wherein to play a Leo's part
> I said, 'Let others cricket, row or race
> I will go in for Art.[43]

At Marlborough the defiant and posturing 'high aesthetic band' celebrated their daring irregularity with the publication of a controversial magazine, *The Heretick*. It was largely taken up with a predictable attack on the Victorian values of virile muscularity. Its cover portrayed a cropped-haired, square-jawed, wide-shouldered athlete, squatting on a large rugby ball, surrounded by mischievous and taunting pixies. Below was the caption 'Upon Philistia I will triumph' – an entirely accurate prognostication.

At Lancing Evelyn Waugh formed the Corpse Club for the world-weary. Its members paraded in black ties, black tassels and buttonholes, and wrote on black-edged notepaper. Their mouthpiece in the school magazine was 'Lavernia Scargill', who defended her published witticisms against the spleen of 'the tedious and self-assured letters from all parts of the Empire' by announcing:

'No humour . . . could be more cadaverous, no pomp more funereal than that of the O.B. trying to restore the school to the high position it had attained in his day.'[44]

Other schools, it seems, had less imaginative, less ambitious and less indulged iconoclasts, but all the magazines reveal a growing unwillingness to parade the former virtues, to maintain uncritical solidarity, to abstain from open disaffection. Increasingly, independent-minded boys nurtured on Shaw, Ibsen, Tawney and Eliot raised their voices in criticism of traditional ways. Even at Loretto, the school magazine – once the purest of ideological texts – published in 1929 a cry for 'A Quiet Life':

> Leave Rugger, Hockey, Fives and
> Such to those blokes athletic
> For they lead hardy lives and
> I'm not energetic.
>
> I always was a loafer
> Away with all these follies
> O give me but a sofa
> And a pile of Edgar Wallace.[45]

If it lacked the venomous sting of 'Lavernia Scargill', it was clearly an attempt to be sacrilegious.

Such things betokened the appearance of a new, openly critical, non-conformist public school boy, embarrassed by his past image and uncertain of his present role.[46]

Constant and fierce anti-athleticism within and outside the schools, competition from the state-educated, the demands of a national examination system, the growth of professional occupations in association with reduced opportunities for imperial careers especially in the armed services, reactions and arguments of medical practitioners, physical educationalists and radical schoolmasters, the new ethos of individualism, a nonconformist spirit of disenchantment – these certainly appear to be among the main reasons for the eventual decline of athleticism. Yet two points must be firmly made: despite the evidence of change presented above, residual elements of the ideology were prevalent until well after the Second World War, and as in other things, the schools of this study were characterised by quite different rates of change.

In 1930 a German observer, Bruno Wachsmuth, claimed in the *Quarterly Review* that athleticism no longer held sway in England; its limitations had been acknowledged.[47] It was a premature observation. At Uppingham the years of R. H. Owen's headship (1915–34) brought a period of intense games regimentation with an accompanying ideological rhetoric, which resulted in Uppingham's 'Second Golden Age of Athleticism'.[48] Some remember Lancing in the 1930s as still excessively given over to games.[49] At Marlborough a member of staff took over a house in 1948 to discover that only five activities were permitted on weekday afternoons: play a game, practise a game, watch a game, go a 'sweat' (run) or garden under supervision.[50] At Loretto in the 1950s one observer considered, 'the tide of Philistinism was only just beginning to turn'.[51] Ideological argument in its most undiluted form could be found as late as 1955: '. . . courage, determination, loyalty, enthusiasm, love of fair play, honest dealing, good temper, self-control, good manners in victory, cheerfulness in defeat, unselfishness – all and much more can be learnt on the playing field.'[52]

As regards the varying speed of change, understandably the closer the study approaches the present, the more reticent witnesses become, the fewer the biographies and autobiographies, and written records in general are in short supply. For comment, one must rely heavily on the school magazine and its coverage is neither encyclopedic nor objective. Statements regarding differing rates of change, therefore, must be most tentative.

Marlborough appears to have anticipated the other schools in the move towards alternative commitment, while Harrow seems to have clung longest to the games tradition.[53] One fact symbolises this difference in time. While the editor of the *Marlburian* announced a reduction of space devoted to games topics in 1926, a similar statement appeared in the *Harrovian* in 1971![54] At Uppingham, Lancing, Loretto and Stonyhurst the three decades after the Second World War seem to have seen the gradual assertion of a new liberalism.

However difficult it is to be exact about the timing of reaction in individual schools, it may be said without fear of contradiction that by the late 1960s athleticism was widely ridiculed, savaged and moribund. As the *Harrovian* recorded:

Since Kipling's 'muddied oafs' and Waugh's 'Loom of Youth', the more obvious excesses of Manliness have been pummelled and derided to the point of death. We can now read with detached amusement and relief the words of a recent writer on the late-Victorian public schools: 'the beauty of athleticism, the salutary effects of Spartan habits . . . the cultivation of all that is masculine, and the rejection of all that is effeminate, un-English and excessively intellectual . . .'[55]

New priorities, extremism and reaction have produced new values. The Welldons, the Bowens and the Almonds are certainly seen and heard no more; the rhetoric is no longer written and the litanies no longer loyally chanted; the badges are fewer, less valued and less flauntingly displayed; the practical manifestations such as compulsion and an expected homage to the major games of cricket and football are far less evident than in earlier times. It is even possible that what is apparently true of Lancing is equally true elsewhere: 'The great post-war reaction against over-athleticism . . . that had such a violent effect . . . is declining into merely an excuse for apathy and cynicism . . . Instead of an athletic hierarchy we [now] have an exclusively intellectual one.'[56]

Whatever ideological beliefs and actions characterise the present, they too will in time stimulate appraisal, reaction, change. Every ideology, its tenets created for a certain moment in time and in response to a particular set of circumstances, carries within itself the seeds of its own destruction. Tempus edax rerum!*

* Time devours all things.

Appendices

Appendix I

Historical documents of special significance in the evolution of athleticism

(a) Harrow: Philathletic Club papers (April/May 1853)
  i. Circular letter dated 15 April 1853 sent out with the prospectus
  ii. The club prospectus
  iii. The club rules drawn up on 13 April 1853
  iv. A printed list of the first honorary and acting members which includes H. M. Butler (headboy 1851; headmaster, after Vaughan, 1859–84).

(The originals of items ii and iii are in the Vaughan Library Collection, Harrow School; the originals of items i and iv are contained in the papers of T. H. S. Sotheron (MS D1571) in the Gloucestershire Record Office. Together these two sets of documents comprise the most complete known collection of early club papers.)

(b) Marlborough: Cotton's 'Circular to Parents' (June 1853)

Appendix I(a)i

Harrow, April 15th 1853.

Sir,

  I beg to lay before your consideration a prospectus of the objects of a Club which has been lately formed at Harrow, for the purpose of promoting among the Members of the School an increased interest in manly sports and exercises. The plan has met with the entire approbation of the Head Master, and will, it is hoped, obtain the support of all old Harrovians who take an interest in the welfare of the School.

  Should you wish to become an Honorary Member of the Club, you will perhaps be kind enough to state your intention of doing so to the Treasurer at as early an opportunity as possible.

  I have the honour to be, Sir,
    Your very obedient Servant,
      J. Wallace Hozier
        President, H.P.C.

Appendix I(a)ii

HARROW PHILATHLETIC CLUB.

PROSPECTUS OF THE OBJECTS OF THE INSTITUTION.

At a Meeting of certain members of the VIth and Vth Forms, held on Tuesday, 22nd February, 1853, it was decided that a Club should be established in Harrow, to be called the HARROW PHILATHLETIC CLUB, with the view of promoting among the members of the School an increased interest in games and other manly exercises.

The project in question has its rise in a desire to obtain a remedy for the general apathy and want of spirit now conspicuous at Harrow. That the excitement and interest formerly displayed in behalf of the games of the School is at present, to say the least, considerably on the decline, is a matter at once of notoriety and regret. Those who knew Harrow some years ago, see a marked change in the spirit and manners of the School, as contrasted with that of olden times. The encouragement of innocent amusements and recreation must tend greatly to the maintenance of order and discipline throughout the School. The sure way to keep boys out of mischief is to find them plenty of modes of amusement during the hours devoted to recreation. There need be no conflict between School-games and School-duties; on the contrary, the encouragement of the former, within proper limits, must undoubtedly assist the due performance of the latter. Those who *play* well, will generally be found to *work* well also. It is on this supposition that the Harrow Philathletic Club has been established.

It is intended that the Club shall have a Reading-room in the town, in which sporting periodicals shall be taken in, and which shall at all times be accessible to members. A monthly meeting will be held here for the despatch of business, when all questions relating to the games of the School will be discussed. The Head of the School and the Head of the Eleven will be always members *ex officio*; and means will always be taken to secure having at least four Monitors, if possible, in the Club, as this will be a guarantee to the Masters for the propriety of all proceedings.

With regard to the objects of the Club, the members will be considered pledged to the promotion and encouragement of all sorts of games, both by pecuniary contributions and by all other means in their power. The commencement of subscriptions for prizes at Football, Racquets, Cricket, &c. will form one of their chief duties; and it must be allowed by all that it is a much easier matter for a body corporate than for a single individual to take the initiative in any steps of this nature. It is also felt that, at present, during two quarters of the year the encouragement of School-games depends so entirely on the personal tastes of the Head of the School that there may be at times a danger of the interests of a large body being sacrificed to the private opinion of an individual. The risk of such a state of things will be considerably diminished by the establishment of the Philathletic Club. The encouragement of house-matches, and the institution of prizes for the Championship in both Cricket and Football, will come under the consideration of the Club. The foundation of a Gymnasium will also be one of its chief objects. It will also feel itself bound to reward any display of peculiar merit on the part of any member of the Eleven in the matches either at Harrow or at Lord's: in fact there will be no difficulty in finding a wide field for its operations.

The benefits resulting from such an institution will, it is hoped, be two-fold. It will in the first place, from its popular character, tend to raise throughout the School a desire of gaining admission to the Club. It will in this manner cause an ambition of excelling in games, while it will necessarily disseminate generally throughout the School a stronger feeling of interest in manly exercises and amusements than now exists, and thus it will probably help to bring forward and stimulate many who, though possessing great weight and influence in the School, do not at present come sufficiently forward in games. In the second place it will certainly (even if it should do nothing more) foster a spirit of sociability and concord throughout the members of the School, the absence of which at present is greatly to be regretted. The various members will be bound together by a common tie, and from meeting frequently for the transaction of necessary business, will become better acquainted with each other, and consequently better able to work together for the general good.

To prevent misapprehension it may be as well to add that the idea of the Philathletic Club being a *Sporting* Club is most entirely repudiated, no such intention having been ever entertained by its originators.

Old Harrovians are most earnestly invited to give their support to the objects of the Club by becoming Honorary Members; and it is believed that the advantages they will derive from the use of the Reading-room, on the occasion of their visits to Harrow, will prove of great convenience to them.

** Subscriptions may be forwarded to the Treasurer, H. E. Platt, Esq. at Harrow.

Appendix I(a)iii

RULES OF THE HARROW PHILATHLETIC CLUB, ESTABLISHED A.D. MDCCCLIII.

I. The chief object of the Club shall be the encouragement and promotion of all manly Sports and Exercises, and every Member shall consider himself pledged to the attainment of this object by all lawful means in his power.

II. Under the head of 'manly Sports and Exercises' shall be included Cricket, Racquets, Football, Races, Jumping, Fencing, Gymnastics, Swimming, Skating, Quoits, or any other game which may meet with the approbation of the Club.

III. Admission to the Club to be confined to Members of the VIth and Vth Forms.

IV. The Head of the School and the Head of the Eleven shall be always Members of the Club *ex officio*.

V. The Members of the Club to be restricted in number to thirty.

VI. The Club shall have a room, in which all Periodicals approved of by the Members shall be taken in. This room shall be at all times provided with a due supply of paper, pens, &c. and all other materials for letter-writing; as well as all appliances for Chess and Backgammon. Attached to the Reading-room shall be a Library, to be augmented by voluntary donations of Members leaving the School, and others.

VII. At the beginning of each Quarter a President, Treasurer, and Committee of

Six Members shall be elected, to hold office during that period, being re-eligible at the commencement of the next Quarter.

VIII. In the discussion of any question, where in Committee or at a general Meeting, in the case of an equal division, the President shall have a casting vote.

IX. A meeting of the Members shall be held within the first week of each Month for the despatch of all business connected with the objects of the Club.

X. Attendance at these meetings shall be compulsory, on pain of a fine of one shilling and sixpence.

XI. It shall be the duty of the Treasurer to present for the inspection of Members, at each Monthly meeting, a Balance Sheet of the expenses of the Club; and he shall not be allowed to incur any expense above the sum of ten shillings within the month, unless empowered by the Committee so to do.

XII. The election of new Members shall take place by ballot at the Monthly meetings; one black ball in five to exclude.

XIII. Notice of the proposal of any new Member must be posted up on a board provided for that purpose in the Club-room, not later than one week previous to the next meeting.

XIV. Notice of the proposal of any alteration in the Rules or addition to the Periodicals supplied to the Club must be declared at length in the same manner, with the proposer's name. All such propositions to be voted upon at the business-meetings and decided by a majority of Members present.

XV. The elective power shall be vested in the whole body of Members.

XVI. At the business-meeting no remarks shall be allowed not immediately connected with the objects of the Club; and any member making such remarks shall be called to order by the President.

XVII. The President shall have the power of convening at any time an extra-ordinary meeting of the Club.

XVIII. All Members shall consider themselves pledged not to attempt any pre-vious canvassing on the subject of the election of a new Member; and any candidate who may be convicted of having used such means for obtaining his admission, shall be excluded from the Club.

XIX. The institution of prizes for distinction in the various School Games shall come under the especial consideration of the Club, which will also feel itself bound to present with some Testimonial any member of the Eleven who particularly distinguishes himself in the matches at Lord's.

XX. The necessary expenses of the Club to be defrayed by an entrance-fee of One Guinea – to be paid immediately after election – and a quarterly subscription of Ten Shillings from each Member, to be paid to the Treasurer within one week after the commencement of the Quarter.

XXI. The names of all Members failing to pay their subscriptions within the appointed time to be posted on a board in the Room; and any Member failing to pay within a fortnight after the posting of his name, to be excluded from the Club until the payment of his subscription.

XXII. All old Harrovians may become Honorary Members on payment of either an immediate donation of Three Guineas, or a yearly subscription of Ten Shillings. N.B. The Club will always be grateful for Subscriptions from any of those interested in its welfare, although not desirous of becoming Honorary Members.

XXIII. A veto on the election of all new Members to be vested in the Head Master.

xxiv. A majority of Members present at any business-meeting has the power of altering or abolishing any former Rule, after the proposal of such a measure in due form.

Harrow Philathletic Club,
April 13th, 1853.

Appendix I(a)iv

HARROW PHILATHLETIC CLUB.
MAY, 1853.

Honorary Members.

** Those to whose names an asterisk is prefixed are members for life; the others are yearly Subscribers.

    * The Earl of Hardwicke.
    * The Earl Spencer, K.G.
    * Joseph Neeld, Esq. M.P.   ⎫ Governors of
    * T. H. S. Sotheron, Esq. M.P.⎭ Harrow School.
    G. F. Harris, Esq. Senior Assistant Master.
    Rev. G. C. Swayne, Assistant Master.

* Hon. R. Grimston.	* H. K. Boldero, Esq.
* Hon. F. Ponsonby.	W. B. Marillier, Esq.
* M. Portal, Esq. M.P.	F. G. Veasey, Esq.
* Rev. K. H. Digby.	H. C. Finch, Esq.
* E. Wigram, Esq.	J. S. Gibson, Esq.
* J. Arkwright, Esq.	* J. R. Maxwell, Esq.
* W. Stone, Esq.	H. M. Butler, Esq.
* C. O. Eaton, Esq.	* W. K. Fenton, Esq.
Hon. George Pepys.	* J. W. Bliss, Esq.
R. N. Young, Esq.	H. S. Cunningham, Esq.
L. H. Daniell, Esq.	J. H. Clutterbuck, Esq.
* Captain Boldero.	W. S. Portal, Esq.

Acting Members.

President.

J. W. Hozier.

Treasurers.

H. E. Platt.   W. H. Stone.

Committee

R. Arkwright.	A. A. De Bourbel.
K. E. Digby.	W. H. Davey.
C. D. Crawley.	S. C. Glyn.

R. D. Wilson.	Lord Althorp.
W. J. Hope.	T. Walters.
F. E. Wigram.	Lord Garlies.
C. Bruce.	Hon. R. H. Stewart.
R. Marker.	P. H. Knight.
A. Smith.	R. G. Currie.
F. M. Birch.	O. Wigram.

F. S. White.

Appendix 1(b)

The Lodge,
Marlborough College.
June 1853.

My dear Sir,

In the course of my first year's experience as Master of this College, I have naturally thought over plans by which the general welfare and discipline of the boys might be promoted, and I wish at the end of it, to lay before you my views on one or two subjects.

I. The first of these, is the important one of the boys' amusements. In most public schools of long standing these are regulated very much by prescription, and the subscriptions, necessary for keeping them up, are levied as a matter of course on every member of the School. Here there has not been time for such a tradition to grow up: and the result is, that both subscriptions and games are very imperfectly organized. To the Cricket Club (which also provides for the expenses of foot-ball and hockey) not half the School subscribe, and the result of this is bad in many ways. The mass of the School are not trained up to cricket and foot-ball at all, which, as healthy and manly games, are certainly deserving of general encouragement. Instead of this, the money, which should be devoted to the legitimate games of the School, is spent on other amusements, often of a questionable character in themselves, or at least liable to considerable abuse, and which have no effect in providing constant and wholesome recreation for the boys. Many do not spend their half-holidays in the play-ground, but in wandering about the country – some in bird's nesting, or in damaging the property of the neighbours, or other undesirable occupations.

The system of fines has of late been discontinued. It seems clear that there were serious objections to it, of which one may be mentioned here, that the fine for trespass or disobedience ultimately came out of the parent's pocket, since if a boy's money was stopped as a punishment, the parent was obliged to give him an additional supply, unless he wished to hear of his running into debt. Detentions and impositions have been substituted for fines (except as far as the payment of actual breakage or other mischief is concerned) but this change, though it must have diminished parents' expenses, has deprived the College of a considerable sum applicable to public objects. A large part of the expense of levelling the cricket ground was paid for from the fine fund.

Although no compulsory extras are permitted by the charter of the College, and though it is most desirable to keep subscriptions low, yet it is obvious that in every large School, there must be some contributions for public objects and amusements. In the hope of encouraging such as will most obviously conduce to the good of the boys, of introducing gradually the feeling that they should keep as much as possible together as one body in the College itself and in the play-ground; of checking abuses of the liberty which it is necessary to allow, if Marlborough is to confer the advantages, and be conducted on the principles of English public Schools, under which any system of entire and compulsory restriction to the College premises is quite impossible; I venture to recommend the following objects for your son's subscriptions, and in doing so I am not advising any increase of the money now given to him for such purposes, but only pointing out how, in my judgement, it can be best bestowed for his own advantage, and the general good of the School.

1. THE CRICKET CLUB:- The present Captain of the Eleven has made a calculation, by which it appears that the expenses of cricket and foot-ball might be liberally provided for, if the great majority of the School were to subscribe half-yearly, on the following scale:-

Lower School 1s
Middle School 2s
Fourth Form 3s
Fifth Form 4s
Sixth Form 5s

with some private contributions from the first eleven. This would include expense of bowler, tent, matches &c.: would enable every subscriber to play, and might possibly be diminished if *all* the School were to subscribe.

2. HOUSE LIBRARIES:- It is proposed to establish in each of the three houses, a library of entertaining and improving books, which the boys may take with them to read where they choose, to be selected by a committee of the boys who subscribe, subject to the approbation of the House-Masters, who will undertake the general superintendence and regulation of the libraries. The subscription proposed is 2s a half-year. It is hoped that, besides the obvious advantages of such an institution in each house, it might provide some occupation for long afternoons in winter and rainy weather, which are now liable to be misused.

3. THE FIVES-COURTS:- The games of fives and rackets, healthy and good in themselves, and particularly useful at School, as filling up many half-hours when there is not time to get up a game at foot-ball or cricket, are suspended at Marlborough from the defective paving of the Courts. A general effort to pave them would be of great advantage to the School, and some external help from its friends has already been promised. This is an object to which the old fine fund would have been properly applicable.

There are other amusements which I hope gradually to see arise, such as carpentering, turning, and some scientific occupations, which have been introduced with success at Woolwich and elsewhere. But it is undesirable to attempt too many things at once. Again, other public objects, such as the Musical Society, though very good in themselves, need not be noticed here, as limited for the most part to those who have some particular taste or talent. Nor do I mention the religious societies now grouped together under our College Church Union, among the institutions to which I venture to call your attention, partly because my chief motives for sending this circular are unconnected with those societies, but still more, because our desire is that the contributions to the Church Union should spring from a conviction on the part of the boys, that they ought to devote a part of their own money to higher and better objects than their own pleasures, and therefore that any sums given to it should not be supplied from extra funds allowed by their parents, but fairly saved from their own ordinary expenses, as a sign that they desire, according to their ability, to promote the glory of God.

II. There is one subject more which I wish to mention, connected with the Education of the School. So many boys are now not intended for an academical career, that the feeling is becoming general, that it would be well if in our large School classes were instituted by the side of the present course of preparation for the Universities, in which modern languages and science should form the principal subjects, and where boys should be prepared for military, naval, engineering, or other pursuits. I do not feel, with my present information competent to submit to the Council a scheme for introducing such a department here, but it is my desire to do so in the course of the next year, and it would much facilitate my plans if I could form any notion as to the number of pupils likely to be placed under such a course.

Possibly, too, we might be able to introduce it gradually, and by way of experiment, before endeavouring to incorporate it in our general School system. It would of course be included in the ordinary charge for education, or at most with the additional expense of a private tutor, which might be necessary till it sufficiently commended itself to public favour, to stand on its own foundation, and to occupy the whole time of one or more Masters.

I must apologise for the length of the communication, which has been occasioned by a deep conviction that no School, least of all one of such recent foundation as ours, can really flourish unless all connected with it, the boys, and their parents, no less than the masters and other authorities, are united in the common desire and effort to raise its general tone, and to make it, in all respects, worthy of the high purposes for which it was instituted.

Believe me,

Yours very faithfully,

G. E. L. Cotton.

Appendix II

Historical documents dealing with various aspects of the economics of athleticism

(a) Uppingham School statement of capital invested and comparative annual expenditure of trust and masters 1853–72

(b) Harrow School tercentenary appeal 1871

(c) Deed of trust associated with the Bessborough Memorial Fund raised 'for the permanent benefit of cricket at Harrow School' 1899 (extracts)

(d) Harrow School: approximate sums collected for the purchase and development of games facilities 1850–1900

Appendix II(a)

A. CAPITAL INVESTED IN BUILDINGS, &C.
(The actual cost is given in each case, unless otherwise stated.)

I. Belonging to the Trust:

	£.	£.	£.
(A) *Supplied by the Foundation*;			
1 House, the Head-Master's: the old School-house, (say)	4,000		
Contributions to the School-room	3,093		
		7,093	
(B) *Presented by Present Masters to the Trust since* 1853;			
The Gymnasium	300		
School-room, remainder of cost of building, including site	2,408		
The Chapel, with Organ and Tower★	9,797		
2 Fives Courts in School Quad	100		
		12,605	
Total belonging to the Trust			19,698

II. Belonging to the Masters:

    (A) *Conjointly;*

Sanatorium★	2,920	
2 Bathing Places cost	250	
2 Cricket Fields, levelled, etc., cost	300	
Pavilion on Cricket Field	360	
Plate and Furniture in Chapel	195	
Furniture in School-rooms	300	
in Music Class-rooms	130	
in Library	73	
in Museum	135	
in Sanatorium (say)	200	
Total belonging to Masters conjointly		4,863

    (B) *Separately;*

        (a) *Used for public purposes:*

Scale Hill, Class-rooms, etc.	1,500	
Old School-room, Carpentry, etc.	500	
Gardens	860	

        (b) *Used by individual Masters:*

11 Boarding Houses, with 10 Fives Courts and 1 covered Play Ground	48,275	
3 Private Dwelling Houses	5,500	

(Other Properties are held in Uppingham by Masters with a view to the benefit of the School, but as they are not used for School purposes they are not here included.)

Total belonging to Masters separately		56,635
Total belonging to Masters		61,498

    Total Capital Invested in Buildings, etc., £81,196

★ *Considerable debts remain upon the Chapel and Sanatorium secured upon the personal bonds of the Masters and in course of liquidation.*

Thus of the Total Capital invested in Buildings, etc., viz., £81,196,

The Trust has supplied	£7,093, or 8¾ per cent.,
And the Present Masters	£74,103, or 91¼ per cent.

    B. Comparative Annual Expenditure of the Trust and the Masters in carrying on the Work of the School.

    (For details of these, so far as they are borne by the Masters conjointly see Appendix.)

I. Masters:

    The School employs 27 Masters and 2 Lecturers. Of these

        The Trust contributes towards 2 Masters £270;

The School supplies the chief income of these 2 Masters, and also
maintains the 25 other Masters and pays the 2 Lecturers.

Thus of the Teaching Staff, the Trust supplies about 2¼ *per cent.,*
and the School supplies 97¾ *per cent.*

II. Houses:

The School employs 21 Dwelling Houses, viz., 12 Boarding Houses and 9
Private Houses. Of these

The Trust keeps in repair, etc., 1 Boarding House (the Head-Master's).
The Masters keep in repair, etc., 14 Houses.
The remaining 6 Houses are rented by the Masters.

III. Chapel: *(Now belonging to the Trust.)*
The Masters supply attendance and repairs.

IV. School-rooms: *(The large School-room, with Library and 1 Class-room, belongs to the Trust.)*
The Masters supply attendance and repairs.
The Masters also supply entirely about 24 other Class-rooms, in their Houses
or at Scale Hill.

V. Examiners:

The School employs 4. Of these

The Trust supplies 1 annually for the highest boys for Exhibitions.
The Masters supply 3, viz.:

1 for Music, half-yearly.
1 for Mathematics, yearly.
1 for Scholarships, yearly.

VI. Scholarships, Exhibitions, and Prizes: *(Exclusive of 3 Exhibitions each year, to boys at College, total value £420,)*

The Trust gives in the School yearly £7 10s. in Prizes.
The Masters give in the School yearly £890.

VII. Other Buildings and Apparatus for public School purposes, which have all
been supplied since 1853 by the present Masters, are repaired by them, viz.:

(*a*) SANATORIUM.
(*b*) SMALLER HOSPITAL.
(*c*) WORK-SHOP FOR CARPENTRY.
(*d*) GYMNASIUM.
(*e*) MUSEUM.
(*f*) GARDENS.
(*g*) 2 CRICKET FIELDS.
(*h*) 2 BATHING PLACES.

APPENDIX DETAILING MONIES ANNUALLY EXPENDED BY
THE MASTERS CONJOINTLY FOR PUBLIC SCHOOL
PURPOSES, AS SET FORTH UNDER B.

	£.	£.
Salaries:		
Classical, etc. Master	250	
Do. do.	162	
Do. do.	162	
Mathematical Master	150	
Singing do.	100	
Reading Lecturer	50	
Other Lecturers	7	
Attendant on Rooms, etc.	60	
	——	941
Examiners:		
Music	30	
Mathematics	15	
Scholarships in School		
	——	45
Scholarships:		
Classical, etc.,	680	
English	80	
	——	760
Prizes:		
Books, etc.		130
Rents:		
Class-rooms, Scale Hill: deficiency	35	
Smaller Hospital	21	
Carpenter's Shop and Museum	30	
Gardens: deficiency about	45	
Cricket Fields	83	
Bathing Places	17	
	——	231
Tradesmen:		
Gas and Coals	52	
Gravel for School Quad, etc.	6	
Printing, etc.	85	
Miscellaneous and Repairs	20	
	——	163

Interest on money borrowed for building purposes is not here included, nor in
the Statement of Capital Invested in A. It has been and is a considerable item.
On the new School-room the Masters paid £394 as Interest, in addition to the
cost as given in A.

TOTAL   £2,270

EDWARD THRING, M.A.,
HEAD-MASTER.

Appendix II(b)

This Circular is respectfully addressed to the Parents of those who are now, or have been previously, members of the School.

Harrow, May 10th, 1871.

I am anxious to be allowed to bring before the Parents of Harrow Boys, past as well as present, a work of much importance to the welfare of the School.

Three hundred years have now passed since the original Charter was granted to JOHN LYON by QUEEN ELIZABETH. We propose to commemorate our 300th birthday by an effort on a large scale to supply the School with such buildings as are still necessary in order to enable it to do its duty fully by its Scholars, and to carry out worthily such additions to its educational system as the progress of sober and cultivated opinion demands.

I.—It may be desirable to explain at the outset the peculiar financial position in which Harrow stands. *Harrow has virtually no endowment.* The Trust Fund administered by the Governors is quite inconsiderable, amounting to a very few hundreds a year, and is practically absorbed by annual and unchanging demands. Hence, when any improvements on a wide scale become necessary, there is no resource but to apply to the friends of the School for voluntary subscriptions. How largely we have been indebted to this system will be seen from a rapid sketch of our recent history.

Till 1819 there appear, so far as I am aware, to have been no considerable additions to the public buildings or resources of the School.

In 1819 a subscription was raised among Old Harrovians and Parents of the Boys for the purpose of building a new Speech-Room, adding one wing to the old buildings (including a Library), and enlarging the School-yard. This subscription received additions till 1829, and amounted at last to about £8,000.

In 1838 a Chapel was erected at a cost of some £4,000, similarly raised.

In 1845 about £3,000 was subscribed, £1,000 being a single gift, to build a Boarding House for the Head Master.

In 1851 the School Bathing Place was improved by DR. VAUGHAN, at a cost to himself of about £1,000.

In 1854–1856 the present new and beautiful Chapel was erected at a cost, from first to last, of some £12,000. The Chancel, which cost about £2,500, was the gift of DR. VAUGHAN.

At the same time new School buildings were raised for about £4,000, to which the Masters very largely contributed.

In 1861–1863 the Vaughan Library was built at a cost, including the purchase of site, of about £10,000.

In 1864 new Racquet and Fives Courts were constructed at a cost of some £2,300, in addition to some £1,400 which had been expended in 1849–1851.

In 1865 followed the School Sanatorium, costing about £5,000.

In 1865 a Spire was added to the School Chapel as a Memorial to the REV. WILLIAM OXENHAM, at a cost of about £1,000.

In 1866 we collected the large sum of £7,000, for the purchase and adaptation of a new and additional Cricket Ground, which had become absolutely necessary for the wants of the School.

It thus appears that in a space of about fifty years sums of not much less than £59,000, nearly £47,000 of which have come during the last quarter of a century, have been expended on permanent School improvements, raised by voluntary contributions from Masters, Old Harrovians, and Parents of Boys actually in the School. These do not include other very large donations to the School in the form of Scholarships and Prizes, representing a capital of some £20,000. A list of them will be found in the enclosed copy of the Commemoration of Benefactors, which is yearly read out in the Chapel on our Founder's Day. Its simple facts are perhaps the best record of the recent historical life of the School.

Our warmest acknowledgments are due, and cannot be paid more fitly than in this year of Commemoration, to all those who during the past half-century have come forward so repeatedly and so generously to meet Harrovian wants.

II.—But the fact remains that other wants are still very pressing, and it is to these that I would now respectfully invite attention.

In the first place, there is no one room in which the School can conveniently be summoned together, a deficiency which is often seriously felt. The present Speech-Room is too small—too small for the annual gathering on our Speech-day, when numerous visitors and all the boys are obliged to be excluded, but also too small for our own School uses, for Lectures, for Concerts, and even for occasional assemblings.

We require a new and very much larger Speech-Room. If this were once standing, the present Speech-Room could be turned to practical account, as it is capable of being divided into several excellent School-rooms.

These last we greatly need, partly because of our numbers, partly because some of those which we are now obliged to use are by no means well adapted for teaching; but still more because the extension of our range of studies absolutely demands greater material appliances.

We need a Museum, a Laboratory, with two good Lecture Rooms for Physical Science, a large and well-lighted room for Drawing, and at least four good Class Rooms besides the three into which the present Speech-Room can be divided.

We have also very great need of a Gymnasium. It would occupy many boys at all times, and would be peculiarly valuable in wet weather.

Besides the number of buildings required, we have special difficulties of *site* to contend with, as is well known to all who are familiar with the locality of Harrow. Nothing on a large scale can be done at Harrow without considerable previous demolition, and this of course adds largely to the cost.

It has been estimated, after much careful thought, that in order to make such purchases of land, and erect even a considerable part of such buildings as we now require, we must endeavour to raise a sum of not less than £30,000.

At a meeting of old Harrovians held a few weeks back in London on March 30th, with the HON. FREDERICK PONSONBY in the chair, it was moved by A. J. B. BERESFORD-HOPE, Esq., M.P., and seconded by the EARL OF GALLOWAY, "That a

Fund be raised to be called the 'Lyon Memorial Fund,' for the purpose of acquiring land and erecting buildings for School purposes, the first object being the erection of a Speech-Room."

This resolution was carried unanimously, and we have since been actively engaged in considering the measures for carrying it into effect. Though we are only just beginning to extend our appeal beyond the body of the Masters and our immediate neighbours, we have already received promises of subscriptions to the amount of some £5,700. These are indicated below.

I trust I shall be pardoned for thus laying our case not only before the Parents of Boys now in the School, but before the friends of past years. It will be felt that we are pleading not for ourselves, but for the School, which has no permanent funds of its own. If we are to carry out our work in a manner worthy of the fame and antiquity of the School, it can only be by the generous and even munificent aid of those who have its interests at heart, and feel the importance, at the present educational crisis, of not only loyally maintaining all that is best in the old classical system, but also making provision for other studies, the claims of which are so loudly and so justly demanding recognition.

My gratitude will be very great if, at the close of our third century of School life, we are enabled to continue with ampler appliances, but with unchanged spirit, those labours of our predecessors which have left their mark—we trust for good—on the public life of England.

H. Montagu Butler.

P.S.—At Messrs. COUTTS AND CO., 59, Strand; Messrs. GLYN, MILLS, AND CO., 67, Lombard Street; and the London and Westminster Bank, accounts have been opened in favour of the "Lyon Memorial Fund." Any Donations that may be kindly given can be paid either to the above Banks or to the Master of the House in which the Donor's son resides; or to the REV. J. A. CRUIKSHANK, Harrow, or to the Head Master. They can, if the Donor prefers it, be spread over a term of three years.

	Subscriptions already Promised
	£ s d
Anderson, Douglas E. Esq. (the late)	50 0 0
Butler, Mrs., Julian Hill	100 0 0
Butler, Mrs. Montagu	25 0 0
Galloway, Earl of	200 0 0
Gilliat, J. S. Esq.	105 0 0
Grant, W. Esq.	200 0 0
Grimston, Hon. R.	100 0 0
Harrow Club at Oxford	100 0 0
Heath, Baron	105 0 0
Leaf, C. J. Esq.	1,000 0 0
Ponsonby, Hon. Fred.	150 0 0
Roundell, C. S. Esq.	50 0 0
Sanderson, Rev. L.	50 0 0

	Subscriptions already Promised
FROM THE MASTERS OF HARROW SCHOOL	£ s d
Accumulation of certain School Funds (about)	750 0 0
The Head Master	1,000 0 0
Bowen, E. E. Esq.	50 0 0
Bull, W. J. Esq.	25 0 0
Bushell, Rev. W. D.	100 0 0
Cruikshank, Rev. J. A.	150 0 0
Gilliat, Rev. E.	25 0 0
Griffith, G. Esq.	50 0 0
Hallam, G. H. Esq.	100 0 0
Hayward, R. B. Esq.	60 0 0
Holmes, C. F. Esq. (1st sub.)	50 0 0
Hutton, H. E. Esq.	150 0 0
Marshall, F. E. Esq.	100 0 0
Masson, Mons. G.	21 0 0
Middlemist, Rev. R. (1st sub.)	50 0 0
Nettleship, H. Esq.	25 0 0
Quick, Rev. R. H.	100 0 0
Rendall, Rev. F.	200 0 0
Ruault, Mons. G.	20 0 0
Smith, Rev. J.	50 0 0
Smith, R. Bosworth, Esq.	50 0 0
Steel, Rev. T. H.	60 0 0
Stogdon, J. Esq.	30 0 0
Tosswill, A. C. Esq.	50 0 0
Watson, A. G. Esq.	100 0 0
Young, Rev. E. M.	100 0 0

Appendix II(c)

DEED OF TRUST ASSOCIATED WITH THE BESSBOROUGH MEMORIAL FUND (EXTRACTS)

This Indenture made the thirtieth day of August 1899 BETWEEN THE RIGHT HONOURABLE THOMAS FRANCIS EARL OF LICHFIELD of 38 Great Cumberland Place London W. ALEXANDER JOSIAH WEBBE of 35 Eaton Square London S.W. Esquire and WILLIAM OXENHAM HEWLETT of Harrow-on-the-Hill in the County of Middlesex Esquire hereinafter called the Trustees of the one part and EDWARD ERNEST BOWEN of the Grove Harrow-on-the-Hill aforesaid Esquire of the other part WHEREAS on the death in 1895 of the late Right Honourable Frederick George Brabazon Ponsonby Earl of Bessborough a fund was raised in his memory called the Bessborough Memorial Fund and

Trust Deed date 30th August, 1899, between the Trustees and Representative of the Committee.

Recites creation of Bessborough Memorial Fund.

the objects for which the same were raised included the erection of a memorial in Harrow School Chapel (which has been erected) and the application of the residue thereof to some purpose or purposes for the permanent benefit of Cricket in Harrow School. And WHEREAS the Committee in charge of the said fund have caused such residue to be laid out in the purchase of the messuages and pieces of land described in the schedule hereto and the same have been conveyed to the Trustees in fee simple And WHEREAS the funds at the disposal of the Committee not having been sufficient for the payment of the whole of the purchase money thereof a sum of £940 or thereabouts has been borrowed by the Committee for that purpose And WHEREAS it is desired that the trusts on which the Trustees hold the said premises should be declared and the following provisions with a view to carrying out the objects of the said fund have been agreed upon by the said Committee and they have authorised the said Edward Ernest Bowen to be a party to and to execute these presents as representing the Committee and in testimony of the approval by the Committee hereto NOW THIS INDENTURE WITNESSETH that to effectuate the said desire and in consideration of the premises it is hereby declared as follows:—

Purchase of property by Committee.

Money borrowed by Committee.

Object of Trust deed.

Sanction of Committee.

Declaration of Trust.

1. The Trustees and the survivors and survivor of them and the heirs and assigns of such survivor or other the Trustees or Trustee for the time being of these presents (hereinafter called the Trustees or Trustee) shall stand possessed of the said messuages and premises so vested in them as aforesaid (which together with any lands or hereditaments added or substituted under the powers herein contained are hereinafter called the Trust Estate) upon trust for the promotion and advancement of the game of Cricket among the Scholars of Harrow School and thereby for the benefit of Harrow School in such manner as the Trustees or Trustee shall from time to time think most expedient to carry into effect such object and in order thereto subject to the trusts and with the powers hereinafter expressed.

Trustees to hold the Trust Estate to promote cricket in Harrow School.

To apply the income of the Trust Estate and any other money whether capital or otherwise held by the Trustees or Trustee for the purposes of the Trust for the promotion of any of the purposes of the Trust or in furtherance of any of the powers of these presents and in any other manner which the Trustees or Trustee shall deem to be conducive to the promotion or advancement of Cricket among the Scholars of Harrow School.

To apply moneys in promotion of the Trust.

.   .   .

To lay out and construct or arrange for the laying out and construction of the Trust Estate or any part thereof, as a Cricket ground and place of recreation for Harrow School in connection with any other ground or otherwise with any fences drains sewers roads paths and other accessories and to make or provide for any alterations works or improvements on the Trust Estate.

To lay out property as Cricket Ground.

To erect alter and repair or arrange for the erection alteration and repair of any pavilions sheds or other buildings on the Trust Estate and to accept maintain and keep in repair any pavilions sheds or other buildings which may be presented to the Trustees or Trustee or erected by their or his leave on the Trust Estate for the use of the Scholars of Harrow School and for the purposes of Cricket.

To erect Pavilions.

To manage plant and cultivate and cut timber on the Trust Estate and to do all other acts of cultivation and management.

To plant trees.

To depute any person or persons appointed by the Head Master or the Cricket Committee for the time being of Harrow School in that behalf to act in the general management and regulation of any part of the Trust Estate appropriated as a Cricket ground or place of recreation and the care and custody thereof.

To regulate use of ground.

To unite partially or wholly temporarily or permanently the management of the Trust Estate or any part thereof with the management by Trustees or others of any other Cricket ground used by the Scholars of Harrow School and in particular the grounds known as the Philathletic Field and the Nicholson Ground, but in the latter or any similar case not beyond the interest for which the same is appropriated for the use of the said School and to convey the Trust Estate or any part thereof to the Trustees of any such other ground (subject to a permanent Trust thereof for such use as aforesaid having been established) upon the Trusts and subject to the powers vested in such other Trustees and as to the estate so conveyed to determine the present Trust.

To unite property with any other Cricket ground.

To do all other acts which in the opinion of the Trustees or Trustee are incidental to the execution of these Trusts and powers or conducive to the attainment of the general object of this Trust.

To act generally.

PROVIDED that after appropriation of any part of the Trust Estate as a Cricket ground the foregoing powers of selling exchanging and leasing or any other power whereby such part of the Trust Estate would be taken away from the use for the time being by the Scholars of Harrow School as a Cricket ground or place of recreation shall not be exercised unless in cases where by change of circumstances or for any

Restriction on certain powers.

As to sale of Cricket Ground.

special reason the portion of the Trust Estate so to be dealt with shall in the opinion of the Trustees or Trustee be no longer capable of being conveniently used as such Cricket ground or place of recreation or another and in the opinion of the Trustees or Trustee a more suitable piece of land will be or is intended to be substituted for the same or it will otherwise be in the opinion of the Trustees or Trustee conducive to the general object of this Trust or in the case of a sale or exchange of small portions for the purpose of altering or rectifying boundaries or other like purpose and no sale or exchange of the whole of the Trust Estate for the time being not so appropriate shall be made unless the same shall have been first offered to the Governing Body of Harrow School to be purchased by them on reasonable terms and shall have been refused by them.

As to sale of Trust Estate.

Appendix II(d)

HARROW SCHOOL: APPROXIMATE SUMS COLLECTED FOR THE PURCHASE AND DEVELOPMENT OF GAMES FACILITIES 1850–1900

Date	Amount	Purpose	Source
1851	£1000	For improvement to school bathing place	C. Vaughan, Headmaster
1864	£2300	For new racquets and fives courts	General subscription
1866	£7000	For philathletic field (9 acres)	General subscription
1873	£4000	For a gymnasium	Lyon Memorial Fund
1884	£3000	For philathletic field (5 acres)	Grimston Memorial Fund
1885	£18,500	For purchase of football field	Butler Memorial Fund
1891	£800	For new fives courts	Parent in memory of his son.
	£1000	For Harrow cricket	Bequest of T. K. Tapling, O.H.
1893	£1000	For Lower Cricket Field	E. Bowen, Assistant Master
1894	£1000	For Harrow cricket	Bequest of A. A. Hadow, O. H.
1895	£200	For Harrow cricket	Bequest of Earl of Bessborough, O.H.
	£5500	For improvement of cricket fields	Bessborough Memorial Fund
	£19,000	For purchase of football fields	General subscription
	£500	For Harrow cricket	Bequest of I. D. Walker, O.H.

Note: The above list does not include items such as additions to the bathing place by former scholars and others in 1881, the 1883 new pavilion on the Old Cricket Ground – a gift from old boys, masters (E. Bowen made a substantial contribution) and friends of the school, the purchase of the Nicholson Field by a former pupil, William Nicholson, for the use of the school and laid out at the expense of old boys and others, and the 1893 new pavilions on the cricket fields in memory of Old Harrovians, William Law and Cyril Buxton. In all these instances the exact amounts involved are not known.

Sources: P. B. M. Bryant, *Harrow*; E. W. Howson and G. T. Warner, *Harrow School*; E. D. Laborde, *Harrow: yesterday and today*; *Tyro*; *Harrovian* (1st, 2nd and 3rd series); *Harrow Notes*; *Harrow School Tercentenary, 1871*.

Appendix III

The school magazine

(a) The school magazine as a primary source.

(b) A page and correspondence analysis of the school magazines 1866–1966

Appendix III(a)

THE SCHOOL MAGAZINE AS A PRIMARY SOURCE

This study has involved a page-by-page scrutiny of the magazines of the various schools from their inception to their present maturity. Such sources provided the researcher with a rich 'lode' for the simple reason that the role of the school magazine is largely an introspective one. The outside world seldom intrudes. In the words of an early commentator: 'the society is close knit . . . and absorbed in its own pursuits. The magazine is a record of this life' (J. R. H. O'Regan, *The Public Schools from Within*, 1906, p. 102). Despite censorship discussed below, it is a record which, in the view of one writer who has made a comparative study of public school magazines, captures 'with remarkable accuracy, the standards, vitality and temper of each school' (Oliver van Oss, 'A Century of School Magazines', *Conference*, April 1976).

The habit of introspection was, from the start, quite deliberate and commercially sensible. 'To be the mouthpiece of the school, to chronicle events, to take notice of all that goes on, to record the incidents of the day, to interest the present school by pleasantly writing down its exploits, the past school by reminding them of their own' was the avowed ambition of the first editors of the *Uppingham School Magazine* (editorial, April 1863). Those elsewhere made similar promises and had similar objectives. In defence of its parochial flavour the *Stonyhurst College Magazine* described itself modestly as chronicler of school life for boys past and present. Erudite treatises and elaborate essays, it stated, were available in *The Times* for those who desired them (editorial, March 1886). The objectives of those early editors remain broadly the same today.

It must never be overlooked, however, that the magazine in its self-appointed role is an *official* record of school life. As such it has always perpetuated established values rather than challenged them. It is significant that the Marlborough aesthetes of the 1920s published their own magazine, *The Heretick*, rather than sought space in the *Marlburian* for their polemics. However, unofficial magazines while permitted greater freedom of expression were not safe from interference. In one such journal, a Harrovian wrote with mournful indignation:

> Another poem here should be
> Born of my fountain pen, sir,
> O gentle reader, weep with me.
> It did not pass the censor!   (*Upshott*, July 1938)

And, in fact, *The Heretick* was suppressed after the second number.

An important question to ask, therefore, in connection with all school magazines is, 'What has been the nature and extent of official censorship?' It is clear that there has always been censorship, the task of an appointed member of the school staff and a deliberately conservative responsibility. By way of illustration, Rev. T. Cooke wrote cuttingly in his Lancing diary of one censor of liberal views who, feeling strongly about a particular subject, was tempted to promote (rather than repress) radicalism: 'His position is to control not to initiate' (entry for 18 October 1908). No surviving examples of unacceptable material have been located. And, indeed, such ephemera are hardly likely to exist still. In general, any material likely to bring the school into bad odour with parents, old boys and possible clients would be declined. Quite reasonably, the aim of the censor was to present the school to such people in its most attractive light.

A further matter of importance is the nature of editorial power. Generally the editors were boys, and exercised the usual editorial prerogatives of initial selection and rejection of material. As in the case of official censorship, the tastes of past editors and their full effect on the content of the magazines can never be known, but the *Uppingham School Magazine* contains some interesting evidence on the subject. It was its practice for a time to state the reason why articles were not accepted. The third number (June 1863) includes the following:

'Victor'   – Declined with thanks; most
                 objectionable in style and
                 matter.
'Pie-Crust' – Utterly unworthy to appear
                 in any periodical.

An earlier number still (April 1863), gave detailed reasons for several rejections: one was a piece of plagiarism, one required overmuch correction and rewriting, one was short on matter and one was 'not of interest to young readers'. In the above cases, therefore, rejection appears to have been on both technical and moral grounds. No doubt where the morality of editor and censor failed to agree, the censor triumphed.

Occasionally editors had strong literary and intellectual aspirations, as discussed briefly in chapters 4 and 5, and favoured aesthetic and scholarly rather than sporting contributions, but until the second quarter of the twentieth century their idealism was invariably thwarted. The reason was elementary: 'a boy would very much rather read how decisive a victory his house achieved over another in the cricket field . . . than any abstract dissertation, and will dwell on the scores made on either side long after an essay on Milton has palled' (F. E. Hulme, *The Town, College and Neighbourhood of Marlborough*, 1881, p. 86). The fate of the editors of the second *Harrovian*, established in November 1878, fully illustrates this brutal truth.

They wished to kindle a literary spirit in their readers, and at first were undaunted 'by the many who will sneer at the idea of a school paper having any serious literature in it . . . wishing to see it given up exclusively to Philathletic news'. Yet eventually they reverted to old styles and litanies. As the first *Harrovian* had knowingly observed, it was rare to hear of a literary paper which survived long at any Victorian public school (editorial, April 1870). There can be little doubt its cynicism was justified. In 1898 the *Public School Magazine* published the details of a survey of some hundred school magazines, and discovered that they contained 'no clever or learned articles'.

Despite the absence of a detailed record of official censorship and a complete analysis of the preferences of editors, and while it is impossible to be exact about the extent to which magazines reflected various shades of school opinion over the years, a careful reading of the magazines indicates that between 1860 and 1920, competently written descriptions of school life, especially its sporting dramas, which were of interest to the majority, invariably won editorial and official favour. Pressure to produce issues, fill pages and win support, circumscribed the power of the most literary editors and made light work for the censor's blue pencil.

It would be unreasonably circumspect, in my opinion, to adopt the view that during this period the preoccupation with games revealed in the correspondence columns, and the extensive reporting of matches, indicated obsequious editorial gestures towards officialdom rather than dominant community values; or that the later increasing emphasis on literary material did not indicate in turn the relative lack of interest in games which gradually came to characterise the subsequent decades.

Finally, apart from indicating general trends of this nature, the magazine, with its devotion to the small world of the school, contains biographical material and the statements of staff, pupils and old boys, which constitute a fund of vocabularies of motive, enthusiasm and nostalgia. These provide insights into the beliefs, attitudes and values of an era, and permit the composition of a picture which, though certainly incomplete, goes a considerable way towards capturing the aesthetic of athleticism.

Appendix III(b)

HARROW
Pages

	1866	1876	1886	1896	1906	1916	1926	1936	1946	1956	1966
Sport	30	—	78	43	45	—	72	95	64	46	51
	21.4%		50.6%	38.7%	34.9%		52.9%	54.0%	38.6%	30.3%	28.5%
All other	110	—	76	68	84	—	64	81	102	106	128
	78.6%		49.4%	61.3%	65.1%		47.1%	46.0%	61.4%	69.7%	71.5%

Correspondence

	1866	1876	1886	1896	1906	1916	1926	1936	1946	1956	1966
Sport	3	—	7	5	16	—	10	7	47	30	14
	50%		41.2%	26.3%	59.3%		47.6%	26.9%	54.6%	34.1%	20.9%
All other	3	—	10	14	11	—	11	19	39	58	53
	50%		58.8%	73.7%	40.7%		52.4%	73.1%	45.4%	65.9%	79.1%

Note: There was no school magazine in 1876.

LANCING

Pages	1880	1890	1900	1910	1920	1930	1940	1950	1960
Sport	20 43.5%	48 43.6%	48 46.2%	40 27.4%	42 37.5%	60 34.5%	—	16 10.2%	49 27.2%
All other	26 56.5%	62 56.4%	56 53.8%	106 72.6%	70 62.5%	114 65.5%	—	142 89.8%	131 72.8%

Correspondence

Pages	1880	1890	1900	1910	1920	1930	1940	1950	1960
Sport	6 50%	15 50%	6 60%	1 8.3%	7 31.8%	10 58.8%	—	3 27.3%	2 40%
All other	6 50%	15 50%	4 40%	11 91.7%	15 68.2%	7 41.2%	—	8 72.7%	3 60%

LORETTO

Pages	1881	1891	1901	1911	1921	1931	1941	1951	1961
Sport	36 54.5%	36 57.2%	32 53.3%	25 48.1%	31 55.4%	55 59.7%	—	18 23.7%	30 31.9%
All other	30 45.5%	24 42.8%	28 46.7%	27 51.9%	25 44.6%	37 40.3%	—	58 76.3%	64 68.1%

Correspondence

	1886	1896	1906	1916	1926	1936	1946	1956	1966
Sport	20 40.8%	13 65%	2 25%	1 14.3%	12 57.2%	5 62.5%	— —	2 33.3%	4 33.3%
All other	29 59.2%	7 35%	6 75%	6 85.7%	9 42.8%	3 37.5%	— —	4 66.7%	8 66.7%

STONYHURST
Pages

	1886	1896	1906	1916	1926	1936	1946	1956	1966
Sport	16 9.8%	35 17.7%	25 10.1%	— —	— —	50 24.5%	42 22.8%	51 41.8%	22 36.7%
All other	146 90.2%	163 82.3%	223 89.9%	— —	— —	154 75.5%	142 77.2%	71 58.2%	38 63.3%

Correspondence

	1886	1896	1906	1916	1926	1936	1946	1956	1966
Sport	3 16.7%	10 55.6%	3 9.7%	— —	— —	0 0%	3 20%	1 20%	0
All other	15 83.3%	8 44.4%	28 90.3%	— —	— —	7 100%	12 80%	4 80%	0

Note: Stonyhurst no longer has copies of the school magazine for 1926.

UPPINGHAM

Pages

	1864	1874	1884	1894	1904	1914	1924	1934	1944	1954	1964
Sport	112 24.5%	101 29.2%	175 46.3%	134 41.1%	—	—	166 44.5%	86 32.8%	—	67 34.7%	37 27.6%
All other	346 75.5%	245 70.8%	203 53.7%	192 58.9%	—	—	207 55.5%	176 67.2%	—	126 65.3%	97 72.4%

Correspondence

	1864	1874	1884	1894	1904	1914	1924	1934	1944	1954	1964
Sport	19 38%	6 35.3%	10 58.8%	1 50%	—	—	2 28.6%	4 44.4%	—	3 13.6%	5 45.5%
All other	31 62%	11 64.7%	7 41.2%	1 50%	—	—	5 71.4%	5 55.6%	—	19 86.4%	6 54.5%

Note: No details are available for 1904.

General notes

1   Details of Marlborough may be found in the text in chapter 4.
2   Both World Wars considerably disrupted life in the schools, military training often replacing conventional games. For this reason an analysis of the war years is omitted above.
3   The contents of magazine pages and occasionally of correspondence, of course, do not divide neatly into sporting and non-sporting material. The above separation must of necessity be only an approximate division.

Comment

The overall picture which emerges from this analysis, as in the case of Marlborough discussed in chapter 4, is one of a distinct emphasis on games reporting and discussion in the late nineteenth and early twentieth centuries at Harrow, Lancing, Loretto and Uppingham. Yet there is some variation between the schools. Harrow, Lancing and Loretto gave considerable space to games literature, while Uppingham, initially under Thring, appears to have taken a more balanced view of life, although games coverage grew in volume towards the end of his headship and subsequently remained substantial for many years. Once again, it may be noted, Stonyhurst proves the exception. As the twentieth century progressed there was a gradual shift away from a preoccupation with sporting matters, and after the Second World War, as the figures above indicate, this was clearly reflected in the school magazines.

Appendix IV

Some nineteenth- and twentieth-century timetables in relation to games

Uppingham

Paul Ford, writing on public school athletics in C. Cookson's *Essays on Secondary Education*, published in 1898, claimed that the average public school boy devoted a considerable amount of time to playing games, and that during the second half of the nineteenth century school timetables were continually rearranged to make this possible. Evidence from Uppingham would certainly support this assertion. This is clear from the comparison below of the timetables for 1857 and 1913. The comparison incidentally reinforces the now general belief that Thring (headmaster 1853–87) was a moderating influence on games zealots rather than the reverse. He allowed fewer hours each afternoon for games than H. W. McKenzie (headmaster 1908–15).

UPPINGHAM: WEEKDAY TIMETABLE

1857		*1913*	
Rise	6.30 a.m.	Rise	7.00 a.m.
First school	7.00 a.m.	Prayers in classroom	7.30 a.m.
		First period	7.45 a.m.
Breakfast	8.30 a.m.	Breakfast	8.30 a.m.
Second school	10.00 a.m.	Second to fourth periods	9.45 a.m.
Extras/free time	12.05 p.m.	Extras/free time	12.30 p.m.
Dinner	1.30 p.m.	Dinner	1.30 p.m.
Three days per week –			
Maths 2.30–4.00 p.m.		*Monday to Saturday – no further school*	
Three days per week – no			
further school		Monday, Wednesday – Two periods	
		and Friday	4.30–6.30 p.m.
No details – 4.30–7.00 p.m.		Thursday	No further school except for upper sixth (5.30–6.30 p.m.)
Preparation 7.00 p.m.		Tea 6.45 p.m.	
Supper, prayers and bed		Preparation 7.30 p.m.	
9.00 p.m.		Supper, prayers and bed 9.00 p.m.	

Note: For details of the 1857 timetable see 'The Reminiscences of Charles Cornish', *USM*, vol. LXXI, no. 535 (April 1933), pp. 42–9. I am indebted to Mr T. B. Belk, the Uppingham School archivist, for the 1913 details. He further informed me that some form of physical activity was compulsory every weekday during this period. On Tuesdays, Thursdays and Saturdays there were school games, and on Mondays, Wednesdays and Fridays there were either house games, runs or fives. The unathletic or unenthusiastic, however, he insists, could occasionally escape this routine. Mr Belk himself has pleasant memories of painting on summer afternoons.

Stonyhurst

It is instructive to compare the Uppingham timetables above with those of Stonyhurst for 1866 and 1894 (to 1920) given below. At Stonyhurst the earlier rising hour and the longer time devoted to academic work illustrate quite clearly its stricter regime. Its relative severity is further emphasised by the details, left by B. E. James in his diary, of Sunday study periods and continual religious services. Uppingham boys, in contrast, attended chapel only twice on Sundays, apparently did no preparation and had a considerable amount of free time.

STONYHURST: WEEKDAY TIMETABLE

1866		*1894*	
Rise	5.30 a.m.	Rise	6.30 a.m.
Mass	6.00 a.m.	Mass	7.00 a.m.
Studies	6.45 a.m.	Breakfast	7.45 a.m.
Breakfast	7.45 a.m.	Morning studies	8.15 a.m.
Schools	8.00 a.m.	Schools	9.15 a.m.
Dinner	12.30 p.m.	Dinner	1.00 p.m.
Recreation	1.00 p.m.	Recreation	1.30 p.m.
Afternoon studies	2.30 p.m.	Afternoon studies	3.00 p.m.
Schools	3.00 p.m.	Schools	3.30 p.m.
Bread and beer	4.50 p.m.	Bread and beer and recreation	5.00– 5.45 p.m.
Chapel visit	5.10 p.m.	Chapel visit	5.45 p.m.
Night studies	5.30 p.m.	Night studies	6.00 p.m.
Supper and recreation	7.00 p.m.	Supper and recreation	7.30 p.m.
Night prayers and bed	8.30 p.m.	Night prayers and bed	8.30 p.m.

Note: It is not clear whether there were half-holidays in 1866 – probably not, as this was a public school device introduced to permit organised team games which at this time were barely established at Stonyhurst. However, one full day each month (the Blandyke) was completely free. In 1894 Tuesdays and Thursdays were half-holidays and the traditional Blandyke was still observed. Details of the 1866 timetable are to be found in the diary of B. E. James for October 1866 (SCA), and the 1894 timetable is recorded in *SCM* vol. XXVIII, no. 357 (July 1945), p. 75.

Appendix V

Captains of school, games and academic awards

In chapter 4 above, it was argued that ideological consolidation in the schools of this study was achieved between 1880 and 1900 rather than during the previous twenty years. It is interesting to note in this context, therefore, the change that occurred in the qualifications of school captains after 1890.

Between 1860 and 1890 at Harrow, Marlborough and Uppingham there was a definite tendency to select as school captains, boys of predominantly intellectual ability – as measured by the winning of internal and external academic awards and non-representation in school games teams. Between 1891 and 1931, on the other hand, the number of school captains of predominantly intellectual ability declined at all three schools, while the number of school captains with games ability increased markedly at Harrow and Marlborough. At Uppingham the all-rounder became favoured. As regards the other schools, at Lancing after 1890 there was a noticeable shift in selection towards the games player. At Loretto, as early as 1862 prowess at games appears to have been a prerequisite for promotion. Unfortunately the qualifications of Stonyhurst school captains are not readily available for analysis.

Of course, a number of factors, in addition to ideological pressure and popularity, affected both the nature of the qualifications of school captains and their selection for promotion: for example, the presence or absence of an academic elite and the corresponding ability to win university scholarships, the number of internal academic awards available and the predilections of headmasters. However, it is suggested that, despite the influence of such variables, the figures below demonstrate a distinct trend in selection, which reveals the considerable importance attached to games in school life in the late nineteenth and early twentieth centuries, in contrast to the earlier periods.

HARROW

1860–1890	1891–1931
Total 34; games awards 8; academic awards 27	Total 44; games awards 23; academic awards 25
Games awards only 1	Games awards only 15
Academic awards only 20	Academic awards only 17
Both 7	Both 8
Neither 6	Neither 4

MARLBOROUGH

1860–1890
Total 29; games awards 9; academic awards 29

Games awards only	0
Academic awards only	20
Both	9
Neither	0

1891–1931
Total 46; games awards 27; academic awards 34

Games awards only	12
Academic awards only	19
Both	15
Neither	0

UPPINGHAM

1860–1890
Total 26; games awards 9; academic awards 23

Games awards only	2
Academic awards only	16
Both	7
Neither	1

1891–1931
Total 44; games awards 29; academic awards 34

Games awards only	6
Academic awards only	11
Both	23
Neither	4

LANCING

1860–1890
Total 25; games awards 20; academic awards 15

Games awards only	10
Academic awards only	5
Both	10
Neither	0

1891–1931
Total 47; games awards 40; academic awards 11

Games awards only	30
Academic awards only	1
Both	10
Neither	6

LORETTO

1860–1890
Total 29; games awards 27; academic awards 14

Games awards only	13
Academic awards only	0
Both	14
Neither	2

1891–1931
Total 62; games awards 62; academic awards 13

Games awards only	49
Academic awards only	0
Both	13
Neither	0

Appendix VI

'Poets' of athleticism

Three of the most fertile writers of the 'poetry' of athleticism from the schools of this study are H. B. Tristram of Loretto, Edward Bowen of Harrow and John Bain of Marlborough. Typical examples of their work are found below. Tristram's 'Cricket Song' and 'Football Song' are so far unpublished, and John Bain's verse has appeared only in the *Marlburian*.

The selection reflects the various moods of athleticism. Tristram represents the mass of verse of the genre: hearty, well-intentioned propaganda. There is much of this in Bowen ('Lord's 1878', 'Tom') but there is also jocular silliness ('The Niner',) and elegiac tenderness ('R.G.'). Bain, inspired by the tragedy of the Great War, wrote poetic obituaries of gentle, unsophisticated sorrow.

H. B. Tristram

Go Like Blazes

Tune: Marching through Georgia

Listen, friends, I beg you, while I sing a football song.
Shout the chorus loudly, you must keep it going strong,
Only use your voice and lungs, and we'll make it swing along
Boys as we are at Loretto.

Chorus
Hurrah! hurrah! for forwards backs and all;
Hurrah! hurrah! We'll carry every maul,
We all can go like blazes and we're always on the ball
While we are boys at Loretto.

Best of games in all the world for those who have the grit,
Far above all other sports, there's none can rival it,
Going strong from first to last, we'll play for all we're fit,
Boys as we are at Loretto.

Charging down the Pinkie Hill, upon the other backs
Never one among us all a single minute slacks;
What care we although we're bumped or what care we for hacks
While we are boys at Loretto.

Grand it is to tackle low, and grip the runner round,
Grand to feel we've got him safe, and swing him to the ground,
Grand to make some glorious kick, when loud the cheers resound
From all who are boys at Loretto.

Shoving hard in every scrum, then quick away we go
All together, dribbling close, the ball wet at our toe,
Till, a winning team again, we hear the whistle blow
While we are boys at Loretto.

Here's to all the gallant souls who've worn the jersey red,
Here's to all the captains who the School Fifteen have led,
Here's to all who've got their pluck and in their footsteps tread,
All who were boys at Loretto.

Going Strong!

Sing Football the grandest of sports in the world,
And you know it yourself if your pluck's never curled,
If you've gritted your teeth and gone hard to the last,
And sworn that you'll never let anyone past . . .

Chorus
Keeping close upon the ball – we drive it through them all,
And again we go rushing along, along, along;
O the tackle and the run, and the matches we have won,
From the start to the finish going strong, strong, strong, going
    strong!

If you live to be a hundred you'll never forget
How they hacked in the scrum, how you payed back the debt;
The joy of the swing when you tackled your man,
The lust of the fray when the battle began.

Long hence when you look with a quivering eye
On the little white tassel you value so high;
You'll think of the matches you've played in and won,
And you'll long for the days that are over and done.

Football Song

The poet oft sings of a sport fit for kings,
But a far grander subject is mine:
Sport for heroes and gods; I will lay any odds
Jove himself would have called it divine.
For football's the sport that I mean
A sport to make anyone keen;
The game we all love,
Where we run and we shove,
Yes, the finest that ever was seen.

Chorus

Then here's to this team of to-day
You bet we can show them the way;
Whether winners or not,
We're a jolly fine lot,
And we'll teach the old crocks how to play.

In the glorious strife, that glad hour of life,
When the blood pulses strong in our veins,
There's nought can compare with enjoyment so rare,
And we care not for hacks or for strains.
That push in the scrummage so strong!
That dash through the thick of the throng,
Coming straight through the pack
We are down on the back
And again we go rushing along.

And when in the fight we may find we're too light,
We must work all the harder instead;
Never mind if you're small, but get hold of the ball,
And fortune will smile on the red.
Then think of that wonderful drop,
Sailing inside the posts at the top,
Of the man whom you downed,
Having gripped him well round,
Or that dribble that no one could stop.

It's the very best fun, but it soon will be done,
So we'll play while we can, never fear;
Generations must fade, and all those who have played
For the School, in their turn disappear;
But although we regret each old friend;
Still fortune another will send;
And Loretto will show
Both to friend and to foe
That she turns out the stuff in the end.

Then here's to the team of to-day
You bet we can show them the way;
Whether winners or not
We're a jolly fine lot,
And we'll teach the old crocks how to play.

Cricket Song

Though cold be our summers
We welcome all comers
And lend them a sub if they're short.
If they give us a beating
It won't spoil our greeting,
And we always can show them some sport.

And when we are winning
We send the ball spinning,
All bowlers' devices defy:
We come down on the shooters
Stop wicket-uprooters,
That make other people's bails fly
  (And steal a sharp run on the sly.)

We hit 'em all round
And all over the ground,
And feel we could stay there all night;
And every fresh fourer
That's notched by the scorer
Makes our century nearer in sight.

But trying too often
Too high do we loft one,
And sadly the wiseacres frown.
Going straight up to heaven
It's fully worth seven,
But no, there's the tenth wicket down.

And though Fettes may beat us,
And others defeat us
Sometimes and it seems a bit rough;
To the very best cap'en
Such accidents happen
And the luck will come back soon enough.

Then from careful beginnings,
We'll run up long innings,
And banish all pitiful blobs;
We'll become wicket takers
With cunning leg breakers,
Or develop some wonderful lobs.

And the past generations
Who've won reputations
Must not be left out in the cold
With due meed and measure
We always shall treasure
The names of the heroes of old.

Then hurrah! for elevens victorious
For cricket, the great and the glorious
For each keenly fought match
And each gallery catch;
And away with all critics censorious.

Edward Bowen

Tom

> Tom!
> Now that the matches are near,
> Struggle, and terror, and bliss,
> Which is the House of the year?
> Who is the hero of this?
> Tom!
> Tom, who with valour and skill, too,
> Spite of the wind and the hill, too,
> Takes it along sudden and strong,
> Going where Tom has a will to;
> And so let us set up a cheer, O,
> That Jaffa and Joppa can hear, O,
> And if a hurrah can waken the Shah,
> Why, then, let us waken him, singing, Hurrah.
>
> Rules that you make, you obey;
> Courage to Honour is true;
> Who is the fairest in play,
> Best and good-temperedest, who?
> Tom!
> Tom, who is sorry and sad, too,
> When there are bruises to add to;
> Why did he crush Jack with a rush?
> Only because that he had to!
> And so let us, &c.
>
> Base is the player who stops
> Fight, till the fighting is o'er;
> Who follows up till he drops,
> Panting and limping and sore?
> Tom!
> Tom, who with scuffle and sprawl, too,
> Knows where he carries the ball to;
> Ankles and toes! look how he goes!
> Through them and out of them all, too!
> And so let us, &c.
>
> Some, who their Houses enthrone,
> Rest, when the victory comes;
> Who will go on till his own
> Boasts an eleven of Toms?
> Tom!
> Tom, who in cloud and in clear, too,
> Goes with the lads he is dear to;
> Is it a dream? There is the team;
> Tom may be real, and here, too!
> And so let us, &c.

Lord's 1878

There we sat in the circle vast,
Hard by the tents, from noon,
And looked as the day went slowly past,
And the runs came, all too soon;
And never, I think, in the years gone by,
Since cricketers first went in,
Did the dying so refuse to die,
Or the winning so hardly win.

Ladies clapped, as the fight was fought,
And the chances went and came;
And talk sank low, till you almost thought
You lived in the moving game.
O, good lads in the field they were,
Laboured and ran and threw;
But we that sat on the benches there
Had the hardest work to do!

Feet that had sped in games of yore,
Eyes that had guarded well,
Waited and watched the mounting score,
And the hopes that rose and fell;
And girls put frolic and wagers by,
As they felt their pulses throb;
And old men cheered – but the cheering cry
Went gurgling into a sob!

What is it, forty, thirty more,
You in the trousers white,
What did you come to Harrow for,
If we lose the match to-night?
If a finger's grasp, as a catch comes down,
Go a thousandth part astray –
Heavens! to think there are folks in town
Who talk of the game as play!

'Over' – batsmen steadily set;
'Over' – maiden again;
If it lasts a score of overs yet;
It may chance to turn the brain.
End it, finish it! such a match
Shortens the breath we draw.
Lose it at once, or else – A catch!
Ah!

The Niner

He may have been little, or may have been tall,
But his tale is so sad, you will weep for it all,

And it happened along of a bat and a ball!
Boo-hoo!
Of Cricketers never a finer,
From Nottinghamshire to China,
But he never could manage a niner!
Boo-hoo! Boo-hoo! Boo-hoo!

Chorus: Of Cricketers never, etc.

He planted his feet – and he lifted his bat –
And his reach you would wonder excessively at:
And the field said, 'For nine he will surely hit that.'
Boo-hoo!
But they ran and they scampered and fielded,
And such was the work that their zeal did,
That merely an eighter it yealded,
Boo-hoo! Boo-hoo! Boo-hoo!

Chorus: Of Cricketers never, etc.

But he finally struck a majestical blow,
And didn't it, didn't it, DIDN'T it go,
If not for a mile, for a quarter or so!
Boo-hoo!
Oh run, I believe you, he then did,
With speed and celerity splendid,
And stopped with the nine of them ended,
Boo-hoo! Boo-hoo! Boo-hoo!

Chorus: Of Cricketers never, etc.

And just as the niner was done and entire,
He threw himself down to rejoice – (and perspire),
'One short,' said the fair and impartial umpire!
Boo-hoo!
So he gave up and went and ate ices,
Of various colours and sizes,
And died of pulmonary phthisis,
Boo-hoo! Boo-hoo! Boo-hoo!

Chorus: Of Cricketers never etc.

R.G.★

Still the balls ring upon the sun-lit grass,
Still the big elms, deep shadowed, watch the play;
And ordered game and loyal conflict pass
The hours of May.

But the game's guardian, mute, nor heeding more
What suns may gladden, and what airs may blow,
Friend, teacher, playmate, helper, counsellor,
Lies resting now.

'Over' – they move, as bids their fieldsman's art;
With shifted scene the strife begins anew;
'Over' – we seem to hear him, but his part
Is over, too.

Dull the best speed, and vain the surest grace –
So seemed it ever – till there moved along
Brimmed hat, and cheering presence, and tried face
Amid the throng.

He swayed his realm of grass, and planned, and wrought;
Warned rash intruders from the tended sward;
A workman, deeming, for the friends he taught,
No service hard.

He found, behind first failure, more success;
Cheered stout endeavour more than languid skill;
And ruled the heart of boyhood with the stress
Of helpful will.

Or, standing at our hard-fought game, would look,
Silent and patient, drowned in hope and fear,
Till the lips quivered, and the strong voice shook
With low glad cheer.

Well played. His life was honester than ours;
We scheme, he worked; we hesitate, he spoke;
His rough-hewn stem held no concealing flowers,
But grain of oak.

No earthly umpire speaks, his grave above;
And thanks are dumb, and praise is all too late;
That worth and truth, that manhood and that love
Are hid, and wait.

Sleep gently, where thou sleepest, dear old friend;
Think, if thou thinkest, on the bright days past:
Yet loftier Love, and worthier Truth, attend
What more thou hast!

* R. G. was Robert Grimston, an Old Harrovian who was for many
years the schools devoted and voluntary cricket coach.

John Bain

*In Memory of Lieutenant E. S. Phillips**

I read – It all rushed back again –
The merry games we played together,
The old squash court, the shine, the rain,
The Boy who'd play in any weather,

The heart not pinned to Honours Lists –
That knew the joy of hard fought matches;
The steady eye, the supple wrists,
The sinewy hands that gripped the catches.
Aye, Marlborough knows you played the game,
Dying you set the gem upon her,
Giving her yet another name
To sparkle on her Roll of Honour.

* Marlborough 1898–1901. Killed in action in Flanders, 8 May 1915.

In Memory of Lieutenant H. J. O. Leather★

In the old days, a Voice would call,
A cheery voice, just after Hall;
To Cotton House, gloves, shoes and all,
I'd run, young Leather,
And there we'd knock a little ball
About together,

And now you've played a grimmer game;
Old England called – you heard and came
To shot and shell, to fire and flame,
To death or glory
To fight and fall, and link your name
With England's story.

O cheery voice that once I knew!
O hand and eye so quick and true!
Its hard to think on death and you,
Old Friend, together.
Goodbye the old days when the fives-balls flew,
Goodbye, young Leather.

* Marlborough 1898–1902. Killed in action in France, 2 December 1915.

In Memory of Second Lieutenant H. J. Goodwin★

I saw your brave face in the *Sphere* –
I had not seen it since the days
When, term by term, and year by year,
You taught the ball to go your ways.

Cricket and Hockey, Rackets, Fives –
Aye, you were the master of them all;
I see your hand as it contrives
The old spin that made the wickets fall.

And now you've played your noblest game,
And now you've won your grandest Blue,

And Marlboro' lads shall read your name
Upon the wall and Honour you.

★ Marlborough 1900–5. Killed in action, 24 April 1917.

In Memory of Captain E. A., Lieutenants B. H. G. and A. G. Shaw★

Three years! and every year has taken one,
Each in its turn has reft away a son.
O, Mother, mourning for your splendid dead,
Let proud drops mingle with the tears you shed.
Falling they leave behind them as they fall
A nobler fame than that of bat and ball.

On English fields life's happiest years they spent,
Now dead for England, lo! they lie content.

★ B. H. G. Shaw killed in action at Neuve Chapelle, December 1914.
A. G. Shaw killed in action in Flanders, December 1915 and E. A.
Shaw killed in action on the Somme, October 1916. All three were
pupils at Marlborough before the Great War.

Appendix VII

Salaries of assistant masters at Harrow in 1874

Schedule H of the school regulations for 1874 below reveals that there were:

21 assistant masters in classics
5 assistant masters in mathematics
2 assistant masters in modern languages
1 assistant master in natural science
1 assistant master on the 'modern side' (at this time a classicist by training).

The financial advantages accruing to a classical qualification are clear from the details on the following pages. Only classics masters could aspire to masterships of large houses and the post of tutor in these residences. In some cases the posts of housemaster, tutor and form master might be held by the same person.

(Details are from Harrow school regulations for 1874 in the Papers and Correspondence of the Marshall Family (Box D/M/1) held in the Cumbria County Record Office. One of the family, Francis Edward Marshall, was an assistant master at Harrow from 1870 to 1904. His papers are published by permission of the Cumbria County Record Office.)

Schedule H.
Number and Salaries of Assistant Masters

A. ASSISTANT MASTERS IN CLASSICS

I. Masters of Large Houses and Tutors

Four at £300 a Year each.
Six at £150 a Year each.

II. Masters of Small Houses and Tutors

Three at £150 a Year each

III. Tutors without Houses

One at £200.
Four at £150 a Year each

IV. Form Masters, not being Masters of Houses nor Tutors

One at £500.
One at £450.
One at £300.

B. ASSISTANT MASTERS IN MATHEMATICS

I. Masters of Large Houses

One at £150 a Year, with a Fee of £1 10s. on each Non-Foundationer, with liberty to receive Private Pupils from his own House.
One with a Fee of £1 on each Non-Foundationer, with liberty to receive Private Pupils.

II. Master of a Small House

One with a Fee of 16s. 8d. from each Non-Foundationer, with liberty to receive Private Pupils.

III. Form Masters, not being Masters of Houses nor Tutors

One at £500 a Year.
One at £400 a Year.

C. ASSISTANT MASTER IN NATURAL SCIENCE

Master of a Small House

One with 10s. Entrance Fee and £1 per annum on each Non-Foundationer and with liberty to take Private Pupils.

D. ASSISTANT MASTERS IN MODERN LANGUAGES

Masters with Small Houses for young Boys destined for the regular Houses.

One with a Fee of £1 2s. 6d. on each Non-Foundationer, and a Salary of £200, and with liberty to receive Private Pupils.
One with a Fee of £1 2s. 6d. on each Non-Foundationer, and a Salary of £100.

E. ASSISTANT MASTER ON THE MODERN SIDE

One at a Salary of £400.

Sealed by the Governing Body of Harrow School this Twenty-first day of February, 1874.

Appendix VIII

Jesus College, Cambridge: educational background of entrants in the nineteenth century

Schools of entrants 1849–85

Total entrants – 1290
Schools
- 217 entrants from small local schools known as grammar schools
- 207 entrants from private schools and private tutors
- 818 entrants from schools commonly called public schools

From English public schools

Harrow 63, Eton 50, Uppingham 33, Haileybury 31, Marlborough 30, Shrewsbury 30, Repton 27, Rugby 26, St Edmund's, Canterbury 24, King's College School, Wimbledon 22, Winchester 22, Lancing 22, Tonbridge 21, Charterhouse 19, Radley 19, Rossall 18, Malvern 17, Brighton 15, Felsted 15, Clifton 15, Oundle 14, Christ's Hospital 13, Wellington 13, Durham 12, Sevenoaks 11, Blackheath Proprietary School 11, Merchant Taylors 10, Bradfield 10.

From other public schools

32 entrants from public schools in 'British lands overseas':

Australia 19
New Zealand 11
Canada 1
Mauritius 1

Also Scotland 16
Wales 9
Ireland 3

Other

48 entrants – details not known
Note: 818 of the 1290 entrants took degrees and 217 of the 818 took honours degrees.

(Details from A. Gray and F. Brittain, *A History of Jesus College, Cambridge*, 1960, pp. 176–7.)

Notes

List of abbreviations

The following abbreviations occur in the notes:

Magazines

LCM   *Lancing College Magazine*
USM   *Uppingham School Magazine*
SCM   *Stonyhurst College Magazine*

Archives

HSA   Harrow School Archives
LCA   Lancing College Archives
LSA   Loretto School Archives
MCA   Marlborough College Archives
SCA   Stonyhurst College Archives
USA   Uppingham School Archives

Reports

PSC   *Report of the Public Schools Commission*
      (Clarendon Commission), 1864
SIC   *Report of the Schools Inquiry Commission*
      (Taunton Commission), 1868

Other

DNB   *The Dictionary of National Biography*
PSM   *The Public School Magazine*

Prologue

1 Simpson (1883–1959) was subsequently to achieve some small measure of distinction in English education. After experience as an assistant master at Gresham's and Rugby, and as a junior inspector at the Board of Education, he had become the first headmaster of Rendcombe College, Cirencester, in 1920. He remained there twelve years. From 1932 to 1944 he was principal of the College of St Mark and St John, Chelsea. He wrote several books dealing with his liberal educational ideas and experiences: *An Adventure in Schooling* (1917), *Howson of Holt* (1925), *Sane Schooling* (1936), *Schoolmaster's Harvest* (1954) and of course *Public Schools and Athleticism* (1923).

2 It has been considered, but only briefly and in very general terms, in histories of the public school system, histories of education and histories of physical education.

3 J. Wakeford, *The Cloistered Elite* (1969), p. 9.

4 For example, Alicia Percival, *Very Superior Men* (1973), pp. 3–10; J. Graves, *Policy and Progress in Secondary Education 1902–1942* (1943), pp. 178–9; Ian Weinberg, *The English Public Schools: the sociology of an elite education* (1967), pp. ix–xiii; Guy Kendall, *A Headmaster Reflects* (1937), p. 22; G. Kalton, *The Public Schools: a factual survey* (1966), pp. 4ff; *The Public Schools and the General Education System* (the Fleming Report, 1944), appendix A, pp. 106ff.

5 Vivian Ogilvie, *The English Public School* (1957), p. 8.

6 Its task may be understood from the full title of the published findings: *Report of Her Majesty's Commissioner Appointed to Enquire into the Reserves and Management of Certain Colleges and Schools, and the Studies Pursued therein; with an Appendix and Evidence* (1864).

7 The last two of these schools were day schools. This study of athleticism is confined to public boarding schools – space forbids a wider sample. An interesting discussion of the evolution of games in two public day schools (Dulwich and Manchester Grammar School) is to be found in John Mallea, 'The Boys' Endowed Grammar Schools in Victorian England: the educational use of sport' (unpublished Ph.D. thesis, Columbia University, 1971). *The Report of the Bryce Commission on Education* (1895) referred to the seven boarding schools of the Clarendon Report as the 'Great Public Schools'.

8 Brian Gardner, *The Public Schools* (1973), p. 164.

9 Robert Merton, *Social Theory and Social Structure* (3rd edn, 1968), pp. 493–509. He makes it clear that the labels should not be taken too literally. They merely reflect trends.

10 T. W. Bamford, *The Rise of the Public Schools* (1967); J. R. de S. Honey, *Tom Brown's Universe: the development of the public school in the nineteenth century* (1977); Gardner, *Public Schools.*

11 J. J. Tobias, *Crime and Industrial Society in the Nineteenth Century* (1967), p. 11.

12 Honey, *Tom Brown's Universe*, pp. 339ff.

13 It would be a step towards the ideal set out recently by an educational historian, namely a history of British education on 'the basis of individual schools combined with an understanding of national developments', see P. J. Wallis, 'Histories of old schools: a preliminary list for England and Wales', *British Journal of Educational Studies* vol. XIV, no. 1 (Nov. 1965) p. 48.

14 For a specific comment about differing responses to athleticism see Honey, *Tom Brown's Universe*, p. 117.

15 Bernard Darwin, *The English Public School* (1931), p. 21.

16 The term is that used by N. P. Mouzelis in *Organization and Bureaucracy* (1967), p. 69. Mouzelis considers the virtues of one-case, intensive-comparative and global investigations. See especially pp. 66–70.

17 Quoted in Ogilvie, *English Public School*, p. 180. Ogilvie states that no reasons were offered for such a categorical list but insists that public opinion had a fairly precise idea as to which schools were the best.

18 These schools also figured in the smaller list of indisputable public schools in the first *Public School Year Book* published in 1889. See Gardner, *Public Schools*, p. 202.

19 The term 'ideology' was coined by the French philosopher Destult de Tracy, at the end of the eighteenth century. For an outline of its creation see Daniel Bell, *The End of Ideology* (1961), pp. 394–5.

20 For a discussion of the emergence of ideologies in social groups see 'Ideology' in David L. Sills (ed.), *International Encyclopedia of the Social Sciences* (1968), pp. 66ff.

21 For a discussion of this wider definition, and for a subtle and seminal consideration of the term 'ideology', see J. M. Burns, 'Political ideology' in N. MacKenzie (ed.), *A Guide to the Social Sciences* (1966), pp. 205–23.

22 The view of Marx and Engels discussed in K. Fletcher, *The Making of Sociology* (1971), p. 406.

23 Gustave Bergmann, 'Ideology' in May Brodbeck (ed.), *Readings on the Philosophy of the Social Sciences* (1968), p. 127.

24 Notice has been taken of the advice of Asa Briggs, namely that history students should seek the assistance of specialists in the social sciences when the insights are relevant. See Asa Briggs, 'History and society' in MacKenzie (ed.) *Guide to the Social Sciences*, pp. 39–40.

25 While widely used as a descriptive and analytical term it is not always defined. In particular, P. C. McIntosh in his *Physical Education in England since 1800* (2nd edn, 1968), devotes three chapters to it but fails to provide a definition!

26 E. C. Mack, *Public Schools and British Opinion Since 1860* (1941), p. 126.

27 W. D. Smith, *Stretching Their Bodies* (1975), p. 18. Circular causality, in fact, existed. It is more appropriate to recognise that middle-class anti-intellectualism and contempt for the classical curriculum prevailing in the schools were major *causes* of athleticism as well as consequences. For a discussion of this point, see chapter 5 below.

28 Edward Lyttelton, 'Athletics in public schools', *Nineteenth Century*, vol. VII, no. 35 (Jan. 1880), pp. 43ff. Lyttelton (1855–1942) was typical of the later nineteenth-century genre of public school headmasters: 'schoolmaster, Divine and cricketer' (*DNB*, 1941–50). He was educated at Eton and Trinity Hall, Cambridge. From 1882 to 1890 he was an assistant master at Eton. After serving as headmaster of Haileybury (1890–1905), he returned to Eton as headmaster (1905–16). In his youth he was a famous cricketer, captain of Eton eleven (1874) and captain of Cambridge (1878). His Cambridge eleven defeated the Australians in 1874, and he was the only man in England to score a century against them. But with regard to athleticism he wore no rose-tinted

spectacles. He took an objective view of it in his writings: *Schoolboys and Schoolwork* (1909) and *Memories of Hopes* (1925).

29 Lyttelton, 'Athletics', p. 57.

30 Cyril Norwood, *The English Tradition of Education* (1929), p. 143. Norwood (1875–1956) represented the new public school headmaster of the twentieth century: layman, academic and games player. In 1901 he abandoned his civil service post at the Admiralty and became an assistant master at Leeds Grammar School. He subsequently became one of the most distinguished educationalists of the first half of the twentieth century. In 1906 he became headmaster of Bristol Grammar School, revived its fortunes and became known as 'its second founder'. Despite a lack of experience of public boarding schools he became headmaster of Marlborough in 1916. Ten years later on the urging of the Archbishop of Canterbury he took up the headmastership of Harrow with a mandate 'to raise the standard of work and discipline' (*DNB*, 1957–60). Norwood was a staunch supporter of the English public school, and a forceful advocate of team games. He wrote a number of books on education in which a discriminating admiration of the English public school is apparent. See in particular *The Higher Education of Boys in England* (1909) (written in conjunction with A. H. Hope) and *English Tradition of Education*.

31 *English Tradition of Education*.

32 Dennis Brailsford, *Sport and Society* (1969), p. 25.

33 Philip Mason, *A Matter of Honour: an account of the Indian Army; its officers and men* (1974), p. 391. The sentiment recalls E. W. Hornung's poem about his son, an Old Etonian, entitled 'Last Post' in his *Notes of a Camp Follower on the Western Front* (1919), p. 2:

> Still finding war of games the cream
> And his platoon a priceless team
> Still running it by sportsman's rule
> Just as he ran his house at school.

34 Ernest Raymond's *Tell England: a study in a generation*, first published in 1922, was a novel of the public school boy at war; its heroes such as Ray, were decent, uncomplicated games-playing men and boys. Arnold Lunn's *The Harrovians*, first published in 1913, was a deliberate attack on the philistine 'aristocracy of muscle' at Harrow before the Great War. Cayley was a callous but courageous member of this aristocracy.

35 E. C. Mack, *Public Schools and British Opinion 1780–1860* (1938), p. 108.

36 D. M. Stuart, *The Boy Through the Ages* (1926), p. 281.

37 R. A. Nisbet, *The Sociological Tradition* (paperback edn, 1970), p. 23.

38 This is clear from many sources including headmasters, assistant masters, ex-pupils and mere admirers. For restrained examples see S. A. Pears (assistant master at Harrow 1847–54, and subsequently headmaster of Repton 1854–74), *Sermons at School: short sermons preached at Repton School Chapel* (1870), p. 10; J. E. C. Welldon (headmaster of Harrow 1884–95), *Recollections and Reflections* (1915), p. 138; Cyril Norwood (headmaster of Marlborough 1916–25 subsequently Harrow 1926–34), 'The boys boarding schools' in J. Dover Wilson (ed.), *The Schools of England: a study in renaissance* (1928), p. 16; Stephen Foot (bursar and assistant master at Eastbourne College 1920–34), 'Public schools' in *Nineteenth Century*, vol. XCIX, no. 587 (Feb. 1926),

p. 1961; Archibald Douglas Fox (Harrow pupil 1892–7), *Public School Life: Harrow* (1911), p. 58; Sir Ernest Barker (ed.), *The Character of England* (1947), pp. 447–8. For particularly committed examples see Oxonian–Harrovian, letter to *The Times*, 30 Sept. 1889, p. 3; Eustace Miles, 'Games which the nation needs', *Humane Review* (1901), pp. 211–22; E. B. H. Jones, 'The moral aspect of athletics', *Journal of Education*, June 1900, pp. 352–4.

39 T. L. Papillon (1841–1926), quoted in Darwin, *English Public School*, p. 21.
40 T. C. Worsley, *Barbarians and Philistines* (1940), p. 107.

Chapter 1   Reformation, indifference and liberty

1 G. M. Young, *Victorian Essays* (1962), p. 135.
2 W. L. Burn, *The Age of Equipoise: a study of the mid-Victorian generation* (2nd edn, 1968), p. 60.
3 H. Perkin, *The Origins of Modern English Society 1780–1880* (1969), p. 438–40.
4 Geoffrey Best, *Mid-Victorian Britain 1851–1875* (1971), pp. 81–91.
5 W. J. Reader, *Professional Men* (1966), p. 84.
6 Sir George Norman Clarke, *English History: a survey* (1971), p. 447.
7 Perkin, *Modern English Society* p. 428; R. Lewis and A. Maude, *The English Middle Classes* (1950), pp. 19ff.; Reader, *Professional Men,* pp. 163–6.
8 G. M. Young, *Victorian England: portrait of an age* (1936), p. 81.
9 See for example R. L. Archer, *Secondary Education in the Nineteenth Century* (1921), p. 23; J. W. Adamson, *English Education 1789–1902* (1930), pp. 66–7; S. J. Curtis, *A History of Education in Great Britain* (1948; 7th edn, 1967), pp. 144–7.
10 T. W. Bamford, *Thomas Arnold on Education: a selection from his writing, with introductory material* (1970), p. 5.
11 Bamford, *Rise of Public Schools*, p. 53.
12 H. C. Barnard, *A Short History of English Education 1760–1944* (1947), p. 79.
13 Gertrude Himmelfarb, *Victorian Minds* (1968), pp. 280–2.
14 A. Whitridge, *Dr Arnold of Rugby* (1928), p. 133.
15 'His lifetime was spent in warfare'. J. J. Findlay, *Arnold of Rugby* (1897), p. viii.
16 Bamford, *Arnold on Education*, p. 8. See also T. W. Bamford, *Thomas Arnold* (1960), pp. 53, 108.
17 This has been summed up rather well by Ogilvie. 'His supreme contribution was his own personality' (*English Public School*, p. 144).
18 For an annotated chronology of the schools see Gardner, *Public Schools.*
19 Quoted in Eustace Miles, *Let's Play the Game* (1904), p. 29.
20 See Sir Ernest Barker, *National Character* (1948), p. 262; R. J. Mackenzie, *Almond of Loretto* (1905), p. 88.
21 Percival, *Superior Men*, p. 115.
22 W. H. G. Armytage, 'Thomas Arnold's views on physical education', *Journal of Physical Education*, vol. 47 (March 1955), pp. 27–8.
23 Arthur Penrhyn Stanley, *The Life and Correspondence of Thomas Arnold D.D.* (3rd edn, 1890), p. 180.
24 Whitridge, *Arnold of Rugby*, p. 109.
25 Thomas Arnold, 'Rugby School', *Quarterly Journal of Education*, vol. VII, no. 14 (1834), pp. 234–9.

26 W. C. Lake, 'Rugby and Oxford 1830–1850', *Good Words*, Oct. 1895, p. 666.

27 David Newsome, *Godliness and Good Learning* (1961), p. 91. Newsome's opinion is strongly supported by the fact that T. W. Bamford, the most distinguished of Arnold's recent biographers, omits games from his index (1960) such was their relative insignificance in Arnold's life and his latest review of Arnold's educational writing (1970) contains no discussion of his attitude to games, apparently for the same reason.

28 Diary of R. A. L. Nunns for 1852, *Supplement to the Marlburian*, Aug. 1931 (MCA).

29 See E. Lockwood, *Early Days at Marlborough College* (1893), p. 106.

30 A. C. Bradley *et al.*, *A History of Marlborough College* (1923), p. 106.

31 *Ibid.*, p. 126.

32 Diary of Boscawen Somerset Feb.–Dec. 1851 (MCA). R. A. L. Nunns's diary for 1852, although less detailed, draws a similar picture of unsupervised and unregulated leisure before Cotton's headmastership.

33 J. W. Mackail, *The Life of William Morris* (1899), vol. I, p. 15.

34 B. W. T. Handford, *Lancing: a history of SS. Mary and Nicolas College 1848–1930* (1933), p. 60.

35 T. Pellatt, *Boys in the Making* (1936), p. 48.

36 *Loretto's Hundred Years 1827–1927: Special Supplement to the Lorettonian* (1927), p. 23.

37 T. G. Bonney, *Memories of a Long Life* (1921), p. 12.

38 H. J. Torre, 'Harrow Notebook 1832–1837' (HSA). Torre was a pupil at Harrow 1831–8, head of school 1838, in cricket eleven 1836–8, captain of eleven 1838. Tufnell was a fellow pupil. For a further description of 'toozling' see *Harrow Association Record* (1907–12), p. 29 (HSA).

39 W. J. McGucken, *The Jesuits and Education* (1932), p. 225.

40 T. Sheil, 'Recollections of the Jesuits', *The New Monthly Magazine*, vol. XXVI, no. 106 (Oct. 1829), p. 361. For pupils' recollections of the close supervision at Stonyhurst see Alfred Austen, *The Autobiography of Alfred Austen (Poet Laureate) 1835–1910* (1911), p. 35; Sir Arthur Conan-Doyle, *Memories and Adventures* (1924), p. 15; Oliver St John Gogarty, *It isn't This Time of Year At All* (1954), p. 27. For a general description of the system as applied to English Jesuit schools see Christopher Hollis, *A History of the Jesuits* (1968), p. 225. A resolute defence when the system was being reviewed in response to demands to conform more closely with Protestant public schools is that of 'S.J.', 'School ideals', *Oxford and Cambridge Review*, 1 Nov. 1912, pp. 64–9.

41 Charles Waterton, *Essays on Natural History; with a biography by the author* (1838), p. xxiv.

42 *SIC*, vol. I, p. 321. The implicit criticism of the commission was made explicit by Rev. W. Petrie in his book *Catholic Systems of School Discipline*, published in 1878. He won support from the *Tablet* (April 1878) but attracted fierce condemnation from the *Dublin Review* (March, July, October 1878) which staunchly defended supervision as the bastion of purity.

Chapter 2   Licence, antidote and emulation

1 Sophia A. Cotton (ed.), *Memoir of George Edward Lynch Cotton D.D.* (1871), p. 13.
2 Bradley *et al.*, *Marlborough College*, pp. 156ff.
3 There is at present controversy regarding the nature and extent of the 'great rebellion' and its contribution to Wilkinson's resignation shortly afterwards. There can be no doubt, however, that acts of vandalism were committed, indiscipline was widespread in the school for a time, and boys were subsequently expelled. Further it is not disputed by anyone that the school was in serious financial difficulties due to the small fees charged. It has also been suggested that Wilkinson's High Church views offended some Evangelical governors. It seems entirely reasonable to the present writer to suppose that the rebellion may have been instrumental in prompting Wilkinson's resignation. It may well have been the proverbial last straw.
4 G. G. Bradley, *The Parting at Miletus* (sermon in memory of G. E. L. Cotton) (1866), p. 18.
5 See appendix 1 below for a complete copy of the 'Circular to Parents'.
6 See Bamford, *Thomas Arnold*, p. 25 for an interesting discussion of this point, the burden of much of the soul searching in the *Dublin Review* in 1878.
7 'Circular to Parents', p. 2.
8 Edward Ashley Scott, Charles Musgrove Bull and Charles Sandford Bere. Scott was at Marlborough 1853–8, Bull 1853–94 and Bere 1853–4.
9 *Marlburian*, vol. XLI, no. 624 (22 May 1906), p. 56.
10 Diary of Henry Palmer (Marlborough 1846–54) (MCA).
11 'Recollections of Marlborough by an old boy' in G. Routledge, *Every Boy's Annual* (1869), p. 296.
12 Cotton, *Memoir*, p. 12. There were, of course, other reasons why Cotton preferred young staff. Young bachelors were inexpensive. See F. B. Malim, *Almae Matres* (1948), p. 110.
13 G. E. L. Cotton, *Sermons and Addresses Delivered in the Chapel of Marlborough College* (1858), p. 406.
14 Mack, *British Opinion 1780–1860*, p. 336.
15 Cotton, *Sermons*, p. 478.
16 *Ibid.*, pp. 220–1.
17 Diary of Henry Palmer, entry for 20 May 1854.
18 F. D. How, *Six Great Schoolmasters* (1904), p. 259.
19 See his obituary in the *Marlburian*, vol. XXXVIII, no. 581 (3 April 1903), pp. 48–51.
20 See Himmelfarb, *Victorian Minds*, p. 314. Her delightful description of Charles Darwin's probable reaction to variations on his theory seems equally appropriate to Cotton.
21 Norwood, *English Tradition*, p. 100.
22 See appendix 1. *Harrow Philathletic Club: prospectus of the objects of the institution*, p. 1.
23 McIntosh, *Physical Education in England*, p. 35.
24 *Ibid.*, p. 38; Mack ignores Uppingham but suggests Marlborough as the source. See Mack, *British Opinion 1780–1860*, p. 336.

25 See appendix 1 for a complete set of copies. The individual parts have been collected from various sources.

26 E. D. Laborde, *Harrow School: yesterday and today* (1948), p. 191.

27 Welldon, *Recollections and Reflections*, p. 108.

28 C. J. Vaughan, *Sermons Preached in the Chapel of Harrow School* (2nd series, 1853), p. 352.

29 C. J. Vaughan, *Memorials of Harrow Sundays* (1859), p. 189.

30 Edward Graham, *The Harrow Life of Henry Montagu Butler* (1920), p. 360.

31 *Harrovian*, vol. x, no. 8 (20 Nov. 1897), p. 102.

32 'Circular to Old Boys'.

33 J. H. Overton and E. Wordsworth, *Christopher Wordsworth, Bishop of Lincoln 1807–85* (1888), p. 52.

34 Charles Wordsworth was a particularly influential figure in the development of games in English education. His somewhat boastful and immodest *Annals of My Early Life 1806–1846*, published in 1891, contained details of his athletic career. He claimed responsibility for the introduction of the Oxford versus Cambridge cricket and rowing (with others) fixtures in 1825; later as second master at Winchester he played a major role in the development of games there; then as principal of Glenalmond he took the public school games tradition to Scotland.

35 Not at least on the evidence of his published sermons. See his *Sermons Preached at Harrow School* (1841).

36 See for example J. G. Cotton Minchin, *Old Harrow Days* (1898), pp. 87–99; letter of H. T. Powell dated 4 Nov. 1816 describing the boys' treatment of Dr George Butler (HSA); *Harrow Gazette and General Advertiser*, 4 Jan. 1864, p. 3 (Croxley House File, HSA); Charles Stretton, *Memoirs of a Chequered Life* (1862), pp. 87–99.

37 H. J. Torre, *Recollections of Schooldays more than Fifty Years Ago*, (1890), p. 29 (HSA).

38 W. O. Hammond, 'Reminiscences of Harrow'. These were written in about 1888 but never printed. Extracts were included in the *Harrovian* in November and December 1950. For details of stone-throwing see *Harrovian*, vol. LXIV, no. 9 (6 Dec. 1950), p. 38.

39 R. R. Williams, *Christianity and Sound Learning: the educational work of C. J. Vaughan* (1954), p. 4.

40 'An Old Harrovian' (Sydney Daryl) *Harrow Recollections* (1867), p. 83.

41 How, *Great Schoolmasters*, p. 143.

42 *Ibid.*, p. 142. Percy M. Thornton gives the figure as 273, see *Harrow School and its Surroundings* (1885), p. 289.

43 See 'The headmaster's address at the Charles John Vaughan centenary ceremonies', *Supplement to the Harrovian*, vol. VVIII, no. 13 (31 Jan. 1945).

44 During a game of football on Tuesday 22 November 1853, Platt, a monitor apparently in charge of the game, rebuked Randolph Stewart, one of the players, for playing badly. Stewart answered back and was subsequently beaten. The beating was severe and Platt was dismissed from his monitorship. His father wrote a letter of protest to Vaughan and receiving no redress, published the exchange of correspondence. The outcome was a public controversy 'The Platt/Stewart Affair' which led to the production of a series of

pamphlets and letters by the interested parties and others, now in the HSA (File 1).

45 *A letter to Viscount Palmerston, M.P., on the Monitorial System of Harrow School* (1854, printed copy), p. 1 (HSA).

46 'Circular to Parents by an Assistant Master' (HSA).

47 *The Times*, 13 April 1854, p. 9. It was argued in an editorial that a boy on the playing field was free from monitorial supervision.

48 Mack, *British Opinion 1780–1860*, p. 346.

49 Cotton, *Memoir*, p. 61.

50 E. Howson and G. T. Warner, *Harrow School* (1898), p. 112; diary of Henry Palmer, entry for 25 Sept. 1854.

51 Reasonable conjecture is necessary since Vaughan left instructions that on his death no one was to write his biography and that all his papers should be burnt. These instructions were no doubt prompted by his desire to keep his homosexual activities at Harrow from becoming public knowledge.

52 Thornton, *Harrow School*, p. 291.

53 Laborde, *Harrow: Yesterday and today*, p. 54.

54 The upper school moved in the autumn of 1857 and the lower school joined them in March 1858 (Handford, *Lancing 1848–1930*), p. 83.

55 Subscription request, New Shoreham Vicarage, Feb. 1847 (Woodard Papers, Lancing College, Drawer 9).

56 Handford, *Lancing 1848–1930*, p. 14.

57 Brian Heeney, *Mission to the Middle Classes* (1969), p. 87; see Nathaniel Woodard, *A Plea for the Middle Classes* (1843), *Public Schools for the Middle Classes: a letter to the clergy of the Diocese of Chichester* (1857) and *The Scheme for the Education of St Nicolas College: a letter to the Marquis of Salisbury* (1869) for full details of this scheme.

58 Heeney, *Mission to the Middle Classes*, p. 39.

59 'It is clear from countless references that the Founder intended Lancing to take its place among the ordinary public schools.' Handford, *Lancing 1848–1930*, p. 86.

60 *Ibid.*, p. 70.

61 Handford, *Lancing 1848–1930*, p. 14.

62 Sir John Otter, *Nathaniel Woodard: a memoir of his life* (1925), p. 123.

63 K. E. Kirk, *The Story of the Woodard Schools* (1937), p. 83.

64 These are housed at Lancing College in two collections: the Woodard Papers and the Lancing Archive Collection.

65 I owe the information on early Shoreham days and plans to Mr B. W. T. Handford (letter dated 11 Aug. 1975).

66 *SIC*, vol. v, p. 102. Evidence of the headmaster, R. E. Sanderson. As a result of the commission's findings, science was begun in 1872.

67 K. E. Kirk, *Woodard Schools*, p. 52.

68 See Handford, *Lancing 1848–1930*, p. 61; for details of Woodard's dismissal of C. E. Moberly (headmaster 1849–51).

69 *Ibid.*, p. 114.

70 See W. S. Raymond, *A Sermon Preached in the Chapel of St Nicolas' College, Lancing* (1859) (LCA).

71 The title of the head of each of the five regional societies of the Corporation of St Nicolas.

72 *Lancing College Register* (3rd edn, 1933), p. v.
73 E. C. Lowe, *The Image of God: a sermon for schoolmasters and schoolboys* (1856) (LCA).
74 E. C. Lowe, *St Nicolas' College and its Schools: a letter to Rt. Hon. Sir J. J. Coleridge* (1867), p. 30 (LCA).
75 *SIC*, vol. v, p. 50, Q.9367.
76 E. C. Lowe, *A Record of Thirty Years Work in the Effort of Endowing the Church of England with a System of Self-supporting Public Boarding Schools for the Upper, Middle and Lower Classes* (1878) (LCA).
77 Handford, *Lancing 1848–1930*, p. 96.
78 Heeney, *Mission to the Middle Classes*, p. 76; Handford, *Lancing 1848–1930*, pp. 33–9, 57–8 and 63–4.
79 Handford, *Lancing 1848–1930*, p. 96.
80 H. N. Dickinson, *Keddy: a story of Oxford*, 1907, p. 46.
81 *Sam Brooke's Journal: the diary of a Lancing schoolboy 1860–1865* (1953). See, for example, entries for 15 May, 20 and 28 Oct. 1860.
82 In 1858 there were 97 pupils; by 1871 there were 121 (Heeney, *Mission to the Middle Classes*, p. 197).
83 A. C. Wilson, educated Westminster and Christchurch, Oxford; second master at Lancing 1851–69; later headmaster of Basingstoke Grammar School.
84 Extract from *The Woodford Times*, 31 July 1869, in his notebook and collection of press cuttings (LCA).
85 There were at least two other notable Christian athletes at the school about this time, Rev. E. H. Morgan (1862–5) later, with Leslie Stephen, a famous athletic don at Cambridge and Rev. E. Field, member of the society from 1853 and chaplain at Lancing from 1860.
86 Honey, *Tom Brown's Universe*, pp. 109ff. Honey states however that Cotton's role is not to be exaggerated and points to the contribution of the universities. They were, as he suggests, important agents of diffusion. They inspired Almond and Thring and lesser men such as William Sterne Raymond. For a discussion of the role of the universities see chapter 6 below.

Chapter 3 Idealism, idealists and rejection

1 See Cormac Rigby, 'The Life and Influence of Edward Thring' (unpublished D.Phil. Thesis, University of Oxford, 1968), p. 6.
2 George R. Parkin, *Edward Thring, Headmaster of Uppingham Schol: life, diary and letters* (2 vols, 1898), vol. I, p. 5.
3 *Ibid.*, p. 27.
4 *Ibid.*, p. 23.
5 *Ibid.*, p. 13.
6 For a description of the regular ecclesiastical preferment of Victorian headmasters to bishoprics see Honey, *Tom Brown's Universe*, pp. 314–16.
7 He wrote love letters to his pupils. See Phyllis Grosskurth, *John Addington Symonds* (1964), pp. 33ff.
8 Edward Thring, *Addresses* (1887), p. 5.
9 See Edward Thring, 'The charter of life' in *The School of Life: addresses to public school men by public school masters* (1885), pp. 86–7ff.

10 J. H. Skrine, *A Memory of Edward Thring* (1889), p. 125.

11 George W. E. Russell, *Fifteen Chapters of Autobiography* (1913), p. 63.

12 W. P. James, 'Thring and Uppingham: an essay of recollections', p. 23 (USA).

13 See M. Tozer, 'The Development and Role of Physical Education at Uppingham School 1850–1914' (M.Ed. Thesis, University of Leicester, 1974), pp. 198ff. Thring entered in his diary for 18 June 1886 that both the Kingsleys had 'a strong feeling for Uppingham and the work here'.

14 James, 'Thring', p. 14.

15 Details are to be found in *Uppingham School: the statement of the Rev. E. Thring, headmaster, respecting the organisation of the school* (1860).

16 Peter Stansky, 'Lyttelton and Thring: a study in nineteenth century education', *Victorian Studies*, vol. v (March 1962), p. 217: 'Thring revolutionised the physical "plant" of the British public school.'

17 Edward Thring, *Education and School* (1864; 2nd edn, 1867), p. 33.

18 *School Delusions: essays by the sixth form* (1860), p. 76. See also pp. 10, 35, 48, 64.

19 Numbers at Uppingham: 1853 – 28, 1854 – 46, 1861 – 175, 1865 – 282, 1869 – 355. See Parkin, *Life of Thring*, pp. 82, 113, 145, 163.

20 Edward Thring, MS diary, entries for 25 Feb. and 8 March 1860.

21 *Ibid.*, entry for 20 Dec. 1858.

22 *SIC*, vol. v, p. 97, Q.9920.

23 Rigby, 'Edward Thring', pp. 90–3.

24 Mallea's 'entry by entry analysis' of the first volume of Thring's diary reveals over seventy references to physical activities, many concerned with the acquisition of facilities ('Endowed Grammar Schools', p. 125).

25 *USM*, vol. ix, no. 70 (Dec. 1871), p. 401. W. F. Rawnsley, *Early Days at Uppingham School under Edward Thring. By an Old Boy* (1904), p. 110.

26 It was often freely given. For details of the expense of these innovations and the contributions of staff see the section in chapter 5 below dealing with the economics of athleticism.

27 His 'triumphalist admirers' include W. F. Rawnsley, H. D. Rawnsley and W. S. Patterson: 'all fanatical athletes' (Rigby, 'Edward Thring', p. 282).

28 See Newsome, *Good Learning*, p. 220.

29 This is a major concern of the recent theses of Cormac Rigby, John Mallea and Malcolm Tozer.

30 W. S. Patterson, *Sixty Years of Uppingham Cricket* (1909), p. 50; For details of his attitude to the professional and rugby union see Mallea 'Endowed Grammar Schools', pp. 131 and 117; Rigby, 'Edward Thring', pp. 290–3 and 299.

31 See Rigby, 'Edward Thring', p. 372 for a frank assessment.

32 Tozer, 'Physical Education at Uppingham', pp. 215ff.

33 H. B. Tristram, *Loretto School Past and Present* (1911), p. 66.

34 Mackenzie, *Almond of Loretto*, p. 16.

35 *Ibid.*, pp. 256–7.

36 Quoted in Ian Thomson, 'Almond of Loretto and the Development of Physical Education in Scotland during the Nineteenth Century' (unpublished M.Sc. Thesis, University of Edinburgh, 1969), p. 80.

37 Herbert Spencer, *Education: intellectual, moral and physical* (1861), pp. 188–9.

38 Quoted in Mackenzie, *Almond of Loretto*, p. 291.

39 Ian Thomson has described him as 'the most articulate Muscular Christian in Scotland' ('Physical Education in Scotland', p. 12).

40 H. H. Almond, 'The Consecration of the Body' in *Sermons of a Lay Headmaster* (1886), p. 152.

41 Guy Kendall, *Charles Kingsley and his Ideas* (n.d.), p. 41.

42 Skrine, *Memory of Thring*, p. 126.

43 Mackenzie, *Almond of Loretto*, pp. 136ff.

44 Quoted in Joan Evans, *John Ruskin* (1952), p. 314.

45 The work of men like J. B. Basedow (1724–90), J. C. Gutsmuths (1759–1839) and J. F. C. L. Jahn (1778–1852) had led to the widespread introduction of gymnastics in Germany by 1850. See P. C. McIntosh (ed.), *Landmarks in the History of Physical Education* (1957), pp. 109ff.

46 G. Beisiegal was a loyal servant of Uppingham until his retirement in 1902 and a distinguished physical educationalist. He was an acquaintance of Archibald MacLaren, founder member and president on three occasions of the National Society of Physical Education, President of the National Physical Recreational Society and member of the British College of Physical Education; see Tozer, 'Physical Education at Uppingham', p. 65.

47 Tristram, *Loretto School*. p. 210. In the 1870s a full-time resident instructor, Sergeant-Major Robinson, was appointed.

48 Archibald MacLaren (1820–84) was a Scot, born in Alloa and educated at Dollar Academy. After a period on the continent he opened a gymnasium at Oxford in 1858 which was well patronised by the students. His work resulted in the introduction of physical education in the British Army.

49 See Tristram, *Loretto School*, p. 210, for details of measuring. Some of the records survive in the Loretto archives. Measuring became common in schools and Marlborough College records are to be found in the British Museum.

50 Thomson has drawn attention to the similarity of ideas in these articles, in his *Training* and in Almond's writings ('Physical Education in Scotland', p. 92).

51 Mackenzie, *Almond of Loretto*, p. 239, letter to R. W. Phillip, MD, 17 Dec. 1898.

52 *Ibid.*, p. 261.

53 R. L. Archer implies the reverse was true but a careful reading of Almond's writings shows him to be quite wrong in his assumption. See Archer, *Secondary Education in the Nineteenth Century* (1921), p. 228. Cf. references in notes 101, 102, 103 and 104 below.

54 Mackenzie, *Almond of Loretto*, p. 188, Almond's letter to James Annan dated 9 Jan. 1902: 'It has been an uphill pull, building up a public school from nothing.'

55 *Ibid.*, p. 313, Almond's letter to H. B. Tristram (undated).

56 *Ibid.*, pp. 262–6. The poem contained, of course, the now famous expression, 'the flannelled fools at the wicket and the muddied oafs at the goal'.

57 *Loretto Register 1825–1925* (1927), p. xvi.

58 *Lorettonian*, vol. IV, no. 15 (17 June 1882), p. 57.

59 Mackenzie, *Almond of Loretto*, pp. 272–4.

60 Almond, *Sermons*, p. 168.

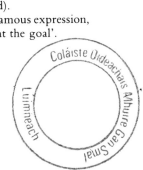

61 Archer, *Secondary Education*, p. 228.

62 Mackenzie, *Almond of Loretto*, pp. 274–7.

63 *Supplement to the Lorettonian*, May 1947, p. 8.

64 R. M. Freeman, *Steady and Strong* (1891), pp. 33–4 and 89. Chudleigh was Loretto's fictional name in the novel.

65 *Ibid.*, p. 177.

66 See for example Ogilvie, *English Public School*, p. 190.

67 For a discussion of the role of physical education in the prevention of cardio-vascular disease see J. A. Mangan (ed.), *Physical Education and Sport: socio-logical and cultural perspectives* (1973).

68 Others of the priesthood were Clement Dukes, *Health at School* (1905) and C. C. Cotterill, *Suggested Reforms in the Public Schools* (1883).

69 There are also marked similarities of attitude, ability and ambition between Woodard and Loyola. Both were men of moderate academic ability, both superb organisers adept at obtaining financial support, and though renowned for establishing educational systems both were more concerned with saving the irreligious.

70 G. Scott, *The RCs* (1967), p. 141.

71 From *Letters and Notices*, vol. 2, pp. 17, 18, quoted in Bernard Bassett, *The English Jesuits* (1967), p. 400.

72 David Mathew, *Catholicism in England 1535–1935* (1936; 2nd edn, 1948), p. 50.

73 A. S. Barnes, *The Catholic Schools of England* (1926), p. 35.

74 Hollis, *The Jesuits*, p. 222.

75 Mathew, *Catholicism in England*, p. 110. The Catholic Relief Act of 1829 improved the position still further; it gave Catholics the right to vote, sit in parliament and hold most offices of state.

76 Douglas Woodruff, *The Tichborne Claimant* (1957), p. 8. 'The Philosophers' were young Catholic gentlemen who pursued their 'undergraduate studies' at Stonyhurst as the universities were closed to them.

77 Quoted in Hollis, *The Jesuits*, p. 225; see also G. Gruggen and J. Keating, *Stonyhurst: its past history and life in the present* (1901), pp. 158–9.

78 Bassett, *English Jesuits*, pp. 408–9. The university ban was the action of the Catholic bishops. It was lifted in 1895 by Cardinal Vaughan, an alumnus of Stonyhurst.

79 Collection of papers on higher Catholic education 1871–95 made by Rev. E. I. Purbrick, p. 10 (Jesuit Society Archives).

80 Obituary, *Letters and Notices*, vol. xv (Dec. 1914), p. 565.

81 H. E. Manning (1808–92) educated at Harrow and Balliol, a Catholic convert in 1851, Archbishop of Westminster 1865, Cardinal 1875. It is an interesting aside that Manning played in the Harrow eleven of 1825 against Eton. Subsequently he was a man 'of ascetic temper'. 'He disliked the ideal of muscular Christianity and of a heaven where cherubs played curates at cricket indefinitely.' Of athletic priests he asked, 'How would you like to appear in the next world with a cricket bat in one hand and a chalice in the other?' Leslie Shane, *Henry Edward Manning: his life and labours* (1921), p. 13.

82 E. S. Purcell, *Life of Cardinal Manning* (1896), p. 756.

83 See Peter Levi, SJ, *Beaumont 1861–1961* (1961), pp. 16–17, 18, 29, 30–7.

84 McGucken, *Jesuits and Education*, p. 19.

85 *Ibid.*, p. 22.

86 J. M. Jeffries, *Front Everywhere* (1935), p. 13.

87 F. P. Donnelly, *Principles of Jesuit Education in Practice* (1934), pp. 9–10.

88 M. Foss, *The Founding of the Jesuits* (1969), p. 167.

89 McGucken, *Jesuits and Education*, p. 151.

90 See Michael Maher, SJ, 'Moral Training and Instruction in the Catholic Schools connected by the Jesuit Order in Great Britain and Ireland' in M. Sadler (ed.), *International Inquiry into Moral Training and Instruction in Schools* (1908), pp. 170–5. This is a passage of considerable importance. The strength of the emphasis was reiterated to the present writer by Rev. Father Holt, SJ, formerly pupil, then master at Stonyhurst and now archivist at the Society's headquarters in Farm Street.

91 Speech of Father Bernard Vaughan, SJ, to the boys of Beaumont on Empire Sunday 1914, reported in *The Tablet*, 13 June 1914. p. 11.

92 Percy Fitzgerald, *Stonyhurst Memories* (1895), p. 141.

93 Several descriptions of Stonyhurst football are available: Gruggen and Keating, *Stonyhurst Past and Present*, pp. 147–51; J. Gerard, *Centenary Record. Stonyhurst College* (1864), pp. 189–91, *SCM*, vol. II, no. 64 (Nov. 1886), p. 195. Fitzgerald has a vivid description of the 'Grand Matches' in *Saxonhurst* (1907), pp. 62–7.

94 Descriptions of Stonyhurst cricket appear in Gruggen and Keating, *Stonyhurst Past and Present*, pp. 151–8 and Gerard, *Stonyhurst College*, pp. 180–2.

95 Diary of B. E. James 1866–7 (SCA).

96 B. Jarret, *Living Temples* (1919), pp. 33–4.

97 W. J. Lockington, *Bodily Health and Spiritual Vigour* (1913).

98 Fitzgerald, *Saxonhurst*, p. 63. See also 'J.W.', 'Stonyhurst life', *The Month*, vol. III, no. 118 (March 1874), pp. 331–2.

99 Quoted in 'Catholic college education in England', *Dublin Review*, vol. XXX, no. 60 (April 1878), p. 358.

100 *Report of H.M. Inspectorate of Schools* (Stonyhurst) (1903), Education 109/2667, p. 15 (Public Record Office).

101 Details are discussed in chapters 7 and 8 below.

102 For an amplification of this point see chapter 4 below.

103 Brian Jackson, review of *The Victorian Public School* in *The Guardian*, 11 Dec. 1975, p. 14.

104 J. R. M. Butler, *Henry Montagu Butler, Master of Trinity College, Cambridge, 1886–1918* (1925), p. 13.

Chapter 4 Compulsion, conformity and allegiance

1 Lionel Ford, 'Public school athletics' in C. Cookson (ed.), *Essays on Secondary Education* (1898), p. 289.

2 Bamford, *Rise of Public Schools*, p. 83.

3 Open allegiance to the belief in games for character training is extremely rare in Stonyhurst literature. For an example, a discussion of unselfishness as the chief merit of soccer, see *SCM*, vol. III, no. 34 (Nov. 1887), p. 42.

4 Press cutting in the Harrow scrapbook (MSD/DU/681/1) of Sir Frederick Green (Harrow 1860–3) included in his papers in the Essex County Record Office.

5 *USM*, vol. XXIX, no. 229 (July 1891), p. 167.

6 *The Pen Vyper* 23 July 1870, p. 4.

7 Edward Thring, introductory notes to diary quoted in Parkin, *Life of Thring*, p. 92.

8 Taken from the *Marlburian*, vol. XXVIII, no. 446 (21 Oct 1893), p. 140.

9 McIntosh, *Physical Education in England*, p. 41.

10 John Stearne Thomas, Marlborough 1848–55, assistant master 1859–97.

11 Extract from a sermon preached in Marlborough College Chapel, 28 Feb. 1897 (MCA). It was, of course, the reflection of an old man looking back on his youth and this may account for his partial accuracy.

12 Entry dated September 1857 in the Marlborough College Cricket Club Book at present in the possession of Mr L. Warwick James. I owe this point to him.

13 For details of the reform see the *Marlborough College Register 1843–52* (9th edn, 1952), p. xxvii.

14 Letter to *The Times* from 'Oxonian–Marlburian', Wed. 2 Oct. 1889, p. 4; Letter from 'Liliput' in the *Marlburian*, vol. XIII, no. 217 (23 Oct 1878), p. 161.

15 *PSC*, vol. I, p. 281, Q.27–30.

16 'An Old Harrovian', *Recollections*, p. 60.

17 H. Merivale, *Bar, Stage and Platform* (1902), pp. 180, 189 (Harrow 1851–6); also B. Russell and P. Russell (eds.), *The Amberley Papers* (1937), p. 165. This includes the letters of John Russell, later Lord Amberley (Harrow 1857–9).

18 Edward Thring, *Three Letters and Axioms on Education* (1866), p. 11.

19 R. C. Rome, 'Uppingham: the story of a school 1584–1948' (1948), appendix, p. 1 (USA).

20 Tozer, 'Physical Education at Uppingham', p. 53.

21 *Ibid.*, p. 90. Mallea also stresses his well-meaning despotism in this context: 'Endowed Grammar Schools' p. 117. The historian of *Uppingham Cricket*, W. S. Patterson, is equally assertive on this point in the narrower context of the development of cricket at the school (pp. 15, 138).

22 Edward Thring, MS diary, entry for 28 Feb. 1860. Althorpe and Clay were senior pupils.

23 The clearest, most succinct outline of Almond's philosophy and practice of good health is A. R. Smith's 'The making of healthy men: Dr Almond's work at Loretto' in E. Maloine (ed.), *Délibérations du Troisième Congrès International d'Hygiène Scolaire* (1910), A. R. Smith (Loretto 1889–94) was headmaster of Loretto 1908–26.

24 'It required some courage to sit down among the ice, and sponge ourselves on frosty mornings!' wrote R. J. Mackenzie (*Almond of Loretto*, p. 69).

25 *Report of Royal Commission on Physical Training* (Scotland) (1903), vol. II, p. 414, Q.9774.

26 *Ibid.*, vol. II, p. 416, Q.9834.

27 For details of the contribution of Clough and Welby see Gruggen and Keating, *Stonyhurst College,* p. 159; for that of Baldwin see *Stonyhurst Association Football Journal*, p. 1 (SCA); for that of Robinson see Gruggen and Keating, *Stonyhurst College,* p. 163.

28 *SCM*, vol. IV, no. 52 (Nov. 1890), p. 563. In 1887 football had been made compulsory once a week for the boys *chosen* to play for the Higher and Lower

Line sets (upper and lower school teams) by a selected committee of five boys for each Line. See *SCM*, vol. III, no. 34 (Nov. 1887), p. 34.

29 Brooke, *Journal*. Brooke was at Lancing 1855–62.

30 *Ibid.*, p. 10.

31 *Ibid.*, p. 39.

32 Brooke, for his part, expressed doubt about the 'unity of games' claim. He considered football was the source of continual disturbance and conflict! (*Journal*, p. 42).

33 It is interesting to note that although Brooke expected support from home, he found his father sympathetic to the official school position.

34 Brooke, *Journal* p. 66.

35 Robert Edward Sanderson, headmaster 1862–89.

36 H. D. Rawnsley, *Thring: teacher and poet* (1889), p. 92.

37 Newsome, *Good Learning*, p. 222.

38 As late as 1901 Almond, who was in contact with many of the English public schools, reported to the Royal Commission on Physical Training (Scotland) that he had had 'most deploring letters from Doctors of English schools stating that boys get far too many exemptions, that there is too little compulsory exercise and too many means of getting free of it' (*Report*, vol. II, p. 416).

39 Not only Newsome discussed above but also Ogilvie, *English Public School*, p. 181.

40 The situation is not wholly clear but it seems that house games themselves were relatively disorganised until the 1880s. Laborde, *Harrow: yesterday and today*, pp. 192 and 196.

41 *Harrow Notes*, vol. VI, no. 46 (Dec. 1885), p. 141.

42 *Harrovian*, vol. I, no. 1 (16 Oct. 1869), p. 8., and vol. I, no. 4 (Nov. 1869), pp. 42–3.

43 *Ibid.*, vol. I, no. 18 (Oct. 1870), pp. 16–17.

44 *Ibid.*, p. 18. The same situation existed at Uppingham. On the single compulsory day of the week only part of the school played games (Mallea, 'Endowed Grammar Schools', p. 135). At Lancing the problem was even more acute than elsewhere. There was one field for 215 boys and the principle of compulsory games was especially difficult to put into practice (*LCM*, vol. I, no. 24, Nov. 1883, p. 305).

45 *Ibid.*, vol. III, no. 27 (1 April 1871), p. 121.

46 *Ibid.*, vol. III, no. 34 (7 Oct. 1871), p. 16.

47 *Ibid.*, vol. IV, no. 4 (6 March 1878), p. 32.

48 *Ibid.*, vol. IV, no. 6 (29 May 1879), p. 61.

49 *Ibid.*, vol. IV, no. 10 (27 Sept. 1879), p. 114; *ibid.*, vol. IV, no. 11 (11 Dec. 1879), p. 126.

50 *Harrow Notes*, vol. I, no. 9 (11 Oct. 1883), pp. 115, 116.

51 *Ibid.*, vol. IV, no. 46 (16 Dec. 1885), pp. 141, 142.

52 P. E. Matheson, *The Life of Hastings Rashdall* (1928), p. 14. (Harrow 1871–7).

53 A reviewer of Cotterill's book in *The Spectator* was, for example, quite unsurprised and most sympathetic towards the recommendation of daily physical exercise. See *The Spectator*, April 1886, p. 457.

54 *The Times*, 29 June 1900, p. 11.

55 Charles Graves, *The Bad Old Days* (1961), p. 28.

56 R. Gurner, *I Chose Teaching* (1937), p. 184 (assistant master at Marlborough 1913–20).

57 E. F. Benson, *Sketches from Marlborough* (1905), p. 55 (Marlborough 1881–7).

58 Charles Hamilton Sorley, *Marlborough and Other Poems* (1916), p. 9 (Marlborough 1908–13).

59 *USM*, vol. XXVIII, no. 248 (Oct. 1893), p. 273.

60 W. N. Roe (ed.), *Public Schools Cricket 1901–1950* (1951), p. 189.

61 R. Meinertzhagen, *Diary of a Black Sheep* (1964), p. 189 (Harrow 1891–5). The historian, George Macaulay Trevelyan (Harrow 1889–93), inveighed against 'the homage paid . . . to athletics' during Welldon's headship, and considered Welldon's liking for 'excellent Philistines' the cause. See Victoria de Bunsen, *Charles Roden Buxton* (1948), p. 20. Buxton, a schoolboy contemporary of Trevelyan, was at Harrow 1889–94.

62 Sir Home Gordon (ed.), *Eton versus Harrow at Lord's* (1926), p. 62.

63 *LCM*, vol. I, no. 56 (April 1888), p. 327.

64 *Ibid.*, vol. II, no. 72 (March 1901), p. 869.

65 N. MacLachlan in *Loretto's Hundred Years 1827–1927: Special supplement to the Lorettonian*, p. 51 (pupil 1872–8, deputy head 1885–92).

66 *Lorettonian*, vol. VII, no. 6 (24 Jan. 1885), p. 24 and vol. VII, no. 7 (7 Feb. 1885), p. 29. The 'Wallyford' was three and a half, the 'long Wallyford' four and a half, the 'Falside' five and 'Three Trees' seven miles long.

67 *Lorettonian*, vol. V, no. 5 (9 Dec. 1882), p. 19.

68 Tristram, *Loretto School*, p. 89.

69 Charles Sorley, 'Song of the Ungirt Runners' in G. C. F. Mead and R. C. Clift (eds.), *English Verse: Old and New* (1922; 3rd edn, 1947), p. 113.

70 J. P. T. Bury in *Marlborough College 1843–1943* ed. H. C. Brentnall and E. G. H. Kempson (1943), p. 75 (Marlborough 1922–7). First Post was about two, Old Eagle four, Training Stables five and Rockley Warren six and a half miles long. These are still Marlborough 'sweats'. I owe this information to the late Gerald Murray and Mr Bruce Tulloch of Marlborough College.

71 C. R. W. Nevinson, *Paint and Prejudice* (1937), p. 77.

72 *USM*, vol. XL, no. 312 (March 1902), p. 8.

73 *LCM*, vol. VII, no. 9 (Dec. 1914), p. 115. The same point was made to the present writer by the Lancing historian, B. W. T. Handford.

74 J. Betjeman, *Ghastly Good Taste* (1933; 2nd edn, 1971), pp. xivff. (Marlborough 1920–5).

75 Nevinson, *Paint and Prejudice*, p. 8.

76 Meinertzhagen, *Black Sheep*, p. 180. Ironically, Bosworth-Smith's son Nigel played for the school at cricket, football and squash. See B. Hollender, *Before I Forget* (1935).

77 D. Savory, 'Marlborough sixty years ago', *Contemporary Review*, vol. CLXXXX (Oct. 1956), p. 212.

78 *Marlburian*, vol. XXXVIII, no. 583 (11 June 1903), p. 87.

79 *PSC*, vol. IV, p. 231, Q.2013.

80 *Idem.*, Q.2027.

81 *Ibid.*, p. 228, Q.1869.

82 George W. E. Russell, *Collections and Recollections* (1898; new edn, 1899), pp. 412–13 (Harrow 1867–72).

83 Russell, *Autobiography*, p. 39.

84 *Tyro*, vol. III, no. 13 (1 Feb. 1866), p. 89.

85 *Ibid.*, vol. III, no. 28 (31 July 1866), pp. 210–11.

86 Rowland Prothero, *Whippingham to Westminster* (1938), p. 42 (Marlborough 1864–71).

87 *Marlborough College Register* (9th edn, 1952), pp. 966–75.

88 Savory, *Contemporary Review*, p. 215. J. D. Penny (Marlborough 1899–1905), commenting on Savory's article in *The Contemporary Review* writes: 'What one could not help seeing was the hero worship of athletes . . . I agree with Savory that it was the athletes rather than the prefects who exercised real power.' (Letter of recollections to Gerald Murray dated 13 Nov. 1975 written for this study.)

89 Cyril Alington, *Things Ancient and Modern* (1936), p. 34 (Marlborough 1886–91).

90 *Marlburian*, vol. XXVIII, no. 585 (15 July 1903), p. 102.

91 See appendix III for the analysis of the contents of the magazines of the other schools. The technique of panel analysis is described in M. W. Riley *Sociological Research* (1963), vol. I, pp. 556–9.

92 *Harrovian*, vol. IV, no. 47 (27 July 1872), p. 169.

93 *USM*, vol. XI, no. 79 (March 1873), p. 415.

94 *Ibid.*, vol. XI, no. 80 (April 1873), pp. 61–2.

95 *Ibid.*, vol. XVI, no. 124 (Oct. 1878), pp. 178–9.

96 *Ibid.*, vol. XVI, no. 132 (Oct. 1879), p. 255.

97 P. Caraman, *A Biography of C. C. Martindale* (1967), p. 41, Martindale was at Harrow 1893–6.

98 Meinertzhagen, *Black Sheep*, p. 189.

99 Stephen Tallents, *Man and Boy* (1947), p. 13 (Harrow 1897–1903).

100 E. M. Venables, 'Bases Attempted: twenty five years at Harrow' (1947), p. 23. (HSA).

101 Evelyn Wrench, *Francis Yeats Brown* (1948), p. 8 (Harrow 1900–3). The obituary of an Uppingham boy who died at school read: 'Not widely known in the school for his feeble health precluded any participation in games' (*USM*, vol. XIII, no. 205, 6 Feb. 1878 p. 10).

102 *PSM*, April 1898, p. 36.

103 *Punch*, 15 May 1875, p. 211.

104 Cyril Heber-Percy, *Us Four* (1963), p. 74 (Harrow 1919–22).

Chapter 5 Conspicuous resources, anti-intellectualism and sporting pedagogues

1 Thring catered for the upper classes because they alone could afford the machinery he thought necessary (Rigby, 'Edward Thring', p. 101.)

2 Best, *Mid-Victorian Britain*, p. 2.

3 *Ibid.*, p. 1.

4 F. Clarke, *Education and Social Change* (1940), pp. 10–11.

5 Thorstein Veblen, *The Theory of the Leisure Class* (1899; Modern Library edn, 1934), p. 45.

6 Diary entries for 30 March 1860, 16 April 1860, 31 Jan. 1861, 29 Aug. 1861,

for example, were all concerned with finding additional cricket fields for the school.

7 For example, R. J. Hodgkinson: 'his wealth saved the school' (Rigby, 'Edward Thring', p. 133).

8 Rome, 'Uppingham', p. 54.

9 For a copy of the complete document see appendix II below.

10 'Statement', p. 2.

11 Between March 1876 and April 1877 the school took up residence in Borth, a small resort on the Cardiganshire coast, to escape an outbreak of typhoid in Uppingham.

12 Letter dated 20 July 1877 (USA).

13 Masters' Agreement (USA).

14 *USM*, vol. xxxviii, no. 298 (March 1900), p. 59.

15 T. B. Rowe, *Guide Book* (1869) (USA).

16 *School Rules* (USA).

17 Formerly the audit was the responsibility of the treasurer of the games committee.

18 Cutting from *The Guardian*, 27 April 1892, in the papers of E. C. Fields (LCA).

19 Paul Ford in Cookson, *Secondary Education*, p. 293.

20 Weinberg, *Elite Education*, p. 45.

21 By the second half of the twentieth century the situation had changed greatly. At Marlborough, for example, by 1963 there were forty-six entirely voluntary extra-curricular clubs in addition to six musical, twenty athletic and fifteen house societies. Details may be found in *Marlborough: an open examination written by the boys* (1963), p. 43. This was a quite typical expansion. The other schools experienced the same phenomenon.

22 Gruggen and Keating, *Stonyhurst Past and Present*, pp. 173–81. Play-acting was a tool of the Jesuit educational system fulfilling the need for drama, ritual symbolism and colour which boys elsewhere found in the ceremonies and trappings of athleticism.

23 Beverley Nichols, *Prelude* (1920; 4th edn, 1929), p. 173.

24 Harold Nicolson, *Sir Arthur Nicolson, Bart.: a study in the old diplomacy* (1930), p. 7.

25 *PSC*, vol. I, p. 55.

26 *The Times*, 28 March 1864, p. 9.

27 *SIC*, vol. v, p. 330, Q.12226ff.

28 *Ibid.*, vol. I, appendix III, p. 162. The winning of scholarships at Marlborough was due in large part to its high percentage of clergymen's sons without money or contacts. See Alington, *Ancient and Modern*, pp. 73, 79, and Bertram Pollock, *A Twentieth Century Bishop* (1944), p. 21.

29 Ogilvie, *English Public School*, p. 188.

30 Ian Hay, *The Lighter Side of School Life* (1914; 2nd edn, 1921), p. 102.

31 John Addington Symonds was at Harrow 1854–8, see Grosskurth, *John Symonds*, pp. 22–41; James Elroy Flecker was at Uppingham 1901–2, see Geraldine Hodgson, *The Life of James Elroy Flecker* (1925), pp. 36–61; John Betjeman was at Marlborough 1920–5, see his verse autobiography *Summoned by Bells* (1960), pp. 65–75; Evelyn Waugh was at Lancing 1917–25, see his

autobiography *A Little Learning* (1964), pp. 85–140; Dudley Carew, *A Fragment of Friendship* (1974), pp. 13ff.

32 Matthew Arnold, *A French Eton* (1892 edn), pp. 110–11.

33 For an interesting description of nineteenth-century anti-intellectual boys at Marlborough for example, see E. F. Benson, *Our Family Affairs 1867–1896* (1920), pp. 150–2. Benson was at Marlborough 1881–7.

34 For details of the respective exchanges see *The Times*, 20 Sept.–10 Oct. 1889. Sir Oliver Lodge, 'Our public schools as a public peril', *Nineteenth Century*, vol. LII, no. 310 (Nov. 1902), pp. 941–50; *Times Educational Supplement*, March–Oct. 1918; *English Review*, vol. XXXVI (June, 1923). For earlier harsh criticism see vol XII (Sept. and Oct. 1912), vol. XXVI (April 1918) and vol. XXVIII (March 1919).

35 Mais was a pupil at Denstone at the turn of the century. He taught at Rossall (1909–13), Sherbourne (1913–17) and Tonbridge (1917–20) and wrote frankly of his experiences in *A Public School in Wartime* (1916), *A Schoolmaster's Diary* (1918) and in his autobiography *All the Days of My Life* (1937). Other severe critics over the years included A. B. Badger, *The Public Schools and the Nation* (1944), H. B. Gray, *The Public Schools and the Empire* (1913), and L. B. Pekin, *Public Schools: their failure and reform* (1932).

36 Mais, *Public School in Wartime*, p. 24.

37 'Public school types', *London Society*, vol. XVI (1869), pp. 37–8.

38 E. F. Benson, *David Blaize* (1916), p. 154.

39 Nichols, *Prelude*, p. 266.

40 The exception was Stonyhurst; the magazine was strongly supported by the staff and the literary standard was consistently high.

41 *Lorettonian*, vol. XXIII, no. 8 (23 Feb. 1901), p. 28 and vol. XXI, no. 7 (30 Jan. 1892), p. 25.

42 J. R. H. O'Regan, 'The school magazine' in *Public Schools from Within: a collection of essays on public school education written chiefly by Schoolmasters* (1906), pp. 165–7. O'Regan was assistant master at Marlborough 1894–1922.

43 *Marlburian*, vol. I, no. 18 (26 Sept. 1866), p. 134.

44 Arnold Lunn, *Come What May* (1940), p. 27; also G. M. Trevelyan, *An Autobiography and Other Essays* (1949), pp. 10–11.

45 J. E. C. Welldon, *Gerald Eversley's Friendship* (1895), pp. 75–6.

46 F. W. Farrar, *In the Days of thy Youth: sermons on practical subjects preached at Marlborough College from 1871 to 1876* (1889), p. 372.

47 Cotterill, *Reforms*, p. 177.

48 Edward Thring, *Sermons Delivered at Uppingham School* (1858), p. 113.

49 Cyril Alington, *Lionel Ford* (1934), p. 102. Ford was headmaster of Harrow 1910–25.

50 A. H. Gilkes, *The Thing that Hath Been or a Young Man's Mistakes* (1894), p. 165.

51 Leslie Stephen, 'Thoughts of an outsider: public schools', *Cornhill Magazine*, vol. XXVII, no. 159 (March 1873), p. 290.

52 William Cory, 'A queen's visit' quoted in Faith Compton MacKenzie, *William Cory* (1950).

53 Stephen Marcus, *The Other Victorians* (1966), p. 283.

54 Augustus Hare, *The Story of My Life* (1896), p. 242 (Harrow 1847–8).

55 *The Spectator*, 29 Oct. 1898, p. 606.
56 Jack Hood, *The Heart of a Schoolboy* (1919), pp. 22 and 27.
57 *Punch*, 19 Dec. 1874, p. 265.
58 Edward Lyttelton, *Schoolboys and Schoolwork* (1909), p. 12.
59 Edward Lyttelton, *Memories and Hopes* (1925), p. 131.
60 A general description of curricular reform, especially the rise of science, may be read in Bamford, *Rise of Public Schools*, pp. 86–115 and 167–8. For a good summary of the subject see *Science Teaching in the Public Schools*, Association of Public School Science Masters, Educational Pamphlets no. 17 (1909).
61 See Mack, *British Opinion since 1860*, p. 336. For details of the development of 'modern sides' see Bamford, *Rise of Public Schools*, p. 25 and J. W. Adamson, *English Education 1789–1902* (1930), pp. 156–7. For details of the qualifications and relative salaries of Harrow staff in the later part of the nineteenth century see appendix VII.
62 *Report of the Headmasters' Conference* (1890), p. 15.
63 In 1914 of the 114 schools of the Headmasters' Conference 92 had headmasters with degrees in classics; 10 had headmasters with degrees in mathematics; 7 had headmasters with degrees in mathematics and science; 4 had headmasters with degrees in science; 1 had a headmaster with a degree in history. V. Seymour Bryant, *The Public School System in Relation to the Coming Conflict for National Supremacy* (1917), p. 5. This faithfully reflected the imbalance among assistant masters. See appendix VIII.
64 J. Davidson Ketchum, *Ruhleben* (1965).
65 A term first used by the sociologist Max Weber in his historical–comparative studies, and now part of the terminology of the discipline of sociology. It represents exaggerated distinction for the purpose of conceptual comparison and analysis.
66 The importance of the Victorian headmaster's freedom to select his staff in promoting internal change has been strongly emphasised by Roger Ellis, the present headmaster of Marlborough (letter to the present writer dated 6 Oct. 1973).
67 Of course an impressive public personality (not least in the pulpit) was a further requirement. For an excellent description of the evolution of the Victorian headmaster see Honey, *Tom Brown's Universe*, pp. 290–317. He fails, however, to give adequate consideration to the part athletic ability played in selection for headships. For a brief consideration of this point see Smith, *Stretching Their Bodies*, pp. 43–4.
68 *PSM*, vol. II (1898), p. 503.
69 This was not quite fair to Warre. He had published less but his academic pedigree was highly respectable. At Oxford (1855–9) he gained a first class in 'Moderations' and 'Greats' and became a fellow of All Souls. Although he was eventually president of the Oxford University Boat Club and won rowing blues in 1857 and 1858, he refused to row in 1856 because of pressure of academic work. His application, incidentally, was successful and he was headmaster of Eton 1884–1905.
70 *The Times*, 26 July 1884, p. 10.
71 Evelyn Waugh, *Little Learning*, p. 156. For typical examples of such men see Graves, *Bad Old Days*, p. 30; Worsley, *Flannelled Fool*, p. 135; James, 'Thring' p. 54.

72 Henry Newbolt, *The Twymans: a tale of youth* (2nd edn, 1911), p. 82.

73 R. Gurner, *For the Sons of Gentlemen* (1926), p. 88.

74 Alec Waugh, *The Loom of Youth* (1917), p. 27. The 'Bull' is believed to be modelled on G. M. Carey, a master at Sherborne for many years. S. P. B. Mais, in his autobiography, described Carey in his prime (*Days of my Life*, pp. 163–5).

75 Gerald Murray, 'The Games Master in the Public Schools' (unpublished paper compiled for the present writer dated 20 Nov. 1973). See also Norwood, *English Tradition*, p. 56; Gray, *Schools and Empire*, pp. 188–9; A. C. Benson, *The Upton Letters* (1904), pp. 163–4. An explicit attack of remarkable ferocity was H. J. Spencer's 'The athletics master in public schools', *Contemporary Review*, vol. LXXVIII (July 1900), pp. 114–17.

76 See for example McIntosh, *Physical Education in England*, p. 60.

77 *LCM*, vol. X, no. 313 (March 1917), p. 17. Hepburn was assistant master at Lancing 1916–17.

78 Brentnall and Kempson (eds.), *Marlborough 1843–1943*, p. 87.

79 Diary of S. L. E. Haslam 1870–3 entry for 24 Oct. 1871. S. A. Haslam was assistant master at Uppingham 1871–1908 and housemaster of Brooklands 1892–1908.

80 Paul Ford in Cookson, *Secondary Education*, p. 303.

81 G. G. Coulton, *Fourscore Years: an autobiography* (1943), p. 73.

82 Tozer, 'Physical Education at Uppingham', p. 28.

83 *USM*, vol. LVIII, no. 95 (March 1920), pp. 36, 39.

84 *Marlburian*, vol. XLIV, no. 667 (17 June 1909), p. 73. Wood was assistant master at Marlborough 1893–1908.

85 *The Times*, for example, 'A Former Head of The School at Harrow', 28 Sept. 1889, p. 8; 'Another Old Etonian', 30 Sept. 1889, p. 4; 'A College Tutor', 3 Jan. 1903, p. 6; 'A Schoolmaster', 7 Jan. 1903, p. 13.

86 *Report of the Headmasters' Conference* (1897), pp. 79–80.

87 *Athenaeum*, 23 July 1898, p. 131.

88 *PSM*, vol. 5 (Jan. 1899), p. 15.

89 Mais, *Days of my Life*, p. 37.

90 Guy Kendall, *A Headmaster Remembers* (1933), p. 193.

91 Arthur Westcott, *The Life and Letters of Brooke Foss Westcott* (2 vols, 1903), vol. I, p. 193.

92 *SCM*, vol. VI, no. 87 (July 1896), p. 246.

93 For an excellent example of one who held strongly to this view, see the tribute to Badger Hale 'An Eton master', *Blackwood's Magazine*, vol. CLVI, no. 845 (1894), pp. 693–9.

94 Newsome, *Good Learning*, p. 227. For a fictional example of the growth of athleticism as a result of pandering to popular demand see A. H. Gilkes, *Boys and Masters: a study of school life* (1887).

95 R. G. Collingwood, *An Autobiography* (1939), p. 9; Ogilvie, *English Public School*.

96 Kendall, *Headmaster Remembers*, p. 193.

97 An outstanding example was Rev. A. J. Tuck at Uppingham, who did, and was all these things (Mallea, 'Endowed Grammar Schools', p. 117).

98 G. G. Coulton, *A Victorian Schoolmaster: Henry Hart of Sedbergh* (1923). Hart

was a pupil at Rugby 1858–62, assistant master at Haileybury 1866–73, at Harrow 1873–80, headmaster of Sedbergh 1880–1900.

99 *Ibid.*, p. 23.

100 B. H. Tower, 'In memoriam' in Coulton, *Victorian Schoolmaster*, appendix. Tower was assistant master at Sedbergh 1882–1902; then headmaster of Lancing 1902–9 where, as a schoolboy, he had been a distinguished scholar and athlete. Thus the process of diffusion was carried on.

101 H. W. McKenzie is another excellent example of a headmaster who greatly assisted the spread of athleticism throughout the public schools, including three of this study, Loretto, Lancing and Uppingham. In particular, he illustrates the considerable power of the nineteenth-century headmaster both to select men with similar inclinations and to raise the pupil athlete to positions of power in the school. In 1889 McKenzie became headmaster of Lancing. He was himself of 'resolute, sure muscular Christianity' (Obituary, *LCM*, vol. xxxv, no. 461, Lent term, 1942, p. 52) and proceeded to recruit a band of notable muscular Christians to the staff, rather it appears for the same reasons as Cotton at Marlborough, to subdue the indisciplined pupils – discipline had deteriorated in the last years of Sanderson's headship (1862–89). McKenzie's recruits included R. D. Budworth, E. B. Brutton and E. H. North (all rugby internationals), H. C. Stewart (county cricketer), F. Yardley (athletics blue), R. A. Ingram (soccer blue international and county cricketer) and L. T. Thring (soccer blue). In 1907 he became headmaster of Uppingham. His reign saw the 'first golden age of Uppingham athleticism' (I owe this point to T. B. Belk, the Uppingham School archivist). He raised non-sixth-form athletes to pre-eminence by making them prefects. Some remembered him chiefly for this action (see J. P. Graham, *Forty Years of Uppingham: memories and sketches*, 1932, pp. 121–2).

Chapter 6   Oxbridge fashions, complacent parents and imperialism

1 This was certainly the case at the schools of this survey as the biographies of masters in the school registers show.

2 Annan, *Leslie Stephen*, p. 30. For an interesting statistical breakdown of entry to a university college in the nineteenth century which supports Annan's assertion see A. Gray and F. Brittain, *A History of Jesus College, Cambridge* (1960), p. 176.

3 H. H. Halsey, 'Education and social mobility in Britain since World War II', paper presented in OECD seminar 'Education, Equality and Life Chances', Jan. 1975, p. 12.

4 *The Times*, 30 Dec. 1859, p. 9.

5 *PSC*, vol. ii, appendix to report, p. 18.

6 *Blackwood's Magazine*, vol. c, no. 612 (Oct. 1866), p. 448.

7 See Taine's *Notes on England*, trans. E. Hyams (1958), p. 120. Hippolyte Taine (1828–93) French philosopher, historian and literary critic.

8 *Ibid.*, pp. 120–1.

9 V. H. H. Green, *Oxford Common Room: a study of Lincoln College and Mark Pattison* (1957), pp. 240–1, 316–17.

10 D. A. Winstanley, *Late Victorian Cambridge* (1947), p. 147.

11 *Ibid.*, p. 146.

12 Pellatt, *Boys in the Making*, p. 67.

13 McIntosh, *Physical Education in England*, p. 62.

14 Prothero, *Whippingham to Westminster*, p. 45.

15 Diary of E. C. C. Firth, entries for 11–19 Oct. 1885 (MCA).

16 T. Thornley, *Cambridge Memories* (1936), p. 17; T. Humphreys, *Criminal Days* (1946), p. 16; T. Collins, *School and Sport: recollections of a busy life* (1905), p. 16; Green, *Oxford Common Room*, p. 286; Mais, *Days of my Life*, p. 26.

17 E. H. Morgan (Red Morgan) and H. A. Morgan (Black Morgan) were two notable sporting dons of Jesus College, Cambridge, in the last quarter of the nineteenth century. Jesus had its own club for leading athletes, the Rhadegunds, and an impressive athletic record. It was Head of the River continuously from 1875 to 1885. The university rugby fifteen of 1889 included six Jesus men, and in some years there were as many as eighteen blues in the college. For a description of its sporting ethos and success see Arthur Gray, *Jesus College, Cambridge* (1902), appendix on Jesus sport.

18 *Report of the Headmasters' Conference* (1897), pp. 79–80.

19 *Blackwood's Magazine*, vol. CLVIII, no. 959 (Sept. 1895), p. 424.

20 Collins, *School and Sport*, p. 19.

21 Thornley, *Cambridge Memories*, p. 25.

22 Lewis R. Farnell, *An Oxonian Looks Back* (1934), pp. 141–2; W. Tuckwell *Reminiscences of Oxford* (1900), p. 124; G. B. Grundy, *Fifty Years at Oxford* (1945), p. 59.

23 *SCM*, vol. VI, no. 89 (Dec. 1896), p. 279.

24 *The Spectator*, vol. 76 (30 May 1896), pp. 767–8.

25 *Punch*, 8 Nov. 1873, p. 184.

26 *Ibid.*, 24 Oct. 1906, p. 293.

27 *Ibid.*, 20 Feb. 1907, p. 128.

28 *Ibid.*, 18 Nov. 1908, p. 368.

29 Trevelyan, *Autobiography*, pp. 14–15.

30 Smith, *Stretching Their Bodies*, p. 45.

31 N. J. Smelser, *Theory of Collective Behaviour* (1962), pp. 319–38.

32 Simpson, *Athleticism*, pp. 3–4.

33 Quoted in P. Smith and G. Summerfield, *Matthew Arnold and the Education of the New Order* (1969), pp. 8 and 15.

34 Numerous contemporary studies make this point. For a recent influential analysis see C. Jencks *et al.*, *Inequality* (1973).

35 E. Wingfield-Stratford, *The Squire and his Relations* (1956), p. 354.

36 Betjeman, *Ghastly Good Taste*, p. 11.

37 John Ford, *A Social History of Cricket* (1972); see also E. W. Bovill, *English Country Life 1780–1830* (1967).

38 *Ibid.*, p. 58.

39 Best, *Mid-Victorian Britain*, pp. 81–91; F. Musgrove, 'Middle class families and schools 1780–1880', *Sociological Review*, vol. 7 (Dec. 1959), pp. 169–78.

40 Musgrove, *Sociological Review*, p. 175.

41 *Fraser's Magazine*, vol. XX, no. 600 (Dec. 1879), p. 832.

42 T. Pellatt, *Public Schools and Public Opinion* (1904), pp. 33–5.

43 *SIC*, vol. I, p. 47.

44 Some fathers would recruit cricket professionals on the estate to coach their sons. See for example, S. A. Heywood, 'Fifty Years of Harrow Cricket 1907–1957' (1957) (HSA). Heywood was professional cricketer to Harrow School 1907–57.

45 W. B. Gallie, *An English School* (1949), pp. 24–5.

46 *Ibid.*, p. 25.

47 See, for example, McIntosh, *Physical Education in England*, p. 177.

48 MacKenzie, *William Cory*, p. 121.

49 Barker, *Character of England*, p. 447.

50 J. Demogeot and H. Montucci, *De l'enseignement secondaire en Angleterre et en Ecosse* (1868), pp. 522ff.

51 Ludwig A. Wiese, *German Letters on English Education*, trans. and ed. L. Schmitz (1877), p. 10.

52 The title conferred on him by Professor Eugen Weber in 'Pierre de Coubertin and the introduction of organised sport into France', *Journal of Contemporary History*, vol. 5, no. 2 (1970), p. 6.

53 Pierre de Coubertin, *L'Education en Angleterre: collèges et universités* (1888), p. 43.

54 *The Quarterly Review*, vol. 125 (July 1868), pp. 473–90, contains a particularly smug evaluation of the English public schools using the report of Demogeot and Montucci as a basis for comment.

55 Pierre de Coubertin, 'Are the public schools a failure?', *Fortnightly Review*, vol. LXXII, no. 432 (1902), pp. 976–86.

56 For example, *The English Schooldays of a French Boy: letters from Maurice de Pange* (1928); *The Times*, 16 Jan. 1903, p. 4.

57 *Marlburian*, vol. XIX, no. 304 (5 March 1884), pp. 24–5.

58 *Harrovian*, vol. XII, no. 7 (21 Oct. 1899), p. 23.

59 *Ibid.*, vol. III, no. 42 (4 May 1872), p. 119.

60 *Report of the Headmasters' Conference* (1873), p. 59.

61 Farrar, *Sermons*, p. 372.

62 Kendall, *Headmaster Remembers*, pp. 240–1.

63 The term is Robert Gibson's for the French writer of childhood Henri Alain Fournier. See his *The Land without a Name: Alain Fournier and his world* (1975).

64 H. A. Vachell, *Brothers* (1904), p. 16.

65 Second stanza of the 'Eton Boating Song'.

66 Of the many discussions of the role of Kingsley and Hughes in the rise of the games ideology, the most elegant and atmospheric is undoubtedly David Newsome's (*Good Learning*, pp. 195–239).

67 The essence of *In Memoriam: Ernest Henry Blyth by his affectionate father* (1886), p. 19 (USA).

68 R. F. Cholmondesley 'A complaint of public schools', *The Independent Review*, Aug. 1904, p. 350.

69 *The Times*, 3 Oct. 1889, p. 8 and 7 Oct. 1889, p. 4.

70 *PSC*, vol. I, p. 40.

71 Darwin, *English Public School*, pp. 24–5.

72 Lyttelton, *Schoolboys and Schoolwork*, pp. 54–6.

73 *The Times*, 4 Jan. 1903, p. 8. After serving as assistant master at Shrewsbury from 1873 to 1885, Gilkes was a distinguished headmaster of Dulwich from 1885 to 1914.

74 *Ibid.*, 11 Jan. 1903, p. 10.

75 Gilkes, *Young Man's Mistakes*, p. 2.

76 *The Times Educational Supplement*, 3 Oct. 1918, p. 46.

77 See in particular, *The Spectator*, 10 Nov. 1917, p. 256; 17 March 1928, p. 409; 24 Aug. 1934, p. 256.

78 Cyril Alington, *A Schoolmaster's Apology* (1914), p. 78.

79 Cyril Norwood in Dover Wilson, *Schools of England*, pp. 140–1.

80 *Report of the Headmasters' Conference* (1919), p. 119.

81 Venables, *Bases Attempted*, p. 27.

82 Welldon, *Eversley's Friendship*, p. 5.

83 Alec Waugh, 'The public schools: difficulties of reform', *The English Review*, vol. XXVIII (March 1919), p. 221.

84 Christian gentility as an ideal is typically depicted by, for example, G. G. T. Heywood in 'Boys at public schools' in E. H. Pitcairn (ed.), *Unwritten Laws and Ideals of Active Service* (1889), pp. 293ff. This ideal is harshly compared with the alleged reality in J. Howard Whitehouse (ed.), *The English Public School. A Symposium* (1919), pp. 21–5. For a discussion of social Darwinism and Victorian social Darwinism see Don Martindale, *The Nature and Type of Sociological Theory* (1961), pp. 168–74 and Himmelfarb, *Victorian Minds*, pp. 314–32 respectively.

85 *Dublin Review*, vol. LVII (July 1865), p. 18.

86 W. H. G. Armytage, *Four Hundred Years of English Education* (1970), pp. 132–5.

87 *Saturday Review*, 8 Dec. 1860, p. 727.

88 Harold Nicolson, *Good Behaviour* (1955).

89 H. Perkin, *The Origins of Modern English Society 1780–1880* (1969), p. 274.

90 David Newsome, 'Public schools and Christian ideals', *Theology*, vol. LXIV, no. 448 (Dec. 1961), p. 489.

91 John Bowles, *The Imperial Achievement* (1974), p. 290.

92 Bertrand Russell, *Education and the Good Life* (1926), p. 54.

93 See J. A. Mangan, 'The concept of duty and the prospect of adventure: images of empire in the late Victorian public school', *Journal of Educational Administration and History*, vol. XII, no. 1 (1980), pp. 31–9.

94 Charles E. Byles, *Rupert Brooke's Grave and Other Poems* (1919), p. 43.

95 Geoffrey Drage, *Eton and the Empire* (1890), p. 40. See also Worsley, *Barbarians and Philistines*, p. 200 and Mack, *British Opinion since 1860*, p. 179.

96 J. E. C. Welldon, *Forty Years On* (1935), p. 119.

97 *Early Days at Uppingham by an Old Boy*, appendix IV, p. 163.

98 James, 'Thring', p. 22.

99 Mack, *British Opinion since 1860*, p. 108.

100 J. G. Cotton Minchin *Our Public Schools: their influence on English history* (1901), p. 113.

101 Michael Edwardes, *A Season in Hell: the defence of the Lucknow Residency* (1973), p. 293.

102 See, for example, Theodore Cook, *Character and Sportsmanship* (1927), pp. 73–4.

103 When A. C. Mann, an Old Uppinghamian, was killed on active service, in a clash with Burmese dacoits, the *USM* proudly recorded that 'in the path of duty, running as he used to run on our football fields, he fell dead' (vol. x, no. 76, Oct. 1872, p. 267).

104 James Morris, *Heaven's Command* (1973), p. 86.

105 J. A. Mangan, 'Imperialism and an ideal of boyhood in fact and fiction', *Book Window*, vol. v, no. 2 (1978), p. 2.

106 See Worsley, *Barbarians and Philistines*, pp. 89–93, for a brief consideration of Newbolt as Darwinian imperialist.

107 J. Wellens, 'The anti-intellectual tradition in the West' in P. W. Musgrave (ed.), *Sociology, History and Education* (1970), pp. 93–6.

108 'Gentleman emigrants', *Macmillan's Magazine,* vol. LVII (Jan. 1888), pp. 32–40.

109 R. W. Service, *Songs of a Sourdough* (60th edn, 1947), pp. 93–6.

110 *Punch*, 6 Sept. 1873, p. 99.

111 Described by C. A. W. Monckton in his *Experiences of a New Guinea Resident Magistrate* (n.d.), p. 111, Monckton himself was deposited in Cooketown, Queensland, with £100, a particularly unsuitable suit, and a letter of introduction to the Lieutenant Governor of British New Guinea.

112 *Lorrettonian*, vol. xv, no. 12 (20 May 1893), pp. 52–3.

113 Quoted in R. H. Tucker, *Memoir of the Life and Episcopate of George Augustus Gardner* (1879), pp. 130–1.

114 A typical example of this process at work is to be found in C. F. Harford-Battersby, *Pilkington of Uganda* (1898), p. 320. G. L. Pilkington (Uppingham 1878–84) was a missionary killed in Uganda during an uprising in 1897, who brought the games of Uppingham to his missionary school; see also J. A. Mangan, 'Eton in India: the imperial diffusion of a Victorian educational ethic', *History of Education*, vol. VII, no. 2 (1976), pp. 105–18.

115 Walter E. Houghton, *The Victorian Frame of Mind 1830–1870* (1951), pp. 201–2.

116 *Ibid.*, pp. 110ff.

Chapter 7   Fez, 'blood' and hunting crop: the symbols and rituals of a Spartan culture

1 John Bunyan, *The Pilgrim's Progress and the Holy War* (Cassell's illustrated edn, 1911), pp. 421, 523–4.

2 Lancing College common room minute book (prefects' book) 1907–13, p. 1.

3 P. B. M. Bryant, *Harrow* (1936), p. 108.

4 J. La Fontaine, *The Interpretation of Ritual* (1972), p. xvii.

5 E. R. Leach, 'Ritualization in man in relation to conceptual and social development', *Philosophical Transactions of the Royal Society of London*, vol. 257, series B (1966), p. 404.

6 See J. H. M. Beattie, 'On understanding ritual' in Bryan R. Wilson (ed.), *Rationality* (1970), pp. 240–71.

7 This is a condensed version of the definition by T. Paterson. 'Rituals are formalised behaviour patterns, methods of communication, verbal and non-verbal, necessary for the establishment of relations among members of a

group or between groups' in 'Emotive rituals in industrial organisms', *Philosophical Transactions*, p. 437.

8 B. Bernstein, H. L. Elwin and R. S. Peters, 'Ritual in education', *Philosophical Transactions*, p. 429.

9 J. Beattie, 'Ritual and social change', *Man*, vol. I, no. 1 (1966), p. 66.

10 D. Godwin, 'Ritual in nineteenth and twentieth century education', *Education, Economy and Politics*, Open University, E352 (1973), block 2, p. 35.

11 Mary Douglas, *Purity and Danger* (1966), p. 63.

12 E. M. Avedon and B. Sutton-Smith, *The Study of Games* (1971), p. 228.

13 M. Douglas, *Purity and Danger*, pp. 63ff.

14 R. Wilkinson, *The Prefects: British leadership and the public school tradition* (1964), p. 46.

15 Witness the reaction of the public schools to A. Waugh's *The Loom of Youth*.

16 L. P. Hartley, 'The conformer' in Graham Greene (ed.), *The Old School* (1932), p. 92.

17 Tallents, *Man and Boy*, p. 104.

18 Caraman, *C. C. Martindale*, p. 42.

19 *Pall Mall Gazette*, 16 July 1866.

20 *Blackwood's Magazine*, vol. CXL, no. 804 (Dec. 1866), p. 76.

21 Lyttelton, *Memories and Hopes*, p. 76.

22 Quoted in Bernard Darwin, *The Game's Afoot: an anthology of sport* (1926), pp. 150–1.

23 H. W. Serpell, 'Old boys societies' in Norwood and Hope, *Higher Education*, p. 472.

24 *Ibid.*, p. 473.

25 Wilkinson, *The Prefects*, p. 46.

26 File 55, Hawley Bequest (USA).

27 Honey, *Tom Brown's Universe*, p. 157.

28 It did not apparently affect Stonyhurst's status as a public school. The college was admitted to the Headmasters' Conference in 1900 and in the Harmsworth Encyclopedia of 1905, as we have seen in the prologue, was listed as one of the more famous public schools.

29 In 1917 a fourth 'playroom' was added due to an increase in school numbers.

30 Tristram wrote of Almond, 'He was a thorough going autocrat' (*Loretto School*, p. 104).

31 This was made possible by the small numbers of boys at the school: about 12 in 1862 rising gradually to about 60 by 1864, down to 38 in 1866, up to 100 by 1878 and then climbing steadily until Almond's death in 1903 when the numbers stood at 136.

32 R. C. T. Taylor, *A Housemaster's Letters* (1912), p. 37.

33 This is made particularly clear, for instance, in J. A. Symonds's unusually honest account of homosexuality at Harrow under Vaughan described in Grosskurth, *John Symonds*, pp. 30–4.

34 An especially good example is Uppingham at the end of the nineteenth century. See Nevinson, *Paint and Prejudice*, p. 8.

35 Witness Symonds's torment in trying to keep quiet (Grosskurth, *John Symonds*, p. 35).

36 The door that separated the housemaster's private apartments from the boys.

37 Russell, *Autobiography*, p. 48. Another Harrow master who seemed quite indifferent to the management of his house was F. Rendall, housemaster 1854–81. (Grosskurth, *John Symonds*, p. 27). For discussions of the distance between boys and housemasters of the Victorian period see Rigby, 'Edward Thring', p. 122 and Noel Annan, *Roxburgh of Stowe* (1965), p. 6.

38 Fitzgerald, *Stonyhurst Memories*, pp. 81–2.

39 Stephen Foot, *Three Lives: an autobiography* (1934), pp. 279–82.

40 Bundle 17, College Papers (Lancing Archives Collection).

41 Bradley *et al.*, *Marlborough College*, p. 85. See also *PSC*, vol. IV, p. 164, Q.284 and vol. IV, p. 209, Q.1202 for details of the situation at Harrow at the time.

42 Venables, *Bases Attempted*, p. 190.

43 Welldon, *Recollections and Reflections*, p. 163; see also P. M. Thornton, *Some Things We Have Remembered* (1912), p. 147.

44 J. A. Mangan, 'Physical education as a ritual process' in Mangan (ed.), *Physical Education and Sport*, p. 97.

45 Laborde, *Harrow: yesterday and today*, p. 175.

46 Handford, *Lancing 1848–1930*, p. 14.

47 Tallents, *Man and Boy*, p. 105. A 'base' is the Harrow equivalent of a goal.

48 Honey, *Tom Brown's Universe*, p. 139.

49 J. Fischer-Williams, *Harrow* (1901), p. 204.

50 *Harrovian*, vol. XVI, no. 2 (14 Dec. 1878), p. 13; Vachell's *Brothers*, contains a chapter 'Billy's versus Poodles' which is a realistic description of a 'footer' house match at Harrow in the 1870s.

51 *Harrovian*, vol. I, no. 19 (22 Oct. 1870), p. 34.

52 Erving Goffman, *Asylums* (Penguin edn, 1971), p. 103.

53 Rome, 'Uppingham', p. 98; see also *LCM*, vol. V, no. 72 (Feb. 1890), p. 817, *Marlburian*, vol. XXXI, no. 492 (3 Dec. 1896), p. 181, *Harrovian*, vol. I, no. 19 (22 Oct. 1870), p. 44 and Lancing College headmasters' notices 1925–9 (LCA) for similar difficulties.

54 J. C. Gibson, *Reminiscences of a Railwayman* (1968), p. 8.

55 Desmond Coke, *The Bending of a Twig* (2nd edn, 1906), p. 155.

56 *Marlburian*, vol. III, no. 20 (2 Oct. 1865), p. 1.

57 *Ibid.*, vol. XXIV, no. 388 (14 Oct. 1889), p. 139.

58 Benson, *David Blaize*, p. 231. Benson also gives vivid descriptions of house matches in his *Sketches from Marlborough* (1905), pp. 50–3.

59 Letter to the author dated 6 Oct. 1973.

60 Letter to the author dated 24 Aug. 1973.

61 Lyttelton, *Memories and Hopes*, p. 42.

62 Hay, *Famous Schoolmasters*, p. 48.

63 Laborde, *Harrow: yesterday and today*, p. 175.

64 H. A. Vachell, *The Hill* (1905; 39th edn, 1947), p. 34.

65 Parkin, *Life of Thring*, vol. I, p. 328.

66 *Ibid.*, pp. 330–5.

67 *Punch*, 30 May 1917, p. 357.

68 *The Spectator*, 15 Feb. 1913, p. 272. R.C.T. made an analysis of 167 men who made up his school cricket and football teams between 1890 and 1900 and who in their final school years devoted themselves largely to games, and discovered that all but three were successful in later life.

69 Description of A. G. Watson, housemaster of Large House 1868–91 in the *Marlburian*, vol. XXIX, no. 5 (29 July 1916), p. 94. In this context Geoffrey Chilton (Marlborough 1910–15, assistant master 1920–58) has informed the author that in the period immediately prior to the Great War, virtually all the housemasters at the school were enthusiastic advocates of games. One excellent indication of their enthusiasm at an even later period is to be found in the school 'Red Book' which contains headmasters' notices to staff. During Turner's headship there was a ruling that superannuated pupils permitted extra terms at school were not allowed to play in inter-house games. Turner wrote that he considered the rule 'unhealthy', but appreciated it existed because housemasters could not trust one another not to make special allowance for their athletes to remain at school, once superannuated, in the interest of house games success (p. 227).

70 'Quid', 'Memoirs of a famous schoolmaster', *Baily's Magazine*, Jan. 1903, p. 11.

71 W. E. Bowen, *Edward Bowen*, p. 146.

72 *Harrovian*, vol. XIV, no. 3 (13 May 1901), p. 31.

73 W. E. Bowen, *Edward Bowen*, p. 231. He played in friendly matches for his house until his late fifties and 'was a dangerous man to be near' (*Harrovian*, vol. LXII, no. 23, 30 March 1949, p. 92).

74 J. Burrow (ed.), *Kings and Commoners: studies in British idealism* (1936), p. 39.

75 H. A. Vachell, *Fellow Travellers* (1923), pp. 25–6.

76 Fourth stanza of 'Lord's 1878' quoted in W. E. Bowen, *Edward Bowen*, p. 410.

77 E. Bowen, 'Games', *The Journal of Education*, 1 Feb. 1884, p. 70.

78 W. E. Bowen, *Edward Bowen*, p. 222.

79 *Ibid.*, p. 197.

80 *Harrovian*, vol. II, no. 2 (7 March 1889), p. 145.

81 *Ibid.*, vol. XXIV, no. 14 (16 Feb. 1961), p. 65). Kemp was an Old Harrovian (1874–80). At school he was captain of cricket (1880) and Public Schools Racquets Champion. At Oxford he represented the university at association football, racquets and cricket and captained the Oxford eleven that beat the Australians. On his appointment to Harrow as assistant master he was referred to in the press as the 'master of games' (*Harrow Association Records*, 1920–4). He took charge of Harrow cricket in 1888 and continued in charge until 1921. It is claimed he was instrumental in raising £10,000 for Harrow cricket over the years (*Harrovian*, vol. LXIV, no. 29, 11 July 1957, p. 124).

82 *Harrovian*, vol. LXI, no. 25 (19 May 1948), p. 100.

83 See J. A. Mangan, 'Athleticism: a case study of the evolution of an educational ideology' in Brian Simon and Ian Bradley, *The Victorian Public School* (1975), pp. 155–9.

84 *Marlburian*, vol. XLIV, no. 671 (5 Oct. 1909), p. 133.

85 A. H. Beesly, *Ballads and Other Verses* (1895), p. 21.

86 Patterson, *Uppingham Cricket*, p. 35.

87 David Tate, *West Deyne, Uppingham 1859–1959* (1959), 8 (USA).

88 Jonathan and Michael Lewis, *Lorne House, Uppingham 1856–1956* p. 10 (USA).

89 *LCM*, vol. IV, no. 4 (May 1911), p. 46.

90 Diary of T. D. Cook, entry for 15 Oct. 1908 (LCA).

91 Handford, *Lancing 1848–1930*, p. 248; also *LCM*, vol. XIX, no. 372 (Nov. 1926), pp. 118–19, for an appreciation of W. B. Harris.

92 Bryant, *Harrow*, p. 145. For a brief but excellent sketch of Bowen the stimulating educational radical, see Archer, *Secondary Education*, p. 227. At Cambridge he was 'one of the most distinguished and brilliant of our graduates' (W. E. Bowen, *Edward Bowen*, p. 45) and was a member of the select group of intellectuals, the 'Apostles'. He contributed to Farrar's *Essays on Liberal Education* (1867).

93 For a sympathic description of Beesly see E. F. Benson, *Family Affairs*, pp. 157–65. Benson considered him 'by far the most gifted I ever came under either at school or the University'.

94 I owe this point to Mr T. B. Belk, the Uppingham School archivist.

95 Lyttelton, *Memories and Hopes*, p. 22.

96 Wilkinson, *The Prefects*, p. 45.

97 Malim, *Almae Matres*, p. 163.

98 Minchin, *Public Schools*, p. 159.

99 Arthur G. Penny, *The Shirt-Sleeved Generation* (1953), p. 113.

100 *Ibid.*, p. 112.

101 This story is recounted in several places. For example, J. E. C. Welldon, *Strand Magazine*, vol. IV (July–Dec. 1892), p. 246 and Laborde, *Harrow: yesterday and today*, p. 107.

102 Simpson, *Howson*, p. 60.

103 Mackenzie, *Almond of Loretto*, p. 248; *Lorettonian*, vol. XXVI, no. 4 (28 Nov. 1903), p. 13.

104 Thomson, 'Physical Education in Scotland', p. 122.

105 F. W. M. Kitto, 'Loretto School', *PSM*, Dec. 1900.

106 'Stonyhurst Association Football Journal', p. 63. (SCA). Father Robinson was the Stonyhurst Bowen. He was a sportsman who did a great deal to encourage football, cricket and hockey while an ordinary member of staff (1877–84) and as first prefect (1888–1907). Obituary in *SCM*, vol. XV, no. 226 (Feb. 1920), p. 94.

107 For details of this correspondence see *SCM*, vol. V, no. 74 (June 1894), p. 326; vol. VI, no. 87 (July 1896), p. 198; vol. VI, no. 86 (June 1896), p. 188; and vol. VI, no. 84 (Feb. 1896), p. 122.

108 Rector's book for matters connected with the interests of the college 1869–93, entry in the year 1888 (SCA).

109 *SCM*, vol. VI, no. 92 (June 1897), p. 368.

110 *Ibid.*, vol. X, no. 153 (July 1907), p. 326.

111 *Ibid.*, vol. XIII, no. 211 (June 1917), p. 1926.

112 Philip Bell, *Idols and Idylls: essays by a public schoolboy* (1917), p. 78. When Father Robinson's 'house' games system was reformed in 1922 the reorganisation was the work of a Father Wilson. A fact that further reveals the boys' subservient role in the control of games.

113 *Harrovian*, vol. LXII, no. 23 (30 March 1949), p. 92.

114 'Harrow Verses' written in 1873–4 by three members of Mr Hutton's House, p. 52 (HSA).

115 *USM*, vol. XXXIV, no. 268 (June 1896), pp. 185–6.

116 Lancing College Games Committee report book 1921. See especially the committee meeting for 5 July 1921 (LCA).

117 *Harrow School Rules and Regulations 1914.*

118 J.G.L. 'To a Certain Friend' in 'Harrow Verses', pp. 51–3.

119 *Harrow School Existing Customs* (n.d.), p. 30 (HSA).

120 *Report of the Headmasters' Conference* (1914), p. 21.

121 Graham, *Forty Years*, p. 132.

122 At Lancing, for example, in 1934 standard house caps were introduced – all for 4s. 6d. Previously prices had ranged from 4s. 6d. to 18s. 6d. At Harrow about this time, when the cost of material became exorbitant, one old Harrovian had the cloth for sports clothing woven, another bought the cloth for the school, yet another had it tailored and the clothing was loaned to teams (*Harrovian*, vol. LXX, no. 12, 30 June 1957, p. 60).

123 See, for example, the colour regulations in the *Harrovian*, vol. LIII, no. 33 (July 1940), p. 130.

124 W. R. I. Crewdson, 'Harrow School', *The Pennant* (house magazine of Benskin's Brewery), vol. 7 (Oct. 1950), pp. 200–1 (HSA).

125 Wakeford, *Cloistered Elite*, p. 124.

126 Arnold Lunn, *The Harrovians* (1913), p. 45. Lunn was at Harrow 1902–7.

127 The first rule book opens: 'The purpose of this book is to provide a permanent record of the various new rules made by successive Heads of House, and to ensure that they shall not merely exist in the memory of the "privs".' These books are no longer used.

128 Fischer-Williams, *Harrow*, p. 152.

129 Arthur Bryant, *English Saga 1840–1940* (1942), p. 286. Bryant was at Harrow 1912–17.

130 Blue jacket worn daily.

131 A. C. M. Croome (ed.), *Fifty Years of Sport at Oxford, Cambridge and the Great Public Schools* (2 vols, 1913), vol. II, p. 127. To have won your flannels at Harrow indicated membership of either the cricket or football eleven.

132 Lunn, *Come What May*, p. 29.

133 Ogilvie, *English Public School*, p. 181.

134 *USM*, vol. XXXIII, no. 261 (Nov. 1895), p. 190.

135 S. W. Gore, 'Jerry' in G. Ewart (ed.), *Forty Years On: an anthology of school songs* (1969) (unnumbered page). Gore was at Harrow 1863–9 and had himself an illustrious athletic career – cricket eleven 1867–9 (captain 1869), football eleven 1866–8, school racquets player 1869.

136 Philathletic Club photograph book 1885–1922 (HSA).

137 Third stanza of 'A Tale of Two Careers' in Sorley, *Poems*, p. 95. A 'forty cap' was the equivalent of a second fifteen place at Marlborough.

138 M. Arlen, *Piracy* (1922), p. 91: 'The difference between a College Prefect and a House Prefect is that a College Prefect can do what he likes everywhere and a House Prefect can do what he likes in his house.'

139 Betjeman, *Summoned by Bells*, p. 155.

140 *Marlburian*, vol. IX, no. 865 (12 Dec. 1925), p. 155.

141 Waugh, *Loom of Youth*, p. 21.

142 Fox, *Harrow*, p. 75. Fox was at Harrow 1892–7.

143 Lunn, *Come What May*, p. 42.

144 E. W. Howson, 'Boy', *Harrow Notes*, vol. I, no. 4 (12 May 1883), p. 46.

145 *Harrovian*, vol. LXXX, no. 9 (Dec. 1966), p. 40.

146 *The Spectator*, 1 June 1912, pp. 865–6.

147 C. Mayo, 'Reminiscences of a Harrow master', *Cornhill Magazine*, vol. LXIV, no. 380 (Feb. 1928), p. 196.

148 'P.P.H.', 'A woman's invasion of a famous public school and how men endured it', *Cornhill Magazine*, vol. LLXXII, no. 436 (Oct. 1932), p. 404.

149 Walter Sichel, *The Sands of Time: recollections and reflections* (1923), p. 99.

150 *USM*, vol. XL, no. 317 (Oct. 1902), p. 181.

151 *LCM*, vol. XXXV, no. 461 (Lent term 1942), p. 52.

152 Bryant, *Harrow*, p. 111.

153 *Marlburian*, vol. XL, no. 611 (17 June 1905), p. 68.

154 *USM*, vol. XIV, no. 355 (July 1907), p. 136.

155 *Marlburian*, vol. XX, no. 324 (3 June 1875), p. 78.

156 *Harrovian*, vol. I, no. 5 (7 June 1888), p. 53.

157 Penny, *Shirt-Sleeved Generation*, p. 111.

158 Rome, 'Uppingham', p. 132.

159 The role of the stigmatised in institutions is interestingly discussed by Erving Goffman in *Stigma* (1963), passim.

160 See Louis MacNeice, *The Strings are False* (1945), pp. 94–9 and 241–5 for a description of the Marlborough aesthetes.

161 A. Blunt, 'Conversation piece', *The Centenary Edition of the Marlburian* (1943), p. 32, and 'From Bloomsbury to Marxism', *Studio International*, Nov. 1973, pp. 164–5.

162 *Marlburian*, vol. LII, no. 772 (19 March 1917), p. 32.

163 *The Union Jack*, Jan. 1883, pp. 147–8.

164 Gentle in manner but vigorous in deed.

165 *Marlburian*, vol. XXXIV, no. 527 (7 June 1899), p. 75. Another more skittish Marlborough verse goes:

> I wish I was a colour
> I wish I was a blue
> I would wear a XV jersey
> And a tie of pretty hue.

(*Marlburian*, vol. XXXVIII, no. 590, 20 Dec. 1903, p. 170.)

166 Howard T. Swage, *Games and Sports in British Schools and Universities* (1926), p. 44.

Chapter 8   Play up and play the game: the rhetoric of cohesion, identity, patriotism and morality

1 *Harrovian*, vol. XX, no. 6 (27 July 1907), p. 64.

2 *PSM*, vol. VIII, no. 46 (Oct 1903), p. 318.

3 Siegfried Sassoon, *The Old Century* (1938), p. 228.

4 Lancing master 1899–1912.

5 G. F. Bradby, *The Lanchester Tradition* (1914; 1954 edn), p. 41.

6 Hugh Dalziel Duncan, *Language and Literature in Society* (1961), p. 5. See Monica Wilson, *Religion and the Transformation of a Society: a study of social*

change in Africa (1971), p. 54, for a discussion of the relative emphasis of symbolism in literate and non-literate societies.

7 Welldon, *Recollections and Reflections*, p. 131.

8 C. E. S. Webb, 'Sports and sportsmen at Harrow', *Sport and Sportsmen*, vol. I, no. 2 (Dec. 1920), pp. 81–92. Appendix VI contains a selection of Bowen's Harrow verses.

9 For Churchill's comments see *Harrovian*, vol. LXXII, no. 10 (4 Dec. 1958), p. 39; also Arthur Bryant, *London Illustrated News*, 1 Jan. 1949, p. 2.

10 H. A. Vachell, *Distant Fields* (1937), p. 30.

11 See Dell Hymes, 'Models of the interaction of language and social life' in J. Gumperez and D. Hymes (eds.), *Directions in Socio-Linguistics* (1972).

12 Quoted in John B. Carroll, *Language, Thought and Reality: selected writings of Benjamin Lee Whorf* (1959), p. 134.

13 Basil Bernstein, 'A socio-linguistic approach to social learning' in *Class, Codes and Control* (1971), vol. I, p. 119.

14 Quoted in S. I. Hayakawa, *Language in Thought and Action* (1959), p. 164.

15 Quoted in John Drinkwater, *Patriotism in Literature* (1924), p. 125. The inclusion above of both these men of letters, Huxley and Cory, is particularly apposite as both were public school masters at some time in their careers and Cory (assistant master at Eton 1845–72) saw the blossoming of the athleticism movement there. The famous 'Eton Boating Song' was one of his compositions.

16 A brief but excellent example of this type of study may be found in E. P. Thompson, *The Making of the English Working Class* (1963), chapter XI 'The transforming power of the cross', in which he analyses the rhetoric of nineteenth-century Methodism.

17 This is also an attempt to meet the request of C. Wright Mills, to locate the 'vocabularies of motive' of actual historical eras. See 'Situated-actions and vocabularies of motive', *American Sociological Review*, vol. V, no. 6 (1940), p. 651.

18 This embraced an astonishing range of publications – autobiographies, biographies, educational treatises, sermons, school histories and articles, verses and letters in literary and educational journals, daily and weekly newspapers and, of course, school magazines.

19 Famous playing fields respectively at Uppingham, Loretto and Harrow.

20 These were first published in 1858, four years after Thring arrived at Uppingham. Later were added 'The Old Boys' Match' (1862) and 'The Football Song' (1866).

21 Quoted in Tozer, 'Physical Education at Uppingham', p. 199.

22 *Ibid.*, p. 118.

23 Red and white are the Loretto school colours. Apparently Almond chose red out of admiration for Sparta where the young warriors wore red cloaks. I owe this point to Mr R. B. Bruce-Lockhart, former headmaster of Loretto.

24 *Loretto School Songs* (n.d.), p. 6.

25 Quoted in W. E. Bowen, *Edward Bowen*, p. 377.

26 For an interesting discussion of this point see J. H. M. Beattie, 'On understanding ritual' in Wilson, *Rationality*, pp. 266–7.

27 *Marlburian*, vol. XLI, no. 620 (7 Feb. 1906), p. 3. E. W. Howson in his 'Five Hundred Faces' anticipated just such a reaction:

> The time may come, as the years go by,
> When your heart will thrill,
> At the thought of the Hill,
> And the slippery fields and the raining sky.

28 *Lorettonian*, vol. xx, no. 8 (March 1898), p. 38.
29 Third verse of the Harrow song 'Stet Fortuna Domus'.
30 *SCM*, vol. x, no. 148 (Oct. 1906), pp. 149–50.
31 *USM*, vol. lx, no. 467 (March 1922), p. 25.
32 *USM*, vol. lix, no. 463 (June 1921), p. 92. See also 'Going Strong' by H. B. Tristram in *Loretto School Songs* the last verse of which goes:

> Long hence when you look with a quivering eye
> On the little white tassel you value so high;
> You will think of the matches you've played in and won
> And you'll long for the days that are over and done.

33 'The Same Old Game' was presented at the Annual Dinner of 1887 (USA).
34 Iain Fletcher (ed.), *The Complete Poems of Lionel Johnson* (1953), p. xx.
35 Hely Hutchinson Almond wrote in an article entitled 'Football as a moral agent', *Nineteenth Century*, Dec. 1893, 'I have never yet known a genuine rugby forward who was not distinctively a man.'
36 *A Housemaster and His Boys by One of Them* (1929), p. 64. 'A Housemaster' was apparently Stephen Foot. He developed his argument further in two articles entitled 'The future of the public schools', *Nineteenth Century*, vol. ci, no. 592 (Jan. 1927), pp. 86–96, and vol. cviii, no. 635 (Jan. 1930), pp. 17–25.
37 From 'Harrow' in *On England and Other Addresses* (1926), p. 265.
38 Martin Crusoe, 'The development of the public school', *Scrutiny*, May 1932, p. 57.
39 See for example Graves, *Bad Old Days*, pp. 21–2; Worsley, *Flannelled Fool*, pp. 74–7; Caraman, *C. C. Martindale*, p. 46; J. W. Keble-Martin, *Over the Hills* (1968), p. 23. For a general discussion of homosexuality in public schools, see 'Our gentlemen's schools' by ex-monitor, *English Review*, March 1923, pp. 155–60 and June 1923, pp. 256–7; Bamford, *Rise of Public Schools*, pp. 279–81 and Honey, *Tom Brown's Universe*, pp. 178ff.
40 Edward Thring, *Uppingham School Songs* (1881), p. 17.
41 See respectively Thomson, 'Physical Education in Scotland', p. 71; *Sports and Sportsmen*, p. 145, F. B. Malim in A. C. Benson (ed.), *Cambridge Essays on Education* (1917), p. 153.
42 Thring, *Songs*, p. 17.
43 *Ibid.*, p. 28.
44 Quoted in W. E. Bowen, *Edward Bowen*, p. 405.
45 *LCM*, vol. v, no. 80 (Dec. 1890), p. 915.
46 R. C. T. Taylor, *Housemaster's Letters* (1912), p. 181.
47 W. Turley, 'Modern athleticism', *Dark Blue*, vol. iv (Sept, 1872–Feb. 1873), p. 297.
48 Norman Gale, 'The Female Boy' in *More Cricket Songs* (1905), p. 15.
49 *Punch*, 27 Feb. 1901, p. 165. (*USM*, vol. xliv, no. 348, Aug. 1906, p. 115.)
50 J. M. Wilson, *Morality in Public Schools and its Relation to Religion* (1882),

pp. 18–19. James Maurice Wilson (1836–1931) was assistant master at Rugby (1859–79) and headmaster of Clifton (1879–90).

51 *Ibid.*, p. 19. A large extract of Wilson's essay, including the above passage, was printed in the *Lorettonian*, vol. IV, no. 4 (26 Nov. 1881), pp. 14–15. No doubt it was considered an uplifting passage for pupils and parents.

52 *The Times Educational Supplement*, 5 Dec. 1918, p. 527.

53 *Lorettonian*, vol. I, no. 5 (13 March 1880), p. 15.

54 *Ibid.*, vol. III, no. 10 (17 March 1881), p. 32.

55 *Ibid.*, vol. XVIII, no. 4 (30 Nov. 1895), p. 15.

56 Quoted in W. E. Bowen, *Edward Bowen*, p. 395.

57 *Lorettonian*, vol. XLIV, no. 9 (18 March 1922), p. 40.

58 Lawrence Moncrieff, 'The Cricketer's "If"' in *The Cricketer* (Winter Annual, 1921–2) ed. P. F. Warner.

59 *The Times*, 13 July 1859, p. 12.

60 Norman Gale, *More Cricket Songs* (1905), p. 57.

61 *Harrovian*, vol. IV, no. 11 (11 Dec. 1879), p. 116.

62 *Lorettonian*, vol. XXIV, no. 6 (1 Feb. 1902), p. 22.

63 Alan R. Haig-Brown, *Sporting Sonnets* (1902), p. 16.

64 Second verse of 'Carmen Marlburiense' by C. W. Moule. Translation: 'Long live the strength of our footballers and that of the eleven! May they fight for their country on football or cricket field – or on the field of battle.' Song and translation from Ewart, *Forty Years On*, pp. 169–70.

65 *Lorettonian*, vol. XXII, no. 5 (17 March 1900), p. 24.

66 *SCM*, vol. XIII, no. 199 (April 1915), p. 112.

67 E. W. Hornung, *The Old Guard* (1919), p. 63.

68 From ' "The Game of Life"; a sermon preached in the Chapel of Stowe House, Broadstairs', 5 July 1914, quoted in S. Chichester (ed.), *E. W. Hornung and his Young Guard 1914* (1936), p. 37.

69 Byles, *Poems*, p. 20.

70 *Marlburian*, vol. LII, no. 776 (12 July 1917), p. 108. ('In Memory of Second Lieutenant H. J. Goodwin'). 'J.B.' was John Bain, assistant master at Marlborough 1873–83, 1886–1913. He himself is celebrated in Charles Sorley's *Marlborough and Other Poems* in the poem entitled 'J.B.', pp. 29–30. Examples of his poetic obituaries may be found in appendix VI.

71 Gurner, *I Chose Teaching*, p. 55. Gurner's *War Echoes* (1917), a small book of poetry composed at the front, significantly contains no verses of the shrill simple patriotism of games-as-war training or war-as-games variety.

72 Dennis Stanhope appeared in R. C. Sherriff's *Journey's End*, the famous play about public school boys in the trenches. At the fictitious Barford (his public school) he had been a clean-limbed skipper of the fifteen and enthusiastic member of the eleven, and as head of house notably severe on drinkers and smokers.

73 Alington, *Ancient and Modern*, p. 31.

74 See A. H. H. Maclean, *Public Schools and the Great War* (1919). Maclean was at Marlborough 1877–81.

75 *Harrovian*, vol. XXX, no. 3 (2 June 1917), p. 41.

76 F. B. Malim in Benson, *Cambridge Essays*, p. 152.

77 Paul Jones, *War Letters of a Public School Boy* (1918), pp. 50–1.

78 *Ibid.*, p. 49.

79 This extract from the poem appeared in the *Lorettonian*, vol. v, no. 10, (17 March 1883), p. 37. The entire poem of three verses, written by Frank Able, was first published in the *Union Jack* (eds. G. A. Henty and Bernard Heldmann) 23 Jan. 1883, p. 263.

80 The *Lorettonian* some forty years later included a poem closer in metre to 'If' but which somewhat distorts Kipling's message:

> If you can keep to all the rules of rugger
> And though you're beaten always play the game
> Yours is the rugger field and all that's on it
> And what is more, you'll tread the field of fame.

(Vol. XLV, no. 7, 10 Feb. 1923, p. 30.)

81 Second verse of 'Tom' by Edward Bowen in W. E. Bowen, *Edward Bowen*, p. 405. Tom is described in Edward Graham's *Some Notes on the Harrow School Songs* as 'the ideal of a school hero of the football field and his House'. The complete poem can be found in appendix VI.

82 Hugh Dalziel Duncan, *Symbols in Society* (1968), p. 168.

83 *SCM*, vol. VIII, no. 120 (Feb. 1902), p. 31.

84 Second verse of 'Farewell to Loretto' by H.F.C.', *Loretto School Songs* (n.d.), p. 6.

85 Third verse of 'Three Yards' written in 1895 by E. W. Howson (assistant master at Harrow School 1881–1905) in Ewart, *Forty Years On*, p. 95.

86 *Ibid.*, p. 109.

87 *Man and Wife* (1873). In mordant vein Collins returned to this theme continually through the book (see pp. 54–5, 140–2, 147–8, 150–1, 184 and 426).

88 *Punch*, 15 April 1871, p. 14.

89 *The Spectator*, vol. 62, no. 3181 (15 June 1889).

90 *USM*, vol. 35, no. 273 (Feb. 1897), p. 7: the headmaster's funeral oration on Stevenson's death.

91 J. P. Graham, pupil (1888–94) and assistant master (1900–27). Graham recounts that Stevenson was in the habit of providing regular 'delicious spreads' for selected groups of boys (*Forty Years*, pp. 56–7).

92 *Harrovian*, vol. XXV, no. 6 (27 July 1912), p. 76.

93 *Ibid.*, vol. XXVI, no. 5 (26 July 1913), p. 86.

94 Welldon, *Forty Years On*, p. 112.

95 Letter dated 14 Jan. 1974 to the author from Michael Birley (Marlborough 1934–39), and at present a Marlborough housemaster. For a cynical view of 'playing the game', see Lunn, *Harrovians*, pp. 66–7; P. G. Wodehouse, *Enter P. Smith* (1935), pp. 10ff.

96 *Boys' Own Annual* (1913–14), p. 406.

97 *LCM*, vol. II, no. 53 (Feb. 1899), p. 638.

98 S. P. Grundy, 'What public school men can do', *Hibbert's Journal*, vol. X (1911–12), pp. 687–8.

99 *Report of the Headmasters' Conference* (1923), p. 53.

100 Welldon, *Recollections and Reflections*, p. 144.

101 *Report of the Headmasters' Conference* (1923), p. 53.

102 J. E. C. Welldon, 'The public school spirit in public life', *Contemporary*

Review, vol. CXXXII, no. 313 (Oct. 1927), p. 620; for a similar outburst see C. H. P. Mayo, 'The public school spirit', *Quarterly Review*, vol. 251, no. 498 (Oct. 1928), p. 212.

103 Sir Geoffrey Lagden, 'On public schools and their influence', *Nineteenth Century*, vol. LXXI, no. 421 (March 1912), p. 574.

104 Quoted in Lord Cromer, 'The teaching of patriotism', *Nineteenth Century*, vol. LXXVIII, no. 465 (Nov. 1915), pp. 1012–13.

105 Miles was editor of Cassell's 'Physical Education' and Routledge's 'Fitness' series, and co-editor of Hurst and Blackett's 'Imperial Athletic Library'. He wrote a number of books on health, diet and exercise, and established a string of health restaurants. He was a talented all-rounder – obtaining a first class (classical tripos) at Cambridge – and at various times amateur tennis and racquets champion of the world. Between 1882 and 1887 he was a pupil at Marlborough and later in his career Cambridge don and public school master. A delightful reminiscence of his frugal existence on biscuits is to be found in the autobiography of Sir E. Dennison Ross, the distinguished Oriental linguist, *Both Ends of the Candle* (1963), p. 27, Ross was at Marlborough 1883–8.

106 Sir Theodore Cook, *Character and Sportsmanship* (1927), p. xiv. Sir Theodore Cook (1867–1927) was educated at Radley, where he was captain of football and boats and head of school, and at Oxford where he won his rowing blue in 1899. In later life he was twice captain of the English fencing team at international competitions.

107 Rudolph Kircher, *Fair Play*, trans. R. N. Bradley (1928).

108 *Baxter's Second Innings* (1892). The allegory was written by Henry Drummond, the Free Church evolutionist, and was a Victorian best seller. I am grateful to Mr Patrick Scott, lecturer in English Literature, Edinburgh University, for this information.

109 *Ibid.*, p. 16.

110 Extract from a letter from Mr R. B. Bruce-Lockhart, former headmaster of Loretto, to the author dated 25 Oct. 1972.

Epilogue

1 This is the practice of A. M. Kazamias in his excellent study of English education *Politics, Society and Secondary Education in England* (1966). And appropriately it was the position adopted in a series of articles, 'The Public Schools: a hundred years of experience' in *The Times* in August 1928.

2 F. W. Farrar, *The Fortnightly Review*, 1 March 1868, p. 237. (Published lecture delivered to the members of the Royal Institute on 31 Jan. 1868.) Farrar clearly included Marlborough in his strictures. Although at the time of the lecture he was a Harrow master (1855–71), he had been assistant master at Marlborough 1853–5.

3 *Harrovian*, vol. XVI, no. 2 (4 April 1903), p. 13.

4 Farrar, *Sermons*, pp. 370–5. Henry Palmer recorded in his Marlborough diary, 'Farrar writes his form a most touching letter on their idleness' (entry for 25 May 1855).

5 Newspaper cuttings, pp. 15, 17, 19, 21 (MCA).

6 See his autobiography, *After Many Days: a schoolmaster's memories* (1937), pp. 123–5.

7 *Marlburian*, vol. LXXXVII, no. 1065 (winter 1954), p. 51. A fuller description of the attitudes of both Fletcher and Bell is to be found in Mangan 'Athleticism: a case-study of an educational ideology' in Simon and Bradley, *Victorian Public School*, pp. 147–67.

8 See for example his articles on social service and the public schools, *The Spectator*, 13 Nov. 1926, pp. 847–8 and 23 Nov. 1929, p. 756.

9 *Marlburian*, vol. LX, no. 810 (13 July 1920), p. 91.

10 I owe this point to Mr E. G. H. Kempson, who was a pupil under Turner. Turner himself was a Marlburian (1904–10). He was school captain, a loyal and enthusiastic supporter of Frank Fletcher and the first secretary of the Literary Society created in his last year as pupil. He returned to Marlborough as assistant master in 1919, became housemaster of B1 and subsequently headmaster.

11 A point made by Turner's obituarist in the *Marlburian*, summer term 1967, p. 5.

12 This is discussed in considerable detail in Mack, *Public Opinion since 1860*, see especially chapters X, XI and XII.

13 Kazamias, *Politics in England*, p. 315.

14 All fee-paying secondary schools in receipt of a government grant had to provide 25% of their places free annually for children from elementary schools.

15 G. A. N. Lowndes, *The Silent Social Revolution* (1937; 2nd edn, 1969), p. 88. He also made this point, with embellishments in conversation with the author.

16 Gerald Bernbaum, *Social Change and the Schools 1918–1944* (1967), pp. 4–5.

17 *The Spectator*, 17 March 1928, p. 407.

18 Norwood in John Wilson, *Public Schools and Private Practice* (1962), p. 121.

19 Vachell, *Distant Fields*, p. 147.

20 W. N. Marcy, *Reminiscences of a Public Schoolboy* (1932), pp. 172–3.

21 A. D. Edwardes, *The Changing Sixth Form in the Twentieth Century* (1970), pp. 16ff.

22 *Grant-earning schools (England and Wales): growth of a university connection*

	Boys	Girls
1908–9	695	361
1920–1	1675	1214
1924–5	1912	1330

(From Board of Education Pamphlets, no. 50, 1927, p. 21.)

23 *USM*, vol. LXXIII, no. 549 (July 1935), p. 179.

24 *Lorettonian*, vol. LXXXIII, no. 3 (30 Sept. 1960), p. 33. In a letter to the author dated 26 Oct. 1974, Mr Forbes McIntosh stressed that in the late 1940s, as a result of the public examinations, the emphasis at Loretto changed. Boys worked harder and there was a broadening of interests.

25 *Harrovian*, vol. LX, no. 26 (18 June 1947), p. 108.

26 *Ibid.*, vol. LXII, no. 31 (22 June 1949), p. 121. Statements about the considerable effect the public examination system had on the traditional schoolboy way of life continued to be made in the *Harrovian* throughout the

following decades, see especially vol. LXXII, no. 14 (12 Feb. 1959), p. 57; vol. LXXV, no. 26 (15 June 1962), p. 129.

27 *USM*, vol. LXXXVIII, no. 623 (Feb. 1950), p. 2. B. W. T. Handford, with over thirty years experience of Lancing, informed the author that, in his view, the development of the examination system was the single most potent factor in destroying athleticism.

28 Inspectorate Reports (Harrow 4196, 4197, 4198; Lancing 6253, 6254; Marlborough 6596, 6597, 6598; Education 109, Public Record Office).

29 Lowndes, *Silent Revolution*, p. 107.

30 Among the officer-instructors was E. M. Grenfell, who became an inspector at the Board of Education in 1909, see Smith, *Stretching Their Bodies*, p. 60. I draw on Smith's excellent description of the emergence of physical education as a discipline throughout the following section.

31 *Report of the Headmasters' Conference* (1924).

32 Symptomatic of this development was the creation in 1930 of the Argonauts Club at Harrow, which encouraged 'every kind of open air life, but especially the wilder kind, such as camping out' (General prospectus of the club, HSA).

33 *Memorandum of Evidence to the Norwood Committee* (1942), p. 56.

34 Gerald Murray, for a number of years in charge of physical education at Marlborough, died in 1978. Between 1971 and 1978 he furnished the writer with letters, papers and source references. His kind interest was a considerable stimulus.

35 S. J. Curtis and M. E. A. Boultwood, *An Introductory History of English Education Since 1800* (1960; 4th edn, 1966).

36 J. F. Roxburgh, *Eleutheros, or the Future of the Public Schools* (1930); for details of his headship at Stowe see Annan, *Roxburgh*, passim.

37 Birley, letter to author.

38 Lord Gornell, '"Forty Years On" with an Old Harrovian', *The Christian Science Monitor* (Boston), 8 March 1938 (HSA).

39 *USM*, vol. CII, no. 690 (March 1965), p. 3.

40 *Lorettonian*, vol. LXX, no. 7 (31 May 1947), p. 39.

41 *LCM*, vol. XXX, no. 434 (March 1937), p. 5; *Marlburian*, vol. LXXXV, no. 1050 (July 1957), p. 87; *Harrovian*, vol. LXIV, no. 27 (June 1957), pp. 114–15.

42 David Thomson, *England in the Twentieth Century* (1964), p. 73.

43 Quoted in James Laver, *Victorian Vista* (1954), p. 197.

44 *LCM*, vol. XV, no. 34 (March 1922), p. 31.

45 *Lorettonian*, vol. LII, (12 Oct. 1929), p. 8.

46 Michael Birley has written of his Marlborough schooldays that the sartorial trappings of colours had become a source of embarrassment 'as they made me out a privileged member of society'. He notes with sympathy that boys nowadays, in an attempt to merge into a common adolescent background, adopt slovenly accents and worship commonplace music (letter to author).

47 *Quarterly Review*, vol. CCLV, no. 564 (30 April 1930), p. 353.

48 I owe this point to Mr T. B. Belk. See also his funeral sermon entitled 'R.H.O.' (USA).

49 I owe this point to Mr R. D. Bell, assistant master at Lancing.

50 Mr R. Jennings, letter to the author dated 21 Feb. 1973.

51 Mr Peter Wood, a senior member of the Loretto staff to the author in conversation.

52 H. L. O. Flecker, 'Character training: the English boarding school', *The Year Book of Education* (1955), p. 264.

53 To read the *Harrovian* of the 1960s and 1970s is to reread the verbal battles over compulsion, regimentation and excessive team games playing which in the other magazines ended some years earlier.

54 *Harrovian*, vol. LXXIV, no. 22 (12 June 1971), p. 125.

55 *Ibid.*, vol. LXXVII, no. 2 (11 Oct. 1963), p. 5.

56 *LCM*, vol. LV, no. 522 (Advent 1962), p. 135.

Bibliography

A. School archives

The schools of this study, with the exception of Loretto, possess sizable archives. All their available nineteenth- and twentieth-century material was inspected. The total is substantial, and only items directly related to the theme of this study are listed below.

HARROW

The main archives are housed in the school museum. The archives of the Philathletic Club and Knoll House were also inspected.

Unpublished sources

Bishop Coplestone: letter to Dr Longley on the indiscipline as a result of the building of the new Birmingham to London Railway, dated 27 June 1835 (MS)

Butler, H. M.: letter to E. Rendale on cricket flannels, dated 10 May 1875 (MS)

'Harrow Verses', written 1873–4 by three members of Mr Hutton's house (bound volume, MS)

Harrow School: captain of the school's book 1852–73 (MS)

Heywood, S. A. 'Fifty Years of Harrow Cricket 1907–1957' (recollections of a Harrow cricket professional) (TS)

Longley, Dr C. T.: letter to the editor of the *Morning Chronicle* rebutting claims of outrages by Harrow pupils, dated 9 April 1831 (MS)

Newlands house books (various) (MSS)

Notes on sermons preached at Harrow School Chapel presented by F. W. Farrar (MS)

Philathletic Club records 1864–93 (MS)

Powell, T. B.: letter on the trials of Dr G. Butler at the hands of his house, dated 4 Nov. 1816 (MS)

Regulations for fagging at football and cricket submitted by the monitors to the headmaster on 9 May 1838 and 7 Oct. 1842 (MS)

Scrapbook of H. W. Greene

Scrapbook of Alec Tweedie

Somervall, D. C. 'Forty Years Back: a paper read to the Essay Club', n.d. (MS)

Torre, H. J. 'Harrow Notebook 1832–1837' (MS)

Thornton, P. M.: letter to E. E. Bowen presented to P. C. Vellacote, dated 21 March 1890 (MS)

Tyssen, C. D.: cricketing record and notebook with newspaper cuttings 1877–1908 (MS)

The Vaughan Papers: letters and testimonials (MSS)

Venables, E. M. 'Bases Attempted: twenty-five years at Harrow' (TS)

West Acre house books (various) (MS)

Printed Sources

A Harrow Dictionary by an Old Boy. n.d.

Annual Cricket Matches between Harrow and Eton and Harrow and Winchester from 1833–1851. 1855

Darlington, W. S. *Chronicles of the Past – Harrow on the Hill.* 1906

Graham, Edward. *Some Notes on the Harrow School Songs.* 1933

Harrow Almanack 1865–1870

Harrow Almanack 1870–1939

Harrow Association School Quarter-centenary Guildhall Dinner Programme

Harrow Association Record (1907 onwards)

Harrow School Existing Customs (three copies: one undated, one dated 1903 and one dated 1950)

'Harrow football: a change to Rugby rules' (cutting from *The Times*, 11 Dec. 1926)

Harrow Hurdle Races (printed programmes for 4 and 24 March and 8 April 1854)

'Harrow memoirs of H. O. D. Davidson' (cutting from the *Morning Post*, 19 March 1913)

Harrow Memorials of the Great War 1914–18. 1919–21

Harrow School Rules and Regulations 1914

Harrow School Songs (various editions)

Harrow School Tercentenary, 1871

Memorials of a Harrow Schoolboy. 1873

Modern Side Prospectus 1869 (signed by H. M. Butler)

Register of Principal Matches played at Harrow and Lord's during the season 1884

'Some Eton and Harrow matches 1858 to 1864' (offprint of an article by G. Lyttleton from the *National Review*)

Also, collated material on various topics at present filed as follows:

'Goulash' and other internal school magazines (File 2)

Older Harrow magazines (File F)

Published articles on Harrow (File K)

Published memoirs of Old Harrovians (File 7)

Platt affair (various pamphlets) (File 1)

Philathletic Club

Match books (Shell, fifth, and sixth forms and Philathletic Club) for various years throughout the nineteenth century

Philathletic Club account books 1893–1922 and 1922–53

Philathletic Club photograph book 1885–1922

Knoll House
House rule books 1913–27 and 1927–45

LANCING

At the time of my visits there were two main sources of material – the Woodard Papers in the bursar's office and the Lancing Archives Collection in the new archive room.

Woodard Papers

Material consulted included items from:
Sermons and pamphlets by Nathaniel Woodard and others (Drawer 1)
Newspaper cuttings (Drawer 2)
Copies of early kalendars (Drawer 3)
Founder's sermons in Lancing Chapel 1857–77 (Drawer 5)
Founder's sermons in St Nicolas Society Chapels (Drawer 6)
Founder's sermons undated (Drawer 7)
Founder's sermons 1844–89 (Drawer 8)
Founder's letters and pamphlets 1847–87 (Drawer 9)

Lancing Archives Collection

Unpublished sources

Complaint to the headmaster by a number of staff regarding certain aspects of the school organisation (including the disproportionate time spent on games). 1932 (MS)
Field, Edmund: miscellaneous papers (MSS)
Games Committee report book 1921 (MS)
Headmasters' notices 1890–9, 1905–9, 1925–9 (MSS)
Hill, Eustace St Clair. 'Notes on Old Mac' (H. W. McKenzie). 1941 (MS)
Letter to the Provost and Fellows of the Corporation of SS Mary and Nicolas and the Provost and Fellows of the Society of SS Mary and Nicolas, Lancing, concerning the unsatisfactory state of the school from a group of old boys. 1897
Lancing College: proposed changes in the timetable and curriculum after the Second World War (MS)
Lancing College common room minute book (prefects' book) 1907–13 (MS)
Wilson, A. C.: notebooks (various) (MSS)
Wilson, A. J. 'Report to the Provost on the Conditions at Lancing'. 1899
Wilson, A. J. 'Suggestions for the Reorganisation of the School'. 1899

Printed sources

Handford, B. W. T. *Lancing College 1848–1948.* 1948
Kalendars of the Corporation of SS. Mary and Nicolas. 1858–1969
Lowe, E. C. *The Image of God: a sermon for schoolmasters and schoolboys.* 1856
  Address delivered at the Wolverhampton Congress. 1867

St Nicolas and its Schools: a letter to Rt. Hon. Sir J. J. Coleridge. 1867
A Record of Thirty Years Work in the effort of endowing the Church of England with a System of Self-supporting Public Schools for the Upper, Middle and Lower Classes. 1878
Published articles on Lancing College (various)
Raymond, W. S. *A Sermon preached in the Chapel of St Nicolas' College.* 1859

LORETTO

Unpublished sources

Almond, H. H.: letter to an unnamed correspondent in defence of his school, games policy and curriculum balance, dated 18 July 1898 (TS copy)
BBC script for programme on H. H. Almond, dated July 1957 (TS)
Loretto School athletics standards book 1907–47 (MS)
Loretto School cricket scorebook 1864–9 (MS)
Loretto School roll of honour (TS)
Photographic albums of school life (various)
Scrapbook of reviews of the writings of H. H. Almond
Tristram, H. B. 'Six School Songs' (TS)

Printed sources

Buchanan, A. *A Quarter at Loretto* (extracts from a school diary privately printed). 1869
H. B. Tristram, Loretto: special supplement to the 'Lorettonian'. 1947 (This includes an obituary of Mrs E. Almond, wife of H. H. Almond and sister of H. B. Tristram.)
Loretto Association Records
Loretto's Hundred Years 1827–1927: special supplement to the 'Lorettonian'. 1927
Loretto Portfolio (prints of drawings of Loretto school life). n.d.
Loretto School Rules. n.d.
Loretto School Songs. n.d.
Nineteen Memorable Years: special supplement to the 'Lorettonian' (a tribute to J. R. C. Greenlees, headmaster 1926–45). n.d.
Prospectus of Loretto School. 1854
Some Memories of the Head. 1903

Also, a collection of Lorettonia contributed by Mrs S. W. Elphinstone, 1963. It contains music programmes, examination papers and reports.

MARLBOROUGH

The main archival sources are the official school archives in a room adjoining the Memorial Library, and in the Adderley. In addition, some of the houses possess partially or wholly complete sets of house record books devoted exclusively to games.

Unpublished sources

(Unless otherwise indicated the location is Marlborough College.)

'Autobiographical Musings from the Shades of Marlborough College by a Doctor of Medicine 1881–1886'. n.d. (TS)

BBC script for programme on Marlborough. 1952 (TS)

Beckurth, E. C. (pupil 1919–23). 'Right and Left: verses of the open air'. 1960 (TS)

Book of annotated press cuttings 1893–1906

Coney, E. C. (pupil 1867–77): letter to his uncle, A. H. Coney, describing life in the school in the early 1870s (MS)

Cotton's 'Circular to Parents' 1853 (TS)

Cricket scorebook belonging to John Sowerby (MS)

Diary of W. F. Adams 1848 (MS)

Diary of Henry Palmer 1854 (TS)

Diary of Boscawen Somerset 1851 (TS)

Diary of E. C. C. Firth 1883–5 (MS)

'E Dormitory Gazette'. 3 vols, 1887–8 (MS)

Games teams 1849–87 (MS)

Harrison, J. W. D. 'Marlborough in the Sixties' (undated recollections of school-days) (MS)

House record books – various (details of teams, matches, results and performances) (MS)

Marlborough College Cricket Club book circa 1855 (MS)

Marlborough College Rugby Football Club books 1861–88, 1889–1907, 1909–32 (MSS)

'Marlborough College Jubilee': scrapbook of J. F. L. Hardy

'Marlborough College and the Victoria Cross'. n.d. (MS)

Penny, Sir John. 'Autobiographical Notes on Marlborough Schooldays'. 1975 (MS)

Photographic albums of school life (various)

'Red Book, The' (headmaster's rules for staff, 1903 onwards) (MS)

Rodgers, H. Mordaunt. 'Magnetic Marlborough'. n.d. (TS)

Annotated book of press cuttings of Marlborough Nomads and Blues 1902–20

Leonard the Lionhearted: 'A Record of Sporting Achievements' (MS)

Senior prefect's report book 1905–50 (MS)

Sorleiana (papers of C. H. Sorley) in the possession of Marlborough College Literary Society, including poetry manuscripts, letters in manuscript, photographs, minutes of the Lower Sixth Literary Society and various manuscript letters of commentary and reflection by relatives and contemporaries of Sorley to the late Gerald Murray

Thomas, J. S.: extract from sermon preached at Marlborough College, 1897 (misc. papers, bursar's office) (MS)

Wilkinson, M.: letters, 1849 onwards (transcribed from the original carbon copies by L. Warwick James) (TS)

Printed sources

A Collection of Poems by Younger Boys of Marlborough College (written for 'A House Magazine' between 1936 and 1942). 1943

Benson, E. F. *Sketches from Marlborough.* 1905

Brentnall, H. C. and Kempson, E. G. H. *Marlborough College 1843–1943.* 1943

Brown, F. A. Y. *Family Notes.* 1917

Butterworth, M. H. *Alexander Kaye Butterworth 1854–1946: a memoir by his niece.* 1967

Cowley, P. (ed.). *St. John Basil Wynne-Willson.* n.d.

Carmen Marlburiense (song sheet). n.d.

Centenary Cavalcade (a musical entertainment marking the centenary of the school). 1943

Davies, J. Llewellyn. *Sermon in Marlborough Chapel on the Feast of St. Michael All Angels.* 1874

Extracts from School Rules 1890

Edward Meyrick 1854–1938 (reprint from 'Obituary Notices of the Royal Society of London', vol. II, no. 7, Jan. 1939)

Heaven, J. W. G. *Marlborough College: by way of reply to John Betjeman's 'Summoned by Bells'.* n.d.

Hulme, F. E. *The Town, College and Neighbourhood of Marlborough.* 1881

John Stearne Thomas (offprint from *Marlburian*, vol. XXXII, no. 504, 4 Nov. 1897)

Littlefield Annals 1872–1905. 1907

Marlborough College Year of Jubilee. 1893

Marlburian Club News Bulletin. 1953–6, 1957–60

Miscellaneous Sermons by Staff, Headmasters and Visiting Preachers (bound volume)

Penny Reading Concert Programmes (various)

Prize Day Programmes (various)

School Rules (various)

Wilkinson, Matthew. *School Sermons Preached in the Chapel of Marlborough College.* 1852

Wilson, Jonathan. *False Starts.* 1943

Also, four box files of memorabilia including athletic cards, song book, Marlborough Nomads fixture lists, Marlborough v. Rugby score cards and the Marlborough Cricket Club accounts book, 1851

STONYHURST

Unpublished sources

Diary of B. E. James 1866–7 (MS)

First prefect's log 1817–21, 1822–32, 1844–67, 1868–76, 1894–1906 (MSS)

Prefect of studies reports
(a) Father John Gerard 1880–4
(b) Father G. R. Kingdon 1861–2, 1864–72, 1873–9 (MSS)
(These reports were made at the end of each term and covered each class in the school.)

Rector's book for matters connected with the interests of the College 1869–93 (MS)

Stonyhurst association football journal 1884–95 (MS)

Stonyhurst biographical dictionary 1794–1825

Stonyhurst cricket journal 1860–72, 1873–84, 1885–93 (MS)
Stonyhurst Cricket Club cash book of subscribers 1864–88 (MS)
Stonyhurst centenary record (annotated book of press cuttings)

Printed sources

*Hints offered to Young Masters in the Colleges of the English Province By One Who has
    known the Difficulties of their Position.* 1882 (1928 edn)
Introduction to Stonyhurst College. n.d.
Memorials of Stonyhurst College. 1881
Reports of the Stonyhurst Association. 1880–9
Souvenir of Stonyhurst. 1882
Stonyhurst. 1909
Stonyhurst and its Tercentenary. 1892
Stonyhurst Handbook for Visitors and Others. n.d.
Stonyhurst Illustrated. 1884
Stonyhurst War Record. 1927
Stonyhurstiana (bound volume of printed memoirs, school lists, etc.). n.d.
Views of Stonyhurst College. 1931

In addition, records (manuscript and published) of Stonyhurst life are contained in
a number of assorted files (E/1/2 to G/2/7/10) in the archive strongroom. Relevant
items include:
Customs, traditions and events (G/2/7/10)
Diary of an unidentified writer 1847–51 (F/vi/22)
Diary of F. Trappe and J. and J. S. O'Ferrall 28 Aug. 1826–10 Nov. 1826.
    (F/vi/23)
Discipline: pupils, school rules, discipline (including flogging) (F/1/2/6)
History: documents on early history (E/iii/5–7)
Inspections by Board of Education 1903, 1910, 1919 (F/vi/71, F/vi/72)
Oxford versus London Dispute 1894–6 (F/1/3/7)
Press cuttings on Stonyhurst (F/2/5)
Printed matter on Stonyhurst (Drawer 28)
Printed articles on Stonyhurst in monthly magazines (E/1/2/5)
'Stonyhurst Chorus' (school song) (E/1/2)
Stonyhurst old prospectuses (F/ii/7/7)
Stonyhurst photographs (F/1/4/9)
Stonyhurst school societies (E/i/11)
Stonyhurst sport (F/1/3/6, F/1/1/4, F/9/2/7)

UPPINGHAM

Unpublished sources

'Archdeacon Johnston's School, Uppingham, 1874–1906' (scrapbook)
BBC script for programme on Edward Thring. 1949
Belk, T. B. 'Fives at Uppingham' (MS)
    'A Copy of the Rules of Uppingham Football'. 1857 (MS)
    'Sources for School History from the School Magazines' (TS)

Bothamley, H. W. 'Some Notes on the History of Uppingham School'. 1951 (MS)
Bell, Dr Thomas. 'A Letterbook 1876–1904'
Howitt, Harold Gibson. 'Reminiscences'. 1966 (TS)
James, W. P. 'Thring and Uppingham: an essay of recollections' (MS)
Memorials of the Rev. Edward Thring, collected by H. F. Wilson. 1887
Photographic albums (various)
Rome, R. C. 'Uppingham: the story of a school 1584–1948'. 1948 (TS)
Thring, Edward: Diary – extant volumes 1853–62, 1886–7 (MS)
   Sermons (MSS)
   'Index Rerum: a notebook' (MS)
Thring, Margaret: 'Memories' (notes) (MS)

Also, a considerable quantity of miscellaneous manuscripts, letters and other Uppinghamia is contained in a series of folders, Uppingham Archive Files 1–102. Much useful material is to be found here. For example File 53(1) and (2) holds the Candler/Thring correspondence on the purchase of the Leicester Field, File 55 holds 'Old Uppingham in India' and File 57 holds various songs of the Uppingham Rovers.

Printed sources

Bingham, C. R. *Our Founder*. 1884
Blyth, W. *In Memoriam: Ernest Henry Blyth by his affectionate father*. 1866
Lewis, J. and M. *Lorne House, Uppingham 1856–1956*
OUFC *Records of the Old Uppinghamian Football Club*. 1913
Rowe, T. B. *Guide Book*. 1869
School Delusions: essays by the sixth form. 1860
School Rules. Circa 1880
Tate, David. *West Deyne, Uppingham, 1859–1959*. 1959
Thring, Edward (The complete set of Thring's printed works is held in the Uppingham archives. This list includes his lesser-known works. For his better-known writings see *secondary sources* below.)
   Translations and Songs. 1855
   School Songs: a collection (with Herr Riccius). 1858
   Uppingham School: the statement of the Rev. Edward Thring, Headmaster, respecting the organisation of the school. 1860
   Truth in Schools. 1862
   Three Letters and Axioms on Education. 1866
   Borth Lyrics. 1881
   An Address delivered before the Education Society. 1885
   The School of Life: addresses to public school men by public school masters. 1885
   An Address on Education. 1886
   Addresses. 1887
Uppingham School: Thring Centenary 1853–1953. 1953
Uppingham Tercentenary. 1864

B. Correspondence and unpublished papers

A number of staff, present and retired, and old boys provided written details of the schools. In addition, the late Gerald Murray generously wrote several papers on various matters.

Correspondence

Mr T. B. Belk, Mr Michael Birley, Mr R. B. Bruce-Lockhart, Mr G. Chilton, Mr D. Forbes McIntosh, Mr B. W. T. Handford, Mr L. Warwick James, Mr R. A. U. Jennings, Rev. F. J. Turner SJ, Mr Raymond Venables, Mr E. J. Whiteley and Mr Peter Wood

Unpublished papers

Gerald Murray. 'Some Notes on the Cotton Letter of June 1853'
  'Ritual in Public Schools'
  'The P.T.I. in the Public Schools'
  'The Games Master in Fact and Fiction'
(In addition, there are thirty-seven letters on matters relating to Marlborough and general public school history.)

C. School magazines

(The official school publications from 1860 onwards are printed in italics.)

Harrow: Harrovian (1828), Harrow Magazine (1836), *Triumphirate* (1859–61), *Tyro* (1863–6), *Harrovian* (1869–72 and 1878–81), *Harrow Notes* (1883–7), *Harrovian* (1888 onwards), Pen Vyper (1870), Bullite (1873), Unicorn (1895), Toad (1900), How's That (1923), Bell (1925–6), Broadsheet (1947–52), Goulash (1953–63)

Lancing: *Lancing College Magazine* (1877 onwards), Beard, Miscellany

Loretto: *Lorettonian* (1880 onwards)

Marlborough: Marlborough Magazine (1842–62 irregularly), *Marlburian* (1865 onwards), Viator (1881–2), Heretick (1924), Kennet (1950s), 'A' House Magazine (1961), Polyglot (1973), Phoenix (n.d.)

Stonyhurst: *Stonyhurst College Magazine* (1881 onwards), Eagle

Uppingham: Hospitaler (1851–3), *Uppingham School Magazine* (1863 onwards)

D. School registers

Harrow: Second edition, 1800–1901
  Fourth edition, 1845–1925
  Fifth edition, 1855–1949

Lancing: Third edition, 1848–1932
  Fourth edition, 1901–54

Loretto: First edition, 1825–1907
  Second edition, 1825–1925
  Fourth edition, 1825–1964

Marlborough: Fifth edition, 1843–1904
  Eighth edition, 1843–1903
  Ninth edition, 1843–1952

Stonyhurst: (No register is published)

Uppingham: First edition, 1824–84
               Sixth edition, 1824–1931
               Seventh edition, 1853–1947
               Eighth edition, 1888–1962
Sedbergh: Second edition, 1546–1909

E. Additional manuscript sources

Carlisle: Cumbria Record Office – Miscellaneous papers and correspondence concerning the Harrow life of Francis E. Marshall, assistant master at Harrow 1870–1904, in the Marshall Family Collection (D/M/1)

Chelmsford: Essex County Record Office – Scrapbook of Harrow schooldays among the papers of Sir Frederick Green (MS D/DU/1681/1)

Edinburgh: National Library of Scotland (Dept of Manuscripts) – Thirteen letters on education and other matters from H. H. Almond to his publisher, and one to J. S. Blackie (MSS 4480, 4495, 4546, 4610, 2639 and f 168)

Gloucester: Gloucestershire County Record Office – (a) Letters from Robert Wynter Blathwayt at Harrow to his family circa 1864 (D1799/C58–60); (b) Harrow Philathletic Club: introductory letter, prospectus, rules, list of honorary members and acknowledgement of donation among the papers of T. H. S. Sotheron (school governor 1843–69) (D1571)

London: (i)   Archives of the Society of Jesus, see below
               (ii) British Museum (Dept of Manuscripts) – Tables of the physical development of Marlborough schoolboys 1874–5 (Add.MSS 32610–32, 20)
               (iii) Headmasters' Conference – Headmasters' Conference Reports (1869 onwards)
               (iv) London Library – The MS autobiography of John Addington Symonds
               (v)   Public Record Office – Inspectorate Reports on Harrow (E109/4196, 4197, 4198), Lancing (E109/6253, 6254), Marlborough (E109/6596, 6597, 6598), Stonyhurst (E109/2667)

Reading: Berkshire County Record Office – (a) Letters to his family from the Harrow schoolboy D. Pleydell-Bouverie together with school reports, circa 1885 (D/Epb C38); (b) Correspondence and papers relating to the sons of Phillip Wroughton at Harrow School 1857–61 (D/EW Fii)

ARCHIVES OF THE SOCIETY OF JESUS (Farm Street, London)

Relating to Stonyhurst

Scholars rules circa 1870
Stonyhurst Handbook. 1947
Notes on Stonyhurst by H. J. Pollen (bound volume)
Foreign correspondence 1819–54

Relating to Beaumont

The Beaumont material proves relevant because of frequent reference to the senior establishment at Stonyhurst, and because of the illuminating contrast with the more traditional, authoritarian Lancashire school.

College Rules and Traditions. n.d.
First Prefect's journal 1878–9, 1881–2
Games log books (various)
Miscellaneous papers circa 1880
Papers of J. Brampton 1902–8
Prefects' journal 1862–97
Record of Beaumont games and athletics by a series of prefects

General

A collection of papers on higher Catholic education, 1871–95, made by Rev. E. Purbrick, SJ (printed)

F. Official documents

Reports of:
The Public Schools Commission (Clarendon Commission). 1864
The Schools Inquiry Commission (Taunton Commission). 1868
The Secondary Education Commission (Bryce Commission). 1895
The Royal Commission on Physical Training (Scotland). 1903
The Public Schools and the General Education System Commission (Fleming Commission). 1944
The Public Schools Commission (Newsom Commission). 1968

G. University Theses

Honey, J. R. de S. 'The Victorian Public School 1828–1902: the school as a community'. D.Phil. Thesis, University of Oxford, 1969
Mallea, John. 'The Boys' Endowed Grammar Schools in Victorian England: the educational use of sport'. Ph.D. Thesis, Columbia University, 1971
Rigby, Cormac. 'The Life and Influence of Edward Thring'. D.Phil. Thesis, University of Oxford, 1968
Spence, M. 'Charles Kingsley and Education'. M.A. Thesis, University of Bristol, 1945
Tozer, Malcolm. 'The Development and Role of Physical Education at Uppingham School 1850–1914'. M.Ed. Thesis, University of Leicester, 1974
Thomson, Ian. 'Almond of Loretto and the Development of Physical Education in Scotland during the Nineteenth Century'. M.Sc. Thesis, University of Edinburgh, 1969

H. Secondary sources

The published literature on public school education is huge. The following secondary source list, by virtue of the specialised nature of the inquiry and methodology adopted, makes no claim to be comprehensive. It concentrates considerably but far from exclusively on the literature of athleticism and the six survey schools. A number of bibliographies elsewhere deal more fully with the public schools in general and have been useful collectively for the acquisition of background knowledge. G. F. Lamb, *The Happiest Days* (1959) and Vivian Ogilvie, *The English Public School* (1957) both contain short lists of books which provide a superficial introduction to the study of the English public schools. More substantial but still only skimming the surface is the bibliography of Brian Gardner, *The Public Schools* (1973). A. B. Badger has an interesting reading list which includes a number of continental authors, periodicals and newspapers in his *The Public Schools and the Nation* (1944). Details of the novels dealing with public school life are to be found in W. R. Hicks's *The School in English and German Fiction* (1933) and J. R. Reed's *Old School Ties: the public schools in British literature* (1964). However, the most scrupulous of bibliographers is unquestionably E. C. Mack with his extensive range of sources including a large number of periodicals, in the two volumes of *Public Schools and British Opinion* (1938 and 1941). A. C. F. Beales's *Education under Penalty* (1963) has a most scholarly bibliography dealing with the Catholic public schools, and Brian Heeney in his *Mission to the Middle Classes* (1969) lists many of the sources for the Woodard Corporation. Finally, the Leeds Institute of Education and Paddington Public Libraries have issued details of available school histories.

A Book of Lancing Verse. Oxford, 1928

Abrahams, H. M. and Kerr, J. B. *Oxford versus Cambridge*. London, 1931

Adamson, J. W. *English Education 1789–1902*. Cambridge, 1930

Alington, Cyril. *A Schoolmaster's Apology*. London, 1914
   Lionel Ford. London, 1934
   Things Ancient and Modern. London, 1936

Almond, Hely Hutchinson. *Christ the Protestant and Other Sermons*. Edinburgh, 1899
   Sermons by a Lay Headmaster. Edinburgh, 1886

Amery, L. S. *Days of Fresh Air*. London, 1939
   My Political Life. vol. I, London, 1953

Annan, Noel. *Leslie Stephen*. London, 1951
   Roxburgh of Stowe. London, 1965

'An Old Harrovian' (Sydney Daryl). *Harrow Recollections*. London, 1867

Archer, R. L. *Secondary Education in the Nineteenth Century*. Cambridge, 1921

Arlen, M. *Piracy*. London, 1922

Armytage, W. H. G. *Four Hundred Years of English Education*. Cambridge, 1964
   The Rise of the Technocrats: a social history. London, 1965

Arnold, Matthew. *A French Eton*. London, 1864 (1892 edn)
   Culture and Anarchy. London, 1869 (3rd edn, 1882)

Arnold, Thomas. *Christian Life at School* (sermons). Cambridge, 1832 (1878 edn)

Ashley-Cooper, F. S. *Eton and Harrow at the Wicket*. London, 1922

Assistant Master Speaks, The. London, 1938

Attick, Richard. *Victorian People and Ideas*. London, 1973

Austin, Alfred. *The Autobiography of Alfred Austin (Poet Laureate) 1835–1910*. London, 1911

Avedon, E. M. and Sutton Smith, B. *The study of Games*. New York, 1971

Badger, A. B. *The Public Schools and the Nation*. London, 1944

Badley, J. H. *A Schoolmaster's Testament*. Oxford, 1937

Baldwin, Stanley. *On England and Other Addresses*. London, 1926

Bamford, T. W. *The Rise of the Public Schools*. London, 1967
   Thomas Arnold. London, 1960
   Thomas Arnold on Education: a selection from his writing, with introductory material. London, 1970

Barbour, Ian G. *Myths, Models and Paradigms*. London, 1974

Barker, Sir Ernest. *National Character*. London, 1948
   The Character of England. Oxford, 1947

Barnard, H. C. *A Short History of English Education 1760–1944*. London, 1947

Barnes, A. S. *The Catholic Schools of England*. London, 1926

Barnett, Corelli. *The Collapse of British Power*. London, 1972

Bassett, Bernard. *The English Jesuits*. London, 1967

Beales, A. C. F. *Education Under Penalty*. London, 1963

Beesly, A. H. *Ballads and Other Verses*. London, 1895
   Poems. Old and New. London, 1912

Bell, Daniel, *The End of Ideology*. New York, 1961

Bell, Philip, *Idols and Idylls: essays by a public schoolboy*. London, 1917

Bell, Robert and Grant, Nigel. *A Mythology of British Education*. London, 1974

Benson, A. C. (ed.). *Cambridge Essays on Education*. Cambridge, 1917
   The Schoolmasters. London, 1902
   The Upton Letters. London, 1904

Benson, E. F. *David Blaize*. London, 1916
   Our Family Affairs 1867–1896. London, 1920

Bernbaum, Gerald. *Social Change and the Schools 1918–1944*. London, 1967

Bernstein, Basil. *Class, Codes and Control*. vol. 1, London, 1971

Best, Geoffrey. *Mid-Victorian Britain 1851–1875*. London, 1971

Betjeman, Sir John. *Ghastly Good Taste*. London, 1933 (2nd edn 1971)
   Summoned by Bells. London, 1960

Bishop, T. J. H. and Wilkinson, R. *Winchester and the Public School Elite*. London, 1967

Blumenau, Ralph. *A History of Malvern College 1865–1965*. London, 1965

Bocock, Robert. *Ritual in Industrial Society*. London, 1974

Bolt, Christine. *Victorian Attitudes to Race*. London, 1971

Bonney, T. G. *Memories of a Long Life*. Cambridge, 1921

Bovill, E. W. *English Country Life 1780–1830*. London, 1962

Bowen, Edward. *Harrow Songs*. London, 1886

Bowen, W. E. *Edward Bowen: a memoir*. London, 1902

Bowles, John. *The Imperial Achievement*. London, 1974

Boys' Own Annual. 1913

Bradby, G. F. *The Lanchester Tradition*. London, 1914 (1954 edn)
   Some Verses. Rugby, 1902

Bradley, A. C. et al. *A History of Marlborough College*. London, 1893
   A History of Marlborough College. rev. edn, London, 1923

Bradley, G. G. *Freedom and Bondage*. London, 1882
   The Parting at Miletus (sermon in memory of G. E. L. Cotton). London, 1866

Brailsford, Dennis. *Sport and Society*. London, 1969

Brauer, George C. *The Education of a Gentleman*. New York, 1959

Briggs, Asa. *The Age of Improvement*. London, 1959

Brodbeck, May. *Readings in the Philosophy of the Social Sciences*. London, 1968

Brooke, Samuel Roebuck. *Sam Brooke's Journal: the diary of a Lancing schoolboy 1860–1865*. Friends of Lancing Chapel, 1953

Browne, Martin. *A Dream of Youth*. London, 1918

Browning, Oscar. *Memories of Sixty Years at Eton, Cambridge and Elsewhere*. London, 1910

Bryant, Arthur. *English Saga 1840–1940*. Reprint Society, London, 1942

Bryant, P. B. M. *Harrow*. London and Glasgow, 1936

Bryant, V. Seymour. *The Public School System in Relation to the Coming Conflict for National Supremacy*. London, 1917

Bryce, James. *Studies in Contemporary Biography*. New York, 1920

Bunsen, Victoria de. *Charles Roden Buxton*. London, 1948

Bunyan, John. *The Pilgrim's Progress and the Holy War*. (Cassell's illustrated edn), London, 1911

Burn, W. L. *The Age of Equipoise: a study of the mid-Victorian generation*. London, 1964 (2nd edn 1968)

Burrow, J. (ed.). *Kings and Commoners: studies in British idealism*. London, 1936

Butler, Henry Montagu. *He Served his Generation* (Funeral sermon for C. J. Vaughan). Cambridge, 1897

　Public School Sermons. London, 1899

　Sermons Preached in the Chapel of Harrow School. Cambridge, 1861 (1st series) and 1869 (2nd series)

　The Death of the Bishop of Calcutta. Harrow, 1886

Butler, J. R. M. *Henry Montagu Butler, Master of Trinity College, Cambridge, 1866–1918*. London, 1925

Byles, Charles E. *Rupert Brooke's Grave and Other Poems*. London, 1919

Caraman, P. *A Biography of C. C. Martindale*. London, 1967

Carew, Dudley. *A Fragment of Friendship*. London, 1974

Carr, John Dickinson. *The Life of Sir Arthur Conan Doyle*. London, 1949 (2nd edn 1954)

Carroll, John B. *Language, Thought and Reality: selected writings of Benjamin Lee Whorf*. New York, 1959

Cazamian, Louis. *Modern England*. London, 1912

Chadwick, Hubert. *St. Omers to Stonyhurst . . .* London, 1962

Cheiropax (pseud.). *Sketches of a School*. London, 1939

Chichester, S. (ed.). *E. W. Hornung and his Young Guard 1914*. Wellington, 1936

Churchill, Sir Winston. *My Early Life*. London, 1930

Clark, G. Kitson. *An Expanding Society, Britain 1830–1900*. Cambridge, 1967

　The Making of Victorian England. London, 1962

Clark, Sir George Norman. *English History: a survey*. Oxford, 1971

Clarke, F. *Education and Social Change*. London, 1940

Cloete, Stewart. *A Victorian Son*. London, 1972

Coke, Desmond. *The Bending of a Twig*. 2nd edn, London, 1906

　The House Prefect. London, 1934

　The Worst House at Sherborough. London, 1915

Coleridge, Sir J. T. *Public School Education: a lecture delivered at the Athenaeum, Tiverton*. London, 1861

Collins, T. *School and Sport: recollections of a busy life*. London, 1905

Collins, Wilkie. *Man and Wife*. London, 1873

Collingwood, R. G. *An Autobiography*. London, 1939

Conan-Doyle, Sir Arthur. *Memories and Adventures*. London, 1924

Connolly, Cyril. *Enemies of Promise*. London, 1939

Cook, Sir Theodore. *Character and Sportsmanship*. London, 1927

Cookson, C. (ed.). *Essays on Secondary Education*. Oxford, 1898

Cotterill, C. C. *Suggested Reforms in the Public Schools*. Edinburgh, 1883

Cotton, G. E. L. *Sermons and Addresses Delivered in the Chapel of Marlborough College*. Cambridge, 1858
Seven Sermons. Cambridge, 1855

Cotton, Sophia A. (ed.). *Memoir of George Edward Lynch Cotton D.D.* London, 1871

Coubertin, Pierre de. *L'Education en Angleterre: collèges et universités*. Paris, 1888

Coulton, G. G. *A Victorian Schoolmaster: Henry Hart of Sedbergh*. London, 1923
Fourscore Years: an autobiography. Cambridge, 1943
Public Schools and Public Needs. London, 1901

Croome, A. C. M. (ed.). *Fifty Years of Sport at Oxford, Cambridge and the Great Public Schools*. 2 vols, London, 1913

Curtis, S. J. *A History of Education in Great Britain*. London, 1948 (7th edn 1967)

Curtis, S. J. and Boultwood, M. E. A. *An Introductory History of English Education Since 1800*. London, 1960 (4th edn 1966)

Dancy, John. *The Public Schools and the Future*. London, 1963

Darwin, Bernard. *The English Public School*. London, 1931
The Game's Afoot: an anthology of sport. London, 1926

David. A. A. *Life and the Public Schools: a Prospect*. London, 1932

Davidson Ketchum, J. *Ruhleben*. London, 1965

Demogeot, J. and Montucci, H. *De l'enseignement secondaire en Angleterre et en Ecosse*. Paris, 1868

Demolins, Edward. *Anglo-Saxon Superiority: to what is it due*. Trans. Louis Bert, London, 1898

Dibelius, W. *England* . . . Trans. Mary Agnes Hamilton, London, 1930

Dickinson, H. N. *Keddy: a story of Oxford*. London, 1907

Dickson, Lovat. *Richard Hillary*. London, 1950

Dilke, Charles. *Greater Britain*. London, 1868

Dobbs, Brian. *Edwardians at Play*. London, 1973

Donnelly, F. P. *Principles of Jesuit Education in Practice*. New York, 1934

Douglas, Mary. *Natural Symbols*. London, 1970
Purity and Danger. London, 1966

Dover Wilson, J. *The Schools of England: a study in renaissance*. London, 1928

Drage, Geoffrey. *Eton and the Empire*. Eton, 1890

Drinkwater, John. *Patriotism in Literature*. London, 1924

Druett, W. W. *Harrow Through the Ages*. Oxford, 1935

Drummond, Henry. *Baxter's Second Innings*. London, 1892

Duckworth, Francis. *From a Pedagogue's Sketch Book*. London, 1912

Dukes, Clement. *Health at School*. London, 1905

Duncan, Hugh Dalziel. *Language and Literature in Society*. London, 1961
    Symbols in Society. London, 1968
Education, Economy and Politics. Open University (E352), Bletchley, 1973
Edwardes, A. D. *The Changing Sixth Form in the Twentieth Century*. London, 1970
Edwardes, Michael. *A Season in Hell: the defence of the Lucknow Residency*. London,
    1973
Ensor, R. C. K. *England 1870–1914*. Oxford, 1936
Evans, Joan. *John Ruskin*. London, 1952
Everett, H. O. *The Catholic Schools of England and Wales*. Cambridge, 1944
Ewart, G. (ed.). *Forty Years On: an anthology of school songs*. London, 1969
Farnell, Lewis R. *An Oxonian Looks Back*. London, 1934
Farrall, A. P. *The Jesuit Code of Liberal Education*. Milwaukee, 1938
Farrar, F. W. *Eric a Little by Little*, London, 1858 (1923 edn)
    Essays on Liberal Education. London, 1867
    *In the Days of thy Youth: sermons on practical subjects preached at Marlborough College
        from 1841 to 1876*. London, 1889
    Julian Home: a tale of college life. 1859 (4th edn 1905)
    St. Winifred's; Or, the World of School. London, 1862
Farrar, R. *Life of Frederick William Farrar*. London, 1904
Findlay, J. J. *Arnold of Rugby*. Cambridge, 1897
Firth, J. D'E. *Rendall of Winchester*. London, 1954
Firth, Raymond, *Symbols: public and private*. London, 1973
Fischer-Williams, J. *Harrow*. London, 1901
Fitzgerald, Percy. *Saxonhurst*. London, 1907
    Stonyhurst Memories. London, 1895
Flecker, James Elroy. *The Grecians*. London, 1910
Fletcher, C. R. L. *Edmond Warre*. London, 1922
Fletcher, F. *After Many Days: a schoolmaster's memories*. London, 1937
Fletcher, Iain (ed.). *The Complete Poems of Lionel Johnson*. London, 1953
Fletcher, K. *The Making of Sociology*. London, 1971
Foot, Stephen. *A Housemaster and His Boys by One of Them*. London, 1929
    Three Lives: an autobiography. London, 1934
Ford, John. *A Social History of Cricket*. Newton Abbot, 1972
Foss, M. *The Founding of the Jesuits*. London, 1969
Fox, Archibald Douglas. *Follow Up*. London, 1908
    Public School Life: Harrow. London, 1911
Freeman, R. M. *Steady and Strong*. London, 1891
Frewin, Leslie. *The Poetry of Cricket*. London, 1964
Gale, F. *The Life of the Honourable Robert Grimston*. London, 1885
Gale, Norman. *More Cricket Songs*. London, 1905
Gallie, W. B. *An English School*. London, 1949
Galton, Charles S. *et al. The History of St. Stanislaus' College Beaumont*. Beaumont,
    1911
Gardner, Brian. *The Public Schools*. London, 1973
Gerard, J. *Centenary Record. Stonyhurst College*. Belfast, 1894
Gibson, J. C. *Reminiscences of a Railwayman*. London, 1968
Gibson, Robert. *The Land Without a Name: Alain Fournier and his world*. London,
    1975

Gilkes, A. H. *A Day at Dulwich*. London, 1905
  Boys and Masters: a study of school life. London, 1887
  The Thing that Hath Been or A Young Man's Mistakes. London, 1894
Glyn, Anthony. *The Blood of a British Man*. London, 1970
Goffman, Erving. *Asylums*. Harmondsworth, 1961 (Penguin edn 1971)
  Stigma. Englewood Cliffs, 1963
Gogarty, Oliver St John. *It isn't This Time of the Year At All*. London, 1954
Goldmann, Lucien. *The Tragic Vision*. London, 1964
Gordon, Sir Home (ed.). *Eton versus Harrow at Lords*. London, 1926
Gore, John. *Charles Gore, Father and Son*. London, 1932
Gould, J. and Kolb, W. C. (eds.). *A Dictionary of the Social Sciences*. London, 1964
Gourlay, A. B. *A History of Sherborne School*. Winchester, 1951
Graham, Edward. *The Harrow Life of Henry Montagu Butler*. London, 1920
Graham, J. P. *Forty Years of Uppingham: memories and sketches*. London, 1932
Graves, Charles. *The Bad Old Days*. London, 1961
Graves, Robert. *Goodbye to All That*. London, 1930
Graves, J. *Policy and Progress in Secondary Education 1902–1942*. London, 1943
Gray, Alexander Hill. *Sixty Years Ago*. London, 1925
Gray, Arthur. *Jesus College, Cambridge*. London, 1902
Gray, A. and Brittain, F. *A History of Jesus College, Cambridge*. London, 1960
Gray, H. B. *The Public Schools and the Empire*. London, 1913
Great Public Schools. London, 1893
Green, Graham, (ed.). *The Old School*. London, 1932
Green, V. H. H. *Oxford Common Room: a study of Lincoln College and Mark Pattison*.
  London, 1957
Grierson, Edward. *The Imperial Dream*. London, 1972
Grogan, Lady. *Reginald Bosworth Smith: a memoir*. London, 1909
Grosskurth, Phyllis. *John Addington Symonds*. London, 1964
Gruggen, G. and Keating, J. *Stonyhurst: its past history and life in the present*. London,
  1901
Grundy, G. B. *Fifty Years at Oxford*. London, 1945
Gumperez, J. and Hymes, D. (eds.). *Directions in Socio-linguistics*. New York, 1972
Gurner, R. *C3*. London, 1927
  (pseud. Kerr Shaw) *For the Sons of Gentlemen*. London, 1926
  I Chose Teaching. London, 1937
  War Echoes. London, 1917
Guttsman, W. L. *The English Ruling Class*. London, 1969
Haig-Brown, Alan R. *My Game Book*. London, 1913
  Sporting Sonnets. London, 1902
Hamilton, Lord Ernest. *Forty Years On*. London, 1922
Handford, B. W. T. *Lancing: a history of SS. Mary and Nicolas College 1848–1930*.
  Oxford, 1933
Hare, Augustus. *The Story of My Life*. London, 1896
Harford-Battersby, C. F. *Pilkington of Uganda*. London, 1898
Harris, Stanley S. *The Headmaster and His Boys*. London, 1925
Harrison, Frederic. *Autobiographic Memoirs*. 2 vols., London, 1911
Hay, Ian (Ian Hay Beith). *Housemaster*. London, 1936 (11th edn 1949)
  The Lighter Side of School Life. London, 1914 (2nd edn 1921)

Hayakawa, S. I. *Language in Thought and Action*. London, 1959

Headmaster Speaks, The. London, 1936

Heber-Percy, Cyril. *Us Four*. London, 1963

Heeney, Brian. *Mission to the Middle Classes . . .* London, 1969

Heitland, W. E. *After Many Years . . .* Cambridge, 1926

Hewitson, A. *Stonyhurst College: past and present*. Preston, 1870

Hicks, W. R. *The School in English and German Fiction*. London, 1933

Himmelfarb, Gertrude. *Victorian Minds*. London, 1968

Hodgson, Geraldine. *The Life of James Elroy Flecker*. Oxford, 1925

Hofstadter, R. *Anti-Intellectualism in American Life*. London, 1964

Holder, C. S. *An Anthology of School*. London, 1928

Hollender, B. *Before I Forget*. London, 1935

Hollis, Christopher. *A History of the Jesuits*. London, 1968
  Death of a Gentleman. London, 1943 (2nd edn 1972)

Honey, J. R. de S. *Tom Brown's Universe: the development of the public school in the nineteenth century*. London, 1977

Hood, Jack. *The Heart of a Schoolboy*. London, 1919

Hope, Anthony. *Memories and Notes*. London, 1927

Hornung, E. W. *Fathers of Men*. London, 1912
  Notes of a Camp Follower on the Western Front. London, 1919
  The Old Guard. London, 1919

Horowitz, I. L. (ed.). *Power, Politics and People: the collected papers of C. Wright Mills*. London, 1973

Horrocks, Sir Brian. *A Full Life*. London, 1960

Houghton, Walter E. *The Victorian Frame of Mind 1830–1870*. New Haven and London, 1951

How, F. D. *Six Great Schoolmasters*. London, 1904

Howarth, T. E. B. *Culture, Anarchy and the Public Schools*. London, 1969

Howson, E. and Warner, G. T. (eds.). *Harrow School*. London, 1898

Hoyland, Geoffrey. *The Man who made a School*. London, 1946

Hughes, Donald. *The Public Schools and the Future*. Cambridge, 1952

Hughes, Thomas. *Memoir of a Brother*. London, 1873
  Notes for Boys, and their Fathers, on Morals, Mind and Manners (by an Old Boy). London, 1885
  The Manliness of Christ. London, 1879
  Tom Brown at Oxford. London, 1861 (Oxford edn 1921)
  Tom Brown's Schooldays. London, 1856 (Penguin edn 1973)

Humphreys, T. *Criminal Days*. London, 1946

Jacks, L. P. *The Education of the Whole Man*. London, 1931

Jarret, B. *Living Temples*. London, 1919

Jeffries, J. M. *Front Everywhere*. London, 1935

Jencks, C. *et al. Inequality*. London, 1973

Jessel, Penelope. *Owen of Uppingham*. London, 1965

Johns, Edward F. *Let the Twig Follow its Bent, recalling Charles Kingsley*. London, 1947

Jones, Paul. *War Letters of a Public School Boy*. London, 1918

Joyce, James. *A Portrait of the Artist as a Young Man*. London, 1916 (Travellers Library edn 1930)

Kalton, G. *The Public Schools: a factual survey*. London, 1966

Kazamias, A. M. *Politics, Society and Secondary Education in England*. Philadelphia, 1966

Keble-Martin, J. W. *Over the Hills*. London, 1968

Kendall, Guy. *A Headmaster Reflects*. London, 1937
   A Headmaster Remembers. London, 1933
   Charles Kingsley and his Ideas. London, n.d.

Kingsley, Charles. *Health and Education*. London, 1887
   Sermons on National Subjects. Cambridge, 1852
   True Words for Brave Men. London, 1878

Kingsley, Mrs C. *Charles Kingsley. His Letters and Memories of his Life*. 2 vols, London, 1877

Kipling, Rudyard. *Stalky & Co*. London, 1900

Kircher, Rudolph. *Fair Play*. Trans. R. N. Bradley, London, 1928

Kirk, E. B. *A Talk with Boys about Themselves*. London, 1905

Kirk, K. E. *The Story of the Woodard Schools*. London, 1937

Laborde, E. D. *Harrow School: yesterday and today*. London, 1948

La Fontaine, J. *The Interpretation of Ritual*. London, 1972

Lamb. G. F. *The Happiest Days*. London, 1959

Lambert, Royston *et al*. *New Wine in Old Bottles*. London, 1968
   The Hothouse Society. London, 1968

Laski, Harold J. *The Danger of Being a Gentleman and Other Essays*. London, 1940

Laurie, A. P. (ed.). *The Teachers' Encyclopedia*. London, 1912

Laver, James. *Victorian Vista*. London, 1954

Leaf, Charlotte. *Walter Leaf 1852–1927. Some Chapters of Autobiography . . .* London, 1932

Leake, W. R. M. *Gilkes and Dulwich 1885–1914*. London, 1938

Leclerc. Max. *L'éducation des classes moyennes et dirigeantes en Angleterre*. Paris, 1894

Leff, Gordon. *History and Social Theory*. London, 1969

Levi, Peter. *Beaumont 1861–1961*. London, 1961

Lewis, R. and Maude, A. *The English Middle Classes*. London, 1950

Lockington, W. J. *Bodily Health and Spiritual Vigour*. London, 1913

Lockwood, E. *Early Days at Marlborough College*. London, 1893

Lowndes, G. A. N. *The Silent Social Revolution*. London, 1937 (2nd edn 1969)

Lunn, Arnold. *Come What May*. London, 1940
   Loose Ends. London, 1919
   Public School Religion. London, 1933
   The Harrovians. London, 1913

Lyttelton, Edward. *A Talk with Boys about Themselves* (Kirk Sex Series). London, 1905
   Memories and Hopes. London, 1925
   Schoolboys and Schoolwork. London, 1909
   The Causes and Prevention of Immorality in Schools. London, 1887

McCullagh, Torrens. *Memoirs of R. L. Sheil*. London, 1855

McCunn, John. *The Making of Character*. Cambridge, 1912

McGucken, W. J. *The Jesuits and Education*. New York, 1932

McIntosh, P. C. (ed.). *Landmarks in the History of Physical Education*. London, 1957 (2nd edn 1964)

Physical Education in England Since 1800. London, 1952 (2nd edn 1968)

Mack, E. C. *Public Schools and British Opinion 1780–1860: an examination of the relationship between contemporary ideas and the evolution of an English institution*. London, 1938

Public Schools and British Opinion Since 1860. New York, 1941

Mack, E. C. and Armytage, W. H. G. *Thomas Hughes. The Life of the Author of 'Tom Brown's Schooldays'*. London, 1952

Mackail, J. W. *The Life of William Morris*. London, 1899

MacKenzie, Faith Compton. *William Cory* . . . London, 1950

MacKenzie, N. (ed.). *A Guide to the Social Sciences*. London, 1966

Mackenzie, R. J. *Almond of Loretto*. London, 1905

MacLaren, Archibald. *A System of Physical Education Theoretical and Practical*. Oxford, 1869

Training in Theory and Practice. London, 1866

Maclean, A. H. H. *Public Schools and the Great War*. London, 1919

Macnaughten, Hugh. *Fifty Years of Eton in Prose and Verse*. London, 1924

MacNeice, Louis. *The Strings are False*. London, 1945 (2nd edn 1965)

Mais, S. P. B. *All the Days of My Life*. London, 1937

A Public School in Wartime. London, 1916

A Schoolmaster's Diary. London, 1918 (2nd edn 1928)

Diary of a Public Schoolmaster. London, 1940

The Education of a Philanderer. London, 1919

Maitland, F. W. *The Life and Letters of Leslie Stephen*. London, 1906

Malim, F. B. *Almae Matres*. Cambridge, 1948

Maloine, E. (ed.). *Délibérations du Troisième Congrès International d'Hygiène Scolaire*. Paris, 1910

Mandelbaum, David G. (ed.). *Selected Writings of Edward Sapir*. London, 1948

Mangan, J. A. (ed.). *Physical Education and Sport: sociological and cultural perspectives*. Oxford, 1973

Mannheim, Karl. *Ideology and Utopia*. London, 1936

Marcus, Stephen. *The Other Victorians*. New York, 1966

Marcy, W. N. *Reminiscences of a Public Schoolboy*. London, 1932

Marlborough: an open examination written by the boys. London, 1963

Marriot, J. A. R. *Charles Kingsley, Novelist*. Oxford, 1892

Marshall, F. M. *Football the Rugby Union Game*. London, 1894 (new edn 1925)

Martin, R. B. *The Dust of Combat. A Life of Charles Kingsley*. London, 1959

Martindale, C. C. *Bernard Vaughan*. London, 1923

Charles Dominic Plater S.J. London, 1922

Martindale, Don. *The Nature and Type of Sociological Theory*. London, 1961

Mason, Philip. *A Matter of Honour: an account of the Indian Army, its officers and men*. London, 1974

Matheson, P. E. *The Life of Hastings Rashdall*. London, 1928

Mathew, David. *Catholicism in England 1535–1935*. London, 1936 (2nd edn 1948)

Mayo, C. H. P. *Reminiscences of a Harrow Master*. London, 1928

Mead, G. C. F. and Clift, R. C. (eds.). *English Verse: old and new*. London, 1922 (3rd edn 1947)

Meinertzhagen, R. *Diary of a Black Sheep*. London, 1964

Merivale, Hermann. *Bar, Stage and Platform*. London, 1902 (3rd edn 1968)

Merton, Robert. *Social Theory and Social Structure*. London/New York, 1957 (3rd edn 1967)

Miles, Eustace. *Let's Play the Game*. London, 1904

Minchin, J. G. Cotton. *Old Harrow Days*. London, 1898

    Our Public Schools: their influence on English history. London, 1901

Monckton, C. A. W. *Experiences of a New Guinea Resident Magistrate*. London, n.d.

Monroe, P. (ed.). *A Cyclopedia of Education*. New York, 1911

Morris, James. *Heaven's Command*. London, 1973

Mouzelis, N. P. *Organization and Bureaucracy*. London, 1967

Mulliner, H. G. *Arthur Burroughs. A Memoir*. London, 1936

Murray, G. W. and Hunter, T. A. A. *Physical Education and Health*. London, 1966

Musgrave, P. W. (ed.). *Sociology, History and Education*. London, 1970

Nevinson, C. R. W. *Paint and Prejudice*. London, 1937

Newbolt, Sir Henry. *Collected Poems 1897–1907*. London, n.d.

    Poems. New and Old. London, 1912

    The Twymans: a tale of youth. 2nd edn, Edinburgh, 1911

    The World as in My Time: memoirs. London, 1932

    This Island Race. London, 1898 (5th edn 1902)

Newsome, David. *Godliness and Good Learning*. London, 1961

Nichols, Beverley. *Father Figure*. London, 1967

    Prelude. London, 1920 (4th edn 1929)

Nicolson, Sir Harold. *Good Behaviour*. London, 1955

    Sir Arthur Nicolson, Bart.: a study in the old diplomacy. London, 1930

Nisbet, R. A. *The Sociological Tradition*. London, 1966 (paperback edn 1970)

Norwood, Cyril. *The English Tradition of Education*. London, 1929

Norwood, Cyril and Hope, A. H. *The Higher Education of Boys in England*. London, 1909

O'Connor, Ulick. *Oliver St. John Gogarty*. London, 1964

Ogilvie, Vivian. *The English Public School*. London, 1957

Oman, Sir Charles. *Memories of Victorian Oxford*. London, 1941

Otter, Sir John. *Nathaniel Woodard: a memoir of his life*. London, 1925

Overton, J. H. and Wordsworth, E. *Christopher Wordsworth, Bishop of Lincoln 1807–1885*. London, 1888

Pange, Maurice de. *The English Schooldays of a French Boy*. London, 1928

Parker, Eric. *Playing Fields*. London, 1922

Parkin, George R. *Edward Thring, Headmaster of Uppingham School: life, diary and letters*. 2 vols, London, 1898

Pascoe, C. E. (ed.). *Everyday Life in Our Public Schools*. London, 1881

Patterson, W. S. *Sixty Years of Uppingham Cricket*. London, 1909

Pears, S. A. *Sermons at School: short sermons preached at Repton School Chapel*. London, 1870

Pekin, L. B. *Public Schools: their failure and their reform*. London, 1932

Pellatt, T. *Boys in the Making*. London, 1936

    Public School Education and the War. London, 1917

    Public Schools and Public Opinion. London, 1904

Penny, Arthur G. *The Shirt-Sleeved Generation*. Quebec, 1953

Percival, Alicia. *The Origins of the Headmasters' Conference*. London, 1969
  Very Superior Men. London, 1973
Perkin, H. *The Origins of Modern English Society 1780–1880*. London, 1969
Petrie, W. *Catholic Systems of School Discipline*. 1878
Philosophical Transactions of the Royal Society of London. vol. 257 (series B), London,
  1966
Pitcairn, E. H. (ed.). *Unwritten Laws and Ideals of Active Service*. London, 1889
Pollock, Bertram. *A Twentieth Century Bishop*. London, 1944
Ponsonby, Arthur. *The Decline of the Aristocracy*. London, 1912
Pope-Hennessy, Una. *Canon Charles Kingsley: a biography*. London, 1948
Prestige, G. L. *The Life of Charles Gore*. London, 1935
Prothero, Rowland. *Whippingham to Westminster*. London, 1938
Pryce-Jones, D. (ed.). *Evelyn Waugh and his World*. London, 1973
*Public Schools from Within: a collection of essays on public school education, written chiefly
  by Schoolmasters*. London, 1906
Public School Yearbook. 1889 onwards
Purcell, E. S. *The Life of Cardinal Manning*. 2 vols, London, 1896
Rawnsley, E. F. *Canon Rawnsley: an account of his life*. London, 1923
Rawnsley, H. D. *Edward Thring: teacher and poet*. London, 1889
Rawnsley, W. F. *Early Days at Uppingham School under Edward Thring. By an Old
  Boy*. London, 1904
  Edward Thring: maker of Uppingham School. London, 1926
Raymond, Ernest. *Tell England: a study in a generation*. London, 1922
Reader, W. J. *Professional Men*. London, 1966
Reddie, Cecil. *John Bull, his Origins and Character*. London, 1907
Reed, J. R. *Old School Ties: the public schools in British Literature*. New York, 1964
Rendall, E. D. and Rendall, G. H. *Recollections . . . of the Rev. John Smith, M.A.*
  London, 1913
Riley, M. W. *Sociological Research*. New York, 1963
Rodgers, John. *The Old Public Schools of England*. London, 1938
Roe, W. N. (ed.). *Public Schools Cricket 1901–1950*. London, 1951
Ross, Sir E. Dennison. *Both Ends of the Candle*. London, 1963
Routledge, G. *Every Boy's Annual*. London, 1869
Roxburgh, J. F. *Eleutheros, or the Future of the Public Schools*. London, 1930
Russell, B. and Russell, P. (eds.). *The Amberley Papers*. London, 1937
Russell, Bertrand. *Education and the Good Life*. London, 1926
Russell, George, W. E. *Collections and Recollections*. London, 1898 (new edn 1899)
  Fifteen Chapters of Autobiography. London, 1913
Ryder, J. and Silver, H. *Modern English Society*. London, 1970
Sadler, M. (ed.). *International Inquiry into Moral Training and Instruction in Schools*.
  London, 1908
Sassoon, Siegfried. *The Old Century*. London, 1938
School of Life. Sermons to Public Schoolmen by Public School Headmasters. London,
  1885
Science Teaching in the Public Schools. Association of Public School Science Masters,
  Educational Pamphlets no. 17. London, 1909
Scott, G. *The RCs*. London, 1967
Scott, J. M. *Gino Watkins*. London, 1935

Scott, Michael. *A Modern Tom Brown's Schooldays*. London, 1937

Searle, F. C. *To a Boy Leaving School for the University*. London, 1892

Second International Congress of School Hygiene. London, 1908

Seeley, J. R. *The Expansion of England*. London, 1883

Service, R. W. *Songs of a Sourdough*. London, 1907 (6oth edn 1947)

Shane, Leslie. *Henry Edward Manning: his life and labours*. London, 1921

Sherriff, R. C. *Journey's End*. London, 1929

Sherwood, John. *No Golden Journey*. London, 1973

Sichel, Walter. *The Sands of Time: recollections and reflections*. London, 1923

Sills, David L. (ed.). *International Encyclopedia of the Social Services*. New York, 1968

Simon, Brian. *Education and the Labour Movement 1870–1920*. London, 1965

   Studies in the History of Education 1780–1870. London, 1960

Simon, Brian and Bradley, Ian (eds.). *The Victorian Public School*. Dublin, 1975

Simpson, J. H. *An Adventure in Schooling*. London, 1917

   Howson of Holt. London, 1925

   Sane Schooling. London, 1936

   Schoolmaster's Harvest. London, 1954

   The Public Schools and Athleticism. Educational Times Booklets, no. 1, London, 1923

Skrine, J. C. *Pastor Agnorum*. London, 1902

Skrine, John Huntley. *A Memory of Edward Thring*. London, 1889

   Under Two Queens 1584–1884. London, 1884

   Uppingham by the Sea. London, 1878

Smelser, N. J. *Theory of Collective Behaviour*. London, 1962

Smith, Allan Ramsey. *Loretto School Sermons by a Layman*. London, 1929

Smith, Bertram. *A Perfect Genius*. London/New York, 1909

   Totty: the truth about ten mysterious terms. London/New York, 1908

Smith, Derek Walker. *Out of Step*. London, 1930

Smith, P. and Summerfield, G. *Matthew Arnold and the Education of the New Order*. Cambridge, 1969

Smith, W. D. *Stretching Their Bodies*. Newton Abbot, 1975

Snead-Cox, J. G. *The Life of Cardinal Vaughan*. London, 1910

Snow, George. *The Public School in the New Age*. London, 1959

Somervell, Robert. *Chapters of Autobiography*. London, 1935

Sorley, Charles Hamilton. *Marlborough and Other Poems*. Cambridge, 1916

   The Letters of Charles Sorley. Cambridge, 1919

Spencer, F. H. *The Public School Question*. London, 1942

Spencer, Herbert. *Education: intellectual, moral and physical*. London, 1861

Stanley, Arthur Penrhyn. *The Life and Correspondence of Thomas Arnold D.D.* London, 1844 (3rd edn 1890)

Stephen, Leslie. *Sketches from Cambridge by a Don*. Cambridge, 1865

Storrs, Ronald. *Orientations*. London, 1937

Strachey, Lytton, *Eminent Victorians*. London, 1918

Stretton, Charles, *Memoirs of a Chequered Life*. 3 vols, London, 1862

Stuart, D. M. *The Boy Through the Ages*. London, 1926

Swage, Howard T. *Games and Sports in British Schools and Universities*. New York, 1926

Swanson, G. E. *Religion and Regime: a sociological account of the reformation.* Ann Arbor, 1967

Swift, D. W. *Ideology and Change in the Public Schools: latent functions of progressive education.* Columbus (Ohio), 1971

Swingewood, Alan. *The Sociology of Literature.* London, 1971

Taine, Hippolyte. *Notes on England.* Trans. E. Hyams, New Jersey, 1958

Talboys, R. St. C. *A Victorian School.* Oxford, 1943

Tallents, Sir Stephen. *Man and Boy.* London, 1947

Taylor, R. C. T. *A Housemaster's Letters.* London, 1912

Thomson, David. *England in the Nineteenth Century.* London, 1964.
England in the Twentieth Century. London, 1964

Thompson, E. P. *The Making of the English Working Class.* London, 1963

Thompson, F. M. L. *English Landed Gentry in the Nineteenth Century.* London, 1963

Thornley, T. *Cambridge Memories.* London, 1936

Thornton, Percy M. *Harrow School and its Surroundings.* London, 1885
Some Things We Have Remembered. London, 1912

Thorton, A. P. *The Imperial Idea and its Enemies: a study in British power.* London, 1959

Thring, Edward. *Education and School.* London, 1864 (2nd edn 1867)
Sermons Delivered at Uppingham School. London, 1858
Uppingham School Songs. London, 1881

Tingsten, Herbert. *Victoria and the Victorians.* London, 1972

Tobias, J. J. *Crime and Industrial Society in the Nineteenth Century.* London, 1967

Tollemache, Lionel A. *Old and Odd Memories.* London, 1908

Torre, H. J. *Recollections of Schooldays at Harrow more than Fifty Years Ago.* Manchester, 1890

Tozer, M. *Physical Education at Thring's Uppingham.* Uppingham, 1975

Trevelyan, G. M. *An Autobiography and Other Essays.* London, 1949
English Social History . . . London, 1942 (2nd edn 1946)

Tristram, H. B. *Loretto School Past and Present.* London, 1911

Tucker, R. H. *Memoir of the Life and Episcopate of George Augustus Gardner.* London, 1879

Tuckwell, W. *Reminiscences of Oxford.* London, 1900

Turner, Sir George. *Unorthodox Reminiscences.* London, 1931

Vachell, H. A. *Brothers.* London, 1904
Distant Fields. London, 1937
Fellow Travellers. London, 1923
The Hill. London, 1905 (39th edn 1947)

Vaughan, C. J. *Memorials of Harrow Sundays.* Cambridge, 1859
Sermons Preached in the Chapel of Harrow School. 2nd series, London, 1853
The Vocation of a Public School (sermon preached on the tercentenary commemoration of Radley School). London, 1857

Veblen, Thorstein. *The Theory of the Leisure Class.* New York, 1899 (Modern Library edn 1934)

Wakeford, J. *The Cloistered Elite.* London, 1969

Wall, Bernard. *Headlong into Change.* London, 1969

Warner, P. F. *The Cricketer* (Winter Annual 1921–22). London, 1921

Waterton, Charles. *Essays on Natural History: with a biography by the author.* London, 1838

Waugh, Alec. *Public School Life.* London, 1922

The Loom of Youth. London, 1917

Waugh, Evelyn. *A Little Learning.* London, 1964

Webster, F. A. M. *Our Great Public Schools.* London, 1937

Weinberg, Ian. *The English Public Schools: the sociology of an elite education.* New York, 1967

Welldon, J. E. C. *Forty Years On.* London, 1935

Gerald Eversley's Friendship. London, 1895

Recollections and Reflections. London, 1915

Sermons Preached to Harrow Boys. London, 1888

The Fire upon the Altar: sermons preached to Harrow boys. London, 1891

Youth and Duty: sermons to Harrow schoolboys. London, 1903

Westcott, Arthur. *The Life and Letters of Brooke Foss Westcott.* 2 vols, London, 1903

Whitehouse, J. Howard. *The English Public School: a symposium.* London, 1919

Whitridge, A. *Dr Arnold of Rugby.* London, 1928

Wiese, Ludwig A. *German Letters on English Education.* Trans. and ed. L. Schmitz, London, 1877

Wiley, Basil. *Nineteenth Century Studies.* Harmondsworth, 1949 (Penguin edn 1973)

Wilkins, H. T. *Great English Public Schools.* London, 1925

Wilkinson, Rupert. *Governing Elites: studies in training and selection.* New York, 1969

The Prefects: British leadership and the public school tradition. London, 1964

Williams, R. R. *Christianity and Sound Learning: the educational work of C. J. Vaughan.* London, 1954

Wilson, Bryan R. (ed.). *Rationality.* Oxford, 1970

Wilson, J. M. *An Autobiography 1836–1931.* London, 1932

Essays and Addresses. London, 1887

Morality in Public Schools and its Relation to Religion. Cambridge, 1882

Wilson, John. *Public Schools and Private Practice.* London, 1962

Wilson, Monica. *Religion and the Transformation of a Society: a study of social change in Africa.* London, 1971

Wingfield-Stratford, E. *The Squire and His Relations.* London, 1956

Winstanley, D. A. *Late Victorian Cambridge.* Cambridge, 1947

Wisden's Cricketers Almanack. London, various years

Wodehouse, P. G. *Enter P. Smith.* London, 1935

Wolfenden, J. F. *The Public Schools Today.* London, 1948

Woodard, Francis J. *The Doctor's Disciples.* London, 1954

Woodard, Nathaniel. *A Plea for the Middle Classes.* London, 1843

Public Schools for the Middle Classes: a letter to the clergy of the Diocese of Chichester. London, 1857

Schools for the Middle Classes: a letter to the clergy of the Diocese of Chichester. London, 1852

The Scheme for the Education of St Nicolas College: a letter to the Marquis of Salisbury. London, 1869 (2nd edn 1883)

Woodruff, Douglas. *The Tichborne Claimant.* London, 1957

Woodruffe, Phillip. *The Men Who Ruled India*. 2 vols, London, 1954
Woolley, G. H. *Sometimes a Soldier*. London, 1963
Wordsworth, Charles. *Annals of my Early Life. 1806–1846*. London, 1891
Wordsworth, Christopher. *Sermons preached at Harrow School*. London, 1841
Worsley, T. C. *Barbarians and Philistines*. London, 1940
    Flannelled Fool. London, 1967
    The End of the Old School Tie. London, 1941
Wortham, H. E. *Oscar Browning*. London, 1927
    Victorian Eton and Cambridge, being the life and times of Oscar Browning. London,
    1956
Wrench, Evelyn. *Francis Yeats Brown*. London, 1948
Wymer, N. *Dr. Arnold of Rugby*. London, 1953
Yate, A. C. *The Life of Lieut. Col. John Haughton*. London, 1900
Yonge, Charlotte M. *Life and Letters of John Coleridge Patteson*. 2 vols, London, 1874
Young. G. M. *Victorian England: portrait of an age*. London, 1936 (2nd edn 1953)
    Victorian Essays (Chosen and introduced by W. D. Hancock). London, 1962
Young, Michael (ed.). *Knowledge and Control*. London, 1971

I. Journals and newspapers

American Sociological Review
Army and Navy Illustrated
Army Quarterly Journal
Athenaeum
Baily's Magazine
Bell's Life
Blackwood's Magazine
British Journal of Educational Studies
British Journal of Physical Education
Child
Christian Science Monitor (Boston)
Church Quarterly
Contemporary Review
Cornhill Magazine
Daily Mail
Daily Telegraph
Dark Blue
Dublin Review
Edinburgh Review
Empire Review
English Life
English Review
Essays by Divers Hands
Fortnightly Review
Fraser's Magazine
Good Words
Greece & Rome
Harrow Gazette and General Advertiser

Harvard Theological Review
Hibbert's Journal
Humane Review
Illustrated Sporting and Dramatic News
Independent Review
Journal of Contemporary History
Journal of Education
Journal of the Royal Historical Society
Journal of the Royal Society of Arts
Land and Water
Letters and Notices (British Jesuit house journal)
Life and Letters
London Mercury
London Society
Ludgate Magazine
Macmillan's Magazine
Man
Morning Chronicle
National Review
New Monthly Magazine
New Review
Nineteenth Century
Oxford and Cambridge Review
Pall Mall Gazette
Pennant (house magazine of Benskin's Watford Brewery)
Progress
Public School Magazine
Punch
Quarterly Journal of Education
Quarterly Review
Sandow's Magazine
Saturday Revue
School World
Scottish Field
Scrutiny
Sociological Review
Sociology of Education
Spectator
Sport and Sportsmen
Sporting Gazette
Sportsman
Strand Magazine
Tablet
Theology
The Times
The Times Educational Supplement
Union Jack
Victorian Studies
Woodford Times

J. General works of reference

Alumni Cantabrigienses 1752–1900

Alumni Oxonienses 1715–1886

An Index to Nineteenth Century British Educational Biography

Aslib. Index to theses accepted for higher degree in the universities of Great Britain and Ireland

British Union Catalogue of Periodicals

Cambridge Bibliography of English Literature

Dictionary of National Biography

Dissertation Abstracts International

General Catalogue of Printed Books of the British Museum

International Encyclopedia of the Social Sciences

List of Researches in Education and Educational Psychology, presented for Higher Degrees in the Universities of the United Kingdom, Northern Ireland and the Irish Republic 1918–1957

Palmer's Index to The Times Newspaper 1790–1941

Poole's Index to Victorian Periodicals

Who was Who

Who's Who

Index